GARDENING WITH PERENNIALS

PERENNIALS

Month by Month

GARDENING WITH

WITH

A DEMETER PRESS BOOK

PERENNIALS

Month by Month

JOSEPH HUDAK

Foreword by Joan Lee Faust

 Quadrangle / The New York Times Book Co.

Book design: Tere LoPrete

Library of Congress Cataloging in Publication Data

Hudak, Joseph.
    Gardening with perennials month by month.

    "A Demeter Press book."
    Bibliography: p.
    Includes index.
    1. Perennials.   I. Title.
SB434.H8   1976   635.9'32   75-36250
ISBN 0-8129-0612-8

To the memory of my maternal grandmother,
who introduced me to horticulture.

ACKNOWLEDGMENTS

To all who contributed time and effort over many arduous months, especially to Kenn Stephens, Jeanne and Richard Cross, Jane Simonds, and Margaret Clover, my sincere thanks and appreciation.

PHOTO CREDITS

We gratefully acknowledge the generosity of *Horticulture* magazine in providing the color photographs from their archives.
All black-and-white photographs are by the author.

CONTENTS

FOREWORD

Just maybe, perennials will be making a comeback. For I like to think that Joseph Hudak's delightful efforts here in their behalf may give them that enthusiastic push that will put them in the mainstream of gardeners' choices. The plants surely deserve it.

That old saw that perennials require extra work and effort does not hold very well. Far more important is the fact that they provide our yards with gorgeous blossoms and handsome foliage for truly minimum effort.

There is security in being led down, pardon, this perennial path by a landscape architect whose profession requires seeing the key elements of design that lowly amateurs never see. Practitioners of the design arts are aware of the subtleties of petal color changes, the fine tracery of foliage, individual plant characters and the perennials' downright durability. This knowledge is shared generously here. The pieces have all been put together. The homework is done.

We can merely page through the monthly calendar to have a glorious time picking and choosing the right plants for the right places. Perhaps an iris for the edge of the fish pond, a border of daylilies by the drive or a mixed blend of summer blossoms to perk up the property fence. And how refreshing to have the plants updated into their proper categories and groups that the professionals have decided to place them in.

Things are going to be much easier for perennials now. Both professional plantsmen and amateurs will find in the monthly calendar, which gets right down to business, intimate biographies of these plants with vital statistics on the growing hurdles and troubles that may or may not appear.

Perhaps the subtitle should be Joseph Hudak's own con-
cept, "plants of a thousand days." Just think, almost guaran-
teed 1,000 days of pleasure from a particular group of plants.
And that's only the half of it, for perennials do last forever—
almost!

JOAN LEE FAUST

INTRODUCTION

In the world of garden horticulture there are the *annuals*, which complete their life cycles in one year's time; the *biennials*, which need the first year to produce roots, stems, and leaves, and the second year to blossom and then die; and the *perennials*, which have ongoing persistence for at least three years just to earn their name. Local conditions may alter a known perennial into a biennial or even an annual, but 1,000 days of endurance is the usual criterion for the hardy perennials covered here.

This book is a comprehensive effort at cataloging the majority of the noticeably attractive and reliable plants for garden use called "hardy herbaceous perennials and winter-tolerant bulbs," which can be grown satisfactorily throughout most of the United States and southern Canada, although a great many of them are also successful in the north temperate zones of other parts of the world.

Trees and shrubs are perennial plants also, but they differ by having persistent, woody stems. In the simplest terms, the soft stems and leaves of herbaceous material and winter-hardy bulbs wither to the ground by the end of their growing season but maintain living roots through the dormancy of winter. The hardiness of any plant is primarily based on its successful adaptation to the rigors of cold; yet enduring drought, debilitating heat, excessive wind, and changes in the light intensity can all influence a plant's durability. The usual planting time for perennials is spring or fall when freshly dug, and the after-care maintenance is certainly a contributing factor in assuring normal growth quickly—even for those stalwarts highly tolerant of neglect.

Recommended spacings are not provided here since there are too many variables dictating how far apart plants should be installed. Their initial size, the effect wanted, the length of the growing season, the exposure, the rate of growth as affected by rainfall, and the time available for maintenance all contribute in some way to spacing modifications. Generously self-seeding perennials set their own rules about this.

Insect and disease nuisances given in the main text are not meant to suggest these are the only possible pests which can disfigure perennials. There are always localized difficulties and the cyclic problems which come even with the best of growing conditions and maintenance. The text information points out those nuisances which are especially troublesome throughout most of the growing areas this book covers.

The aim of the text is to place all pertinent growing information in one convenient location as a time-saving aid to both the novice and the experienced gardener. The format is consistent throughout and was planned to make entertaining reading that would also be informatively sound.

It began as a simple up-dating of the 1907 volume by Mabel Cabot Sedgwick, *The Garden Month by Month*, but it quickly assumed a life of its own that expanded her capsuled data into fully detailed explanations of cultural requirements, descriptions of the growth differentiations between similar species, the inclusion of insect and disease nuisances, plus extended essays for the complex major categories such as Narcissus, Peony, and Tulip, which could not have had meaningful coverage from brief commentaries alone.

The main text is divided chronologically into seven monthly installments, the usual growing span for gardens in the Boston, Massachusetts, area—the one with which I am the most familiar. Personal observations of many years as part of my professional design activities have provided me with some clues to the behavior, endurance, and garden usefulness of perennial plants in many other sections of the country, but it seemed less than clear in a work of this focus to include material not reliably hardy to a wide range of temperate zone growing conditions. I have, therefore, reluctantly omitted some highly satisfactory perennials because of their limited range of endurance—not their limited number of admirers. Plants with inferior habits of weediness, an especially demanding culture, or inconspicuous flowering traits are not included since they are usually more appealing to the botanist and specialist than to the horticulturist.

Because there is approximately a week's time difference for each degree of latitude from Boston, those living to the north should add to the given start of flowering spans, while those south of Boston should subtract an appropriate number of days or weeks to balance local conditions. Blossoming anywhere is highly variable from year to year, because gardening effects are no more predictable than the weather conditions which make them happen.

Since color is an important element in any landscape layout, each of the monthly divisions is preceded by an alphabetized list of the color values of flowers blossoming in that period excluding, for the sake of brevity, those carryovers from the previous month. As with all descriptions, the true color of any flower may exist only in the eye of the beholder. While the individual text entry tries to be specific, each coloring represents only a gamble of nomenclature offered in good faith. At least one factor about color is consistent: it changes with the light intensity and with aging.

Because ferns are botanically nonflowering plants, they are not able to be compartmentalized under any month but have a fully developed section of their own. The concluding lists of suggested plants for specialized growing conditions or preferred needs are arbitrarily limited in number and obviously could expand to include many other kinds of problems. The ones provided represent those most commonly requested.

It seems somewhat puzzling that there is still no general agreement by the international authorities of the botanic community about the scientific or common naming of many established perennials. Throughout this book, the majority of the taxonomy was taken from *Standardized Plant Names*, supplemented by current information endorsed by the Royal Horticultural Society of Great Britain, and represents a reasonable consistency of what most authorities prefer to call each plant today.

Generally economical to buy and grow well, the hardy perennial represents a generous range of garden opportunities for ongoing flowering and foliage effects no other plant can produce in quite the same way. If they have any particular drawback, it is their generalized need to be lifted and divided after a few years in one place since most deplete the soil by eager growth and need replanting in a fresh location. All in all, perennials are stalwart members of the plant kingdom deserving wider popular acceptance and far greater use than they now receive. I hope this book will encourage that rewarding discovery.

JOSEPH HUDAK
Westwood, Massachusetts

The Monthly Calendar

MARCH

A General Guide to the Color Values Available in March:
(Each division includes shades, tints, and tones of the dominant value.)

WHITE: Crocus chrysanthus, Crocus vernus, Galanthus elwesii, Galanthus nivalis, Galanthus plicatus, Helleborus niger, Puschkinia scilloides, Scilla tubergeniana
YELLOW: Crocus chrysanthus, Crocus vernus, Eranthis cilicica, Eranthis hyemalis, Iris danfordiae
PINK: Erica carnea *hybrids*
PURPLE: Bulbocodium vernum, Crocus tomasinianus, Crocus vernus, Erica carnea, Helleborus orientalis
BLUE: Chionodoxa luciliae, Chionodoxa sardensis, Crocus chrysanthus, Iris reticulata, Scilla bifolia, Scilla sibirica
BICOLOR: Crocus chrysanthus

Bulbocodium vernum (Spring Meadowsaffron) 2–4 in. Sun
Flowering span: Late March to late April
Color: Bright violet purple
Native habitat: Central and southern Europe, Asia Minor

The flower looks much like the fall-blooming *Colchicum* except that 3 straplike leaves appear with it. The foliage is first purple-toned, then green. Very hardy, the tuber enjoys a moist, well-drained sunspot in rock gardens. New plantings should be made in the autumn, and for best flowering, divide every 3 years. There are no bothersome pests or diseases.

Chionodoxa luciliae (Glory-of-the-snow) 4–6 in. Sun
Flowering span: Late march to mid-April
Color: Violet blue
Native habitat: Western Turkey

Chionodoxa luciliae sports large, open blossoms for several weeks.

Six-pointed, 1-inch, upward-facing flowers with large white centers, generally 8 to 10 on a stalk, emerge from deep green, straplike foliage. Easily naturalized by self-seeding and bulb offsets, this fall-planted bulb enjoys cool, moist, well-drained locations in either sun or light shade. Ants have an attraction for the sugar coating of the seeds and often move them to nests some distance away, thereby starting new colonies inadvertently. Hybridizing readily with some *Scilla*, it produces a hybrid called *Chionoscilla*. Foliage disappears by early summer, and disease or insect problems are nonexistent. Varieties include: *alba*, white and rare; *gigantea*, larger-flowered; *tmolusi*, clear blue but dwarfed, later-flowering; *rosea*, violet-pink but skimpy-flowering; "Pink Giant," blush-pink and floriferous.

Chionodoxa sardensis 4–6 in. Sun
Flowering span: Late March to mid-April
Color: Porcelain blue
Native habitat: Turkey

Deeper blue and more open than *C. luciliae,* the flower here has 6 to 8 blossoms with small white centers, ¾ inch across, on purplish brown stems. Culture is the same for both. Pink and white forms are known but are scarce.

Crocus chrysanthus 3 in. Sun
Flowering span: Mid-March to mid-April
Color: Yellow, blue, white, often interblended
Native habitat: Greece, Asia Minor

Many chalice-shaped, stemless flowers emerge from each tiny bulb before the white-lined, grassy leaves develop fully. Readily colonizing into dense masses in rockeries, borders, and lawn displays where winters are consistently cold, these mountain crocus prefer full sun or light shading in enriched, well-drained loam. Foliage elongates after flowering and should remain until it is dried. Natural self-seeding or fall planting and division of crowded colonies propagate it easily. While insects are no difficulty, a sooty

Self-colonizing *Crocus chrysanthus* brightens the dull days of late winter.

fungus on the corms can spread rapidly. Chipmunks like them too, unfortunately.

Named varieties are many: "Advance," yellow-bronze outside, buttercup yellow inside; "Blue Bird," light blue outside, buttercup yellow inside; "Blue Pearl," pale blue outside, yellow inside with an orange stigma; "Blue Peter," purple outside, blue with a gold throat inside; "Cream Beauty," creamy yellow with an orange stigma; "Goldilocks," golden yellow with an orange stigma; "E. P. Bowles," lemon yellow; "Ladykiller," deep mauve outside, lilac-white inside; "Princess Beatrix," clear light blue with a golden base; "Snowbunting," white with an orange stigma; "Warley," cream and deep blue outside, white and yellow inside; "Zwanenburg Bronze," garnet-brown outside, saffron-yellow inside.

Crocus tomasinianus 3 in. Sun
Flowering span: Early March to April
Color: Purple to mauve
Native habitat: Southern Italy, Yugoslavia

Very hardy, free-flowering, and probably the easiest crocus to grow, the prominent orange stigma is the identifying characteristic. Impervious to being dry or being inadvertently disturbed when dormant, it self-seeds readily. New plantings and division are fall operations in sunny, average-fertility locations. No pests or diseases bother them. Hybrids include: "Barr's Purple," mauve-white outside, purple-lilac inside; "Ruby-Giant," purple outside, silver-mauve inside; "Taplow Ruby," reddish purple; and "Whitewell Purple," purple-mauve outside, mauve-white inside.

Crocus vernus (Common Crocus) 4–6 in. Sun
Flowering span: Mid-March to mid-April
Color: White, yellow, purple
Native habitat: Southern Europe

The largest-flowering of all, these "Dutch Hybrid" crocus have showier flowers and wider, thicker foliage. They self-seed readily. Care for them as for the other crocus. Hybrids are many: "Blizzard," white; "Cinderella," striped pale and deep lilac; "Enchantress," pale blue, silvery; "Flower

Boldly stretching to the warming sun, *Crocus vernus* announces spring's arrival.

Record," rich violet-blue; "Grand Maitre," dark blue-purple; "Haarlem Gem," pale lilac-mauve; "Jeanne d'Arc," pure white; "Kathleen Parlow," white with orange stigma; "King of the Striped," white-striped lilac; "Little Dorrit," lilac; "Negro Boy," deep purple; "Peter Pan," ivory white; "Pickwick," purple-striped lilac; "Purpureus Grandiflorus," deep purple, silvery; "Queen of the Blues," blue-lavender; "Remembrance," silvery violet; "Sky Blue," heliotrope-blue; "Snowstorm," white; "Striped Beauty," white-striped lavender; "The Bishop," deep reddish purple; "Vanguard," pale silvery lilac; "Victor Hugo," light purple; and "Yellow Mammoth," golden yellow.

Eranthis cilicica (Cilician Aconite) 4 in. Sun
Flowering span: Mid-March to early April
Color: Deep yellow
Native habitat: Asia Minor

A sizable, frilly collar of leafy bracts supports solitary, fragrant, 1-inch flowers above bright green true leaves. Spring sun needs to be followed by summer shading after the foliage disappears. Moist, alkaline soil is best but they are not fussy. Plant new tubers immediately in the fall because they dry out quickly. Once established it seeds freely. The foliage here is heavier than *E. hyemalis,* and flowering is slightly later. Diseases and insects are not bothersome.

Eranthis hyemalis (Winter Aconite) 3–5 in. Sun
Flowering span: Early March to April
Color: Lemon yellow
Native habitat: Western Europe, Asia Minor

Similar to *E. cilicica,* the green foliage is topped by solitary, buttercuplike, 1-inch flowers surrounded by a jagged rosette of green bracts. Culture is the same for both.

Erica carnea (Spring Heath) 8–12 in. Sun
Flowering span: Mid-March to May
Color: Reddish purple
Native habitat: Europe, British Isles

Widely creeping and trailing thin stems with needlelike whorls of tiny, ½-inch evergreen leaves produce long-lasting terminal clusters of bell-shaped flowers. Best in full sun, it prefers a well-drained, sandy loam enriched with peat or acid humus; however, it is the only Heath to tolerate lime soils well. Summer tip cuttings or layered stems are the reliable propagation methods since older plants do not divide or move well. No problems are apparent with insects and diseases. The hybrids are all superior to the parent: "Atrorubra," deep pink, late-flowering; "Eileen Porter," carmine red; "King George," deep pink, dwarf; "Ruby Glow," ruby red, compact; "Sherwood Early Red," rosy red; "Snow Queen," white, dwarf; "Springwood Pink," bright pink; "Springwood White," white, showy-flowered; "Vivelli," dark red, dwarf; and "Winter Beauty," rosy pink.

Galanthus elwesii (Giant Snowdrop) 6–9 in. Semi-shade
Flowering span: Late March to mid-April
Color: White
Native habitat: Western Turkey

Grayish, 1-inch-wide leaves surround a taller flower stalk with 1-inch nodding blossoms having 3 outer petals that flare out to reveal a narrow, notched tube colored green at both ends. They naturalize slower than other species and enjoy a rich, moist, well-drained loam that is cool in all seasons. Division after flowering, when the foliage disappears, is best, but new plantings should be made in the fall. Pests and diseases are not problematic.

Galanthus nivalis (Common Snowdrop) 4–6 in. Semi-shade
Flowering span: Early March to April
Color: White
Native habitat: Central Europe

The gray-green, ¼-inch-wide leaves here emerge pressed together at the base. The drooping, 1-inch flowers have outer petals much longer than the green-rimmed inner cylinder. They naturalize freely from self-seeding, and new plantings should be made in the fall in woodsy, well-drained, enriched soil. Spring foliage disappears completely by early summer. No pests or diseases of consequence. Several hybrids are known: "Arnott's Seedling," fragrant, robust, 6 to 10 inches tall; *flore-pleno*, somewhat double; and *simplex*, larger-flowered.

Galanthus plicatus (Crimean Snowdrop) 6–9 in. Semi-shade
Flowering span: Early March to April
Color: White
Native habitat: Russian Crimea, Rumania

Very grayish, 1-inch-wide leaves emerge face-to-face but with the edges rolled back to form a pleat. Blooming earlier than the other species listed, they have a broad, dark green collar on the inner flower tube. Culture is the same.

Helleborus niger (Christmas Rose) 9–12 in. Semi-shade
Flowering span: January through March
Color: Greenish white or pinkish
Native habitat: Europe

Five-petaled, 3-inch flowers centrally ringed with a prominent band of yellow stamens emerge from an evergreen clump of long-stalked, very thick, deeply indented leaves with few serrations on the margins. They dislike heat, intense sunlight, and transplanting. Established plants have long, deep roots and thrive in rich, acid soil that is always moist and well-drained. Nursery plants or seeding, which is very slow, are the better propagation methods. Slugs occasionally feed on the foliage or flowers, and a fungus discolors the foliage in humid weather. The varieties include: *angustifolius*, smaller-flowered; and *altifolius* with longer flower stalks.

Helleborus orientalis (Lenten Rose) 15–18 in. Semi-shade
Flowering span: Early March to mid-May
Color: Purple pink to greenish white
Native habitat: Asia Minor, Greece

Similar in foliage to *H. niger* except the leaves are lighter-colored and have many small teeth, the 2-inch flowers appear on leafless, branched stems with 2 to 6 blossoms. Culture is the same for both. The variety, *atrorubens*, is shorter and carries only 2 to 4 flowers.

Iris danfordiae (Danford Iris) 4 in. Sun
Flowering span: Mid-March to early April
Color: Lemon yellow
Native habitat: Eastern Turkey

Often neglected because its habit of quickly subdividing into many tiny bulblets diminishes annual flowering, the bulb has squat blossoms 2 inches wide before any foliage appears. Light fertilizing annually helps stimulate flower production. Initial plantings are made in the fall and are best in protected, well-drained sites with average soil. Insects are no problem, but a fungus called "ink disease" can destroy the bulbs after planting.

Iris reticulata (Netted Iris) 6 in. Sun
Flowering span: Mid-March to mid-April
Color: Deep violet blue
Native habitat: Asia Minor

Violet-scented, these showy flowers appear between narrow, upright leaves that disappear by early summer. Best used in drifts in rock gardens or borders, they like any well-drained, average soil in full sun. They can also be afflicted with the "ink disease" fungus. Hybrids offer interesting variations: "Cantab," light blue; "Clarette," violet blue with white markings; "Harmony," deep sky blue with gold markings; "Royal Blue," deep Oxford blue; and "Violet Beauty," dark purple with orange markings.

Puschkinia scilloides (*libanotica*) (Striped Squill) 4–8 in.
  Sun
Flowering span: Late March to mid-April
Color: Blue-white
Native habitat: Lebanon, Asia Minor

Related to both *Chionodoxa* and *Scilla*, it has stalks of 5 to 20 florets growing from a pair of fleshy, narrow leaves at ground level. The ¾-inch, white blossoms have a central blue stripe on each petal. Preferring cool, moist locations in sun to light shading, it will not long survive in sun-baked areas. Overcrowded colonies can be separated when the foliage disappears by early summer, but new plantings should be made in the fall. Pests and diseases are unknown.

Scilla bifolia (Twinleaf Squill) 3–6 in. Sun
Flowering span: Mid-March to mid-April
Color: Bright blue
Native habitat: Southern Europe, Asia Minor

Appearing before *S. sibirica*, the starlike, ¾-inch flowers have noticeable anthers jutting beyond the petals. They appear on slender, reddish stalks in arrangements from 3 to 8 above twin, bronze-green leaves. Not quite as vigorously spreading as other species, it likes cool, moist, humusy soil, well-drained, in full sun to light shade. Self-seeding usually takes care of propagation, and new colonies can be planted in the fall. Pests and diseases are not a worry, but in severe climates a winter mulch is helpful. Several varieties are offered commercially: *alba*, white; *praecox*, bright blue, earlier and larger; *rosea*, pale purple-pink; and *splendens*, cobalt blue.

Dwarfed but vibrant, the bright flowering of *Scilla bifolia* enlivens March days.

Scilla sibirica (Siberian Squill) 3–6 in. Sun
Flowering span: Late March to late April
Color: Bright Prussian blue
Native habitat: Southern Russia, Siberia

Readily colonizing by self-seeding into huge mats almost anywhere that conditions suit them, these vibrant, 1-inch flowers appear 3 to 4 to a stalk with several stems from each bulb along with straplike foliage that disappears by summer. Best in cool, moist, well-drained locations of average fertility with sun to light shading, they should be fall-planted initially. Nothing seems to bother them. The white form, *alba*, is rare, but the variety *atrocoerulea*, which is usually carried as "Spring Beauty," has larger, taller, and earlier flowers.

Scilla tubergeniana 4–6 in. Sun
Flowering span: Late March to late April
Color: Pale blue-white
Native habitat: Northwest Iran

Unquestionably blue, the *Scilla sibirica* colonizes with perfect ease.

Very hardy and blooming with S. *sibirica*, the 1-inch, upright blossoms come 2 to 4 to a stem with several stalks from each bulb. Each petal has a dark blue dividing line at the top, giving it a close resemblance to *Puschkinia*. The bright green foliage completely fades away by summer, when overcrowded colonies can be divided. New plantings are best made in the autumn in moist, cool locations in sun to semi-shade; they dislike hot, dry exposures. Slugs are sometimes a springtime pest, but there are no problematic diseases.

APRIL

A General Guide to the Color Values
Available in April:

(Each division includes shades, tints, and tones of the dominant value.)

WHITE: Actaea alba, Actaea rubra, Anemone blanda *hybrids*, Anemone caroliniana, Anemone nemorosa, Anemone pulsatilla *hybrids*, Anemone quinquefolia, Arabis alpina, Arabis caucasica, Arabis mollis, Caltha palustris alba, Claytonia caroliniana, Dentaria diphylla, Dicentra canadensis, Dicentra cucullaria, Dicentra eximia alba, Erythronium albidum, Erythronium dens-canis *hybrids*, Fritillaria meleagris *hybrids*, Hepatica acutiloba, Hepatica americana, Hyacinthus orientalis *hybrids*, Iris bucharica, Iris pumila, Leucojum aestivum, Leucojum vernum, Muscari botryoides album, Narcissus *hybrids*, Ornithogalum nutans, Pachysandra procumbens, Pachysandra terminalis, Phlox subulata, Primula denticulata, Primula sieboldi alba, Sanguinaria canadensis, Trillium grandiflorum, Trillium nivale, Trillium undulatum, Tulipa *hybrids*, Tulipa clusiana, Tulipa fosteriana *hybrids*, Tulipa kaufmanniana *hybrids*, Tulipa turkestanica, Vinca minor *hybrids*, Viola blanda, Viola cornuta *hybrids*, Viola odorata *hybrids*

YELLOW: Adonis amurensis, Adonis vernalis, Alchemilla alpina, Allium moly, Alyssum saxatile, Anemone ranunculoides, Aquilegia canadensis flavescens, Caltha palustris, Caulophyllum thalictroides, Draba sibirica, Erythronium americanum, Euphorbia epithymoides, Euphorbia myrsinites, Fritillaria imperialis lutea, Fritillaria pallidiflora, Hyacinthus orientalis *hybrids*, Iris pumila, Narcissus *hybrids*, Primula auricula, Primula polyantha, Primula veris, Primula vulgaris, Tulipa *hybrids*, Tulipa fosteriana *hybrids*, Tulipa greigi *hybrids*, Tulipa kaufmanniana, Tulipa kolpakowskiana, Tulipa tarda, Viola cornuta *hybrids*, Viola pensylvanica, Viola pubescens, Viola rafinesquii

ORANGE: Fritallaria imperialis, Narcissus *hybrids*, Primula polyantha, Tulipa *hybrids*, Tulipa whittalli, Viola cornuta *hybrids*

RED: Anemone blanda *hybrids*, Anemone pulsatilla *hybrids*, Aquilegia canadensis, Fritillaria imperialis *hybrids*, Hyacinthus orientalis *hybrids*, Iris pumila, Phlox subulata *hybrids*, Primula auricula *hybrids*, Primula polyantha, Primula vulgaris *hybrids*, Tulipa *hybrids*, Tulipa eichleri, Tulipa fosteriana, Tulipa greigi, Tulipa kaufmanniana *hybrids*, Tulipa linifolia, Tulipa pulchella, Tulipa praestans, Tulipa stellata chrysantha, Viola cornuta *hybrids*

PINK: Anemone blanda *hybrids*, Anemone caroliniana, Anemone pulsatilla *hybrids*, Arabis alpina rosea, Arabis caucasica *hybrids*, Aubretia deltoides *hybrids*, Bergenia cordifolia, Bergenia crassifolia, Claytonia virginica, Dicentra eximia, Epigaea repens, Erythronium dens-canis *hybrids*, Fritillaria meleagris *hybrids*, Hepatica acutifolia, Hepatica americana, Hyacinthus orientalis *hybrids*, Mertensia virginica, Narcissus *hybrids*, Phlox procumbens, Phlox subulata, Primula sieboldi, Pulmonaria saccharata *hybrids*, Tulipa *hybrids*, Tulipa aucheriana, Tulipa fosteriana *hybrids*, Tulipa greigi *hybrids*, Tulipa kaufmanniana *hybrids*, Viola odorata *hybrids*

PURPLE: Anemone caroliniana, Anemone nemorosa *varieties*, Anemone patens, Anemone pulsatilla, Aubretia deltoides, Dicentra eximia gracilis, Erythronium denscanis, Fritillaria meleagris, Iris pumila, Primula denticulata, Primula sieboldi, Pulmonaria angustifolia rubra, Pulmonaria officinalis, Pulmonaria saccharata, Trillium sessile, Tulipa *hybrids*, Vinca minor *varieties*, Viola conspersa, Viola cornuta, Viola odorata, Viola palmata, Viola papilionacea, Viola rafinesquii, Viola tricolor

BLUE: Anemone apennina, Anemone blanda, Brunnera macrophylla, Delphinium tricorne, Hepatica americana, Hyacinthus orientalis *hybrids*, Iris magnifica, Iris pumila, Iris verna, Muscari armeniacum, Muscari botryoides, Muscari comosum, Muscari latifolium, Muscari tubergenianum, Omphalodes verna, Phlox subulata *hy-*

brids, Polemonium reptans, Primula polyantha, Primula vulgaris *hybrids,* Pulmonaria angustifolia, Vinca minor, Viola cornuta *hybrids*

BICOLOR: Aquilegia canadensis, Fritillaria meleagris, Iris bucharica, Iris magnifica, Iris pumila *hybrids,* Mertensia virginica, Narcissus *hybrids,* Primula auricula *hybrids,* Primula denticulata *varieties,* Primula polyantha *hybrids,* Tulipa *hybrids,* Tulipa clusiana, Tulipa fosteriana *hybrids,* Tulipa greigi *hybrids,* Tulipa kaufmanniana *hybrids,* Tulipa stellata chrysantha, Tulipa tarda, Viola cornuta *hybrids,* Viola tricolor.

Actaea alba *(pachypoda)* (White Baneberry) 12–18 in. Shade
Flowering span: Late April to June
Color: White
Native habitat: Southeastern Canada to Georgia, west to Oklahoma

Compact spikes of small flowers appear atop large, smooth, compound leaves on stout stems and are then followed by conspicuous clusters of ⅜-inch, football-shaped white fruit (occasionally reddish) in late summer. The fruit is attached by noticeable, stiff, pink-red pedicels, and each berry has a forward colored dot that provides the common name of "doll's eye" in some areas. Good for moist, rich woodlots with acid or neutral soil in full to semi-shade. Divide in early spring or sow seed in the fall for propagation. There are no pests or diseases to worry about.

Actaea rubra (Red Baneberry) 18–24 in.   Shade
Flowering span: Late April to June
Color: White
Native habitat: Southern Canada to New Jersey, west to Iowa and Oregon

Similar to *A. alba* except the stems are slender, the fruit is red (but sometimes ivory white) on green pedicels, and the leaves are usually downy with soft hairs. Culture is identical.

Adonis amurensis (Amur Adonis) 10–12 in. Sun
Flowering span: Early April to May
Color: Golden yellow
Native habitat: Siberia, Manchuria

Multiple, 2-inch, terminal flowers, much like an Anemone, rise from an attractive ball of fernlike foliage. Enjoying moist, rich, sandy loam, it is a good rock garden accent in full sun or semi-shade. The plant goes completely dormant by midsummer. Careful division of the fibrous roots in spring is best, but spring or fall seeding also works well. Insects and diseases are no bother. The double-flowered form, *plena*, has greenish yellow blossoms 6 inches tall. The Japanese have evolved white, orange, pink and copper-toned hybrids, but they have not yet been widely distributed.

Adonis vernalis (Spring Adonis) 12–15 in. Sun
Flowering span: Mid-April to mid-May
Color: Bright yellow
Native habitat: Southern Europe

Taller and later-flowering than *A. amurensis*, this species has 3-inch, solitary blossoms. Culture is the same for both. White and double-flowered forms are known but are scarce.

Alchemilla alpina (Mountain Lady's-mantle) 6 in. Sun
Flowering span: Late April to mid-May
Color: Greenish yellow
Native habitat: Europe

Tiny flowers appear in large, loose clusters above a vigorous set of silvery green, rounded leaves which spread quickly to form mats by creeping stems. A moist, average-fertility soil is suitable in sun to semi-shade. Seeding works better than division. There are no disease or insect problems.

Allium moly (Lily Leek) 6–10 in.   Sun
Flowering span: Late April to June
Color: Bright yellow
Native habitat: Southwestern Europe

Erect flower heads, 2 to 3 inches across, of noticeable, star-shaped florets dominate the paired, gray green, 1-inch-wide leaves. Full sun in any well-drained, average loam with reasonable moisture creates colonies readily from self-seeding and bulbous offsets. Divide overcrowded clumps after the foliage fades, and install new bulbs in the autumn. Pests and diseases are rare.

Alyssum saxatile (Goldentuft Alyssum, Basket-of-Gold)
    6–12 in.   Sun
Flowering span: Mid-April to late May
Color: Bright yellow
Native habitat: Mediterranean Europe

Compact clusters of tiny flowers in great masses envelop the heavy, lancelike, grayish leaves of this rambling perennial. Vivid in full sun for plant walls, rock gardens, and border edgings, it thrives on neutral, sandy-gravelly soil with excellent drainage. Division of the thick, long roots is difficult, so spring or fall seeding is preferred. Summer stem cuttings root satisfactorily. A club-root disease, however, destroys the feeding roots and requires complete removal of the afflicted plants. Flea beetles occasionally bother the foliage. Attractive hybrids are often available: *Citrinum*, pale lemon yellow; *compactum*, bright yellow, dwarfed; *florepleno*, bright yellow, double-flowered, long-lasting; and "Silver Queen," pale, creamy yellow.

Anemone apennina (Apennine Anemone) 4–9 in. Semi-
    shade
Flowering span: Early April to May
Color: Sky blue
Native habitat: Italy

Similar to *A. blanda* in appearance and culture, the rootstock is an elongated rhizome rather than a fat tuber and tolerates slightly more shading to bloom. The daisylike flower is carried above light green, coarsely cut foliage which fades after blossoming. Its proximity in looks to A. *blanda* keeps it commercially scarce, and the white and pink forms are rare.

Anemone blanda (Greek Anemone) 4–6 in. Semi-shade
Flowering span: Early April to mid-May
Color: Intense sky blue
Native habitat: Greece, Asia Minor

Daisy-petaled, 1½-inch vivid flowers are carried above delicately divided leaves. Effective in drifts that can remain undisturbed, it likes a moist, well-drained, humusy soil in dappled light. Divide the fat tubers when dormant in late summer or plant new groupings in early fall. No insect or disease is bothersome. Hybrids extend the colorings: "Blue Star"; "Pink Star"; "Radar," raspberry-mauve; "Bridesmaid," white; and "White Splendor."

Anemone caroliniana (Carolina Anemone) 8–12 in. Sun
Flowering span: Mid-April to mid-May
Color: White, pink, violet
Native habitat: Indiana to Florida, west to Texas and Minnesota

Solitary, 1½-inch blossoms with up to 20 petals on slender stems rise above a basal clump of narrowly incised leaves when naturalized in large rock gardens or open woodlots with rich, moist, alkaline soil. Tolerant to dryness when dormant, it produces densely woolly seed heads useful for reproduction. Insects and diseases are not a concern.

Anemone nemorosa (European Wood Anemone) 3–8 in. Semi-shade
Flowering span: Mid-April to mid-May
Color: White, purplish
Native habitat: Europe, British Isles, Siberia

Individual, 1½-inch flowers with 5 to 8 large petals extend above low foliage with long leafstalks and deeply lobed leaves. Attractive as woodlot carpeting where the soil is acid, constantly moist, humusy, and semi-shaded, this rampant species is intolerant of dryness or high heat. Division of the thick rootstock in spring or fall gives better results than seeding. It appears to have no important pests or diseases. The hybrids include: *alba flore-pleno,* double white; *allenii,* silvery, pale lavender; "Blue Bonnet," rich blue; *major,* white, large-flowered; *robinsoniana,* pale lavender-blue; *rosea,* reddish purple; "Royal Blue," deep blue; and "Vestal," double white with a pompon center. The parent often hybridizes readily with *A. rananculoides* to produce a creamy white offspring sold as *A. seemannii.*

Anemone patens (Spreading Pasque-flower) 4–10 in. Sun
Flowering span: Mid-April to mid-May
Color: Lilac
Native habitat: Wisconsin to Texas, west to Washington, Alaska and Siberia

Cup-shaped, 2-inch terminal flowers appear above a basal clump of ferny leaves with silky, white hairs and soon develop into a distinctive plume of seed heads. Tolerant of dryness when summer-dormant, it likes a sandy, alkaline, well-drained loam in sun to light shading. Root cuttings and seed work best for propagation, and insects or diseases are rare.

Anemone pulsatilla (*Pulsatilla vulgaris*) (Pasque-flower)
    6–12 in. Sun
Flowering span: Mid-April to mid-May
Color: Rich violet purple
Native habitat: Europe, British Isles

Showy, 2½-inch, cup-shaped flowers with a heavy ring of gold stamens bloom before the fernlike foliage fully develops. Fluffy, long-lasting, glistening seed heads follow. Well-drained, gravelly, neutral soil is best in full sun to light shading. Spring division, root cuttings, or seed work equally well. A root-decay fungus requires quick removal and soil sterilization before replanting. Hybrids are available but scarce: *alba,* pure white; "Mrs. van der Elst," soft pink; and *rubra,* maroon to brick-red.

Anemone quinquefolia (American Wood Anemone) 6–10 in.
    Semi-shade

Flowering span: Mid-April to mid-May
Color: White, pinkish
Native habitat: Southeastern Canada to Georgia, west to
  Iowa

Delicate, 1-inch, solitary blossoms are usually surrounded by a single, much-divided leaf lighter in color than *A. nemorosa.* Consistently moist, acid, humusy soil in open woodlots suits it best. Spring or fall division of the wiry root system is easily accomplished. Serious pests or diseases are unknown.

Anemone ranunculoides (Yellow Wood Anemone) 3–8 in.
  Semi-shade
Flowering span: Early April to May
Color: Golden yellow
Native habitat: Europe, Siberia

Except for color, the species is similar in habit, appearance, and culture to *A. nemorosa.* A double-flowered form, *flora-plena,* is rare.

Aquilegia canadensis (American Columbine) 15–24 in.
  Semi-shade
Flowering span: Late April to June
Color: Red and yellow
Native habitat: Southeastern Canada to Alabama, west to
  Texas

Novel in shape, the nodding flowers have 1-to 2-inch red spurs around a rosette of inner, yellow sepals and come on branched, thin stems conspicuously above the rounded, blue-green, compound leaves. Best in light shade in wild gardens or rockeries, it wants a moist, sandy loam, well-drained, in protected locations. Seed is superior to root division. Root borer and leaf miner are destructive insects, while crown rot and mildew are serious diseases. The yellow-flowered variety, *flavescens,* requires the same culture.

Arabis alpina (Alpine Rockcress) 4–10 in. Sun
Flowering span: Late April to June

Color: White
Native habitat: Europe

Blooming conspicuously in dense clusterings of many-petalled flowers above the tufts of hairy, green leaves, this compact groundcover is useful in sunny rock gardens, plant walls, and between stepstones. Shear off the faded flowers after blooming for continued compactness and possible repeat flowering. It wants well-drained, gravelly soil, marginally fertile, and can be propagated equally well from spring divisions, summer stem cuttings, or seeding. Less vigorous than *A. caucasica,* it has no bothersome pests or diseases. Varieties in cultivation are: *flore-pleno,* double, long-lasting; *nana compacta,* dwarfed; *rosea,* soft pink; and *variegata,* with leaves striped in white.

Arabis caucasica (albida) (Wall Rockcress) 4–10 in.   Sun
Flowering span: Late April to June
Color: White
Native habitat: Caucasus Mountains

Slightly fragrant, ¼-inch florets crowd the many tall stalks rising above a vigorous, broad mat of gray green, hairy leaves, coarsely toothed at the tips. Disliking poor drainage, excessive fertilizing, and damp springtimes, it enjoys gravelly, sun-baked locations throughout the year. Severely cut back faded flowers and some foliage after blooming to encourage compactness. Propagate the same as *A. alpina.* It has no pests or diseases. Hybrids include: *flore-pleno,* a showy, double-flowered, long-lasting form; "Rosabella," bright pink, less rampant; and *variegata,* with yellowish white leaf stripes.

Arabis mollis (Downy Rockcress) 1–6 in.   Sun
Flowering span: Late April to June
Color: White
Native habitat: Southeastern Europe

Oblong, 1-inch, glossy leaves that are slightly hairy beneath form flat rosettes of evergreen foliage slowly produced by thin, surface-creeping stems. The domed, 1-inch clusters of tiny florets appear in an airy pattern on wiry stems where

The conspicuous flowering of *Arabis caucasica flore-pleno* is matched by durable gray-green foliage.

sunshine is generous and the well-drained soil somewhat sandy and of average fertility. Spring division, summer stem cuttings, or seed all reproduce it readily, and it is untroubled by pests or diseases of consequence. Often listed as a form of *A. procurrens,* the two plants appear interchangeable.

Aubretia deltoides (Common Aubretia) 3–6 in. Sun
Flowering span: Late April to June
Color: Mauve to deep purple
Native habitat: Mediterranean Europe, Asia Minor

Hundreds of 1-inch flowers can cover a well-grown specimen of this moundlike perennial in sun or light shading where the soil is sandy, well-drained, neutral, and of average fertility. Shear the faded flowers after bloom to improve the compactness of its dark, gray-green foliage. Division, layering of long shoots, fall stem cuttings, or seed all work easily for propagation. Pests and diseases are unknown. Many hybrids are available: "Cardinal Richelieu," royal purple; "Dawn," clear pink, semi-double; *eyrei*, deep violet, large-flowering; *graeca*, blue-purple, dwarfed; *hendersoni*, purple, large-flowered; *leightlini*, pink, dwarfed; "Magician," bright purple; and "Whitewell Gem," bright pink.

Bergenia cordifolia (*Saxifraga cordifolia*) (Heartleaf
    Bergenia) 12–15 in. Semi-shade
Flowering span: Late April to June
Color: Clear rose
Native habitat: Siberia

The 6- to 10-inch wide, leathery, wavy-margined leaves of this hardy plant are probably as interesting as the stout flower stalk with its head of waxy, bell-like blossoms. Turning somewhat limp and bronze green throughout the winter, the semi-evergreen leaves are glossy green and upright when new. Preferring moist, semi-shaded locations with average fertility, it tolerates full sun and some dryness satisfactorily. Division of the thick rootstock in spring or fall is the usual propagation method. A fungus may disfigure the emerging foliage occasionally, and summer chewing insects often create a mild nuisance.

Bergenia crassifolia (*Saxifraga crassifolia*) (Leather
    Bergenia) 12–18 in. Semi-shade
Flowering span: Late April to June
Color: Rose lilac
Native habitat: Mongolia

Similar in appearance to *B. cordifolia*, this species has smaller, oval, flat leaves and a flower stalk rising 12 inches above the foliage. Culture is identical.

Brunnera macrophylla (*Anchusa myosotidiflora*) (Heartleaf
    Brunnera) 12–18 in. Semi-shade
Flowering span: Late April to mid-June
Color: Clear blue
Native habitat: Siberia, Caucasus Mountains

Delicate sprays of forget-me-not-like florets appear abundantly above a mound of rough-textured, broad, 6-inch leaves in the moist, humusy sites this perennial enjoys best. Division in early spring or seeding are the usual propagation methods, and pests are uncommon, although crown rot may be a nuisance in poorly drained locations. The scarce variety, *variegata*, has wide leaf margins of creamy yellow but may prove tender in many locations.

Caltha palustris (Marsh Marigold) 12–18 in. Semi-shade
Flowering span: Mid-April to June
Color: Golden yellow
Native habitat: Canada to Alaska, south to Nebraska and South Carolina

Golden, 2-inch flowers profusely cluster the branched stems rising above shiny, deep green, heart-shaped leaves that are often collected for cooking like spinach. At home in wet, acid soil in semi- to full shade, it thrives natively along stream banks, swamps, and bogs. For garden use it will adapt to rich, moist loam and can be divided when summer-dormant or seeded where wanted. Pests and diseases are no problem. The variety *alba* has white flowers, while *florepleno* produces double, yellow, very showy blossoms.

Caulophyllum thalictroides (Blue Cohosh) 24–36 in. Shade
Flowering span: Late April to June
Color: Yellowish green
Native habitat: Southeastern Canada to Alabama, west to Missouri

Unshowy tufts of tiny, star-shaped flowers in loose panicles rise above a neat foliage mass that is actually a single, much-divided leaf. The admired value is the clustering of deep blue, berrylike fruit in late summer as the foliage withers. Plant in rich, woodsy soil in heavy to semi-shade. Propagate by root cuttings or seed. There are no diseases or pests.

Claytonia caroliniana (Carolina Spring Beauty) 10–15 in. Semi-shade
Flowering span: Early April to June
Color: White with red stripes

Native habitat: Southeastern Canada to North Carolina, west
to Minnesota

A solitary stalk carries widely separated, ¾-inch cupped
flowers on long pedicels above broad, lancelike leaves that
disappear after flowering. The tuber generates new foliage
in late fall that endures the winter. Best in large drifts in
damp, acid woodlots in semi-shade, it self-seeds readily and
can be transplanted from the wild with ease. Insects and
diseases are uncommon.

Claytonia virginica (Virginia Spring Beauty) 8–12 in.
   Semi-shade
Flowering span: Mid-April to June
Color: Pink with red stripes
Native habitat: Southeastern Canada to Georgia, west to
   Texas and Minnesota

Blooming later than *C. caroliniana,* this species has a pair
of grasslike, fleshy leaves, a sprawling habit, and ½-inch
pink flowers. Culture is the same for both.

Delphinium tricorne (Rock Larkspur) 12–24 in. Semi-
   shade
Flowering span: Late April to June
Color: Purple blue
Native habitat: Pennsylvania to Alabama, west to Nebraska

Sporting 1-inch, long-spurred flowers on an erect stalk,
this wildflower has a basal tuft of small, finely divided
leaves that wither after flowering. Some may have pale blue,
white or even blotched colorings. It likes humusy, moist
hillsides or woodlots with light shading. Self-seeding is
likely and the easiest propagation method. Pests and diseases are unimportant.

Dentaria diphylla (Crinkleroot Dentaria) 6–10 in. Semi-
   shade
Flowering span: Early April to June
Color: White
Native habitat: Southeastern Canada to Alabama

From a pair of 3-inch leaves, deeply divided into 3 segments, develops a slender stalk clustered with ½-inch florets with noticeable yellow stamens. Enjoying rich, moist, woodsy soil in deep to semi-shade, it takes to division of the toothed rootstock at any time. Seed works well, too. No diseases or pests bother it.

Dicentra canadensis (Squirrel-corn) 6–10 in. Semi-shade
Flowering span: Early April to mid-May
Color: White
Native habitat: Southeastern Canada to Tennessee

Erect flower stalks with heart-shaped, fragrant blossoms rise above a basal foliage cluster of feathery, gray green leaves in woodsy, moist, sandy soil in semi-shade. Division of the bright yellow tubers, which resemble kernels of corn, should be made soon after flowering and before the mid-summer disappearance of the foliage. Dry rot may prove a nuisance following transplanting, but insects are no problem.

Dicentra cucullaria (Dutchmans-breeches) 6–10 in. Semi-
    shade
Flowering span: Early April to June
Color: White with gold tips
Native habitat: Southeastern Canada to Georgia; Oregon and
    Washington

Similar in habit, form, and culture to *D. canadensis*, here the flowers are more showy with golden yellow tips and wide-spreading end spurs. A purple and orange form is known but rare.

Dicentra eximia (Fringed Bleeding-heart) 12–18 in. Semi-
    shade
Flowering span: Late April to September
Color: Pink purple
Native habitat: New York to Tennessee

Durable and long-flowering, this hardy wildflower has grayish green, heavily dissected foliage persisting until frost. Long, nodding stalks of rounded flowers with short spurs appear generously in spring and intermittently through the heat of summer. Sandy loam enriched with peat or humus, reasonable moisture, and a semi-shaded location suit it well, but it tolerates full sun if kept well-watered. Division of the fibrous rootstock can be made even when in flower, and it self-seeds generously to the point of over-crowding. For best bloom, divide and reset every 3 years. Dry rot and aphids are the nuisances. Varieties are known but scarce to find: *alba*, white with a pink flush, sparse-flowering; and *gracilis*, deep purple with slender flowers and leaves. This species is often confused with the later-blooming *D. formosa* (see May).

Draba sibirica (Siberian Draba, Whitlow-grass) 1–3 in.
      Sun
Flowering span: Early April to May
Color: Bright yellow
Native habitat: Siberia

A ground-hugging mat of creeping stems with ⅛-inch green leaves spreads well in sun or light shade to produce an overwhelming coverage of bright flowers on wiry stems lasting for a month. Repeat bloom in fall is possible, but it will be sparse. Light, gritty soil enriched with peat or leaf mold suit it well, but it may require a light mulch to survive difficult winters. Division after flowering is simple and promotes thriftier plants. There are no problems with insects or diseases.

Epigaea repens (Trailing Arbutus or Mayflower) 2–4 in.
      Semi-shade
Flowering span: Late April to mid-May
Color: Pale pink to white
Native habitat: Southeastern Canada to Mississippi

Tiny clusters of very fragrant, waxy, tubular flowers appear between the broad, leathery, evergreen leaves of this slow-growing, vinelike creeper in late spring. The scent is so attractive that wild stands of this unusual plant have been incautiously eliminated by reckless collectors. Its long roots resist transplanting from the wild, and finicky aftercare is essential to its survival. Use nursery-grown potted stock instead, and keep the plants moist at all times during the first year of reestablishment. It prefers a cool, open woodlot with dappled light where the soil is acid leaf mold over a sandy-loam base with excellent drainage. Its chief pest is man's clumsiness with it.

Erythronium albidum (White Trout-lily, Dogtooth Violet)
    6–9 in. Semi-shade
Flowering span: Late April to June
Color: White
Native habitat: Southeastern Canada to Texas

Showy when colonized, this bulbous perennial has a narrow set of 1½-inch leaves either all green or mottled brown. The reflexed petals of the solitary, lilylike flower reveal a yellow center. Cool, semi-shaded, moist soils, enriched with peat or humus, suit it best. When established it dislikes being moved, but transplanting immediately after flowering has some success. Plant new corms in the fall when received to keep them from drying out. Diseases and insects are uncommon.

Erythronium americanum (Common Trout-lily, Dogtooth
    Violet) 6–10 in. Semi-shade
Flowering span: Late April to June
Color: Yellow
Native habitat: Southeastern Canada to northern Florida

This species enjoys the close proximity of a deep-rooted tree, which may remove any excess water that could keep the corm sulking. Its leaves are entirely mottled, and the blossom is flushed with brownish red outside and is pale to deep yellow inside. Culture is the same as for *E. albidum*. An annual topdressing with bonemeal and wood ashes promotes generous flowering of all species.

Erythronium dens-canis (European Dogtooth Violet) 4–6
    in. Semi-shade
Flowering span: Early April to May
Color: Rose purple
Native habitat: Central Europe, Siberia, Japan

Twin elliptical leaves of mottled green and brown spread close to the ground to produce a solitary, 2-inch, drooping flower that varies naturally from rosy purple to pink to white. Each has orange-red markings at the base and a slight fragrance. Culture is the same as for *E. albidum.* Many hybrids now exist: "Congo," rosy-purple; "Frans Hals," light red-violet; *japonicum,* deep violet, 3-inch flowers; "Pink Perfection," bright pink; "Rose Beauty," deep pink; "Rose Queen," clear pink; and "Snowflake," white.

Euphorbia epithymoides (polychroma) (Cushion
    Euphorbia) 12–18 in. Sun
Flowering span: Late April to June
Color: Chartreuse-yellow
Native habitat: Europe

From a hemispherical clump of many thin stems with ½-inch, dark green leaves come heads of 1-inch, bright yellow bracts surrounding the true, greenish flowers. Spreading widely but neatly, the foliage turns deep red in autumn. Preferring a marginally fertile, sandy loam with good drainage, it grows best in full sun but will take light shading. Division, stem cuttings, or seed work equally well, and there are no difficulties with pests or diseases.

Euphorbia myrsinites (Myrtle Euphorbia) 6–12 in. Sun
Flowering span: Late April to June
Color: Greenish yellow
Native habitat: Mediterranean Europe

Prostrate and sprawling when flowering, this semi-evergreen has cupped, gray-green leaves arranged spirally on fleshy stems that terminate with 3-inch heads of showy yellow bracts around insignificant, greenish, true flowers. Needing protection in severe climates, it prefers full sun and a well-drained, sandy soil that is often dry. Division or seed propagation is easy. Blight or stem rot can be serious diseases, but insects do not bother it.

Fritillaria imperialis (Crown Imperial) 30–42 in. Sun
Flowering span: Late April to June

Color: Reddish orange
Native habitat: Iran to India

Imposing when in flower, the very large, bulbous underground stem produces large, glossy, straplike leaves and a tall flower stalk capped with a dense crown of green, leafy bracts. The 2½-inch flowers beneath the cap are bell-like, musky-scented, and form a generous circle of elevated color. They thrive in full sun on clay soil enriched with humus that is well-drained. The foliage disappears by midsummer when transplanting can occur. New plantings should be made in late summer or fall. Install the 4-inch bulbs on a sand cushion and less than upright to prevent rot. Avoid bruising the bulb since they are offensively strong-smelling. Pests and diseases are not problematic. Hybrids are vividly colored: "Aurora," deep orange-red; *lutea*, bright yellow; *lutea maxima*, deep lemon yellow; "Orange Brilliant," deep orange; and *rubra maxima*, rusty red.

Fritillaria meleagris (Checkered Fritillaria, Guinea-hen)
6–12 in. Sun
Flowering span: Late April to June
Color: Brown-purple checkered with white
Native habitat: Europe, British Isles

Drooping, egg-shaped, solitary flowers, 2 inches long and wide, appear above slender, gray green leaves. The uniquely mottled blossoms naturalize well in constantly damp, acid-humus soil with sun to light shading. Divide overcrowded clumps after the foliage withers, and plant new colonies in the fall. There are no disease or pest problems. Dutch growers have developed many interesting variations: *alba*, pure white; "Aphrodite," white, vigorous; "Charon," deep purple; "Pomona," white with violet markings; "Poseidon," purple pink, 3-inch flowers; and "Saturnus," bright red-violet.

Fritillaria pallidiflora (Siberian Fritillary) 6–15 in. Sun
Flowering span: Late April to June
Color: Creamy yellow
Native habitat: Southern Siberia

Staggered, bell-shaped, 1½-inch flowers with red dots inside are produced terminally in drooping clusters above large, bluish green leaves clumped near the ground. Very hardy and tolerant of almost any soil that is moist and well-drained, this bulb wants full sun and can be divided in midsummer after the foliage withers. Fall planting of new bulbs is recommended. Diseases and insects are unknown.

Hepatica acutiloba (Sharplobe Hepatica) 4–6 in. Shade
Flowering span: Mid-April to June
Color: Pale blue, white, pink
Native habitat: Southeastern Canada to Georgia

Pastel-colored, anemonelike, 1-inch flowers with prominent stamens appear with 3-lobed, pointed leaves on hairy stems that often persist, although browned, through the winter. Wanting no direct sun, the plant likes a rich, neutral, moist soil, well-drained. Spring division or seed propagate it well. Smut fungus is troublesome, but insects are no problem.

Hepatica americana (triloba) (Roundlobe Hepatica) 4–6 in.
    Shade
Flowering span: Mid-April to June
Color: Pale blue, white, pink
Native habitat: Southeastern Canada to northern Florida

Similar to *H. acutiloba* in every way except for the rounded outline of the leaves. Culture is identical.

Hyacinthus orientalis (Common or Dutch Hyacinth) 8–12
    in. Sun
Flowering span: Mid-April to mid-May
Color: Various
Native habitat: Mediterranean Europe and Asia

Enticingly fragrant, this popular bulb has retained a featured place in gardens since the seventeenth century. A stiff spike of heavy-textured, bell-shaped florets rises centrally from a ring of light green, erect, fleshy leaves. Best in full sun in a light, neutral, sandy loam, they display winningly in large drifts or beds. Because the newer bulbs have a dis-

Delightfully scented, the grand flowering of *Hyacinthus orientalis* commands immediate attention.

appointing habit of quickly degenerating into smaller, skimpy-flowering divisions, replanting in the fall with fresh stock every 3 years is a good idea. Bulbs less than top size withstand wind and rain much better, too. Propagation is highly complex and is best left to the growers. Problems with insects and diseases are not critical.

While the newest strains include double-flowered forms, the main appeal continues for these single varieties: "Amethyst," violet; "Amsterdam," rose red; "Anne Marie," clear pink; "Bismark," pale blue; "Blue Jacket," deep blue; "Carnegie," pure white; "City of Haarlem," primrose yellow; "Delft Blue," porcelain blue; "Jan Bos," crimson red; "King of the Blues," indigo blue; "Lady Derby," shell pink; "L'Innocence," ivory white; "Lord Balfour," rose violet; "Myosotis," pale blue; "Orange Boven," orange pink; "Ostara," bright blue; "Princess Irene," deep pink; "Princess Margaret," rose pink; "Prince Henry," clear yellow; "Pink Pearl," deep pink; "Queen of the Pinks," rose pink; "Salmonetta," salmon pink; "Wedgwood," clear blue; and "Yellow Hammer," creamy yellow.

Iris bucharica (Bokhara Iris) 18–24 in. Sun
Flowering span: Late April to mid-May
Color: Creamy white with golden yellow falls
Native habitat: Southern Russia, Iran, Turkey

The bulb has persistent, fleshy roots requiring careful handling when initially planted or later divided. A member of the *Juno* Iris division, it follows the usual pattern of descending flowering with 7 blossoms of 3-to4-inch size appearing between bright green, stem-wrapping leaves. Vigorous when established, it prefers full sun, some wind protection, and a heavy soil that dries out thoroughly for its summer dormancy. Pests and diseases are unknown.

Iris magnifica (*vicaria*) 18–24 in. Sun
Flowering span: Late April to mid-May
Color: Pale lavender blue with white falls
Native habitat: Turkestan

Except for coloring, this hardy *Juno* Iris has the same vigor, appearance, and cultural needs as *I. bucharica*. A white form, *alba*, is scarce.

Iris pumila (Minature Dwarf Eupogon Iris) 4–9 in. Sun
Flowering span: Late April to mid-May
Color: Blue, violet, white, yellow, red
Native habitat: Horticultural hybrid

The American Iris Society has recently unscrambled much of the confusion surrounding recent Iris categories and now places this rhizomatous plant (with others) under the heading of *Miniature Dwarf Bearded Iris* of the Eupogon or "true bearded" grouping. They define the category as being under 10 inches with leaves shorter than the flower stalk and blossoms 2 to 3 inches across. The other 5 horticultural divisions of Eupogon are: *Standard Dwarf, Intermediate, Miniature Tall, Border,* and *Standard Tall Bearded.*

Many of these colorful *pumila* types are fragrant and all usually produce several unbranched flower stalks from each rhizome when established. Good as rock garden or front-of-the-border accents, they like a sunny, well-drained, sandy-clay soil enriched with humus and a light application of balanced fertilizer annually. Propagation is easiest by dividing the clumps right after flowering (until September). Reduce the foliage by half, replant in a deeply prepared location by barely covering the rhizome, and water well. Mulch them lightly the first winter to prevent heaving loss. Various leaf diseases can be disfiguring, but the chief pest is the iris borer, which requires a carefully programmed series of controls.

The following brief listing of hybrids is recommended: "Already," 7 in., purple-red; "Angel Eyes," 5 in., white with blue spots on the falls; "April Mist," 5 in., clear light blue; "Barium Gold," 6 in., deep yellow; "Cherry Spot," 6 in., white with cherry red falls; "Claire," 5 in., medium blue; "Curtsy," 9 in., white with lavender falls; "Fashion Lady," 8 in., orange-yellow; "Little Charmer," 6 in., chartreuse; "Red Gem," 8 in., deep red; and "Verigay," 6 in., yellow with red-brown falls.

Iris verna (Vernal Iris) 3–6 in. Semi-shade
Flowering span: Late April to June
Color: Violet blue
Native habitat: Maryland to Florida, west to Mississippi

Although the rhizome is fussy about adapting permanently with ease, its 3-inch-wide flowers with orange-gold crests are showy, and in mild climates the 3- to 8-inch spike foliage is evergreen. In semi- to full shade where the soil is constantly moist and acid-peaty, it performs well. Division either in early spring or after flowering is recommended, and there are no pests or diseases. *I. cristata* makes a reasonable substitute of appearance. Both are listed in the *Apogon* subsection by the American Iris Society.

Leucojum aestivum (Summer Snowflake) 12–18 in. Sun
Flowering span: Late April to mid-May
Color: White
Native habitat: Southern Europe, British Isles, Asia Minor

Producing more foliage than flowers in typical growth, the bulb has bright green, 9- to 12-inch straplike leaves and taller stalks with several ¾-inch, drooping, bell-shaped flowers carrying noticeable green dots along the rim. It prefers heavy, clay soil near water but can adapt to any rich, moist soil in sun to light shade. Divide overcrowded colonies when the foliage withers in midsummer but avoid unnecessary transplanting. No pests or diseases bother it. The hybrid, "Gravetye" or "Gravetye Giant," has up to 9 florets per stem.

Leucojum vernum (Spring Snowflake) 8–12 in. Sun
Flowering span: Early April to May
Color: White
Native habitat: Central Europe

Differing from *Galanthus* by having all floral parts the same length, the bulb has 1 or 2 bell-like flowers tipped with green or yellow-green on slender stems rising above deep green strap leaves. Thriving in rich, damp meadows in sun to semi-shade, it self-seeds readily to produce sizeable colonies quickly. Diseases and insects are no problem.

Mertensia virginica (Virginia Bluebell) 18–24 in. Semi-shade
Flowering span: Early April to mid-May
Color: Pink, aging to blue violet
Native habitat: New York to Alabama, west to Kansas

Broad, lanceolate, pale green leaves surround flower stalks with heavy clusterings of 1-inch, funnel-shaped, nodding, bluish blossoms beginning as pink buds. Naturalizing easily in moist, cool, humusy woodlots or semi-shaded borders, the foliage disappears by midsummer. Seeding is more reliable than attempts at dividing the dormant, chunky roots. Bothersome pests and diseases are not known.

Muscari armeniacum (Armenian Grape-hyacinth) 6–8 in. Sun
Flowering span: Mid-April to mid-May
Color: Azure blue
Native habitat: Balkans, Turkey

Scented like ripening grapes, the tiny, clustered, white-rimmed florets line erect spikes above a fleshy clump of

Richly scented with the odor of grapes, these spikes of *Muscari armeniacum* provide vivid blue accents.

semi-prostrate leaves that originally appeared in early fall. Colonizing easily by self-seeding, these adaptable bulbs grow in any moist, light soil in sun to light shade. By early summer the foliage disappears and separating can be accomplished. Plant new beds in autumn. Diseases and pests are unimportant. Hybrids are several: "Blue Spike," flax blue, cauliflowerlike, double flower stalks, later-blooming; "Early Giant," cobalt blue, early; and "Heavenly Blue," deep sky blue.

Muscari botryoides (Common Grape-hyacinth) 6–8 in. Sun
Flowering span: Mid-April to mid-May
Color: Pale blue
Native habitat: France, Italy, Japan

Less vigorous than *M. armeniacum*, it resembles it except for being odorless. Culture is the same. The variety *album* is pure white and slower to colonize heavily.

Muscari comosum (Tassel Grape-hyacinth) 12–15 in. Sun
Flowering span: Late April to June

Color: Purple blue
Native habitat: Mediterranean Europe, Asia Minor

Unusual by having purple-blue upright, sterile florets at the top and pendant, greenish brown, fertile florets below. Growing well in sun or light shade in any moist location, self-seeding propagates it readily. Plant new colonies in the fall. Pests and diseases are unknown. The variety *monstrosum* (*plumosum*) is showier with all-sterile, feathery, mauve-blue flower heads and 1-inch-wide, floppy leaves.

Muscari latifolium　9–12 in.　Sun
Flowering span: Mid-April to mid-May
Color: Indigo blue
Native habitat: Turkey

Vividly contrasting in color, this bulb has a solitary, 1½-inch wide leaf and pale lilac blue, sterile top florets above dark purple-blue, fertile ones. Culture is the same as with *M. armeniacum.*

Muscari tubergenianum (Tubergen Grape-hyacinth)　6–8 in.
　Sun
Flowering span: Late April to June
Color: Bright blue
Native habitat: Iran

Dense clusterings of both bright blue upper florets and lighter blue lower ones give this bulb the added name of "Oxford and Cambridge." Straplike, ½-inch wide leaves are dark green. Culture is the same as with *M. armeniacum.*

Narcissus (Daffodil or Jonquil)　4–18 in.　Semi-shade
Flowering span: Early April to mid-May
Color: Yellow, white, orange, many blends
Native habitat: Portugal, Spain, southern France, northern
　Africa, Japan

With the continuing worldwide interest in hybridizing these popular bulbs during the past 150 years, it was inevitable that *Narcissus* would eventually become a huge catalogue of confusing names. To bring order to the over 10,000 wild and hybridized varieties, the Royal Horticultural Society of London was appointed in 1955 by the fourteenth Horticultural Congress to be the official international authority. It devised a series of divisions (the last was added in 1969) for a current total of 12. With the exception of divisions 10, 11, and 12, each division includes only the flowers that are of a cultivated, not wild, origin. Separate classes within the divisions further aid identification, and only the flower's appearance—not its height, size, or blooming time—provides its placement in the listings.

Each *Narcissus* has two major parts to its flower. A ring of 6 flattish petals adjacent to the stalk collectively are the *perianth*. Attached to it, and projecting forward around the stamens and pistil, is another petal group called the *corona*, which is also labeled the *cup, crown,* or *trumpet*. The length and color of the *corona* predominately separate individual flowers into the main divisions.

Classification of Cultivated Narcissi

DIVISION 1: *Trumpet Narcissi*
Definition: Single-flowered with the length of the cup or trumpet equal to or longer than that of the perianth segments.

Class A: All parts yellow

Examples: "Dutch Master," golden yellow with fringed mouth of trumpet; "Golden Harvest," golden yellow, early; "Golden Top," primrose yellow perianth with a canary yellow trumpet; "King Alfred," rich yellow; "Little Gem," clear yellow, miniature; "Rembrandt," golden yellow, large; and "Unsurpassable," deep gold, large.

Class B: Bicolor: Perianth white, trumpet yellow

Examples: "General Patton," ivory-white perianth with a canary yellow, ruffled trumpet, early; "Little Beauty," white perianth with soft yellow trumpet, miniature; "Music Hall," deep gold trumpet and a white perianth; "Spellbinder," trumpet greenish lemon maturing to an almost white interior; and "Trippie Wicks," lemon yellow trumpet with a fringed mouth.

Class C: All white or almost white

Examples: "Beersheba," pure white; "Mount Hood," pure white perianth with a cream trumpet fading to pure white; "Mrs. E. H. Krelage," sulphur-white perianth and trumpet; and "W. P. Milner," sulphur-white perianth and trumpet, miniature.

DIVISION 2: *Large-cupped Narcissi*
Definition: Single-flowered with the cup measuring from one-third to nearly the length of the perianth segments.

Class A: Yellow perianth, cup colored same or darker than the perianth

Examples: "Aranjuez," soft yellow perianth with cup of deep yellow margined with deep orange-red; "Carlton," entire flower soft yellow; "Fortune," yellow perianth with a copper red cup, tall; "Scarlet Elegance," yellow perianth with an intensely red cup; and "Yellow Sun," uniformly golden yellow.

Class B: White perianth, cup colored same or darker than the perianth

Examples: "Duke of Windsor," pure white perianth with a broad, flat, orange-red cup; "Flower Record," creamy white perianth with a flat, yellow cup edged with red; "John Evelyn," pure white perianth with a flat, apricot cup, frilled; and "Mercato," pure white perianth with a yellow cup edged in orange.

Class C: All white

Examples: "Ice Follies," white perianth with a flat, greenish white cup fading to white; "Iceland," pure white perianth with a pale apricot cup; and "Jules Verne," creamy white perianth with a soft yellow cup, early.

Class D: Yellow perianth, paler cup

Examples: "Binkie," entire flower opening clear, sulphur-yellow, then cup fades to almost white.

NOTE: Within this division are included the so-called pink *Narcissus* types. Most of these are seedlings from the original variety, "Mrs. R. O. Backhouse," and often fail to show pink colorings until the flower is fully developed. *Examples:* "Louise de Coligny," pure white perianth with an apricot-pink trumpet, good fragrance; "Pink Rim," white perianth with a cup of creamy white edged in rose; "Mrs. R. O. Backhouse," ivory white perianth with a slim trumpet of clear apricot; and "Rosy Sunrise," primrose-white perianth with a trumpet of salmon-apricot outside and pale yellow inside.

DIVISION 3: *Small-cupped Narcissi*
Definition: Single-flowered with the cup measuring less than one-third of the perianth segments.

Examples: "Edward Buxton," soft yellow perianth with a flat yellow cup edged in orange; "Jezebel," perianth deep red-gold with a reddish cup; "La Riante," pure white perianth and a deep red cup; "Polar Ice," snow-white perianth with a greenish white cup; and "Pomona," white perianth with a sulphur yellow cup margined in red.

DIVISION 4: *Double Narcissi*
Definition: Single-flowered with double blossoms.

Examples: "Mary Copeland," outer petals creamy white with a center mix of orange-red; "Mrs. William Copeland," white and primrose-yellow, generously double; "Texas," golden yellow with a sprinkling of bright orange; "Twink," creamy yellow and golden orange; and "White Lion," creamy white with a yellow center.

DIVISION 5: *Triandrus Narcissi*
Definition: Clusters of 2 to 6 flowers per stem, generally white, with a bowl-shaped cup.

Examples: "Liberty Bells," lemon yellow throughout; "Moonshine," creamy white throughout; "Silver Chimes," pure white perianth and a pale yellow cup; "Thalia," pure white throughout; and "White Marvel," white throughout but the cup is very double.

DIVISION 6: *Cyclamineus hybrid Narcissi*
Definition: Single-flowered, drooping blossoms, perianth segments curve backward noticeably, cup is thin with a fringed mouth.

Examples: "February Gold," golden yellow throughout; "February Silver," silvery white; "Jack Snipe," creamy white perianth with an orange-yellow cup; "March Sunshine," deep yellow, dwarfed; and "Peeping Tom," deep golden yellow throughout, long-lasting.

DIVISION 7: *Jonquilla hybrid Narcissi*
Definition: Clusters of 2 to 6 flowers per stem, gen-
                generally yellow, with a noticeable fragrance.

Examples: "Cherie," perianth ivory white with small cup flushed pink; "Golden Sceptre," golden yellow throughout; "Suzy," canary yellow perianth with an orange cup; and "Trevithian," pale lemon perianth with a darker yellow cup.

DIVISION 8: *Tazetta or Poetaz Narcissi*
Definition: Clusters of 4 to 8 small flowers per stem,
                perianth generally white, fragrant.

Examples: "Cheerfulness," white perianth with a fully double, creamy white center having some yellow shading; "Cragford," creamy white perianth with a dark orange cup; "Geranium," pure white perianth with an orange-scarlet cup; "Orange Wonder," white perianth with an orange-red cup; "St. Agnes," pure white perianth with a citron-yellow cup; and "Yellow Cheerfulness," all yellow.

NOTE: None of the "Paper-white" *Tazettas* of indoor forcing will survive planting outdoors here.

DIVISION 9: *Poeticus Narcissi*
Definition: Single-flowered, perianth usually white, cup
                short and yellow with a wavy, red-edged
                border, fragrant.

Examples: "Actaea," snow-white perianth with a canary yellow cup edged in bright red; "Margaret Mitchell," pure white perianth with a soft yellow cup rimmed in red; and "Old Pheasant's Eye," white perianth with a yellow cup edged in orange-red, late.

DIVISION 10: *Species Narcissi*
Definition: All botanical species and their wild var-
                iations.

Examples: Bulbocodium citrinus, 6 in., pale citron; *bulbocodium conspicuus,* 4 in., dark yellow; *canaliculatus,* 6 in., white perianth with a gold cup, cluster-flowering; *minor,* 6 in., perianth lighter than the deep yellow trumpet; *triandrus,* 8 in., pure white; and *watieri,* 5 in., pure white.

DIVISION 11: *Split-cup Narcissi* (Commercially sold as
                "Orchid," "Butterfly," and "Collar" types.)

Definition: Corona splits for at least one-third its length into 6 separate parts which form a flared collar against the perianth.

Examples: "Baccarat," light yellow perianth with a deep yellow, ruffled, split cup; "Evolution," white perianth with a yellow split cup; "La Argentina," white perianth with a white split cup striped in orange and yellow; "Dr. de Mol," soft yellow perianth with a darker yellow split cup; "Split," white perianth with an ivory split cup; and "White Butterfly," creamy white perianth with a white split cup streaked in yellow and green.

DIVISION 12: *Miscellaneous Narcissi*
Definition: All that do not fit into any other division.

Blooming times of the various *Narcissi* vary with the locality and with the spring weather, but the progression roughly follows this order: the *cyclamineus* and *species* of divisions 6 and 10 often appear by late March or early April; the *trumpets* of division 1 and the *large-cupped* of division 2 quickly follow; the *small-cupped* of division 3, the *doubles* of division 4, the *triandrus* of division 5, and the *split-cups* of division 11 begin by mid-April; while the especially fragrant *jonquilla*, *tazetta*, and *poeticus* of divisions 7, 8, and 9 complete the sequence by late April.

Growing Narcissi is uncomplicated. Because they tolerate a wide variety of soils and do well in light shading, they can be incorporated into any garden space. They prosper and colonize best in fertile, humusy, well-drained locations that are moist to wet in spring and moist to dry in summer. Avoid sun-baked exposures and placement near highly competitive roots of vigorous trees and shrubs. Fertilize annually after blossoming with a top-dressing of bonemeal, but do not use fresh manure in planting or as a dressing since it creates disease problems.

Retain all the foliage until it naturally withers. Grassy areas sprinkled with these bulbs should be left unmowed until early July. To disguise the fading leaves in borders, plant later-blooming perennials having spreading foliage.

Knotting or plaiting the leaves is a decorative chore but does not hasten their demise.

All *Narcissi* resent drying out, and because they have only a short resting period, install new bulbs as early as they appear in the marketplace in the fall. Division of overcrowded clumps after flowering means replanting immediately since they must produce a large root system for effective flowering. Some foliage may appear in late fall, but it is hardy and needs no mulching protection.

Occasionally the larva of the narcissus fly burrows through the bulb to cause rot; destroy all infected bulbs quickly. Fusarium rot can cause mushiness of stored bulbs, too, requiring discard. All in all, these perennial bulbs are unbothered by important problems.

Omphalodes verna (Creeping Navelwort) 4–5 in. Semi-
    shade
Flowering span: Mid-April to June
Color: Bright blue
Native habitat: Austria

Easily naturalized, this slow-creeping perennial has forget-me-not-like flowers in delicately branched sprays above broad, heart-shaped leaves. A cool, moist, woodsy soil in semi-shade is best. Division in spring or fall is recommended. Diseases and pests are not a concern.

Ornithogalum nutans (Nodding Star-of-Bethlehem) 9–12
    in. Sun
Flowering span: Mid-April to late May
Color: Greenish white
Native habitat: Southern and central Europe, British Isles

Tall, slender leaves surround spikes of nodding, 1½-inch, star-shaped florets of jade green edged in white. While preferring light, sandy soil in full sun, it tolerates light shading well, too. Foliage disappears after flowering. Since it self-seeds prodigiously, it can become invasive. New colonies should be fall-planted, and there are no disease or insect problems.

Pachysandra procumbens (Allegheny Pachysandra or
    Spurge) 8–10 in. Semi-shade
Flowering span: Early April to mid-May
Color: Purplish white
Native habitat: Kentucky to Louisiana

This native woodlot plant is unlike its showier Japanese
cousin by having dull green, semi-evergreen leaves on long
petioles. Flowering is from a slender, 5-to-6-inch, ground-
emerging stalk with conspicuous feathery-looking flowers.
Since the leaves generally are prostrate through the winter,
the early flowering is more noticeable. Spreading slowly in
rich, humusy soils with semi-shade to full shade, it can be
propagated most easily by division. There seem to be no important pests or diseases.

Pachysandra terminalis (Japanese Spurge) 6–10 in. Semi-
    shade
Flowering span: Mid-April to mid-May
Color: Greenish white
Native habitat: Japan

A popular, glossy, evergreen groundcover for shady locations, it is tolerant of a wide variety of exposures and soil
conditions, but its terminal flower spikes are rarely produced in any showy quantity. The long, fleshy stem with its
close bunching of 2-inch, jagged-edged leaves tends to
sprawl but soon makes a dense appearance in short order
from vigorous, stoloniferous growth. Although tolerant to
dryness beneath trees, it thrives best in rich, moist, acid soil
in light to heavy shade. Exposure to full sun and arid conditions will turn the foliage yellowish and scorched. Division
or summer stem cuttings make propagation very simple, but
for more flowering effect, use only cuttings which have pre-
viously blossomed. Pests and diseases are not problematic.
A slower-growing form with cream edges and veining,
variegata, needs some shading to maintain its foliage contrast.

Phlox procumbens (amoena) 3–6 in. Sun
Flowering span: Late April to June

Slow-growing but worthwhile, *Pachysandra terminalis variegata* enjoys a bit of morning sunshine.

Color: Purple-pink
Native habitat: Kentucky

From a dark green mat of glossy foliage appears prolific flowering in dense clusters. Thriving on dry sites, it likes sun or light shade and good drainage. Division is the usual propagation method, and insects and diseases seem to avoid it. The variety *foliis variegatis* has yellow-striped leaves and offers a startling color combination in the blooming period.

Phlox subulata (Moss Phlox) 3–5 in. Sun
Flowering span: Mid-April to mid-May
Color: Pink, magenta, white
Native habitat: New York to Michigan, south to North Carolina

Needlelike, evergreen leaves form a dense, mossy groundcover, especially in dry, well-drained, gritty soils that are neutral to alkaline. Loose clusters of ½-inch, flat blossoms proliferate over the entire foliage mat in sunny rock gardens, borders, and plant walls. Shearing back halfway after flowering, then topdressing with compost, promotes thrifty foliage and flowering. Division in early spring of non-woody stems or stem cuttings taken in summer work well, especially with hybrids. Root nematodes can be a serious pest; destroy infected plants. Mildew may also prove troublesome.

Hybrids are far superior to natural colorings, and some of the better ones are: "Alexander's Aristocrat," deep pink; "Alexander's White"; "Brilliant," deep rose; "Camla," salmon-pink; "Emerald Cushion," lavender-blue; "G. F. Wilson," pale lavender-blue; "Intensity," cerise; "Scarlet Flame," scarlet-ruby; "Schneewitchen," a tiny white; and "Vivid," rich pink.

Polemonium reptans (Creeping Jacob's-ladder) 8–12 in.
    Semi-shade
Flowering span: Mid-April to July
Color: Pale blue to bluish white
Native habitat: New York to Alabama, west to Oklahoma
    and Minnesota

Attractive, fernlike, compound leaves of dark green appear early in the spring in heavy tufts, but they do not creep. The weak flower stems, however, sprawl easily, especially in hot, humid weather. Bell-like, ½-inch flowers in generous clusters fill the stalks. They naturalize easily and are attractive in rock gardens. A consistently moist, well-drained site in semi-shade to sun suits them best. Division in spring or fall, along with summer stem cuttings, are the propagation methods, although seed germinates well. Bothersome insects or diseases are no worry, but snails may feed on the rootstocks.

Primula auricula (Auricula Primrose) 6–8 in. Semi-shade
Flowering span: Late April to June
Color: Clear yellow
Native habitat: Mountains of middle Europe

From a wide-leaved, evergreen rosette of light-green foliage come the sturdy flower stalks with generous heads of 1-inch, fragrant blossoms that today are a far cry from the dwarfed original of the mountains. Hybridizing has created every imaginable shade and mix of yellow and red, including some with double flowers and a darker "eye" for contrast. Precise cataloging is impossible with new improvements offered so constantly.

All primroses need a rich, acid loam, ample water throughout the growing season, and organic matter generously available. A light mulching in winter may be necessary to prevent heaving. They naturalize ideally along woodlot streams in semi-shade, but they also adapt to other sunnier garden sites if the soil remains moist and humusy. Division in the spring immediately after flowering, or careful removal of the offsets at the base of the plant, give assured results for a particular color combination; seed germinates easily but will produce some color novelties. Pests are unfortunately many, with slugs, aphids, flea beetles, and spider mites the worst offenders. Botrytis blight and "damping off" can be serious nuisances.

Primula denticulata (Himalayan Primrose) 10–15 in. Semi-shade
Flowering span: Mid-April to late May
Color: Purple, lilac, white
Native habitat: Himalaya Mountains

Even before the lancelike, crinkly leaves are developed, this Indian wildflower produces 2-inch, globose flower heads with noticeable effect. The enlarging light green foliage shows a conspicuous dusting of yellow-white flecks and grows with a heavy bunching effect that, unfortunately, does not remain attractive by midsummer. Culture is the same as for *P. auricula* and it will even tolerate wet, muddy situations if the winter drainage is good. Pests and diseases, too, are consistent. There are a few varieties: *alba*, pure white with a yellow center; and *cachemiriana* (Kashmir Primrose), rich purple with a yellow center, later-flowering.

Primula polyantha (Polyantha Primrose) 10–15 in. Semi-shade
Flowering span: Late April to June
Color: Various
Native habitat: Horticultural hybrid

By far the most prominently grown for its large, flat clusters of fragrant, 1½-inch individual florets in every conceivable coloring, this primrose has dark green, crinkled foliage that is reasonably evergreen. Culture is identical with *P. auricula*, but summertime shading is very important to restrain attacks of red spider mites.

Primula sieboldi (Siebold Primrose) 8–12 in. Semi-shade
Flowering span: Late April to June
Color: Purple, rose
Native habitat: Japan

Scalloped, light green, wrinkled leaves in heavy clumps almost dominate the slender flower stalks with clusters of 1½-inch, deeply indented florets having a crepe-paper texture. The foliage disappears entirely by midsummer, exposing the creeping rootstalk for easy division. This species is more tolerant of drought and sunlight than any other, but the general cultural rules still apply. The attractive variety *alba* is pure white.

Primula veris (officinalis) (Cowslip Primrose) 4–8 in.
    Semi-shade
Flowering span: Late April to June
Color: Bright yellow
Native habitat: Central Europe, British Isles, Asia

Tubular clusters of sweet-scented, nodding flower heads cover the soft green foliage of this evergreen wildflower, and while it is not nearly as showy as *P. polyantha*, it has been hybridized for additional colorings and even some double-looking flowers. Culture is the same as for other primroses.

Primula vulgaris (acaulis) (English Primrose) 4–6 in.
    Semi-shade
Flowering span: Late April to June
Color: Cream yellow
Native habitat: Europe, British Isles

Individual 1½-inch flowers appear on slender, hairy stems directly above the dark green, roughened, evergreen foliage of this widely distributed wildflower, familiar since the time of Shakespeare. Hybridizing has produced pure white, pure blue, and pure red variations, along with other showy combinations having darker-colored "eyes." Tolerant to more sun than other primroses, the general cultural recommendations should be followed under *P. auricula*.

Pulmonaria angustifolia (Cowslip Lungwort) 8–12 in. Semi-shade
Flowering span: Late April to June
Color: Bright blue
Native habitat: Central Europe

Resembling the coloring and flower shape of *Mertensia*, the lungworts are more dwarf and more pronouncedly blue as the pink buds mature. This species has spreading clumps of hairy, lancelike, all-green leaves with weak-stemmed clusters of drooping flowers useful in rock gardens, borders, as edgings, and even as groundcovers under shrubs. It enjoys a rich, moist, light-textured soil in a semi-shaded location but will tolerate sun if the soil can be kept consistently moist. Division in early summer, followed by heavy watering, is the simplest propagation method, but seeds sown in midsummer also work well. There are no disfiguring diseases or insect nuisances. Some varieties are available: *azurea,* intensely blue; "Johnston's Blue," gentian blue; and *rubra,* a rose-violet.

Pulmonaria officinalis (Common Lungwort) 8–12 in. Semi-shade
Flowering span: Late April to June
Color: Blue violet
Native habitat: Europe

In this species the flower bud is a deep rose fading to blue-violet in the ½-inch flowers, while the leaves are light green with conspicuous silver-white mottling. Quick to spread in the woodsy, semi-shaded locations it likes best, the foliage mounds are consistently attractive after the blossoms fade. Culture is the same as for *P. angustifolia*.

Pulmonaria saccharata (Bethlehem Sage) 8–14 in. Semi-
shade
Flowering span: Late April to mid-June
Color: Reddish violet, occasionally white
Native habitat: Europe

Dark green, oval leaves here are noticeably flecked with
white spots, while the buds and ¾-inch flowers remain reddish violet. The variety "Mrs. Moon" has pink buds turning
gentian blue when fully open. The cultural recommendations are the same as for the other lungworts.

Sanguinaria canadensis (Bloodroot) 6–8 in. Semi-shade
Flowering span: Mid-April to mid-May
Color: White
Native habitat: Southeastern Canada to Florida, west to
Mississippi River

Tightly rolled, rounded leaves with silvery pubescence on
the underside act as a slender sheath for the single, emerging, 8-petaled flower that tolerates both sunny and semi-
shaded locations with moist, light-textured, woodsy soil. By
early summer the foliage disappears, and late summer division of the dormant roots, which have reddish yellow sap,
provides easy propagation. There are no pest problems or
diseases. The double-flowered form, *plena,* is superior for
showiness with up to 50 petals in a rounded head, plus
greater longevity than the single form.

Trillium grandiflorum (Snow Trillium) 12–18 in. Shade
Flowering span: Late April to June
Color: White
Native habitat: New England to Carolinas, west to Min-
nesota

From a single collar of 3 broad, pointed leaves held well
above the ground comes a solitary, heavy-petaled, showy
flower which alters from waxy-white to dull rose as it ages.
There is much natural variation in flower coloring, especially where they are planted in large drifts and can readily
interbreed. The fruit is a blue-black berry almost an inch

wide. Preferring rich, deep loam that is consistently moist, acid, and cool in heavily shaded woodlots, this colonizing wildflower can tolerate semi-shade if kept constantly moist. Division of the thick rhizomes in late summer is the best propagation method since seedlings from the wild adapt sluggishly. Rust is the chief disease problem, but there are no insect nuisances. This is the easiest trillium for a garden development. On the Pacific coast, *T. ovatum* is very similar in all respects.

Trillium nivale (Dwarf Trillium) 4–5 in. Shade
Flowering span: Mid-April to mid-May
Color: White
Native habitat: Western Pennsylvania to Minnesota, south
    to Missouri

Here the leaves of this scarce wildflower are only 2 inches long and have compact, 1-inch long flower petals. Culture is the same as for *T. grandiflorum,* except for a neutral soil preference easily accomplished by adding garden lime in spring and fall.

Trillium sessile (Toad Trillium) 9–12 in. Shade
Flowering span: Mid-April to June
Color: Deep crimson purple
Native habitat: New York to Georgia, west to Missouri

The long-pointed, solitary flower here rests directly on the whorl of red-spotted, very broad, green leaves. Natural variation produces some green-yellow flowers occasionally. Culture is the same for all trilliums. The west coast species, *T. chloropetalum (sessile californicum)*, is larger in all respects.

Trillium undulatum (Painted Trillium) 12–18 in. Semi-
    shade
Flowering span: Late April to June
Color: White with magenta markings
Native habitat: Southeastern Canada to Georgia, west to
    Missouri

Undoubtedly the showiest of the trilliums, this wild-flower is very particular about having exactly what it wants to survive transplanting. The large, white flowers are similar to *T. grandiflorum* except the center of each of the three petals is streaked with noticeable magenta coloring and the leaves are blue-green. The fruit is a bright red, three-sided berry. It thrives naturally in acid, moist locations that are almost boggy and often appears under mature stands of Hemlock next to mountain ponds. Propagation is the same as for *T. grandiflorum*. Mice sometimes bother the rhizomes in winter.

Tulipa (Tulip) 2–32 in. Sun
Flowering span: Mid-April to late May
Color: Every conceivable coloring and mixture of coloring
Native habitat: Mediterranean Europe, Africa, Asia Minor, and China for the botanical species; Europe for the hybridization of the cultivated types

Parallel with the nomenclature difficulties described under *Narcissus,* the myriad numbers of *Tulipa* in cultivation also became confused and misrepresented until an international agreement was reached about an authorized catalogue. The first official register of named tulips was published in 1915 by the Royal General Bulbgrowers' Society of Holland. Constantly updated and revised, the current list includes over 4,000 names separated into 15 divisions that recognize the flowering sequence and the shape of the blossom. The first 11 divisions cover all the cultivated tulips, and each is further subdivided into 3 sections: *early-blooming, midseason,* and *late.* The 4 remaining divisions describe the botanical species and their hybrids. New introductions are constantly being made, however, and further modification to the present divisions is likely as commercial breeding expands significantly.

Because the description of the divisions of cultivated tulips was composed to be more relevant to the botanist than the horticultural gardener, logic suggests that the sequence of flowering would be more useful here than precise descriptions of the official categories. The alphabetical listing of the botanical species tulips follows this grouping. May-flowering tulips are separately catalogued in that month.

April-Flowering Sequence of Cultivated Tulips

EARLY (Mid-April to early May)

1. *Single Early* (Derived from hybridizing between *T. gesneriana* and *T. suavoelens.*)

   Description: Single cup, 10 to 18 in., generally fragrant.

   Examples: "Bellona," 15 in., deep golden yellow, large; "Brilliant Star Maximus," 12 in., bright scarlet with black center, early; "Couleur Cardinal," 12 in., velvety crimson with a dewy gray outside sheen; "General de Wet," 13 in., bright orange with scarlet striping, yellow center; "Ibis," 12 in., dark, glowing pink; "Keizerskroon," 13 in., bright red with wide gold-yellow border, large; "Pink Beauty," 14 in., deep rose with white blush; "Prince Carnival," 15 in., red-orange with yellow streaks; "Prince of Austria," 15 in., bright orange red outside, brilliant scarlet interior; "Princess Irene," 12 in., salmon orange with buff streaks; and "White Hawk," 12 in., pure white.

2. *Double Early* (Known since the seventeenth century as a chance mutation or "sport.")

   Description: Wide-opening cup filled with many rows of petals, 10 to 12 inches, slight fragrance, resembles the shape of the peony flower.

   Examples: "All Gold," 11 in., buttercup yellow; "Bonanza," 11 in., carmine red edged with bright yellow; "Carlton," 11 in., bright scarlet; "Dante," 11 in., deep blood-red; "Electra," 11 in., carmine red shading to light violet; "General Dean," 13 in., scarlet red; "Golden Victory," 13 in., golden yellow, large; "Goya," 11 in., light orange red with yellow base; "Marechal Niel," 11 in., soft orange yellow; "Mr. van der Hoeff," 11 in., pure golden yellow; "Orange Nassau," 11 in., deep orange red, large; "Peach Blossom," 11 in., bright rose pink; "Scarlet Cardinal," 11 in., bright scarlet, early; "Schoonoord," 11 in., pure white; "Wilhelm Kordes," 11 in., orange yellow flushed red; and "Wellemsoord," 11 in., carmine with a white edge.

MIDSEASON (Late April to mid-May)

1. *Mendel* (Derived from hybridizing between the *Duc van Tol* variety and *Darwin*.)

Description: Large, single cups, 14 to 24 inches, not quite as sturdy as *Triumph*.

Examples: "Apricot Beauty," 14 in., soft salmon rose outside, rich apricot interior with a light green base; "Athleet," 18 in., pure white; "Her Grace," 20 in., white with a flush of cerise red; "High Society," 20 in., orange with a bright golden orange edge; "Orange Wonder," 22 in., bronze orange with flush of scarlet and a deep yellow edge, large; "Olga," 18 in., violet red with a white edge; "Peerless Pink," 14 in., clear pink; "Pink Trophy," 18 in., pink with a flush of rose; "Remagen," 18 in., deep pink; "Sulphur Triumph," 22 in., primrose yellow; and "White Sail," 18 in, creamy white.

2. *Triumph* (Derived from hybridizing between *Single Early* and *Darwin*.)

Description: Large, single cup, 18 to 26 inches, heavy-textured flowers on sturdy stems with complementary stripes and margins not usually found in other types, usually blooms after *Mendel*, which it has largely supplanted commercially.

Examples: "Arabian Mystery," 18 in., purple with silvery white edges, long-lasting; "Aureola," 26 in., bright red with golden yellow edges; "Bandoeng," 22 in., dark brown-red with deep yellow edges; "Blizzard," 20 in., pure white, large; "Border Beauty," 18 in., white with pink edges; "Bruno Walter," 26 in., light orange; "Crater," 20 in., bright scarlet; "Denbola," 22 in., cerise red with creamy white edges; "Elmus," 24 in., bright red with white edges; "First Lady," 26 in., violet rose, long-lasting; "Garden Party," 18 in., white with wide, vivid rose edges; "Golden Eddy," 20 in., cerise with yellow edges; "Kansas," 20 in., snow white; "La Suisse," 24 in., vermilion red with a yellow base; "Lucky Strike," 26 in., deep red with pale yellow edges; "Madame Spoor," 20 in., mahogany red with yellow edges; "Makassar," 22 in., deep canary yellow; "Mirjoran," 20 in., carmine red with broad primrose yellow edges; "Nivea," 26 in., pure white; "Orange Sun," 26 in., bright pure orange;

"Orange Wonder," 20 in., bronze orange with a scarlet flush; "Paris," 18 in., orange red with yellow edges; "Pax," 18 in., pure white; "Princess Beatrix," 22 in., scarlet with an orange flush and deep yellow edges; "Reforma," 18 in., sulphur yellow; "Roland," 26 in., bright scarlet with ivory white edges; "Rose Beauty," 22 in., creamy white with deep rose edges; "Sulphur Glory," 22 in., chrome yellow; "Tambour Maitre," 24 in., deep cardinal red with a yellow base, long-lasting; "Telescopium," 24 in., violet rose; "Wildhof," 20 in., pure white; and "Yellow Present," 18 in., canary yellow.

3. *Darwin Hybrid* (Derived from hybridizing between *T. fosteriana* and *Darwin*.)

Description: Very large, single cups, 24 to 28 inches, strong, erect stems, brilliant colorings, long-lasting blooms with or after the *Triumph.*

Examples: "Apeldoorn," 26 in., bright scarlet with pale mauve flush and a black base, edged with yellow; "Beauty of Dover," 26 in., soft yellow with salmon rose flush outside, golden yellow inside with a black base; "Big Chief," 26 in., magenta with a rose flush; "Diplomate," 26 in., vermilion red with green-yellow base, large; "Dover," 26 in., vivid red with a dark blue base; "Elizabeth Arden," 26 in., dark salmon pink flushed with violet; "Empire State," 26 in., vivid scarlet red with a yellow base; "General Eisenhower," 26 in., orange-red with a brilliant black base edged in creamy white; "Golden Springtime," 26 in., clear golden yellow, large; "Gudoshnik," 28 in., sulphur yellow with flush of salmon red, large, some variability of colorings; "Holland's Glory," 26 in., orange scarlet with a black base; "Jewel of Spring," 28 in., sulphur yellow with a faint red flush, very large and long-lasting; "Lefeber's Favorite," 24 in., glowing scarlet with a yellow base; "London," 26 in., bright scarlet red; "My Lady," 28 in., salmon orange with a bronze-green base, very large; "Oranjezon," 24 in., bright orange; "Oxford," 26 in., clear orange-red with a yellow base, very large; "Parade," 26 in., scarlet with a black base edged in yellow; "President Kennedy," 26 in., buttercup yellow with an orange flush edged with a red rim; "Queen Wilhelmina," 24 in., scarlet with a yellow rim; "Spring

Song," 26 in., bright red flushed with orange and a white base; "Striped Apeldoorn," 24 in., yellow with stripes of red; "Vulcano," 28 in., carmine red, large, long-lasting; and "Yellow Dover," 26 in., soft yellow with a black base.

Success in raising cultivated tulips is simple. Preferring open, sunny sites and a moist, porous soil of average fertility, they excel where drainage is excellent in a sandy-textured loam that has been fortified for prolonged growth with humus and bonemeal dug deeply into the planting area. A recent commercially sponsored program in Holland of using a light application of sewerage sludge in place of bonemeal shows good promise and should be tried. Avoid using fresh manure near tulips, since it promotes the spread of infectious diseases. Well-rotted, aged manure is considered safe if separated from the bulbs by a thin layer of plain soil. Late fall planting suits them best, and in the southern United States preparation by 8 weeks of cold storage (to simulate northern winter) is necessary for bloom.

Showing no real preference for either acid or alkaline soils, tulip varieties will continue their annual flowering if the planting areas are sun-baked and somewhat dry during the summer dormancy—a throwback to their original native conditions. If the soil remains very moist and wet in summer, lift the dormant bulbs and store them in a cool, well-ventilated room until fall replanting time. This removal and storage is a very laborious and time-consuming process that is readily balanced by the low cost of buying new bulbs with an assured uniformity of flowering.

Expect subdivision of tulips into smaller bulbs as a natural condition annually so that by the third season most bulbs will be weak-flowered or "blind." The humid heat of summer in the southern United States usually exhausts the bulb completely after one season, making tulips there more of an annual than a perennial. Any spring growth showing only a single, broad leaf will not blossom at all and should be discarded as found. It is usually nonproductive to use the tulip bulblets for propagation; leave that to the expert growers.

Retaining all the foliage until it shrivels fully is important to the future flowering of the bulb, as is the removal of any forming seed-heads which only diminish the bulb's energies. Mask the withering leaves with nearby foliage from annuals, perennials, or ferns. For the plant's future survival, cut tulips for decoration either leafless or with no more than one leaf.

Tulips will bloom well in the intermittent, light shading of deciduous trees but will then flower slightly later than normal. Shady locations will, however, quickly debilitate the bulb, as will the competitive root systems from nearby shrubs or trees—especially evergreens—that are vigorous.

Cultivated tulips can be seriously disfigured at any stage of growth by a sooty fungus infection called *botrytis tulipae,* which is mainly transmitted by aphids. Quickly discard all affected bulbs and clean up any fallen petals showing signs of stunting or abnormality since the disease spreads rapidly, especially in wet, humid weather. Serious infections demand that replanting with tulips in the same area be delayed for up to 3 years. Mice sometimes gnaw at the bulbs through tunnels made by the insect-eating mole.

Tulipa aucheriana (Aucher Tulip) 2—3 in. Sun
Flowering span: Late April to mid-May
Color: Clear rose with a yellow center
Native habitat: Iran and Syria

Suitable for rock garden accent, this miniature species tulip has prostrate, narrow green leaves and star-shaped flowers that can range from deep rose to almost white. The outer petals have a thin, greenish yellow stripe. Provide full sun, average soil, and dry dormant conditions. There are no pests or diseases. This species is often cataloged as a form of *T. humilis* (Ground Tulip).

Tulipa clusiana (Clusius or Lady Tulip) 12–15 in. Sun
Flowering span: Mid-April to early May
Color: White with broad streaks of pink-crimson on outside
    petals
Native habitat: Iran, Iraq, Afghanistan

Cultivated since the seventeenth century, the long-tapered, 3-inch flower can colonize well if left undisturbed. The narrow, linear leaves are edged with red, and the inner white flower coloring is set off with a deep purple center. It wants a warm, well-drained location in full sun. Pests and diseases are not bothersome.

Tulipa eichleri (Eichler Tulip) 12–15 in. Sun
Flowering span: Mid-April to early May
Color: Brilliant crimson
Native habitat: Iran, Turkestan, Azerbaijan Russia

Readily colonizing, this conpicuous, sharp-pointed flower opens to a 5-inch spread above wide, gray-green leaves occasionally bordered with red. The inside center of the flower has a black, yellow-bordered blotch. Full sun, average soil, and summertime dryness are its preferences. No trouble from pests or diseases.

Tulipa fosteriana (Foster Tulip) 12–15 in. Sun
Flowering span: Early April to May
Color: Bright crimson scarlet
Native habitat: Central Asia

By far the showiest and largest of all the botanical tulips, the bulb produces enormous, wide-petaled flowers often opening to 10 inches across. It is, however, more visually comfortable clustered in a sunny border or as a solid bedding plant than as a rock garden accent. The large leaves are gray-green and floppy, and the glossy sheen of the inner flower coloring is blotched noticeably at the base with black markings. Pests and diseases are few, and summertime dryness is preferred.

Hybrids with a constantly expanding color range are now available: "Candela," soft golden yellow; "Cantata," vermilion red; "Easter Parade," pure yellow flushed with bright red on the outside; "Golden Eagle," deep yellow with red markings on the outside petals; "Orange Emperor," true orange without pink overtones; "Pink Empress," soft pink with a pencil marking of green on the outer petals; "Princeps," orange scarlet; "Purissima" or "White Empress," pure white throughout; "Red Emperor" or "Madame Lefeber," bright vermilion red; "Solva," rose pink; "Yellow Em-

Companionably arresting, *Tulipa fosteriana* "Orange Emperor" punctuates a bed of *Doronicum caucasicum*.

press," golden yellow; and "White Emperor," creamy white.

Tulipa greigi (Greig Tulip) 6–20 in. Sun
Flowering span: Early April to May
Color: Scarlet
Native habitat: Central Asia

Distinguished by their novel foliage colorings, these broad-flowered tulips open to about 5 inches across with petals more pointed than *T. fosteriana* and with a yellow center marked in black. The broad, gray green leaves are conspicuously spotted or streaked with dark purple markings, an attractive variation not found in any other tulip type. Sensitive to extreme cold, the vigorous bulb likes a sunny, well-drained location with average soil and prefers to be very dry during dormancy. Its problem with botrytis disease is carried in the general *Tulipa* description.

Cultivated hybrids of this interesting botanical tulip have extended its color range and blooming height: "Annie Salomons," 12 in., vermilion inside and out with a brown center; "Cape Cod," 14 in., orange red, edged yellow outside, inside bronze-yellow striped with scarlet; "Donna Bella," 14 in., cream with soft carmine outside, creamy yellow inside with a black base and large scarlet blotches; "Dreamboat," 10 in., rich salmon inside and out blending into amber yellow at the base; "Golden Day," 14 in., red outside, edged yellow, inside lemon yellow with a streaking of red; "Orange Elite," 14 in., apricot, edged orange, outside, orange with deep green streaks, yellow center; "Oriental Splendor," 20 in., scarlet red with a lemon yellow border inside and out; "Pandour," 8 in., pale yellow with red streaks; "Perlina," 8 in., rose with a lemon yellow base inside and out, purple stamens; "Plaisir," 10 in., red and white outside, white with a broad, strawberry red center streak, center bright yellow; "Red Riding Hood," 6 in., scarlet red with a noticeable black center and dark brown-purple leaf streaking; "Royal Splendor" or "Margaret Herbst," 20 in., vermilion red inside and out; "Sweet Lady," 14 in., rose-peach inside and out with a bronze-green base; and "Zampa," 12 in., primrose yellow with a flush of red.

Tulipa kaufmanniana (Waterlily Tulip) 4–12 in. Sun
Flowering span: Early April to May
Color: Yellowish white to pale yellow with pink outer coloring on the petals
Native habitat: Southern Russia

Compact in habit, it lives up to its name by opening 3-inch pointed petals almost flat in full sun. Excellent for rock gardens and borders, the robust bulb naturalizes readily in well-drained, sunshine locations that are dry in summer. The leaves are broad and slightly gray; any hybrids created with *T. greigi* have brown-mottled leaves. Pests are not bothersome, but botrytis disease can be a hazard.

A wide range of colorful variations have been hybridized: "Alfred Cortot," 8 in., deep scarlet with a coal black center, foliage mottled purple; "Ancilla," 4 in., rosy red exterior with a red-ringed white interior; "Caesar Franck," 8 in., bright crimson exterior edged bright yellow, deep yellow interior; "Concerto," 12 in., sulphur white with a black, yellow edged base; "Daylight," 8 in., scarlet with a black, yellow striped base, lightly mottled foliage; "Fritz Kreisler," 8 in., salmon pink; "Gaiety," 4 in., white with rose-red stripes outside, pure white inside; "Gold Coin," 8 in., scarlet with a gold-yellow edge; "Heart's Delight," 8 in., carmine red outside with a rose edge, soft rose with a yellow base inside, leaves mottled; "Shakespeare," 7 in., blended salmon, apricot, and orange; "Stresa," 8 in., golden yellow exterior with a red-orange border, inside deep yellow with red markings; and "Vivaldi," 8 in., clear yellow outside with red shadings, yellow interior with a crimson ring at the base, foliage deep green and mottled with dark streaks.

Tulipa kolpakowskiana (Kolpak Tulip) 8–12 in. Sun
Flowering span: Mid-April to May
Color: Golden yellow
Native habitat: Southern Russia, eastern Turkestan

Tapered and graceful 1½-inch flowers rise above narrow, crinkly edged, prostrate leaves. The outside petals are yellow with a broad streak of pink-red coloring; the inside is entirely golden yellow. It likes full sun, a well-drained location, and dryness in summer. Pests and diseases are not problematic.

Tulipa linifolia (Slimleaf Tulip) 6–12 in. Sun
Flowering span: Late April to mid-May
Color: Scarlet
Native habitat: Southern Russia, Turkestan

Vibrantly colorful and late to bloom, the shimmering glow of its slender flower adds a graceful accent to a rock garden or border where it has good drainage, full sun, and dry dormant conditions. The slightly gray, linear leaves have a faint red edge and are arranged in a rosette about the flower stalk. The lancelike petals are spaced in sets of slightly unequal lengths, and the center has a dark purple blotch. Diseases and pests are not much of a worry. A primrose-yellow counterpart is *T. batalini* (Batalin Tulip).

Tulipa pulchella (Dwarf Taurus Tulip) 4–6 in. Sun
Flowering span: Early April to late April
Color: Deep pinkish crimson
Native habitat: Southern Russia, northern Iran

Olive-green, slender leaves with a purple tip usually stretch 3 inches to reveal a globular, flat-opening flower on a short stalk with a pronounced purple-black center. Occasionally 2 flowers appear from a bulb. Colorings are highly variable, however, and it is often botanically listed as *T. humilis* (Ground Tulip) or *T. violacea* (Violet Tulip). It wants a warm, well-drained location in good sunlight and may require light winter mulching. There are less problems with pests and diseases than with the proper botanical identification of this bulb.

Tulipa praestans (Leatherbulb Tulip) 8–12 in.   Sun
Flowering span: Mid-April to early May
Color: Vermilion scarlet
Native habitat: Central Asia

Multiple-flowering with up to 5 cup-shaped, 2½-inch blossoms on a stout stem, it creates a showy, rock garden accent in well-drained, sunny sites of average soil conditions. Reliably hardy, it shows similarities to *T. fosteriana* in appearance with large, broad, slightly gray leaves and vigorous growth. It is, however, susceptible to botrytis disease. The variety "Fusilier" is bright scarlet, 14 inches, with 3 to 5 flowers per stem.

Tulipa stellata chrysantha (Golden Tulip) 6–8 in.   Sun
Flowering span: Mid-April to early May
Color: Cerise outside, bright yellow inside
Native habitat: Afghanistan, northwest India

A graceful, rockery bulb, it has narrow, wavy leaves with a pinkish margin. The showy, 2-inch flowers are wide-petaled and open flat. Keep it dry through summer and in full sun. No problems with pests.

Tulipa tarda (*dasystemon*) (Kuenlen Tulip) 4–6 in.   Sun
Flowering span: Late April to mid-May
Color: Canary yellow and white
Native habitat: Southern Russia, eastern Turkestan

Clusters of noticeable starlike flowers crowd the slender stems of this easily colonized bulb for rock gardens, edg-

Starlike clusters of bright flowering come readily from the colonizing *Tulipa tarda.*

ings, and borders in full sun, average soil, and reasonably
dry dormant conditions. The 3-inch, wide-spreading flowers
usually come 5 to a stem and are white on the outside while
the interior is glossy yellow with a white edge above a
clump of narrow, almost-prostrate leaves. This species readily seeds itself to form good-sized clumps, and the matured
flower heads make attractive dried accents. There are no
serious problems with pests or diseases.

Tulipa turkestanica (Turkestan Tulip) 8–10 in. Sun
Flowering span: Early April to May
Color: White
Native habitat: Russian Turkestan

Branched, starlike flowering from a slender stem provides
an erect accent to the sunny rock garden or border with
good drainage and dry summertime conditions. Up to 7 individual, 1½-inch, creamy white flowers with yellow interiors
fill the stem above a narrow cluster of gray green, long
leaves in this colonizing bulb. There are no particular pest

or disease problems of concern. Sometimes it is listed as a form of *T. biflora* (Twoflower Tulip).

Tulipa whittalli (Whittall Spartan Tulip) 8–12 in. Sun
Flowering span: Mid-April to early May
Color: Bright orange
Native habitat: Greece, Turkey

Distinctively colored with a tawny-buff exterior and a bright orange interior having a dark green base, the star-shaped flower opens to a 4-inch spread above narrow, green leaves with a dark purple or reddish margin. Full sun, good drainage, and a dry dormancy suit it best. It naturalizes where the conditions suit it well. It has no pests or diseases. Some botanists include it under *T. orphanidea* (Spartan Tulip) or with *T. hageri* (Hager Tulip), which bloom, however, slightly later.

Vinca minor (Common Periwinkle or Creeping Myrtle) 4–6
   in. Sun
Flowering span: Late April to late May
Color: Violet blue
Native habitat: Europe

Shallow-rooted and a suitable companion for vigorous, spring bulb collections like Tulip and Narcissus, this thin-stemmed, evergreen creeper has a showy display of 1-inch, trumpet-shaped flowers appearing from the axils of the ¾-inch, dark green, glossy leaves. It flowers best in locations with sun for at least half the day in consistently moist, humusy loam close to a neutral balance. Prostrate stems root at the nodes easily in loose soil, but division at any time or summer stem cuttings make propagation simple. There are no pests or diseases of importance. Many hybrids and varieties exist: *atropurpurea*, purple but scanty; *aurea*, leaf margins and veins yellowish; "Bowles," the best for vigor, size, flower production and durability; "Miss Jeckyll's White," diminutive in all respects, slow-growing, white flowers thinly produced; *multiplex*, double purple, sparse-flowering; and *plena*, double blue, few flowers.

Viola blanda (Sweet White Violet) 3–6 in. Semi-shade
Flowering span: Late April to June
Color: White
Native habitat: New England to Georgia, west to Minnesota

In either cool, moist woodlots or in heavy, wet soil in meadows this sweetly fragrant wildflower displays noticeable purple streaking in the central petal of the ½-inch, smooth, narrow flowers. Leaves are heart-shaped, glossy, and about an inch wide. Growing in a tuft, it is easily transplanted, but large plants can be divided readily in early spring. Like all the *Violas* it can be prone to many pests such as aphids, slugs, red spider mites, caterpillars, nematodes, and the violet sawfly, along with leaf spot and root rot diseases.

Viola conspersa (American Dog Violet) 3–6 in. Semi-shade
Flowering span: Late April to June
Color: Pale violet
Native habitat: Southeastern Canada to Georgia, west to Minnesota

Here the side petals are tufted with tiny hairs and the central petal is recurved like a trough. Dull green, arrow-pointed leaves appear on the same stem as the flower. They enjoy shaded, moist sites with humus and can be divided easily. Disease and pest problems are the same as for *V. blanda*. A form with white or lavender-white flowers is known.

Viola cornuta (Horned Violet) 5–8 in. Sun
Flowering span: Late April to September
Color: Violet with many hybrid variations
Native habitat: Spain, Pyrenees Mountains

A durable, long-flowering, rock garden plant for well-drained, humusy locations that will not become sun-baked, this showy wildflower has a multitude of 1½-inch, erect flowers arising from oval leaves with slight hairyness on the underside. If cut back severely after the main flowering and fertilized and watered well, the second crop should be almost as profuse. It dislikes intense heat and open, wet

Freshly enticing, the bloom of *Viola cornuta* "Apricot" embellishes cool sites for weeks on end.

winters (mulch with a light cover) and can tolerate light shading. Division in early spring, seed, or nonflowering stem cuttings made in late summer work equally well. The problems with pests and diseases remain the same as with *V. blanda*.

Hybridization has greatly improved the color range, size, and length of flowering. Among the best are: "Apricot," apricot bronze; "Ardross Gem," dull gold and blue; "Arkwright Ruby," terra-cotta, fragrant; "Chantreyland," apricot; "Jersey Gem," violet-blue, large; "Lord Nelson," violet purple; "Purple Heart," purple with yellow center, 12 in.; "White Perfection," white, large; and "Yellow Vixen," soft yellow.

Viola odorata (Sweet Violet) 3–6 in. Semi-shade
Flowering span: Mid-April to June
Color: Deep violet
Native habitat: Europe, North Africa, Asia

Parent to the "Parma" or "florist's violet," this sweet-scented, stemless wildflower grows in low tufts with a blunt, shovel-shaped central petal. It likes light to half shading in moist, humusy sites and is best propagated by division since seeding often produces some murky colorings. Bothersome pests and diseases are listed under *V. blanda.* Cultivated forms are available: "Double Russian," a double purple in late May; "Rosina," deep rose, 6 in. with good fragrance; "Royal Robe," deep violet blue, 8 in., very fragrant; and "White Wonder" or "White Czar," white with faint yellow and blue streaks.

Viola palmata (Palmate Violet) 3–6 in. Semi-shade
Flowering span: Mid-April to June
Color: Violet-purple
Native habitat: New Hampshire to Florida, west to Minnesota

The fingered leaves of this stemless plant are deeply lobed into 5 to 11 thin segments with the middle one the widest. The ¾-inch, bearded flowers have a pale yellow center and grow in dry, open woodlots or meadows with some shading. Division or seeding works well for propagation, and closed, self-pollinating flower forms at the base make prolific seed capsules. The nuisances of pests and diseases are described under *V. blanda.*

Viola papilionacea (Butterfly Violet) 3–6 in. Semi-shade
Flowering span: Mid-April to June
Color: Light to deep violet
Native habitat: New England to Georgia, west to Oklahoma

This commonest of all native violets is at home in a variety of moist woodlots or meadows and has wide-spreading, bearded, side petals shaded to white or yellow green at the center. The dull green, triangular leaves stretch as tall as the flower stalks in robust profusion. Divison is easy, and this species also has voluminous seeding from dwarfed, self-pollinating flower forms at the base. Diseases and pests listed under *V. blanda* apply. There is also a variety, *priceana*, with pale lilac petals, noticeably veined with violet that is known as "Confederate Violet," growing natively from New England westward to Wyoming. Both can be invasive from self-seeding.

Viola pensylvanica (Smooth Yellow Violet) 4–7 in. Semi-shade
Flowering span: Mid-April to mid-May
Color: Bright yellow
Native habitat: Massachusetts to Georgia, west to Oklahoma

Both leaves and flowers appear on the same stem, with the long-stalked, ¾-inch, axillary flowering having purple veins and the broad leaves shaped like arrowheads. It prefers moist woodlots and can be divided or sown as seed. The problems with pests and diseases are given under *V. blanda.*

Viola pubescens (Downy Violet) 8–12 in. Semi-shade
Flowering span:: Mid-April to mid-May
Color: Light yellow
Native habitat: Maine to Mississippi, west to North Dakota

Similar to *V. pensylvanica* except the stems are downy with soft hairs and the flower stalk may be leafless. Petals also taper to a sharper point. It likes rich soil in dry woodlots and can be propagated by seed or by division. Potentially bothersome insects and diseases are listed under *V. blanda*

Viola rafinesquii (Johnny-jump-up) 3–12 in. Sun
Flowering span: Mid-April to June
Color: Cream yellow to blue violet
Native habitat: New York to Texas, west to Colorado

Tiny flowers on long stalks appear with narrow, hairy, tapered leaves on constantly elongating stems in moist, semi-shade to sun. Seed or division work well, and the pests remain a slight hazard, as given under *V. blanda.*

Viola tricolor (Wild Pansy) 4–12 in. Sun
Flowering span: Late April to June
Color: Mix of yellow, purple, and white
Native habitat: Europe, British Isles, northern Asia

The parent of the large-flowered pansy of cultivation, this ubiquitous wildflower is a prolific self-seeder in rich, moist soil in either full sun or light shade. The natural color blending gives the look of a "face," and the soft, brittle stems flop over as they age to produce a wide-spreading mat. The lower leaves on the stem are rounded and the upper ones become heart-shaped. While the pests and diseases listed under V. *blanda* are a potential threat, this vigorous plant is rarely bothered with anything but overproduction.

MAY

A General Guide to the Color Values Available in May:

(Each division includes shades, tints, and tones of the dominant value.)

WHITE: Ajuga reptans alba, Anemone alpina, Anemone narcissiflora, Anemone canadensis, Anemonella thalictroides, Aquilegia alpina alba, Aquilegia caerulea alba, Aquilegia chrysantha alba-plena, Aquilegia hybrida, Arenaria verna caespitosa, Arisaema stewardsonii, Arisaema triphyllum, Armeria maritima alba, Armeria plantaginea leucantha, Asperula odorata, Aster alpinus albus, Baptisia leucantha, Cerastium arvense, Cerastium grandiflorum, Clintonia umbellata, Convallaria majalis, Cornus canadensis, Corydalis nobilis, Cypripedium candidum, Dianthus alwoodii *hybrids,* Dianthus deltoides, Dianthus plumarius *hybrids,* Dicentra formosa *hybrids,* Dicentra spectabilis alba, Dodecatheon meadia, Dryas octopetala, Endymion hispanica *hybrids,* Endymion nonscripta alba, Epimedium youngianum, Galax aphylla, Gentiana acaulis alba, Geranium sanguineum album, Geum rivale album, Houstonia caerulea, Houstonia purpurea, Hutchinsia alpina, Iberis saxatilis, Iberis sempervirens, Ipheion uniflora violaceum, Iris cristata alba, Iris gracilipes alba, Iris *rhizomatous hybrids,* Iris tectorum alba, Jeffersonia diphylla, Lamium maculatum album, Linum perenne alba, Lychnis viscaria alba, Ornithogalum umbellatum, Paeonia lactiflora *hybrids,* Paeonia officinalis alba plena, Papaver alpinum, Phlox divaricata laphami alba, Podophyllum emodi, Podophyllum peltatum, Polemonium caeruleum album, Polygala paucifolia alba, Polygala senega, Polygonatum multiflorum, Potentilla tridentata, Primula japonica, Rananculus aconitifolius, Rananculus amplexicaulis, Saxifraga virginiensis, Sedum acre album, Silene alpestris, Silene caroliniana, Sisyrinchium angustifolium album, Sisyrinchium douglasi album, Smilacina racemosa, Symphytum officinale, Thalictrum aquilegifolium album, Tiarella cordifolia, Tiarella wherryi, Tradescantia virginiana alba, Tulipa *hybrids,* Veronica gentianoides alba, Veronica repens alba, Viola canadensis, Viola pedata alba, Xerophyllum asphodeloides

YELLOW: Anemone alpina sulphurea, Anemone narcissiflora chrysantha, Aquilegia caerulea *varieties,* Aquilegia chrysantha, Aquilegia formosa, Aquilega hybrida, Clintonia borealis, Corydalis lutea, Cypripedium calceolus, Doronicum caucasicum, Doronicum clusi, Doronicum pardalianches, Doronicum plantagineum, Douglasia vitaliana, Dryas octopetala, Epimedium pinnatum, Geum chiloense *hybrids,* Geum montanum, Geum peckii, Hypoxis hirsuta, Iris pseudacorus, Iris *rhizomatous hybrids,* Lithospermum canescens, Lithospermum caroliniensis, Papaver alpinum, Patrinia triloba, Polygonatum biflorum, Polygonatum canaliculatum, Potentilla argentea, Potentilla anserina, Ranunculus aconitifolius luteo-plenus, Ranunculus acris, Ranunculus ficaria, Ranunculus montanus, Ranunculus repens, Sedum acre, Stylophorum diphyllum, Thalictrum dasycarpum, Thermopsis mollis, Thermopsis montana, Trollius asiaticus, Trollius europeus, Trollius japonicus, Tulipa *hybrids,* Uvularia grandiflora, Uvularia perfoliata, Uvularia sessilifolia, Viola hastata, Viola lutea, Waldensteinia fragaroides

ORANGE: Delphinium nudicaule, Epimedium warleyense, Geum chiloense *hybrids,* Geum rivale, Iris *rhizomatous hybrids,* Papaver alpinum, Papaver rupifragrum, Trollius europeus *hybrids,* Tulipa *hybrids*

RED: Aquilegia formosa, Aquilegia hybrida, Armeria maritima *hybrids,* Armeria plantaginea *hybrids,* Dianthus alwoodii, Dianthus deltoides *hybrids,* Dianthus gratianopolitanus *hybrids,* Dicentra formosa *hybrids,* Dicentra spectabilis, Dodecatheon amethystinum, Dodecatheon meadia *varieties,* Epimedium macranthum, Epimedium rubrum, Geranium sanguineum, Geum borisi, Geum chiloense, Geum triflorum, Iris *rhizomatous hybrids,* Paeonia lactiflora *hybrids,* Paeonia officinalis *varieties*, Paeonia tenuifolia, Papaver alpinum, Papaver bractaetum, Papaver rupifragum, Primula japonica, Tiarella cordifolia *varieties*, Tradescantia virginiana coccinea, Tulipa *hybrids*

PINK: Aethionema cordifolium, Aethionema grandiflora, Aethionema warleyense, Ajuga genevensis rosea, Anemonella thalictroides, Aquilegia caerulea rosea, Aquilegia hybrida, Armeria maritima *hybrids*, Aster alpinus roseus, Dianthus alwoodii, Dianthus deltoides, Dianthus gratianopolitanus, Dianthus plumarius, Dodecatheon meadia, Endymion hispanica *hybrids*, Endymion nonscripta rosea, Geranium endressii, Geranium maculatum, Geranium sanguineum lancastriensis, Iris gracilipes, Iris *rhizomatous hybrids*, Lamium maculatum roseum, Lychnis viscaria *varieties*, Myosotis alpestris *hybrids*, Myosotis sylvatica, Paoenia lactiflora *hybrids*, Paeonia officinalis *varieties*, Oxalis adenophylla, Podophyllum emodi, Primula rosea, Silene caroliniana, Symphytum officinale, Thalictrum aquilegifolium, Tradescantia virginiana rubra, Tulipa *hybrids*, Veronica pectinata rosea, Veronica repens, Veronica spuria elegans carnea

PURPLE: Aquilegia hybrida, Armeria maritima, Armeria plantaginea, Asarum europaeum, Aster alpinus, Camassia cusicki, Campanula garganica, Campanula portenschlagiana, Corydalis bulbosa, Cypripedium acaule, Dianthus deltoides, Dicentra formosa, Dodecatheon meadia, Epimedium macranthum violaceum, Erigeron bellidifolius, Geum rivale, Houstonia purpurea, Ipheion uniflora, Iris gracilipes flore-pleno, Iris prismatica, Iris *rhizomatous hybrids*, Lamium maculata, Lychnis viscaria, Phlox pilosa, Phlox stolonifera, Polygala paucifolia, Symphytum officinale, Thalictrum aquilegifolium, Tiarella cordifolia *varieties*, Tradescantia virginiana *hybrids*, Tulipa *hybrids*, Viola pedata, Viola sagittata

BLUE: Ajuga brockbanki, Ajuga genevensis, Ajuga pyramidalis, Ajuga reptans, Amsonia angustifolia, Amsonia tabernaemontana, Anchusa barrelieri, Aquilegia alpina, Aquilegia caerulea, Aquilegia hybrida, Aster alpinus *hybrids*, Baptisia australis, Camassia quamash, Camassia scilloides, Endymion hispanica, Endymion nonscripta, Erigeron glaucus, Gentiana acaulis, Geranium endressii *hybrids*, Globularia trichosantha, Houstonia caerulea, Ipheion uniflora caerulea, Iris cristata, Iris *rhizomatous hybrids*, Iris tectorum, Jeffersonia dubia, Linum narbonnense, Linum perenne, Mazus reptans, Myosotis alpestris, Myosotis scorpiodes, Myosotis sylvatica, Phlox divaricata, Phlox stolonifera *hybrids*, Polemonium caeruleum, Sisyrinchium angustifolium, Symphytum officinale argenteum, Tradescantia virginiana, Veronica chamaedrys, Veronica gentianoides, Veronica officinalis, Veronica pectinata, Veronica repens, Veronica spuria, Veronica teucrium

BICOLOR: Aquilegia caerulea, Aquilegia formosa, Aquilegia hybrida, Arisaema triphyllum, Corydalis nobilis, Dianthus alwoodii, Dianthus deltoides, Epimedium pinnatum, Epimedium rubrum, Epimedium warleyense, Iris *rhizomatous hybrids*, Paeonia lactiflora *hybrids*, Tulipa *hybrids*, Veronica chamaedrys

Aethionema cordifolium (Iberis jucunda) (Lebanon Stonecress) 8–10 in. Sun
Flowering span: Mid-May to mid-June
Color: Rosy lilac to pink
Native habitat: Lebanon

Cooperative plants for hot, dry locations in plant walls and sunny rock gardens, these close relatives of *Iberis* differ by having flowers with same-sized petals but pink coloring. Fragrant, dense, terminal flower heads appear on stiff, upright stems with ½-inch, blue-green leaves. Liking light, sandy soil in full sun, they do best in an alkaline condition (add lime to acid soils). In mild climates they are mostly evergreen, but colder areas without winter's snowcover will cause die-back of stems; mulch with straw or evergreen boughs. They resent being moved when established, but propagate well with summer cuttings or spring-sown seed. There are no pest or disease difficulties.

Aethionema grandiflora (Persian Stonecress) 10–12 in. Sun
Flowering span: Late May to late June
Color: Deep pink
Native habitat: Iran

Similar but later-blooming than *A. cordifolium*, the leaves are 1½ inches, blue green, and more loosely spaced. Culture is the same. Some growers believe this plant is actually *A. theodorum*.

Aethionema warleyense (Warley Stonecress) 3–5 in. Sun
Flowering span: Mid-May to mid-June
Color: Deep rosy pink
Native habitat: Horticultural hybrid

Nonfragrant, it forms a wide-spreading mat when it is growing contentedly. Leaves are gray green and tightly compressed on the stem. Being sterile, it is reproduced only by summertime cuttings. Culture is the same as *A. cordifolium*.

Ajuga brockbanki (Brockbank Bugle) 6–10 in. Sun
Flowering span: Mid-May to mid-June
Color: Deep blue
Native habitat: Horticultural hybrid

All *Ajuga* forms make interesting low groundcovers where grass will not grow, since they adapt well to sun or light shading and a variety of soils. Here the leaves are green—and may be evergreen where it is mild in winter—and the plant is a noncreeper but moundlike. The erect spikes of clear blue flowers should be removed after the flowering for a neater appearance and better foliage growth. Liking a dry, well-drained soil, it needs a winter snowcover or mulching to keep it from dying out in exposed locations. Summer cuttings root easily. Crown rot disease may be bothersome in hot, humid weather; discard affected plants quickly.

Ajuga genevensis (Geneva Bugle) 3–8 in. Sun
Flowering span: Mid-May to mid-June
Color: Bright blue
Native habitat: Europe

Bright green, upright, 3-inch leaves form rounded mats and display erect flowering in bright sun or light shade. Noncreeping, it enjoys a moist, average soil and propagation by spring division. No pests, but crown rot may be troublesome. Several varieties are available (and are not agreed upon where they officially belong): *crispa*, with wavy leaves and blue flowers; *metallica*, with bronze leaves and blue blossoms; *rosea*, with green leaves and pink flowers that last longer than the type; and "Bronze Beauty," with bronze leaves and deep blue flowers.

Ajuga pyramidalis 8–12 in. Sun
Flowering span: Mid-May to mid-June
Color: Deep blue
Native habitat: Europe

Rich, dark green, oval, 4-inch leaves form a compact pyramid with erect flowers on tall stems. Enjoying full sun or semi-shade in moist locations, its appearance is improved by cutting off the old flower stalks. Division in spring or fall works equally well, and only crown rot seems to be a problem.

Ajuga reptans (Carpet Bugle) 3–6 in. Sun
Flowering span: Mid-May to mid-June
Color: Violet blue
Native habitat: Europe

Invasively creeping in any but dry, sun-baked soils, this groundcover has a vigorous habit in either full sun or deep shade (where it flowers only lightly). It can dominate adjacent lawns readily if left unchecked. The upright flowering comes from 2-inch, flat leaf rosettes, and there are many varieties (often confused with those of *A. genevensis*): *alba*, light green leaves and white flowers on plants that are not remarkably hardy; *atropurpurea*, purple leaves with purplish blue flowers; *multicolor*, green and bronze mixed in the leaves and deep blue flowers; *rubra*, deep bronze to purple leaves with purple-blue flowers; and *variegata*, with a mix of cream and gray green leaves, blue flowers, slower growth, and a need for greater shading since its leaves scorch easily.

Amsonia angustifolia (ciliata) (Feather Amsonia) 18–30 in.
     Semi-shade
Flowering span: Early May to mid-June
Color: Pale blue
Native habitat: Missouri

Dense terminal clusters of ½-inch, star-shaped flowers appear atop slender stems with many, very narrow, lanceolate leaves that are downy when young. Useful in moist shrub borders or in wild gardens, they are durable and colonize well if not disturbed. The foliage lasts attractively until frost. Seed, spring division or summer cuttings all work well for propagation. There are no known nuisances from pests or diseases.

Amsonia tabernaemontana (Willow Amsonia) 24–36 in.
     Semi-shade
Flowering span: Late May to July
Color: Pale blue
Native habitat: New Jersey to Georgia, west to Kansas and
     Texas

Here the leaves are consistently smooth and more openly spaced than with *A. angustifolia.* The flower form is also very similar. Culture is the same.

Anchusa barrelieri (Early Bugloss) 18–24 in. Sun
Flowering span: Mid-May to mid-June
Color: Dark blue
Native habitat: Europe, British Isles

Rough, wide leaves produce stems of clustered, tiny flowers with white or yellow throats that resemble *Myosotis* for the border or wild garden. A porous, well-drained soil in light shade is critical since the roots rot in wet, clay soils. Old plants do not move well, and seed or spring division of younger plants is recommended. Division every 2 to 3 years is necessary to maintain good flowering. Crown rot is the only problematic affliction.

Anemone alpina (Pulsatilla alpina) (Alpine Anemone)
     12–18 in. Sun

Flowering span: Early May to June
Color: White
Native habitat: Europe

From woolly buds develop 2- to 3-inch daisylike flowers that begin cup-shaped and open flat above a heavy clump of fernlike, much-divided foliage of rich green. The exterior of the flower is often tinted bluish purple, and the center cluster of stamens is bright gold. Long, feathery seed heads similar to those of *A. pulsatilla* develop last, and these are the best propagation method when ripe, since the root system is thick, deep and taprooted. Established plants resent being relocated. They enjoy full sun in a moist, well-drained, neutral soil on the gravelly side in rock gardens or borders. There is one variety, *sulphurea*, with large, sulphur yellow flowers. Pests and diseases are not worrisome.

Anemone canadensis (pennsylvanica) (Meadow Anemone)
    24–30 in. Semi-shade
Flowering span: Early May to mid-July
Color: White
Native habitat: Southeastern Canada to Maryland, west to
    Kansas

Broad, 1-inch petals surround a bright globe of yellow stamens above a clump of deeply cut, dark green leaves on this prolific wildflower. Enjoying moist to wet locations of average soil in semi-shade to sun, its thin, brown roots ramble along perhaps invasively, and it can be divided at any time. Diseases and pests present no handicaps.

Anemone narcissiflora (Narcissus Anemone) 12–18 in.
    Semi-shade
Flowering span: Early May to mid-June
Color: Creamy white
Native habitat: Europe and Asia

Curiously named, this attractive plant displays clusters of 1-inch, daisylike flowers above a set of deeply incised, dark green leaves. Mainly white with a bright yellow center of stamens, the flowers can be pinkish, too. It likes a moist, well-drained soil with light shading in a border or rock garden. Fresh seed germinates best. There are no pest or disease problems. A bright yellow form from the Caucasus Mountains, *chrysantha*, may be a true variety.

Anemonella thalictroides (Rue-anemone) 6–8 in. Semishade
Flowering span: Early May to mid-June
Color: White, pink
Native habitat: Maine to Florida, west to Oklahoma

Closely related to the true *Anemones*, it has a set of heavily compounded basal leaves on black, wiry stems. The 1½-inch flower displays 5 to 10 petal forms around a massing of gold-tipped stamens. If cut back after the main bloom, it will usually reflower. It enjoys light shading in moist, sandy-loam situations, and the fingerlike tubers can be separated right after blooming. Double forms are not uncommon for either color. There are no disease or pest problems.

Aquilegia alpina (Alpine Columbine) 10–12 in. Sun
Flowering span: Late May to late June
Color: Light to dark blue
Native habitat: Switzerland

Long-spurred, 2-inch flowers, several to a stem, appear with three-part, widely spaced leaflets from a neat clump in sunny or lightly shaded locations in the rock garden or border. They want a well-drained, sandy loam that is consistently moist. Seed and spring or fall division work well. Pests and diseases are the same as for *A. canadensis* (see April). A pure white variety, *alba*, is available.

Aquilegia caerulea (Colorado Columbine) 24–30 in. Sun
Flowering span: Mid-May to late June
Color: Blue and white
Native habitat: Colorado (state flower)

Long-spurred, 2-inch flowers of sky-blue and white on thin, erect stems make a noticeable accent in sunny garden borders. Culture is the same as with *A. alpina*. The foliage of this plant often disappears in hot summers. Hybrids include: *alba*, white; *citrina*, lemon yellow; *lutea*, clear yellow; and *rosea*, pink.

Aquilegia chrysantha (Golden Columbine) 36–42 in. Sun
Flowering span: Mid-May to late July
Color: Deep yellow
Native habitat: New Mexico and Arizona

Long-lasting, slender-spurred, 2- to 3-inch flowers above a dark green clump of foliage contribute a bright addition to sunlit borders or at the edges of woods. Its culture is the same as for the other columbines. There are several varieties: *Alba-plena*, pale yellowish white and double-flowered; *flavescens*, yellow with a reddish tinge and shorter-spurred than the type; and *nana*, dwarfed, not exceeding 18 inches.

Aquilegia formosa (californica) (Sitka Columbine) 24–
    36 in. Sun
Flowering span: Mid-May to mid-June
Color: Yellow and red
Native habitat: Southern California to Alaska, east to Montana

Larger in flower size and taller than its eastern cousin, *A. canadensis*, this wildflower has gray green leaves and pendant, long-spurred blossoms, if grown in moist, thin woods in sun or light shade. Culture is the same as with the others. A natural variation in form occasionally produces dwarfing or flowers with no spurs.

Aquilegia hybrida (Hybrid Columbine) 18–36 in. Semi-
    shade
Flowering span: Late May to July
Color: Crimson, pink, purple, yellow, blue, white
Native habitat: Horticultural hybrid

These long-spurred hybrids of *A. vulgaris* (European Columbine) produce 3- to 4-inch flowers with bright and unusual colorings for a lengthy time. They do better in moist, semi-shade to preserve the colorings longer. Propagate the general types by seed and divide the named hybrids. New, outstanding strains are: "Langdon's Rainbow," 30 in., very long-spurred in various colorings; "Mrs. Scott Elliott Hybrids," 24 in., long-spurred, mixed colors; "McKana Giants," 36 in., extra-large flowers in a rare set of colorings; and "Spring Song," 30 in., long-spurred and almost-double large flowers set closely on the stems, multicolored. Named varieties include: "Crimson Star," 24 in., crimson and white, long-spurred; "Rose Queen," 36 in., soft rose and white; and "Snow Queen," 18 in., pure white.

Arenaria verna caespitosa (Moss Sandwort) 1–2 in. Semishade
Flowering span: Late May to mid-July
Color: White
Native habitat: Europe, Rocky Mountains of United States

As low as almost every letter in its name, this flat film of bright green, mosslike foliage becomes dotted with large pinhead flowers in either semi-shade or sun in moist, well-drained locations. To be used decoratively as a plant filler in stepping-stone layouts, the shallow-roots need daily watering in hot, dry summers to survive. Division works easily and best in spring. There are no difficulties with pests or diseases.

Arisaema triphyllum (Indian Jack-in-the-Pulpit) 18–30 in.
      Semi-shade
Flowering span: Late May to late June
Color: Green with purple stripes
Native habitat: Canada to Florida, west to Kansas

Unusually shaped and colored, this stately wildflower has large, single, green leaves widely divided into 3 lancelike segments. The 6-inch hooded blossom stands erect with an enveloping spadix ("pulpit") around a 3-inch brown-spotted spathe ("Jack") which later develops a showy cluster of scarlet, berrylike fruit as the foliage disappears in midsummer. It wants a humusy, moist, rich soil in light to half-shade and can best be propagated by seed. The mature, flat-topped, roundish corm is difficult to locate when spring-dormant, and fall transplanting is often easier. Where spring frosts linger, mulch heavily to protect the tender new growth from damage. Pests and diseases are uncommon, but chipmunks relish the seeds. The variety, *stewardsonii,* is somewhat scarce and has green and white flowers.

Armeria maritima (Common Thrift) 4–8 in. Sun
Flowering span: Mid-May to mid-June
Color: Pink lilac
Native habitat: British Isles

Dense, narrow, grasslike cushions of bright green foliage produce 1-inch globular heads of tightly packed flowers on short stems. A neat edging in sunny locations with light, well-drained soil, this plant needs division after 3 to 4 years since the center part rots away. Fresh seed also works easily for new plants. There are no pest or disease problems. Several varieties are available: *alba,* pure white, 4 in.; *alpina,* bright pink; *laucheana,* crimson; "Royal Rose," rose-pink, 12 in.; and "Vindictive," deep pink.

Armeria plantaginea (Plantain Thrift) 18–24 in. Sun
Flowering span: Mid-May to July
Color: Lavender
Native habitat: Central and southern Europe

Broad, 4- to 6-inch foliage has tall but bare flower stalks topped with globular flowers similar to *A. maritima.* Culture is the same. There is a white-flowered form, *leucantha,* and a horticultural hybrid, "Bee's Ruby," which is bright crimson.

Asarum europaeum (European Wild Ginger) 6–9 in. Semi-
    shade
Flowering span: Mid-May to June
Color: Green-brown, maroon red
Native habitat: Europe

As an attractive groundcover in moist, rich, humusy woodlots, this glossy-leaved spreader is not grown for its inconspicuous flowering but for its deep green, thick, kidney-shaped foliage on long, fleshy stems. The short-stalked, tubshaped flowers are well hidden beneath the leaves. In mild areas the foliage can remain evergreen. Spring division of the rootstalks is simple, and they smell like tropical ginger when bruised. There are no pests or diseases of concern.

Asperula odorata (Sweet Woodruff) 6–8 in. Semi-shade
Flowering span: Mid-May to mid-June
Color: White
Native habitat: Europe, western Asia

The dried leaves and stems of this groundcover are fragrant like new-mown hay and are used to flavor liqueurs and wines as well as to make durable sachets. Lanceolate, 1- to 2-inch leaves arranged in whorls of 8 are topped by wide clusters of tiny flowers. It does best in moist, humusy, well-drained, acid soils in semi- to full shade, but it can tolerate dryness beneath Maples if the soil is fertile and loose. Spring or fall divisions work satisfactorily. No pests or diseases bother it.

Aster alpinus (Alpine Aster) 3–10 in. Sun
Flowering span: Late May to July
Color: Rose purple
Native habitat: Europe, Rocky Mountains of United States

Daisylike, 2- to 3-inch sturdy flowers with a golden set of stamens rise well above a low mound of pale green leaves in sunny, alkaline sites that are well-drained in winter. Summer cuttings, seed, or spring division work equally well, and there are no insect pests, but mildew, rust, and wilt can be troublesome. Several hybrids are known: *albus*, cloudy white; "Beechwood," lavender-blue; "Dark Beauty," deep violet; "Goliath," purple-blue, taller; and *roseus*, bright rose.

Baptisia australis (Blue Wild Indigo) 3–4 ft. Sun
Flowering span: Late May to July
Color: Indigo blue
Native habitat: Pennsylvania to Georgia, west to Indiana

Showy wildflowers with bushy foliage like their cousins *Lupinus* and *Thermopsis*, they enjoy a sunny, permanent location in the border or along the edges of woods. The compound leaves have 3-inch segments, are blue-green, and last attractively until frost. Flowering is on 12-inch spikes with 1-inch loosely arranged, pealike florets. Moist, humusy soil suits them best, and because they have deep taproots, they rarely become invasive. Seed or spring division work well, and there are no pests or diseases.

Baptisia leucantha (Atlantic Wild Indigo) 36–60 in. Semi-
    shade
Flowering span: Late May to July
Color: White
Native habitat: Ohio to Texas, west to Nebraska and Min-
    nesota

Fussier than *A. australis*, it wants semi-shade and consistent, deep moisture to do its best. The leaf segments are only 2 inches long, but the flower stalk often stretches to 24 inches with 1-inch florets. A sandy, loose soil in open woodlots is its preference. Seed or spring division when dormant are the recommended propagation methods. Pests and diseases are no concern.

Camassia cusicki (Cusick Camass) 24–36 in. Sun
Flowering span: Late May to July
Color: Pale blue-violet
Native habitat: Oregon

A handsome spike with from 30 to 100 star-shaped florets 1½ inches long emerges from a ring of broad, gray green leaves up to 15 inches tall. Thriving in sunny, permanent locations where winters are wet and summers dry, this very large, hardy bulb should be fall-planted in moist, average soil and left to grow undisturbed. Propagation is by seed or by bulbous offshoots, which are uncommon. There are no problematic diseases or pests.

Camassia quamash (Common Camass) 12–24 in. Sun
Flowering span: Late May to July
Color: Purple blue
Native habitat: California to Utah, north to British Colum-
    bia

Once a staple in the diet of western Indians, this vigorous, onion-like bulb has grasslike, 1-inch leaves and 10 to 40 irregularly shaped, starlike flowers on slender spikes. Enjoying full sun in fertile, damp meadows, it should be used on borders and be planted in the autumn in permanent locations improved for good drainage with coarse sand dug into the bottom of the hole. Variable trace elements in the soil may produce paler colorings—even white—in some localities. Pests and diseases are unimportant.

Camassia scilloides (fraseri) (Atlantic Camass) 10–15 in.
    Semi-shade
Flowering span: Early May to June
Color: Pale blue
Native habitat: Ohio to Texas, west to Kansas

Smaller-leaved and smaller-flowered than *C. quamash*, the florets here are broadly star-shaped with golden stamens and more closely arranged on the spike. Preferring fertile, moist, open woods or prairies in its natural wild state, the onion-sized bulb can be readily added to a border with semi-shade to almost full sun. Late summer or early fall planting of dormant bulbs is recommended, and seeds can be sown when ripe. Bothersome pests and diseases are uncommon, but field mice eat the bulbs and can be a nuisance.

Campanula garganica 3–6 in. Sun
Flowering span: Late May to September
Color: Pale blue-violet
Native habitat: Southern Italy

Bell-shaped, five-petaled, numerous flowers appear for many months on trailing stems for sunny rock gardens with room to accept its vigorous spread. Leaves are ivy-shaped and small. Blossoming is fullest early in the season with sporadic flowering until autumn. It likes a moist, average soil and can be propagated by early spring division or summer stem cuttings with a piece of root attached; however, seeds freely fling themselves around. Slugs have a liking for all *Campanula* foliage, and rust disease can disfigure it. The hairy variety, *hirsuta*, needs semi-shade.

Campanula portenschlagiana (*muralis*) (Dalmatian
     Bellflower) 6–9 in. Semi-shade
Flowering span: Late May to September
Color: Pale blue-violet
Native habitat: Southern Europe

It is similar to *C. garganica* except the flower petals are not so deeply cut and the stems are more erect. Having shiny green, pointed leaves on long petioles and abundant flowering, it makes large but neat mats in rock gardens with light shade. Gritty, well-drained soil, perhaps in the shade of a stone wall, suits it nicely. Division, stem cuttings, or seed work equally well for propagation. Pests are the same as *C. garganica*.

Cerastium arvense (Starry Grasswort) 4–6 in. Sun
Flowering span: Early May to July
Color: White
Native habitat: United States, Europe, Asia

Widely distributed naturally, this rock garden perennial has pale green to grayish, 1-inch leaves along mostly recumbent 8- to 12-inch stems. It forms a vigorous, low-lying mat on dry, rocky sites in either sun or light shade. Flowers are ½ inch across with a noticeable cleft in each petal, and clustered, bright yellow stamens. Scissor off the old flower heads after the initial spring bloom for continued blossoming. Division in either spring or fall is workable. Pests or diseases are of no consequence. There is a dwarf form, *compactum*, which is only 3 inches high and flowers slightly later.

Cerastium grandiflorum 6–8 in. Sun
Flowering span: Mid-May to July
Color: White
Native habitat: Spain, Portugal, Hungary

Pleasantly gray, hairy leaves form a compact of reasonably persistent, year-round foliage with erect stems that produce

1-inch flowers in generous coverage through most of the spring season. Adaptable to almost any well-drained soil in sun to light shade, this edging or rock garden plant can be spring- or fall-divided as well as propagated by summer stem cuttings. Pests and diseases are uncommon.

Clintonia borealis (Yellow Beadlily) 12–18 in. Shade
Flowering span: Mid-May to early June
Color: Greenish yellow
Native habitat: Southeastern Canada to Georgia, west to Wisconsin

Thriving best in cool, moist, upland woods, these shade-loving wildflowers can be tried for shady lower elevations where there is very acid, humusy soil enriched with bone-meal or well-rotted manure and consistent moisture. From 3 to 8 nodding, bell-shaped, ¾-inch flowers appear on a thin stem from several very broad, dark green, shiny leaves close to the ground that remain attractive all season. Bright blue berries follow by autumn. Fall planting of original stock—better from nurseries than collected—or fall division of the creeping rootstock in established colonies is best. Sow seed when ripe and expect sluggish response for years until flower production. There are no problems with diseases or pests, except for occasional slugs.

Clintonia umbellata (Speckled Beadlily) 8–12 in. Shade
Flowering span: Mid-May to early June
Color: White
Native habitat: New York to Georgia

Between 10 and 30 tiny, ⅓-inch flowers appear in rounded heads above several broad leaves of this shady woodlot perennial. Petals are dotted with green and purple, and the fruit is blackish. Tolerant of less acidity, moisture, and coolness than *C. borealis*, it enjoys the same general culture.

Convallaria majalis (Lily-of-the-Valley) 6–8 in. Semi-shade
Flowering span: Mid-May to early June

Color: White
Native habitat: Europe, Asia

Remarkably long-lived and adaptable to all degrees of shading, it is a hardy, vigorous groundcover with small, bell-shaped, sweetly fragrant flowers on an arching stem, along with 2 broad, green leaves from each "pip" or "eye," the fleshy, underground stem. Enjoyed since the sixteenth century, it thrives best in rich, moist, shaded locations that receive an annual top-dressing of well-rotted manure or humus, along with some balanced fertilizer. When the bed becomes overcrowded, flowering dwindles and division is necessary. Carefully separate the dormant plants in very early spring or fall and replant in humusy, moist new soil. The sparse, orange-red fruit helps in natural propagation. Leaf spot fungus is an occasional nuisance, but there are no insect problems. Pink-toned, double, and colored-margin leaf forms are known but scarce.

Cornus canadensis (Bunchberry Dogwood) 4–6 in. Shade
Flowering span: Late May to mid-June
Color: White
Native habitat: Greenland to Alaska, south to Indiana and New Mexico

Where conditions are to its liking, this semi-evergreen groundcover will present an annual display of perky flowering followed by clusters of shiny, bright red, persistent fruit and colorful autumn foliage tints. Detesting heat and dryness, it thrives in upland woods to form dense mats where soil is well-drained, consistently moist, cool, and acid-humusy. The showy "flower" is actually 4 white, 1½-inch bracts (or modified leaves) useful in attracting insects for pollinating the minute cluster of green-yellow true flowers in the center. Fall or spring division of the creeping rootstalk is possible but risky; collection of solid sods works better; fall-sown seeding works the best. Pests and diseases are few and far between.

Corydalis bulbosa (Bulb Corydalis) 4–6 in. Sun
Flowering span: Early May to late May

Color: Rosy purple
Native habitat: Switzerland

Closely related to *Dicentra*, especially in its blue-green, lacy foliage appearance, this dwarf, tuberous plant has clusters of small, trumpet-shaped, recurved florets in early spring and a quick descent into total dormancy by June. Colonizing well from self-sown seed or tuber increase, it likes a well-drained, moist, humusy, slightly acid soil in sun or semi-shade. Division of the tubers is best after flowering. It seems to have no pests or diseases.

Corydalis lutea (Yellow Corydalis) 6–10 in. Semi-shade
Flowering span: Late May to October
Color: Pale yellow
Native habitat: Europe

Loose sprays of short-stemmed, tubular, ½-inch flowers provide a long-lasting accent above a lacy mound of vigorous, pale gray-green foliage attractive in its own right. Adaptable to sun and shade, it does best in well-drained, gravelly soil with a slightly alkaline condition in semi-shade. It seems to thrive next to rocks. Self-seeding prolifically, it is difficult to transplant except when very small. There are no pests or diseases.

Corydalis nobilis (Siberian Corydalis) 10–14 in. Semi-shade
Flowering span: Mid-May to mid-June
Color: White, tipped yellow
Native habitat: Siberia

Sturdier in appearance than *C. bulbosa,* the foliage here is vivid green with much-incised, wedge-shaped leaflets below dense heads of 1-inch spurred florets with purple-brown spots. It goes dormant right after flowering, when division of the husky tubers can be made. It likes semi-shade to light shade in well-drained, humusy soil, and has no pests or diseases of concern.

Cypripedium acaule (Pink Lady's-slipper) 8–12 in. Semi-shade

Flowering span: Mid-May to mid-June
Color: Pink purple
Native habitat: Newfoundland to Georgia, west to Minnesota

Showy and one of the more widely distributed of our native wood orchids, this challenging plant—like all its cousins—wants exactly the right growing conditions or it may disappear entirely. The unusual, single, 3-inch flower comes from a set of 2 oblong, wide leaves close to the ground and has brownish and thin-pointed petals at the top and a "lip" or inflated pouch outline below with a cleft in the middle. Veins in the pouch are usually darker colored.

There is a balanced relationship with soil microbes where it grows well naturally, and collecting small plants from the wild is less hazardous when dug with as much soil as possible clinging to their coarse, stringy, and brittle roots. Protect the roots from wind and sun until replanted, then water heavily and often until established. Seed is difficult to germinate, and nursery-grown plants are often the wisest choice. Mulch with humusy litter each fall.

Sandy, well-drained, acid woodlot soil in semi- to full shade is preferred, with adequate moisture during spring blooming, yet summer dryness seems to have no ill effects. There is more anxiety trying to grow them successfully than with any infrequent pests or diseases.

Cypripedium calceolus (pubescens) (Yellow Lady's-slipper)
    10–20 in. Semi-shade
Flowering span: Late May to mid-June
Color: Bright yellow
Native habitat: Southeastern Canada to Georgia, west to New Mexico

One of the easiest wood orchids to establish, it has 1 to 2 flowers on leafy stems with 3-inch chocolate-brown petals above and a clear yellow pouch. Readily forming large clumps in moist, open woods with a neutral, humusy soil, it can also be adapted to rich garden loam in semi-shaded, moist locations. Lift the clumps in early spring or in fall dormancy for simple division. Ease the crowns apart, with roots attached, carefully; replant immediately and water well. Slugs, snails, and fungi can be a bother at times. Some botanists now believe *parviflorum* (Small Yellow Lady's-slipper) is only a variety of the larger one and not another species.

Cypripedium candidum (White Lady's-slipper) 8–12 in.
    Semi-shade
Flowering span: Late May to mid-June
Color: Milky white
Native habitat: New York to Kentucky, west to North Dakota

Seemingly just a white form of *C. acaule* at first glance, this flower has a 1-inch lip below greenish white, twisted terminal parts with crimson veining. There also are 3 to 5 broad leaves along the flower stalk. Found naturally only in bogs and wet meadows, it is much rarer and difficult to locate and transplant successfully. Lifting the small rhizomes in fall dormancy offers the most success, but nursery-grown plants are still the best value. It has some preference for a slightly alkaline soil, which can be made by adding garden lime to the planting bed. Slugs and rodents can occasionally be bothersome.

Delphinium nudicaule (Orange Larkspur) 12–18 in. Sun
Flowering span: Early May to mid-June
Color: Orange red
Native habitat: Northern California to southern Oregon

Unusually colored but not very showy unless heavily grouped, this slender wildflower has widely separated, long-spurred, and drooping flowers, coral-colored on the inside and generally yellow outside. Foliage is small, gray-green, and concentrated at the base. Cut back the old stalks after blooming for possible repeat flowering in the fall. Preferring a well-drained, sandy, and alkaline soil that is not too moist, it does well in sun or light shade. Propagate by seed or division in the spring. Mildew, black spot fungus, and crown rot bother it in wet, humid seasons, while red spider mites are a foliage nuisance in hot, dry ones. In severe climates a light winter mulch helps prevent heaving.

Dianthus alwoodii (Alwood Pink) 12–15 in. Sun
Flowering span: Late May to September
Color: Various blends of pink, red, and white
Native habitat: Horticultural hybrid between *D. plumarius*
    and *D. caryophyllum*

   A very fragrant introduction from England, it is a hardy
hybrid between the old-fashioned garden pink and the per-
petually flowering carnation. Flowers are 2 to 2½ inches
across, double or semi-double, multiflowered, repeat-bloom-
ing when frequently cut, and interestingly variable in the
color range. The compact foliage is gray-green and narrowly
straplike. All enjoy a well-ventilated location, humusy-rich
soil with a touch of garden lime in full sun, and a light
winter mulch. They make a superior edging for borders or
walks. Propagate hybrid selections by summer stem cuttings; seeding will produce variable color results. Pests and
diseases are few. There are many hybrids: *Alpinus*, single-
flowered, mixed colorings, 6 inches; "Blanche," pure white;
"Doris," light pink with a deep pink center; "Helen," deep
salmon; "Ian," rich red; "Lilian," pearly white; "Robin,"
bright scarlet; and "Timothy," silvery pink with heavy
cerise stripes.

Dianthus deltoides (Maiden Pink) 6–9 in. Sun
Flowering span: Mid-May to mid-June
Color: Reddish purple, rose, or white, all with a crimson
    center
Native habitat: Northern Europe, British Isles, Japan

   Variable in flower coloring from plant to plant, the loose
mat of grasslike, evergreen leaves is covered fully with
½-inch, lightly scented blossoms on slender stems. Useful
for rock gardens, edges of borders, or in pavement seams
where there is good air circulation, excellent drainage, full
sun, and a highly alkaline soil (add garden lime yearly to
acid soils). To improve compactness shear back the old foliage heavily after flowering, and in severely cold areas
mulch lightly in winter. This species self-sows easily and
readily grows replacements—perhaps too many to be useful
in small spaces. Crown rot and root rot are occasionally a
nuisance, as is an infestation of red spider mites in hot, dry

summers. There are a few hybrids: "Brilliant," deep pink; and "Hansen's Red," bright crimson.

Dianthus gratianopolitanus (caesius) (Cheddar Pink) 6–8 in. Sun
Flowering span: Mid-May to mid-June
Color: Rose pink
Native habitat: Central Europe, British Isles

Stiff, blue-gray, grassy leaves form dense, evergreen mats covered with 1-inch, spicy-sweet, fringed flowers for rock gardens or border edges with the same cultural requirements as *D. deltoides.* Spring-sown seed or summer stem cuttings work better than division. Dwarf and double forms are available: "Petite," single, bright pink, 3 inches; "Rose Queen," double, bright rose, 6 inches; and "Tiny Rubies," double, rose red.

Dianthus plumarius (Grass or Scotch Pink) 10–12 in. Sun
Flowering span: Late May to July
Color: Rose
Native habitat: Austria to Siberia

Fringed or deeply toothed, 1½-inch, single to semi-double flowers grow in generous quantities from a tuft of blue-green foliage with thick, recurved leaves. Very fragrant with a clove scent, this species is long-lived where the soil is moist and humus-enriched in sunny, open locations. Very acid soils need correction with garden lime. For compactness and greater vigor, cut back the old flower stalks and foliage severely after flowering. Propagate by summer stem cuttings. Pests are the same as for *D. deltoides.* The hybrid selection includes: "Cyclops," bright red; "Dinah," rose with a maroon center; "Evangeline," rose pink; "Pink Princess," coral rose; and "Moon Mist," pure white.

Dicentra formosa (Pacific Bleeding-heart) 6–10 in. Semi-shade
Flowering span: Mid-May to July
Color: Rose purple
Native habitat: Central California to British Columbia

Very similar in appearance to *D. eximia* (see April), it has coarser, heavier foliage and increases by underground rhizomes. Best in cool, humusy, acid, and moist woodlots with semi-shade, it likes an annual top-dressing of compost or humus for continued good growth. In severe climates, plants should be mulched. Spring division is recommended. Pests and diseases are few. The hybridization of this plant has produced some interesting color developments: "Adrian Bloom," ruby red, large flower clusters; "Arrowsmith," creamy white; "Bountiful," fuschia red, sun-loving, repeat flowering in early autumn; and "Sweetheart," pure glistening white with constant bloom.

Dicentra spectabilis (Common Bleeding-heart) 18–30 in.
   Semi-shade
Flowering span: Early May to mid-June
Color: Deep rose red
Native habitat: Japan, Siberia

Arching sprays of 1-inch, heart-shaped, pink flowers with white tips gracefully complement the large, gray green, cut leaves of this popular perennial. Enjoying a rich, light, moist soil in cool shading, the entire plant will quickly go into dormancy in hot, dry summers. Spring or fall division, along with self-seeding, propagate it easily. It is not bothered by pests or diseases. There is a white form, *alba,* which is scarce and less vigorous.

Dodecatheon amethystinum (Jewel Shooting-star) 6–12 in.
   Semi-shade
Flowering span: Early May to June
Color: Crimson
Native habitat: Pennsylvania to Kentucky, north to Minnesota

Relatives of the *Primula* and *Cyclamen,* these open woodlot plants have smooth, wide, dull green leaves in a basal rosette and a slender stalk topped by delicate, pendant flowers with sharply recurved petals around a tube of protruding stamens that suggests a star. Well-drained, constantly moist, sandy-humus soil in cool, semi-shade to shade

Both foliage and flowers provide interest with *Dicentra spectabilis*.

suits them best. The foliage disappears by midsummer, even with seedlings. Fall division of the dormant rootstalk and seeding in permanent locations work well. There are no pests or diseases of concern.

Dodecatheon meadia (Common Shooting-star) 6–20 in. Semi-shade
Flowering span: Early May to mid-June
Color: Purple, lavender, pink, white
Native habitat: Pennsylvania to Georgia, west to Texas and Wisconsin

More easily cultivated than *D. amethystinum* and tolerating less summer moisture, it has a ground rosette of leaves 1 to 2 inches wide, dull green, and produces a flower stalk with 10 to 20 dartlike, narrow-petaled flowers in color tones varying from plant to plant. Culture is the same for both. Several varieties exist: *album*, a graceful white form; *elegans*, deeper-toned, shorter, more floriferous; *giganteum*, all parts larger; and *splendidum*, with crimson flowers and a yellow center.

Showy and long-lasting, these *Doronicum caucasicum* "Madame Mason" complement any garden.

Doronicum caucasicum (Caucasian Leopardbane) 12–18 in.
    Sun
Flowering span: Early May to mid-June
Color: Bright yellow
Native habitat: Southern Europe, Asia Minor

Glossy-green, 3-inch toothed leaves form a spreading foliage mound close to the ground from which come sturdy stems and all yellow, daisylike, 2-inch flowers with long-lasting, cutting quality. As a border or edging, it is neat but has the potential drawback of going dormant by August. It likes rich, deep, moist soil in sun or light shade, and can successfully be divided *before* it blossoms to avoid the constant wilting of the foliage that occurs with after-flowering separation. No pests or diseases seem to bother it. Hybrids have superior qualities: "Madame Mason," free-flowering in spring with persistent foliage until frost; *magnificum,* taller with much larger flowers; and "Spring Beauty," with double, deep yellow flowers.

Doronicum clusi (Downy Leopard's-bane) 18–24 in. Sun
Flowering span: Mid-May to mid-June
Color: Bright yellow
Native habitat: Switzerland, Austria

Later-blooming with larger flowers than *D. caucasicum,* this plant has long, silky hairs and minute teeth on the leaves. Culture is the same.

Doronicum pardalianches (Goldbunch Leopard's-bane) 24–30 in. Sun
Flowering span: Mid-May to July
Color: Canary yellow
Native habitat: Europe

Unusual for the group, the species has clusters of 2 to 5 flowers on each stalk above a mat of hairy, toothed leaves. Culture is the same as for *D. caucasicum.*

Doronicum plantagineum (Plantain Leopard's-bane) 3–4 in. Sun
Flowering span: Mid-May to mid-June
Color: Bright yellow
Native habitat: Western Europe

Appropriate for the background of a border because of its size and coarse leaves, the robust plant has tuberous roots and generous flowering. Cultivation and propagation are the same as for *D. caucasicum.* The hybrid "Harpur Crewe" (or *excelsum*) grows 5 feet tall with 4-inch flowers.

Douglasia laevigata (Smooth Douglasia) 1–3 in. Sun
Flowering span: Early May to June
Color: Deep rose
Native habitat: Northern Oregon to northern Washington

A dense mat of prostrate stems with gray-green, 1-inch leaves crowded toward the tips produces a showy cover of clustered, ¼-inch flowers in very sunny rock gardens with excellent drainage and gravelly, alkaline soil. Best propagated from seed. There are no pests or disease problems.

Douglasia vitaliana 2–3 in. Sun
Flowering span: Early May to June
Color: Bright yellow
Native habitat: Europe

A matted plant with clusters of stemless, ½-inch, tubular flowers that are mildly fragrant is best suited to sunny rock gardens with alkaline, gritty, well-drained soil. Seed is the best propagation method. No pests or diseases bother it.

Dryas octopetala (Mount Washington Dryad) 4–6 in. Sun
Flowering span: Late May to July
Color: Creamy yellow, white
Native habitat: Oregon to Alaska, Europe

A low, evergreen groundcover with an interesting texture, this wildflower has thick, crinkly, 1-inch leaves, wide-spreading, 1½-inch flowers resembling an anemone, plus noticeable, feathery seed plumes. Adaptable to rock gardens in full sun or light shade, it wants a well-drained, acid, leaf-mold soil that is not too dry. Seeds, layered stems, or stem cuttings work equally well for propagation. Bothersome insects or diseases are uncommon. Several varieties are known: *minor,* with compact growth and dwarfed parts, plus white or pale yellow blossoms; and *tenella,* with gray-woolly, ½-inch leaves.

Endymion hispanica (*Scilla campanulata*) (Spanish Squill)
      8–12 in. Semi-shade
Flowering span: Late May to mid-June
Color: Blue
Native habitat: Spain, Portugal

A hardy bulb that colonizes easily in shaded borders and open woodlots, the Spanish squill is larger and more vivid than its cousin *E. nonscripta,* but unfortunately is almost scentless. The ¾-inch, nodding florets line the tall stalks between long, straplike leaves up to an inch wide. It likes a well-drained, moist, humusy loam in semi-shade to sun. The foliage disappears by midsummer, when the dormant bulbs can be lifted for propagation. New plantings should be made in autumn. They self-seed readily and hybridize with

E. nonscripta if planted nearby. Pests and diseases are not commonplace.

Quite a few hybrids are available: "Excelsior," deep blue, large-flowered; "King of the Blues," deep sky blue; "Mount Everest," white; "Myosotis," sky blue; "Queen of the Blues," purplish blue; "Queen of the Pinks," deep rosy pink; and "White Triumphator," white, tall, large-flowered.

Endymion nonscripta (Scilla nonscripta) (Common Blue
    Squill) 8–18 in. Semi-shade
Flowering span: Mid-May to mid-June
Color: Violet blue
Native habitat: Western Europe, British Isles

Similar to *E. hispanica,* the hardy bulb has ½-inch wide leaves that can elongate to 18 inches. Fragrant, bell-shaped, ½-inch flowers are arranged 6 to 15 to a stalk. The botanically noticeable difference between the two flowers is that the anthers are cream-colored here and are blue on *E. hispanica.* Culture is identical. The varieties include: *alba,* white; *caerulea,* blue; *cernua,* nodding, violet blue; *lilacina,* lilac blue; and *rosea,* rosy pink.

Epimedium macranthum (Longspur Epimedium) 6–9 in.
    Semi-shade
Flowering span: Early May to June
Color: Violet red with white spurs
Native habitat: Japan

These flowers have 4 noticeably longer spurs flaring out from the center. All epimedium types have large, compound leaves with thin, heart-shaped leaflets. Usually, too, the spring foliage is light green with prominent streaking of red that turns glossy green by summer. Autumn leaves are bronze-toned, and the foliage may remain persistent, although scorched, through the winter. The ½-inch, delicate flowers are carried on thin, airy stems and have good cutting quality. Flower coloring and size are the usual differentiations between the various look-alike kinds.

The entire genus does best in semi-shade with moist, humusy soil, but any species will tolerate a surprisingly wide range of exposures, soils, and degrees of moisture. Because of their rapid early growth, division of the thick rootstock in the fall is preferred. They can remain permanently in one site if conditions encourage prospering. Pests and diseases are rare. Several varieties of *E. macranthum* are available: *Roseum*, pale rose-red; and *violaceum*, pure violet spurs. The species is sometimes labeled *E. grandiflorum* by growers.

Epimedium pinnatum (Persian Epimedium) 15–18 in.
　　Semi-shade
Flowering span: Early May to June
Color: Canary yellow with red-purple spurs
Native habitat: Iran, Caucasus Mountains

Less dense than others in its foliage mass and lightly hairy on all its parts, it is slow to spread. Culture is identical with *E. macranthum*. The known varieties are: *colchicum*, brilliant yellow and probably the one most found in cultivation; *elegans*, brighter, larger flowers; and *sulphureum* (or *versicolor sulphureum*), pale yellow flowers.

Epimedium rubrum (*alpinum rubrum*) (Red Epimedium)
　　6–9 in. Semi-shade
Flowering span: Early May to June
Color: Crimson with pale yellow or white spurs
Native habitat: Japan

Juvenile foliage is noticeably reddish and the showy, 1-inch flowers are more abundant in this species. The culture is the same as with *E. macranthum*.

Epimedium youngianum (*grandiflorum niveum*) (Snowy
　　Epimedium) 12–15 in. Semi-shade
Flowering span: Early May to mid-June
Color: White
Native habitat: Japan

There is still botanical disagreement about the correct placement for this interesting plant. The flowers are supposedly heavier with short spurs above finer textured, smaller leaves, but other experts claim the spurs are longer. It should be treated like the others for culture.

Epimedium warleyense (Warley Epimedium) 9–12 in.
  Semi-shade
Flowering span: Early May to June
Color: Orange with brown spurs
Native habitat: Horticultural hybrid

A novel color breakthrough of large flowers and vigorous growth. Cultivation is the same as for *E. macranthum.*

Erigeron bellidifolius (pulchellus) (Poor Robin's Plantain)
  18–24 in. Sun
Flowering span: Early May to mid-June
Color: Lavender to bluish white
Native habitat: Maine to Florida, west to Texas and Minnesota

Daisylike, solitary flowers with wide yellow centers on hairy stems arise from a base of several dark green, narrow leaves for this better-than-average representative of the many types of *Erigeron.* Preferring a hot, dry site with sandy, almost impoverished, and well-drained soil, they can also be grown successfully in light shade and slightly moist conditions. Spring division, seed, or rooted offsets are the propagation methods. There are no insect pests of consequence but "aster yellows" disease causes stunting or yellowing of the foliage.

Erigeron glaucus (Beach Fleabane, Seaside Daisy) 3–10 in.
  Sun
Flowering span: Early May to mid-June, continual on the Pacific coast
Color: Lavender blue
Native habitat: Coastal California to central Oregon

Generous flowering from 1-inch blossoms with upturned petals around a golden center make this wildflower useful for rock garden areas with sandy, alkaline soils of good drainage in sunny, exposed locations. It is propagated the same as *E. bellidifolius,* and probably has less disease nuisance at its natural seashore habitat. A variety, *semperflorens,* is dwarf and more heavily flowered.

Galax aphylla (Galax) 6–24 in. Semi-shade
Flowering span: Late May to July
Color: White
Native habitat: Virginia and Kentucky, south to Alabama

These evergreen leaves have long been used in florists' decorative work because of their color, size, and durability. In the garden the new foliage is bright green but changes to a glossy bronze by fall. Leathery, rounded 3- to 6-inch-wide leaves appear on long, wiry stems coming from an underground stem. The tall flower spikes are compactly filled with tiny blossoms. It likes a moist, cool, acid-humusy soil in semi-shade to shade and thrives especially well in conjunction with members of the Rhododendron family. Spring or fall division, along with seeding, work well for propagation. Pests and diseases are uncommon.

Gentiana acaulis (Stemless Gentian) 2–4 in. Sun
Flowering span: Early May to June
Color: Dark blue
Native habitat: Mountains of western Europe

Vivid in flower, this alpine plant has a great reluctance to blossom—even with every growing condition letter-perfect. With luck, trumpet flowers an inch wide and 2 inches long poke up out of a low, evergreen mat of dark green, glossy, broad leaves. Plant in full sun where the soil is well-drained, rich, sandy, and moist. Division of the clump is best, but seed works well, too. No pests or diseases seem to bother this plant. The rare variety *alba* has white blossoms, while *dinarica* is supposed to be superior in form and flower. There are more similarities than substantial garden differences between this gentian and *alpina, angustifolia,* and *clusii,* which need the same care and have the same blooming reluctance.

Geranium endressii (Pyrenean Crane's-bill) 15–18 in. Sun
Flowering span: Late May to September
Color: Rose pink
Native habitat: Pyrenees Mountains

Heavy mounds of dull, dark green, but nicely incised leaves are enlived by showy, 1½-inch flowers, two to a stalk in generous profusion, early in the season and spotty through the summer. Enjoying full sun or light shade equally, this vigorous perennial will do well in any moist, well-drained soil of average fertility. Spring or fall division, summer stem cuttings, or seed give equally good results. Various leaf spot diseases, botrytis blight, and an affliction called "crinkle" can create nuisances, but insects seem to shun it. Hybrids have superior color qualities: "Johnson's Blue," lavender blue; and "Wargrave Pink," a deep pink.

Geranium maculatum (Wild Geranium) 12–18 in. Semi-
   shade
Flowering span: Late May to July
Color: Pale rose
Native habitat: Maine to Georgia, west to South Dakota

From a basal cluster of deeply cut, dull green leaves come erect stems bearing loose clusters of 1½-inch, noticeable flowers. Any average soil with good moisture in semi-shade suits it well, and humus mulch keeps it from drying out as well as protecting the plump buds near the ground level from loss by winter freezing. Spring or fall division of the stout rhizomes, along with seeding, give good results. The pests are the same as for *G. endressii.*

Geranium sanguineum (Blood-red Geranium) 12–18 in.
   Sun
Flowering span: Late May to October
Color: Purple red
Native habitat: Europe, western Asia

Vigorous in sunny borders or on the edges of woods in full sun or light shading, the plant has very hairy, 7-parted, lacy leaves and 1½-inch vivid flowers in large mounds for the en-tire summer. Adaptable to almost any well-drained, moist soil, the foliage turns a noticeable red with frost in mid-autumn. Seed or division in spring or fall work well, and the few pest nuisances are listed under *G. endressii.* A white form, *album,* is 9 inches and prostrate in growth, while the

Delicate foliage and flowering make this *Geranium sanguineum
lancastriensis* prominently attractive.

variety, *lancastriensis* (*prostratum*), has light rose pink blossoms, a creeping, carpetlike habit, and is only 6 inches tall.

Geum borisi (Hybrid Avens)   9–12 in.   Sun
Flowering span: Late May to July, repeating in early au-
    tumn
Color: Orange scarlet
Native habitat: Horticultural hybrid of *G. bulgaricum* and
    G. reptans

Wedge-shaped, deeply toothed leaves form heavy mounds
of dark green foliage close to the ground and produce sprays
of showy, double-petaled, 1½-inch flowers resembling its
distant cousin, the rose. Blossom color ranges from orange-
scarlet to yellow-orange. A light, rich, moist, and well-
drained soil (especially in winter) in full sun or light shade
enhances performance. Protect with a light mulch in severely cold areas. Division in spring or fall plus spring seeding, are the recommended propagation methods. Sow bugs
seem to be their worst pest, and diseases are not problematic.

Geum chiloense (Chilean Avens) 18–24 in. Sun
Flowering span: Late May to July, repeating in early autumn
Color: Scarlet
Native habitat: Chile

While not reliably hardy in every locality, they offer a vivid color range in hybrids that is difficult to find elsewhere. The double flowers are 1½ inches across with leaves 3-parted and deeply cut. Their culture is the same as for *G. borisi.* The many hybrids include: "Dolly North," orange-yellow; "Fire Opal," flame-colored; "Lady Stratheden," yellow, 24 in.; "Mrs. Bradshaw," crimson, 24 in.; "Prince of Orange," orange-yellow, 18 in.; and "Princess Juliana," bright orange, 24 in. Both "Lady Stratheden" and "Mrs. Bradshaw" appear to weaken and diminish more quickly than the other varieties.

Geum montanum (Yellow Mountain Avens) 3–6 in. Sun
Flowering span: Late May to July
Color: Bright yellow
Native habitat: Southern Europe

As a rock garden plant it works well where it has bright sun and ample moisture. Low mounds of heart-shaped leaves with erect, single, 1½-inch flowers are followed by long, feathery seed-heads. See *G. borisi* for cultivation.

Geum peckii 9–12 in. Semi-shade
Flowering span: Early May to July
Color: Deep yellow
Native habitat: New Hampshire, Maine, Nova Scotia

This wildflower is not as showy as some of the other *Geum* types, but it has value in the mountainous locales where it is native. The leaves are glossy, rounded, and sharply toothed, while the single, 1-inch flower is a conspicuous mass of stamens. It prefers damp but well-drained, acid locations with generous humus. Division or seed propagate it best. There seem to be no particular pests or diseases.

Geum rivale (Water Avens) 18–24 in. Semi-shade
Flowering span: Late May to mid-July
Color: Purple orange
Native habitat: Southeastern Canada to New Jersey, west to
    Illinois and Minnesota, Europe, British Isles

Drooping, clawlike flowers on reddish, unbranched stems rise from a ground-hugging clump of 3-parted leaves with noticeable teeth. It likes wet meadows or bogs in semi-shade. Seed or division suit it well, and there is a white form, *album*. Pests or diseases are uncommon.

Geum triflorum (Apache Plume) 9–12 in. Semi-shade
Flowering span: Early May to July
Color: Purplish red
Native habitat: Western New York to British Columbia,
    south to New Mexico and California

Unusual for having feathery, pinnately compound leaves covered with soft hairs, this compact wildflower has at least 3 drooping, jug-shaped flowers per stalk and a strange, 2-inch-long fruit resembling an elongated whisk-duster. It likes a light, consistently moist, humusy soil in semi-shade and can be divided or seeded where more plants are wanted. Pest or disease problems are unknown.

Globularia trichosantha (Syrian Glove-daisy) 4–8 in.
    Semi-shade
Flowering span: Late May to July
Color: Light blue
Native habitat: Asia Minor, Syria

In a rock garden with light shading this slow groundcover displays dull green, narrow leaves around stout flower stalks with 1-inch round-headed blossoms in generous profusion. It wants a moist, well-drained, average soil with a dash of garden lime. Division or seeding work equally well. There appears to be no problem with insects or diseases.

Houstonia caerulea (Common Bluets) 1–6 in. Sun
Flowering span: Early May to June

Color: Pale blue to white
Native habitat: Southeastern Canada to Alabama

Tufts of narrow, dark green, 1-inch leaves produce a host of slender flower stalks topped with single, 4-pointed tiny flowers having a deep yellow center. Thriving in moist, well-drained, average soil almost anywhere, it is better given a wild area to itself because it self-seeds readily into nearby lawns or loose pathways in full sun or light shade. No pests or diseases seem to bother this stalwart.

Houstonia purpurea (Purple Bluets) 4–18 in. Semi-shade
Flowering span: Late May to July
Color: Pale violet to white
Native habitat: Pennsylvania to Georgia, west to Iowa

Lancelike, 3- to 4-inch leaves form a tuft from which appear long flower stalks with ½-inch, funnel-shaped flowers. It enjoys a dry, rocky, acid soil in the semi-shade of open woods. Spring division is best, and there are no pest or disease problems.

Hutchinsia alpina (Alpencress) 2–4 in. Semi-shade
Flowering span: Mid-May to mid-June
Color: Pure white
Native habitat: Pyrenees Mountains

As a rock garden groundcover for light shade, this long-flowering plant has glossy, dark green, feathery leaves in tufts. Clusters of flowers resembling *Draba* cover the foliage, and it will thrive with ample moisture in well-drained, alkaline soils. Seeds, summer cuttings, or division work well. Pests and diseases are unknown.

Hypoxis hirsuta (Yellow Star-grass) 9–12 in. Sun
Flowering span: Late May to August
Color: Bright yellow
Native habitat: Southeastern Canada to Florida, west to Texas

Tufts of tall but narrow, grassy leaves produce clusters of 6-pointed, 1-inch, wide-spreading flowers that can continue blooming well into the summer if moisture is ample. Acid, well-drained, sandy loam in sun to semi-shade helps them prosper. Division of the dormant corms is the reliable propagation method. Diseases and pests are rare.

Iberis saxatilis (Rock Candytuft) 3–6 in. Sun
Flowering span: Mid-May to mid-June
Color: White
Native habitat: Southern Europe

Noticeable in rock gardens with full sun, the flat-topped, 1½-inch flower heads of this prostrate evergreen rise above an irregular assortment of twisted stems with short, cylindrical leaves. Enjoying a well-drained, gravelly soil most, it likes alkaline conditions that can be created by adding garden lime to acid soils. Seed or summertime cuttings are best for propagation. No pests or diseases are known.

Iberis sempervirens (Evergreen Candytuft) 9–12 in. Sun
Flowering span: Mid-May to mid-June
Color: White
Native habitat: Southern Europe

Used as a shrubby evergreen edging or a rock garden accent, the neatly spreading foliage and profuse flowering of this durable plant are rarely matched. Small, dark green, elongated leaves on slender, arching stems are fully masked by 1½-inch, slightly pyramidal flower heads. Leggy plants can be sheared back heavily after flowering. It thrives in full sun on well-drained, rich soil and is easily propagated by seed or summer stem cuttings. Diseases and pests are not bothersome. Many hybrids exist: "Autumn Snow," 7 in., reblooms lightly in the fall; "Christmas Snow," 6 in., blooms occasionally in late fall and winter in mild areas; "Little Gem," 5 in., compact; "Purity," 7 in., dense and long-flowering; "Snowflake," 6 in., compact and large-flowered; and "Snowmantle," 10 in., wide-spreading and heavily flowered.

Ipheion uniflora (*Tritelia uniflora*) (Spring Star-flower) 6–8 in. Sun
Flowering span: Early May to June

Color: Pale lilac
Native habitat: Argentina, Peru

Solitary, 1-inch, trumpet-shaped blossoms open into a star above narrow, grassy foliage which withers by midsummer. Not entirely durable, the bulbs can increase easily into large mats from offshoots in sun or light shading. It prefers a rich, well-drained soil, and new plantings should be made in the fall. Pests and diseases are unknown. The variety *violaceum* is almost white with violet striping, while *caerulea* has porcelain-blue flowers.

Iris cristata (Crested Iris)   4–9 in.   Semi-shade
Flowering span: Early May to June
Color: Lavender blue
Native habitat: Maryland to Georgia, west to Arkansas

Forming wide mats readily, this creeping perennial has a slender, underground stem which often rises to the surface. The 1-inch wide, flat leaves are taller than the blooms but arch backward. The wide-spreading, 4-inch flowers have narrow petals crested with white or yellow. Enjoying a moist, rich, acid-humusy soil best, they will adapt to sunny locations if kept consistently moist. Division after flowering

Nestled into a woodlot setting, *Iris cristata* adds a winsome note of color and texture.

is recommended, and they have no bothersome pests or insects. There is a pure white form, *alba,* but it is scarce. The American Iris Society places this species under the *Evansia* or "crested iris" subsection.

Iris gracilipes (Slender Iris) 6–9 in. Semi-shade
Flowering span: Late May to mid-June
Color: Lilac pink
Native habitat: Japan

Ruffled, wide-petaled blossoms with conspicuous orange crests will appear on slender, branched stalks above a heavy clump of ½-inch-wide arching leaves in shady woodlots or wild garden areas. It enjoys a moist, acid, humusy loam in light to heavy shading and can be easily divided before its spring flowering. Pests and diseases do not seem to faze this sturdy wildflower. A less vigorous variety, *alba,* has pure white blossoms, while the scarce *flore-pleno* has semi-double flowers of lavender. The American Iris Society lists this in the *Evansia* subsection.

Iris prismatica (gracilis) (Slender Blue Flag) 24–36 in. Sun
Flowering span: Mid-May to mid-June
Color: Bright lilac
Native habitat: Nova Scotia to coastal Georgia

Clumps of grasslike, ¼-inch-wide leaves up to 2 inches long produce slender, graceful flower stalks with blossoms about 3 inches across on marshes, swamps, and wet meadows in sun or light shade. Surprisingly, this wildflower will also grow well in drier, acid soil, but its place is still by the waterside. Division of the creeping rhizome is difficult and fall seeding is more successful for propagation. The pest and disease list is negligible. *I. virginica* (Southern Blue Flag) is somewhat similar. The American Iris Society places both under the *Apogon* subsection.

Iris pseudacorus (lutea) (Yellow Flag) 36–48 in. Sun
Flowering span: Late May to July
Color: Bright yellow

Native habitat: Europe, North Africa, Asia Minor, eastern United States

A naturally adaptive waterside plant making generous clumps of tall, 1-inch-wide leaves, this widely distributed plant can also be raised satisfactorily in drier situations of sun or light shading, well supplied with moisture and humus. The 2-inch-wide flowers are center-marked with noticeable brown veins. Early spring or fall division, along with fall seeding, gives good results, and there seem to be no pests or diseases. A scarce variety, *variegata,* has foliage with creamy white striping. This species is listed as an *Apogon* in classification by the American Iris Society.

Iris: rhizomatous hybrids 10–40 in. Sun
Flowering span: Early May to mid-June
Color: All those of the rainbow
Native habitat: Horticultural hybrids

As with other plant categories having great appeal for both the commercial grower and the gardener, the horticultural iris has had its share of confused naming and irregular assignments to proper groupings. The American Iris Society has now devised a reclassification placing the initial emphasis on the two main forms of the underground stem: the *bulb* and the *rhizome.* Because the rhizomatous iris is the largest group in cultivation, it has been further divided into the *bearded,* the *beardless,* and the *crested.* The rhizomes of the spring-flowering bearded iris are usually large and fleshy, while those of the early summer, beardless iris are generally fibrous.

The plant height in flower, the blooming season, and the size of the individual blossom are the main determinants used to classify those iris which are in the *Eupogon* or "true bearded" category. The 6 horticultural divisions of bearded iris are: *Miniature Dwarf, Standard Dwarf, Intermediate, Miniature Tall, Border,* and *Standard Tall Bearded.* Since the rhizomatous Miniature Dwarfs bloom mostly in April, they are so referenced in that month under *Iris pumila.* The culture for all bearded rhizomatous iris is also detailed under that heading.

Standard Dwarf Bearded Iris

Classified as being 10 to 15 inches tall with leaves nearly as high as the flowers and blossoms 3 to 4 inches across; starts blooming in early May.

White: "Baby Snowflake," "Moonspinner," "Small Cloud"

Cream: "Baria," "Blonde Doll," "Lemon Flare"

Yellow: "Brassie," "Coreop," "Golden Fair"

Yellow and brown: "Centerpiece," "Lilli-Var"

Blue: "Blue Denim," "Small Sky," "Small Wonder," "Tinkerbell"

Purple: "Dark Fairy," "Pagan Midget"

Black: "Little Grackle," "Shine Boy"

Red-toned: "Royal Thumbprint," "Velvet Caper"

Blends: "Aqua Green," "Little Witch," "Sky Torch," "Spring Mist"

Intermediate Bearded Iris

Classified as being 15 to 28 inches tall with flowers 2 to 4 inches across; starts blooming in mid-May, slightly later than the Standard Dwarfs.

White: "Arctic Flare," "Cloud Fluff," "Little Angel"

Yellow: "Barbi," "Butterbit," "Lime Ripples"

Yellow and white: "Frosty Lemonade," "Interim"

Blue: "Arctic Ruffles," "Blue Fragrance," "Moonchild"

Lavender: "First Lilac"

Purple: "Black Magic," "Elfin Royal," "Marine Wave"

Black: "Black Hawk," "Dark Eden"

Red-toned: "Maroon Caper," "Red Orchid," "Ruby Glow"

Pink: "Lillipinkput," "Pink Fancy," "Pink Reward," "Sweet Allegro"

Miniature Tall Bearded Iris

Classified as being 18 to 26 inches tall with flowers 2½ inches across and slender, wiry stems; commonly known as "table iris"; starts blooming in late May: "Cherwink," light blue; "Daystar," white with orange beards; "Kinglet," yellow; "Little Helen," white with violet falls; "Tom Tit," deep blue-violet; "Warbler," yellow.

Border Bearded Iris

Classified as being under 28 inches tall with 3- to 4-inch-wide smaller-scaled flowers and stalks than the *Tall Bearded* and with 3 to 4 blossoms per stalk; starts blooming in late May: "Black Forest, blue-black; "Bluet," blue; "Botany Bay," violet; "Chocoleto," brown; "Echoette," white; "Fairy Jewels," white and gold; "Glacier Bay," white and blue; "Lady Kay," orchid; "Little Dude," blue; "Pagoda," pink; "Pinata," violet and buff; "Pink Ruffles," orchid-pink; "Priscilla," white; "Summer Sunset," apricot; "Timmie Too," deep violet; "Tulare," golden yellow; "Yellow Dresden," yellow.

Standard Tall Bearded Iris

Classified as being over 28 inches tall with 3 to 4 blossoms per stalk and 4- to 8-inch flowers; starts blooming in late May. Color patterns are: *self*, all one color; *plicata*, veined with a second color; *bicolor*, standards one color, falls another; *bitone*, standards and falls two values of one coloring; and *blend*, two or more intermixed colors.

SELFS

White: "Celestial Snow," "Cliffs of Dover," "Helen Hayes," "Irish Linen," "Poet's Dream," "Snow Goddess," "The Citadel"

Cream: "Country Cream," "Crinkled Ivory," "Paleface," "Soaring Kite"

Light yellow: "Cool Comfort," "Golden Anniversary," "Waxing Moon"

Dark yellow: "Bravado," "Front Page," "Gold Piece," "Golden Masterpiece"

Buff to brown: "Brass Accents," "Bronze Bell," "Butterscotch Kiss," "Carmela," "Dark Chocolate," "Olympic Torch"

Red: "Ahoy," "Bang," "Captain Gallant," "Garnet Royal," "Tall Chief"

Pink: "Garden Party," "Lynn Hall," "Mary Randall," "Pink Fulfillment," "Rose Flame," "Spring Charm"

Apricot to orange: "Apricot Dancer," "Apricot Lustre," "Glittering Amber," "Magnet," "Orange Crush," "Orange Frills"

Blue: "Blue Raven," "Demetria," "Fox Grapes," "Jean Sibelius," "Marriott," "Pacific Panorama," "Sparkling Waters"

Violet: "Indiglow," "Jersey Beauty," "Polka Time," "Violet Hills"

Orchid to lilac: "Alpine Rose," "Hope Divine," "Lilac Festival"

Black: "Black Onyx," "Early Dusk," "Edenite," "Licorice Stick"

PLICATAS

"Benton Susan," cream and brown; "Chinquapin," cream and golden brown; "Dot and Dash," black and white; "Gene Wild," cream and rose; "Golden Spice," yellow and brown; "Memphis Lass," rose and burgundy; "Moongate," white and blue; "Tea Apron," white and blue.

BICOLORS

"Arctic Skies," pale blue standards and white falls; "Baby's Bonnet," white standards and salmon-pink falls; "Bright Hour," purple standards and white falls; "Kahili," pale gold standards and red falls; "On Parade," beige standards and reddish falls; "Panay," white standards and green-yellow falls; "Pretender," yellow standards and dark blue falls.

BITONES

"Arcady," pale blue tones; "Braithwaite," lavender and purple tones; "Helen Collingwood," pale lavender-blue standards with deep purple falls; "Melodrama," pale blue-violet standards and deep lilac falls; "Toll Gate," pale yellow tones.

BLENDS

"Allaglow," golden brown with blue overtones; "Hindu Wand," chartreuse, yellow, buff, and brown; "Jungle Bird," violet, rose, and claret; "Lula Marguerite," pale blue with gold overtones; "Melbreak," rose-pink with brown overtones; "Smoke Mist," apricot with mauve overtones; "Watermelon," bright pink with yellow-green overtones.

Iris tectorum (Roof Iris) 12–15 in. Sun
Flowering span: Late May to mid-June
Color: Lavender-blue
Native habitat: China, Japan

Although this hardy plant is actually grown on thatched roofs in the Orient, it does come down to earth well in gardens. The 3-inch, wavy flowers are broad-opening and appear between the typical flat leaves of this iris type. Except for enjoying more sun, its culture and propagation are the same as for *I. cristata*. There is a less hardy white variety, *alba*, with noticeable yellow crests. The American Iris Society catalogues this as an *Evansia* or "crested" iris.

Jeffersonia diphylla (American Twinleaf) 8–10 in. Semi-shade
Flowering span: Late May to mid-June
Color: White
Native habitat: Southeastern Canada to Alabama, west to Iowa

Closely resembling *Hepatica* in blossom appearance, the unusual characteristic of this wildflower is its deeply cleft green leaves that resemble a set of lungs in outline. After the 1-inch, single flowers fade, the leaves continue elongating, and by late summer unique, pear-shaped seed pods appear. It likes an acid-humusy soil in open to light shade and can be propagated by seed or fall division of the thick rootstock. Pests and diseases seem to be negligible.

Jeffersonia dubia (*Plagiorhegma dubia*) (Chinese Twinleaf) 6–9 in. Semi-shade
Flowering span: Late May to July

Color: Light lavender blue
Native habitat: Manchuria

This scarce oriental species has 1½-inch, bowl-shaped flowers and 3-inch-wide, heart-shaped leaves with ragged edges. Its culture is the same as with *J. diphylla.*

Lamium maculatum (Spotted Dead-nettle) 8–12 in. Semi-shade
Flowering span: Late May to August
Color: Pink-purple
Native habitat: Europe, British Isles, and New England to North Carolina

A vigorous, sprawling plant, it is useful for shaded borders or rock gardens as a summer "filler" after spring bulb displays. Hooded, 1-inch flowers in ascending whorls around the stem bloom for a long period. The small, crinkled leaves have a central gray green to cream green blotch, and the plant is tolerant to reasonable dryness without strain. It grows in almost any soil and will endure deep shading comfortably. Spring division or seed are the usual propagation methods. There are several varieties: *album,* with pale green leaves and white blossoms, plus a need for shade; *aureum,* with yellowish leaf veining; and *roseum,* with shell pink flowering.

Linum narbonnense (Narbonne Flax)   18–24 in. Sun
Flowering span: Late May to late June
Color: Azure blue
Native habitat: Southern Europe

A delicate accent for borders or rock gardens with much sunshine, this somewhat tender perennial has 5-pointed, 1½-inch flowers with white centers arranged in loose clusters on slender, erect stems. The narrow, 1½-inch leaves are bluish green. It enjoys a moist, sandy loam with good drainage and can be propagated by summer stem cuttings or seed since spring division of the long roots is not always dependable. Cutworms and rust diseases are its chief afflictions.

Linum perenne (Perennial Flax) 18–24 in. Sun
Flowering span: Late May to mid-July
Color: Pale blue
Native habitat: Europe

Less robust than *L. narbonnense* and marginally tender, it has graceful, slender stems with arching tips carrying all-blue flowers in continuing display even though individual blossoms last but one day. In late summer reduce the foliage by half to prevent the plant from exhausting itself by over-blooming. Culture, propagation and pests are the same as for *L. narbonnense*. There is a white-flowered form, *alba*.

Lithospermum canescens (Hoary Gromwell or Yellow
    Puccoon) 9–15 in. Sun
Flowering span: Early May to June
Color: Orange yellow
Native habitat: Southeastern Canada to Georgia, west to
    Texas

Bright, 1/2-inch florets appear in arching sprays above 1/2-inch-wide, willowlike leaves on this wildflower. Short, white hairs on the leaves and stems give a gray cast to the plant in locations from sun to semi-shade. It prefers an infertile, sandy-gravelly soil on the acid side. Seed or root cuttings are recommended since the long, woody roots are difficult to divide well. Pests and diseases seem to avoid this plant.

Lithospermum caroliniensis (Caroline Gromwell) 18–24 in.
    Sun
Flowering span: Early May to June
Color: Orange yellow
Native habitat: Ontario to Mexico

Somewhat similar to *L. canescens*, this species has 1-inch blossoms in generous terminal clusters and heavier and larger leaf hairs. Culture is the same for both.

Lychnis viscaria (German Catchfly or Campion) 6–20 in.
    Sun

Flowering span: Late May to July
Color: Red purple
Native habitat: Europe, Siberia

Profusely flowering in sun-drenched locations, these strong-colored blossoms are often troublesome to incorporate into a mixed border. Branched stalks with single, flat-faced, 1-inch flowers rise from tufts of grasslike foliage. The stem beneath the flower is slightly sticky. Withstanding drought well, it prefers a moist, sandy soil that is well-drained. Self-sowing readily, it can be quickly dominant in small spaces. Smut disease is bothersome, but it has no insect nuisances. The varieties offer some interest: *alba*, white and longer flowering; *splendens*, rose pink; and *splendens flore-pleno*, very double, long-lasting, deep pink to magenta.

Mazus reptans 1–2 in. Semi-shade
Flowering span: Late May to July
Color: Purplish blue
Native habitat: Himalaya Mountains

As a neat carpeting between stepstones in shade, this mat of bright green foliage is attractive even out of flower. The tiny, Lobelia-like blossoms appear in ground-hugging clusters of 2 to 5 on erect, slender stems in profusion. Rooting easily at the leaf nodes, it spreads quickly on rich, constantly moist soil in light to deep shading. It often fails to survive, however, in open, severe winters. Division is the simplest propagation method and there are no pests or diseases worth mentioning.

Myosotis alpestris (rupicola) (Alpine Forget-me-not) 3–8 in.
  Semi-shade
Flowering span: Late May to August
Color: Azure blue
Native habitat: Europe

While not always reliably hardy, this wildflower is appealing for its long-blooming habit and coloring. Lancelike, green leaves with blunt tips form low tufts in semi-shaded, humusy rock gardens and borders that stay consistently moist. Clusters of tiny, yellow-centered flowers appear well above the leaves throughout the summer. Seed (which is scarce), summer stem cuttings, and spring division are the propagation methods. Mildew is destructive in hot, humid summers, as is the red spider mite in hot, dry weather. Quite a few hybrids exist: "Blue Ball," 6 in., clear blue; "Carmine King," 6 in., carmine pink; "Pink Beauty," 6 in., shell pink; "Royal Blue," 10 in., dark blue; and "Ultramarine," 6 in., dark blue.

Myosotis scorpiodes (*palustris*) (True Forget-me-not) 6–18 in. Sun
Flowering span: Late May to August
Color: Bright blue
Native habitat: Europe, Asia, Southeastern Canada to Louisiana

For streamside embankments in full sun to semi-shade, the mat-forming habit of this long-blooming perennial comes into its own. Pinkish buds produce ongoing clusters of 1/3-inch flowers with white, pinkish, or yellow centers above light green, narrow leaves. It enjoys a wet, gravelly soil but will take other locations if the soil can be kept well-moistened at all times. Spring division of the fibrous rootstalk or summer stem cuttings work better than seeding. Mildew and red spider mites can be bothersome. The 8-inch variety, *semperflorens*, lives up to its name by blooming constantly until frost.

Myosotis sylvatica (Woodland Forget-me-not) 12–20 in. Semi-shade
Flowering span: Late May to August
Color: Sky blue, occasionally white or pink
Native habitat: Europe, northern Asia, Quebec to Michigan

These noticeable clusters of 1/3-inch flowers can enliven the summer months of any shaded woodlot with reasonably moist, humusy soil. Here the leaves are gray green, and the stems have a tendency to sprawl. This wildflower is actually a biennial that keeps reseeding itself prodigiously in the same area. Pests and diseases are uncommon.

Ornithogalum umbellatum (Common Star-of-Bethlehem)
    6–9 in. Sun
Flowering span: Early May to June
Color: White
Native habitat: North Africa, southern France, Asia Minor

Grassy clumps of deep green foliage produce a centered multitude of short-stemmed, 1-inch flowers with thin green striping on the outside and pure white inside. They open flat only on sunny days and close even then by midafternoon. Tolerant of full sun or light shade, culture of this bulb is the same as for the April-blooming species, *nutans*. It has a tendency to self-seed readily, and there are no pests or diseases.

Paeonia lactiflora (albiflora) (Chinese Peony) 24–48 in.
    Sun
Flowering span: Late May to late June
Color: White to pink in the wild; hybrids' colorings are myriad
Native habitat: Siberia, Mongolia, China

If any perennial can be said to be truly long-lived in one place, this is the champion. Thriving clumps known to be eighty years old or more are frequently recorded from many locations throughout the world, and the historical background of their cultivation goes back two thousand years. With such longevity and appeal, peonies deserve close attention to being placed and planted correctly, especially since they are not demanding—only selective—about growing enthusiastically for generations in gardens throughout most of the temperate climates. The majority of them are attractively fragrant and long-lasting when cut.

The often-reddish new growth of spring emerges much like asparagus but soon produces a tall, unbranched stem with broad, much-divided, glossy green leaves and the blossoming. The weight of such large foliage plus the sizeable flower head usually requires early staking. Since the Chinese peony has the distinction of carrying more than one flower per stem, the need for quick disbudding of the smaller side flowers is a matter of choice which may or may not improve the size of the main blossom. Unless the seed is wanted for propagation, all faded flowering should be re-moved early. The neat foliage mass will continue as an effective backdrop to other plants until frost and may offer some reddish autumn tinting. To forestall future disease problems, cut all current year's foliage to the ground in late fall and destroy it off the site.

All peonies enjoy a well-drained, sandy-clay soil on the alkaline side that has never before been used for peony cultivation. Intolerant of heavy shade and the invasive roots of nearby vigorous plants, they grow best in full sun in open bedding, although the delicately colored varieties can benefit from some light shading to preserve their tints longer. Frequent deep cultivation and thorough watering in dry summers, along with an annual application of balanced fertilizer after flowering improves future blossoming.

The planting technique is important to long life and generous flowering. Purchase nursery stock or divide old plants in mid-August or September (late October in the southern United States). Excavate a pit at least 2 feet deep and 2 feet wide—more if time and budget allow—for each plant, discarding any rock, sand, or hardpan layers as unsuitable. Pile the acceptable earth to one side and mix it with generous amounts of humus, moist peat moss, or compost (fresh manure is harmful, but well-rotted is satisfactory), a pound of bonemeal or superphosphate, plus lime if the soil is very acid. Redeposit this mix in the hole to a depth about 10 inches below the top, water well to settle it thoroughly, then add 2 inches of dry soil for centering the roots snugly.

Rootstalks are thick and brittle with large, fragile, underground buds or "eyes." Cut off any damaged or raggedy root edges cleanly to avoid rot. Select a plant or division with at least 3 large eyes and place it in the middle of the pit with the buds pointing upward and the tip of the lowest eye *no more than* 2 inches below the surrounding ground level. Planting too deep will eliminate future flowering. Backfill with unfertilized but humus-enriched soil and work it gently between the roots. Water thoroughly and complete by back-filling any depressions. Mulch the first winter to prevent heaving.

Botrytis bud blight, a sooty fungus afflicting buds and foliage, is a serious wilting disease spread by wind and rain—

not by ants as long supposed—and requires immediate spraying control and discarding of infected plant parts. Scraping away the top inch or so of soil often forestalls future infections, too; replace the spore-contaminated soil with limed, fresh topsoil. Other diseases and pests are not so problematic.

The wealth of new hybrids created from inter-breeding this and other peony species is vast and complex. Blossom appearance is a handy guide for differentiation, and the American Peony Society uses these 4 major descriptions: *Single*, having 5 or more large outer petals set around a broad clustering of pollen-bearing stamens; *Japanese* or *Anemone*, having 5 or more petals and a center of either non-pollen-bearing yellow staminoides or a fluffy massing of narrow petals colored similar to or complementary to the main petal hues; *Semi-double*, having 5 or more outer petals and a center of broad petals intermixed with numerous rings and a prominent center of pollen-bearing stamens; and *Double*, having 5 or more outer petals and a center almost fully transformed into heavy clusters of petals from modified stamens no longer apparent.

In the following list of highly regarded varieties, the time of bloom is provided in a general fashion: "E" is early, "M" is midseason, and "L" is late. Color indications are also simplified to fit the main color value.

WHITE

White Single: "Dunlora" (E), "Krinkled White" (M), "Le Jour" (E)

White Japanese: "Ada Priscilla" (M), "Isani-Gidui" (M), "Moon of Nippon" (M)

White Semi-double: "Mildred May" (M), "Miss America" (E), "Rare China" (M), "White Rose" (L)

White Double: "Ann Cousins" (M), "Elsa Sass" (L), "Festiva Maxima" (E), "Florence Nicholls" (M), "George W. Payton" (L), "Kelway's Glorious" (E), "Le Cygne" (E), "Major A. M. Krekler" (M), "Moonstone" (M), "Mother's Choice" (M), "Mrs. J. V. Edlund" (M), "Nauvoo" (M), "Nick Shaylor" (M), "Ramona Lins" (L), "The Fleece" (M), "Victory" (L)

LIGHT PINK

Light Pink Single: "Dainty" (E), "Dancing Nymph" (L), "Dawn Pink" (M), "Moon Mist" (E), "Seashell" (M)

Light Pink Japanese: "Ama-no-sode" (M), "Rose Valley" (M), "Tamate-Boku" (L), "Westerner" (M)

Light Pink Semi-double: "Flamingo" (M), "Lady Alexandra Duff" (M), "Minnie Shaylor" (M), "Silvia Saunders" (E), "Zuzu" (M)

Light Pink Double: "Alice Harding" (M), "Amberglow" (M), "Florence Ellis" (M), "Gertrude Cox" (E), "James Pillow" (L), "La Lorraine" (M), "Marilla Beauty" (M), "Mary Auten" (L), "Mrs. Harry F. Little" (M), "Nancy Dolman" (M), "Pleiades" (M), "Retta" (L), "Solange" (M), "Therese" (E), "Wabash" (M), "Westhill" (E)

DARK PINK

Dark Pink Single: "Cinderella" (M), "Harriet Olney" (M), "L'Etincelante" (M), "Mischief" (M)

Dark Pink Japanese: "Betty Groff" (M), "Filigree" (M), "Magnolia" (M), "Sky Pilot" (M)

Dark Pink Double: "Doris Cooper" (L), "Edulis Superba" (E), "Frances Mains" (M), "Monsieur Jules Elie" (E), "Mrs. Franklin D. Roosevelt" (M), "Mrs. Livingston Farrand" (L), "Reine Hortense" (M), "Sarah Bernhardt" (M), "Tempest" (M), "Walter Faxon" (L)

RED

Red Single: "Acturus" (M), "Kaskaskia" (M), "Man o' War" (E), "Red Key" (M)

Red Japanese: "Dignity" (M), "Fuyajo" (M), "Hari-ai-nin" (M), "Mount Palomar" (E), "Nippon Brilliant" (E), "Nippon Chief" (L)

Red Semi-Double: "Chippewa" (M), "Red Goddess" (M), "Rosalie" (M), "The Mighty Mo" (M)

Red Double: "Bonanza" (L), "Dearborn" (E), "Felix Crousse" (L), "King Midas" (M), "Longfellow" (M), "Matilda Lewis" (M), "Philippe Rivoire" (L)

Paeonia officinalis (Common Peony) 24–36 in. Sun
Flowering span: Mid-May to early June
Color: Dark crimson
Native habitat: France to Albania

Similar in foliage and growth to *P. lactiflora,* this European wild plant has also been used extensively for hybridizing. Its usual form is a single, 5-inch, wide-opening flower on each stalk along with coarsely cut, glossy leaves. Because of its time of bloom, it is often referred to in the United States as the "Memorial Day" peony. Culture is identical with that for the Chinese peony, but its tuberous roots are more brittle to handle. A few varieties are known: *alba plena* with pink buds and pure white, double flowers; *rosea plena* with bright rose, double flowers; *rosea superba plena* with watermelon pink, double flowers; and *rubra plena* with vivid, ruby red, double flowers.

Paeonia tenuifolia (Fernleaf Peony) 15–18 in. Sun
Flowering span: Early to late May
Color: Dark crimson
Native habitat: Asia Minor, eastern Europe

The distinction here is the greatly subdivided, lacy foliage resembling that of a cosmos and the single, 3-inch flower terminally resting on the leaves. It, too, has been used for extensive cross-breeding. By late summer the foliage disappears, and locating established plants for early autumn division of the creeping, underground rhizome requires prior location-staking. Culture is the same as for the other peony species. There is a later blooming, deep red, double-flowering variety called *flore-pleno.*

Oxalis adenophylla 3–6 in. Sun
Flowering span: Late May to late June
Color: Rose pink to white
Native habitat: Chile, Argentina

A South American bulb hardy in all but severe climate sections, it produces a novel gray green foliage mound made up of 1/2-inch, cloverlike leaves with 10 to 20 minute leaflets. From this arise many solitary 1-inch, funnel-shaped flowers with a deeper red throat that make a noticeable rock garden or border accent where the soil is rich, well-drained, limed, and sun-warmed throughout the year. The foliage disappears by late summer and the bulb masses can then be separated. New ones should be fall planted. Pests and diseases are unknown.

Papaver alpinum (Alpine Poppy) 4–8 in. Sun
Flowering span: Mid-May to early June
Color: White, yellow, orange, orange red
Native habitat: Alps Mountains

A bright accent for rock gardens and sun-lit borders, this erect, tissue-thin, bowl-shaped, 2-inch blossom has a mass of bright yellow stamens in the center above a goodly mass of gray-green, finely divided, basal foliage. As with all poppies, the globular, green bud is down-turned noticeably before it opens. The individual plant is short-lived but reseeds readily and generously. It likes a moist, gravelly soil, well-drained in full sun or light shade. Since the roots are deli-

Tissue-thin, the blossoms of *Papaver alpinum* have remarkable color values.

cately brittle and resist transplanting, seed is the best propagation method. Aphids and stem blight are the worst nuisances. The variety *rhaeticum* has larger flowers of deep yellow. It may also cross-hybridize with the other colors, however, if planted nearby.

Papaver bractaetum (Great Scarlet Poppy) 30–36 in. Sun
Flowering span: Mid-May to early June
Color: Deep red
Native habitat: Mediterranean Europe to Iran

Similar to the June-flowering Oriental poppy in blossom size and foliage, this species also has large, leafy bracts beneath the 6- to 9-inch flower. The cup-shaped blossom usually has conspicuous, dark violet markings at the bottom. It tolerates any soil in full sun but prefers moist, well-drained locations. Spring-sown seed and division of the fleshy taproots in late summer, after the foliage has disappeared, are the common propagation routines. Pests and diseases are not problematic.

Papaver rupifragum (Spanish Poppy) 6–15 in. Sun
Flowering span: Late May to July
Color: Pale red to orange
Native habitat: Spain

Flat clumps of gray green, deeply incised leaves produce tall flower stems with 5- to 6-inch-wide blossoms. Any sunny, well-drained location in a border will suffice, and its preference is for a sandy loam. Either seed or divison of the fleshy roots in late summer works well. Diseases and pests are inconsequential.

Patrinia triloba (palmata) 8–16 in. Sun
Flowering span: Mid-May to late June
Color: Deep, golden yellow
Native habitat: Japan

Basal mounds of deeply cut, palmate leaves produce reddish flower stems and sizable heads of 1/3-inch florets resembling Valerian. It thrives in well-drained, damp locations in sun to semi-shade and can be propagated by seed or by spring division. There seem to be no pest or disease nuisances.

Phlox divaricata (Sweet William Phlox) 9–15 in. Semi-shade
Flowering span: Mid-May to late June
Color: Lavender blue
Native habitat: Southeastern Canada to Florida, west to Texas and Minnesota

A workable companion for late spring bulbs in a border, this slow-creeping wildflower provides a long-lasting display of loose, terminal flower clusters with 1-inch flat-petaled blossoms on thin stems with 2-inch green leaves. It wants a well-drained, humusy, and constantly moist soil in semi-shade to sun. Shearing off the old flower heads can extend the blooming appreciably. Summer stem cuttings of 1-year-old plants and spring division of plants at least 3 years old are the best propagation choices. Mildew and drought are the worst problems. The variety *laphami* has deeper blue flowers, while *laphami alba* is white.

Phlox pilosa (aristata) (Downy Phlox) 12–20 in. Sun
Flowering span: Mid-May to late June
Color: Reddish lavender to pink
Native habitat: Connecticut to Florida, west to Texas

Here the plant is noncreeping and has very narrow, 3-inch, sharp-pointed leaves with stiff, downy stems producing blossoms similar in shape to those of *P. divaricata*. Full sun and dryness, plus an acid, sandy loam, well-drained, suit it best, and if the old flower heads are cut off,, the plant usually reblooms in August. Collected wild stock or seed is the better propagation method, but nursery-grown material is even more assured of succeeding. Pests and diseases are unknown.

Phlox stolonifera (reptans) (Creeping Phlox) 6–8 in. Semi-shade
Flowering span: Early May to June
Color: Light purple to rosy pink
Native habitat: Pennsylvania to Georgia, west to Kentucky

Glossy, rounded evergreen leaves form a ground-hugging mat spreading quickly in suitable growing conditions of rich, acid, peaty soil in either shade or semi-shade. Nodding clusters of large florets give a generous spring show and then appear intermittently throughout the summer. Division of the creeping stolons in either spring or fall is recommended. There are no diseases or insects worth mentioning. Several selections of more interesting colors are: "Blue Ridge," a large-flowered, light blue; "Cecil Davies," a mauve blue; and "Lavender Lady," an intensely deep mauve.

Podophyllum emodi (Himalayan Mayapple) 12–18 in.
    Semi-shade
Flowering span: Late May to mid-June
Color: White to pale rose
Native habitat: India

A curious wildflower conspicuous for its leaves and fruit far more than its flowering, it has umbrella-like, 12-inch leaves that are bronze red and down-turned when emerging and expanding from pink-brown stems that also carry the solitary, 2-inch flower beneath the foliage canopy. The blossom is ragged-petaled with prominent yellow stamens, but its edible fruit is brilliant red and the size of a hen's egg. It thrives and expands into large colonies where the shaded soil is deep, rich, moist, and generously endowed with humus or peat moss. Spring separation of the underground rhizomes or fresh seed easily propagates this plant. Pests and diseases are unimportant. In severe climates this plant needs winter protection.

Podophyllum peltatum (Common Mayapple) 12–18 in.
    Semi-shade
Flowering span: Early to late May
Color: Creamy white
Native habitat: Southeastern Canada to Florida, west to
    Texas and Minnesota

Either a single, noticeably white-veined leaf on a long stem or a flowering stem with 2 very broad, palmately divided, dark green leaves emerges from the underground, thick rootstock of this interesting wild plant. Poking out from beneath the umbrella foliage is a single, 2-inch flower with a sickeningly sweet fragrance (to some, at least). The edible fruit can be 1 inch in diameter and yellowish; all other parts of this plant are considered potentially poisonous. The culture is the same as for *P. emodi*, except that fall division is preferred.

Polemonium caeruleum (Jacob's-ladder, Greek Valerian)
    12–36 in. Semi-shade
Flowering span: Early May to July
Color: Sky blue
Native habitat: Europe

Bushy mounds of pinnately compound leaves, resembling the rungs of a ladder, add a neat textural accent in borders or wildflower areas. The stiffly erect stems carry terminal, loose clusters of ¾-inch, bell-shaped flowers. It does best in deep, rich well-drained soil that is kept moist in semi-shade to sun. Division spring or fall, summer stem cuttings, and seed work equally well. There are few pests, but mildew can be an occasional problem. The dwarf hybrid "Blue Pearl" has cobalt-blue florets with a yellow eye, and the variety *album* is white.

Polygala paucifolia (Fringed Polygala or Milkwort) 3–6 in.
    Shade
Flowering span: Mid-May to July
Color: Rosy purple
Native habitat: Southeastern Canada to Tennessee, west to
    Minnesota

This trailing plant offers 1½-inch, glossy, clustered, bronzy leaves on purple stems and produces 1 to 4 orchid-like, winged, 2-inch flowers with a fringed lip. It does best in moist woods or bogs that are acid and humusy in deep to light shade, but it is difficult to establish beyond its natural site because it has a parasitic interrelationship with other woodlot plants. It also has a ground-hugging set of closed, self-pollinating flowers that keep it spreading easily once established. Nursery stock or large, collected sods with plenty of soil are probably the best propagation methods. There are no diseases or pests worth mentioning. A white form, *alba,* exists, but it is rare.

Polygala senega (Seneca Snakeroot) 6–18 in. Sun
Flowering span: Mid-May to July
Color: White to greenish white
Native habitat: Southeastern Canada to Georgia, west to South Dakota

Just as difficult to establish as *P. paucifolia,* it has different needs because it prefers dry, rocky sites with good drainage in full sun. The narrow stems have willowlike, green leaves and terminate with a slender spike of egg-shaped, tiny flowers and pealike seeds. The long taproot resists transplanting on mature plants, but summer stem cuttings or fresh seed can probably succeed. Pests and diseases are unknown.

Polygonatum biflorum (Small Solomon's-seal) 12–36 in. Semi-shade
Flowering span: Late May to mid-June
Color: Pale yellow to greenish yellow
Native habitat: New Hampshire to Florida, west to Texas and Minnesota

Zig-zagged, arching, unbranched stems carry double rows or more of pendulous, ¾-inch, tubular flowers from the axils of the 2-inch, pale green leaves. Dark blue or black fruit develops by midsummer. It does best in semi- to full shade in humus-rich, semi-dry, acid soils. Division of the knobby rootstock in early spring or seed is the best propagation method. No special problems exist from pests or diseases.

Polygonatum canaliculatum (commutatum) (Great Solomon's-seal) 48–72 in. Semi-shade
Flowering span: Late May to mid-June
Color: Pale yellow to greenish yellow
Native habitat: New Hampshire to Florida, west to Texas and Minnesota

More robust than *P. biflorum,* the leaves are up to 6 inches long and 4 inches wide, while the 1-inch flowers frequently come in clusters of 8. Culture is the same, except its preference for constant moisture. It colonizes readily.

Polygonatum multiflorum (Eurasian Solomon's-seal) 24–36 in. Semi-shade
Flowering span: Late May to mid-June
Color: White to greenish white
Native habitat: Europe, British Isles, northern Asia

Here the leaves are bright green, lance-shaped, and up to 6 inches long. It does best in shaded woodlots with a neutral or slightly acid soil that is reasonably moist. Propagate by spring or fall division of the rootstock, although seed can work satisfactorily too. No pests or diseases bother it.

Potentilla argentea (Silver Cinquefoil) 4–12 in. Sun
Flowering span: Late May to August
Color: Sulphur yellow
Native habitat: Europe, Asia, and southern Canada to Virginia, west to Montana

Although not florally distinguished, this long-blooming perennial can establish itself well on dry, sterile soils readily. The deep green, narrow, 5-part leaves are densely silvery beneath, while the ½-inch flowers are repeatedly produced on tall, branched stems above the foliage mounds. It enjoys a light, sandy soil and can be propagated by division or seed. Leaf spot is its only difficulty. A variety from Italy, *calabra,* has fan-shaped leaves whitened on both sides and 1-inch flowers.

Potentilla anserina (Silverweed Cinquefoil) 12–24 in. Sun
Flowering span: Late May to August
Color: Golden yellow
Native habitat: Every temperate-zone country, plus southeastern Canada to New York, west to Iowa and New Mexico

A widely distributed creeping wildflower, it is especially attractive for its fernlike, pinnate leaves of dark green with solid undersides of long, silky white hairs. The creeping red stems root where they touch, making a generous mat of erect, glossy foliage with ongoing single flowers 1 inch across. It likes moist, sandy soils on the alkaline side. Separation of the stolons is the simplest method for propagation. It has no problems with pests or diseases.

Potentilla tridentata (Wineleaf Cinquefoil) 2–6 in.   Sun
Flowering span: Late May to August
Color: White
Native habitat: Southeastern Canada to Georgia, west to Iowa and North Dakota

This prostrate evergreen creeper spreads rapidly and has tiny, star-shaped flowers in clusters. The 1½-inch, glossy, 3-parted leaves often turn slightly orange-red in the fall. Good for dry banks and rock gardens, it enjoys an acid, sandy loam in full sun. Division is the easiest propagation technique. There are no difficulties at all with pests or diseases.

Primula japonica (Japanese Primrose) 8–18 in.   Semi-shade
Flowering span: Late May to late June

Primula japonica eventually elongates into a three-tiered floral display.

Color: Magenta, crimson, white
Native habitat: Japan

Unusual for its 3-tiered flowering, the Japanese primrose is a candelabra type with 2-inch-wide, 8- to 12-inch light green leaves, and blooms for a long time with one whorl of flowers opening atop another. It wants constant moisture and a humusy soil, like all primroses, but will tolerate greater sun if the soil tends to be wet. Self-seeding is generous to the point of overcrowding, and since cross-hybridizing is typical within its own group, color variations are likely. Red spider mite is troublesome in hot, dry weather. Individual color selections are often available, such as "Postford White" or "Miller's Crimson."

Primula rosea (Rose Primrose) 4–10 in. Semi-shade
Flowering span: Mid-May to mid-June
Color: Rose pink
Native habitat: Himalaya Mountains

Another primrose that blossoms before the leaves fully emerge, the florets here are ¾ inch in loose clusters and have a yellow center. The smooth, light green foliage elongates with the fading flower stalk. Preferring a streamside location that is constantly moist to the point of wetness, it can also be used satisfactorily in gardens with peaty, moist loam. Division after flowering and fresh seed are the propagation methods. Slugs, leaf beetles, aphids, and spider mites are an occasional bother, and botrytis disease can be troublesome in hot, humid weather. The variety *grandiflora* has larger blossoms, while "Visser de Greer" has bright rose flowers. In severe climates this plant needs winter mulching.

Ranunculus aconitifolius (Aconite Buttercup) 6–36 in. Sun
Flowering span: Mid-May to July
Color: White
Native habitat: Central Europe

From a clump of palmately divided, green leaves resembling the foliage of an Aconite, come tall, slender flowering stalks, each with several widely spaced blossoms. In a sunny border or light-shaded wild area that is moist, rich, and well-drained, they flower long and can be expected to self-seed readily. Division in early spring or fall is also workable. Mildew is the chief nuisance. The variety *flore-pleno* has double, white, rounded flowers, while *luteo-plenus* has double, golden yellow blossoms.

Ranunculus acris (Tall Buttercup) 8–48 in. Sun
Flowering span: Mid-May to July
Color: Golden yellow
Native habitat: Europe, British Isles, eastern United States
    and Canada

This is the common buttercup of England and has pubescent stems and leaves with 1-inch flowers on tall, branched stems. The basal leaves are palmately divided with many sharp-pointed tips. Culture is the same as with *R. aconitifolius.* The preferred variety, *flore-pleno*, has very double, long-lasting blossoms.

Ranunculus amplexicaulis (Yelloweye Buttercup) 3–12 in.
    Sun
Flowering span: Early May to early June
Color: White
Native habitat: Southern Europe

Here the blossom is wide-petaled and made more conspicuous by a large mass of yellow stamens. The branched flower stalks are slender and the gray-green leaves are lancelike and clasp the stem. Useful in sunny rock gardens or borders, it likes a moist, well-drained, rich soil. Spring division or seed is the propagation method. It appears to have no pests or diseases.

Ranunculus ficaria (Figroot Buttercup, Lesser Celandine)
    2–5 in. Sun
Flowering span: Early May to June
Color: Bright yellow
Native habitat: Europe, British Isles, western Asia, eastern
    United States

The heart-shaped, shiny, green leaves are on long petioles and form attractive, dense mats. Its 1-inch flowers are unusual by having 10 to 12 petals on heavy stems. Good for a wild garden with sun to semi-shade in any well-drained, average soil, this perennial self-seeds readily and can become overcrowded. Dividing the knobby tubers in early spring or fall easily starts new colonies. Pests and diseases are no problem. The variety *major* has larger leaves and flowers and is less rampant-growing.

Ranunculus montanus (Mountain Buttercup) 3–6 in.   Sun
Flowering span: Mid-May to July
Color: Bright yellow
Native habitat: Asia, Europe

This creeping, rock garden perennial creates slowly expanding mats of dark green, much-divided foliage with single, 1-inch, glistening flowers on short stalks. It prefers a rich, rocky soil with good drainage in sun to semi-shade. Division of the stoloniferous rootstock in either spring or fall propagates equally well, and while it is not bothered by insect pests, mildew can be occasionally disfiguring in hot, humid seasons. The variety *dentatus* has larger flowers and leaves.

Ranunculus repens (speciosus) (Creeping Buttercup) 8–12
    in.   Sun
Flowering span: Mid-May to July
Color: Golden yellow
Native habitat: Europe, Siberia, Bermuda, Jamaica, plus
    southeastern Canada to Kentucky, west to Minnesota

Not a true candidate for the garden border, this meadow wildflower has a sprawling habit with stems that grow to 24 inches in length and flop over easily. The dull green leaves are divided into 3 segments, and the glistening flowers are 1 inch across. Moist, rich loam is best. Its stoloniferous root habit allows easy division in spring or fall, and self-seeding is likely. Pests and diseases are not important. The double-flowered form, *flore-pleno*, offers greater attractiveness.

Saxifraga virginiensis (Early Saxifrage) 3–12 in. Sun
Flowering span: Early May to mid-June
Color: White
Native habitat: Southeastern Canada to Georgia, west to
   Oklahoma

   Thick, roundish, gray-green leaves form a broad rosette
for the erect, hairy stems of the widely branched, 2- to
3-inch-broad flower head. They grow naturally in rock clefts
and on dry, sandy hillsides in full sun and are an obvious
rock garden choice. Offsets, spring division, and seed are
the usual propagation methods. Aphids and beetles enjoy
the foliage, but diseases are not prevalent. The double-
flowered form, *flore-pleno,* blooms longer.

Sedum acre (Goldmoss Stonecrop) 1–3 in. Sun
Flowering span: Late May to mid-June
Color: Bright yellow
Native habitat: Europe, British Isles, northern Africa, Asia
   Minor

   The commonest of all the many *Sedums* in cultivation, the
mat-like, tight habit of growth is useful for groundcovering
dry, arid, sunny locations—even those with only a thin soil
layer over rock outcroppings. Dependably hardy, the plant
has cylindrical, ¼-inch, bright green leaves and star-shaped,
somewhat greenish yellow, ½-inch flowers in clusters that
can disguise the foliage completely. The easiest propagation
method is simple separation of the almost-evergreen mats at
any time. Important pests and diseases are unknown. Collectors can investigate these varieties: *album,* white-
flowered; *aureum,* bright golden yellow leaves in spring
only, slower-growing; *elegans,* silvery leaf tips throughout
the season; and *majus,* larger-flowered.

Silene alpestris (Heliosperma alpestris) (Alpine Silene) 4–6
   in. Sun
Flowering span: Mid-May to mid-July
Color: White:
Native habitat: Eastern Europe

An attractive, long-flowering rock garden accent, this alpine has tight clusters of satiny, ¾-inch flowers on wiry stems above narrow, sticky leaves in clumps. Any sandy loam, well-drained, in full sun suits them, and they enjoy occasional lime. Seed, summer cuttings, and division all work well for propagation, and no pests or diseases are a nuisance. The double-flowered form, *flore-pleno*, is showier.

Silene caroliniana (pennsylvanica) (Peatpink Silene) 6–9 in. Sun
Flowering span: Early May to July
Color: Rose, white, pink
Native habitat: New Hampshire to Alabama, west to Missouri

Dense clumps of narrow, 2-inch-wide leaves, sticky and hairy, produce stems with 1-inch, slightly notched flowers closely clustered at the tips in sun to light shading. It prefers a dry, sandy, acid soil. Careful division of the taproot in spring or fall, root cuttings, or seed is the propagation method. There are no diseases or pests worth noticing.

Sisyrinchium angustifolium (Common Blue-eyed Grass) 12–18 in. Sun
Flowering span: Mid-May to early June, occasionally continuing to fall
Color: Violet blue
Native habitat: Southeastern Canada to Florida, west to Texas and Minnesota

Clumps of irislike, flat, ¼-inch-wide leaves produce slender stems with terminal, glossy, ¾-inch flowers having golden centers. They open only on sunny days and spread easily on acid-sandy loam with good drainage. Dividing the fibrous root-mat in spring or fall assures propagation, but self-seeding is likely, too. Diseases and pests are unknown. A scarce variety, *album*, has white blossoms. The Bermuda native, *S. bermudiana*, might well be tried in southern gardens; its flowers are similar but darker-colored.

Sisyrinchium douglasi (grandiflorum) (Douglas Blue-eyed Grass) 10–12 in. Sun
Flowering span: Mid-May to early June
Color: Bright purple
Native habitat: Northern California to British Columbia

This is probably the most attractively flowered of the species, and its culture is the same as for *S. angustifolium.* The plant does, however, go into total dormancy by late summer, and division can then take place. The scarce variety *album* is also attractive.

Smilacina racemosa (Feather Solomon's-plume) 12–30 in. Semi-shade
Flowering span: Mid-May to early June
Color: Creamy white
Native habitat: Southeastern Canada to Virginia, west to Missouri

Although this perennial wildflower is often called False Solomon's-seal and is associated with *Polygonatum,* botanically it is closer to *Smilax,* a group of native vines. The zig-zagged, unbranched stems are terminally capped with 6- to 8-inch feathery clusters of tiny flowers above large, pointed, deep green leaves 3 to 6 inches long. The durable foliage combines well with other plantings in rich, humusy, acid soil that is well-drained in semi-shade to full shade. Its late summer clusters of red berries brighten any woodlot. It colonizes readily but will not reflower until the second season when transplanted. Fall or spring division of the horizontal, thick rootstock is the easiest propagation method, although seeds can be satisfactory but slow. Pests and diseases are not problematic.

Stylophorum diphyllum (Celandine Poppy) 10–18 in. Semi-shade
Flowering span: Mid-May to early June
Color: Golden yellow
Native habitat: Pennsylvania to Missouri

A pair of deeply cut, pinnately formed, gray-green leaves appear just beneath the showy, 2-inch flower. The buds nod like those of a true poppy and come in clusters of 3 to 5. It likes moist, humusy soil of average fertility, well-drained, in light shade. Fall division and seed work equally well, and it transplants easily. Diseases and insect pests are unknown, but chipmunks enjoy the seeds. In protected areas it may bloom weeks earlier.

Symphtum officinale (Common Comfrey) 24–36 in. Sun
Flowering span: Late May to mid-July
Color: White, pink, purplish, rose
Native habitat: Europe, British Isles, Asia

This coarse-leaved plant is durable and long-flowering. The branched, slightly hairy stems carry 3-inch, lanceolate leaves and clusters of tubular, drooping flowers. Any moist, average soil in full sun to light shade is suitable, and seed or division propagates them readily. Pests and diseases are not known. The variegated-foliage form, *argenteum,* is superior with its noticeable creamy white leaf edges and pallid blue flowers.

Thalictrum aquilegifolium (rubellum) (Columbine
    Meadow-rue) 12–36 in. Sun
Flowering span: Late May to early July
Color: Lavender, rose pink
Native habitat: Europe, northern Asia

Large, hollow stems produce gray-green, finely divided, compound leaves and heavy terminal heads of feathery, long-lasting, ½-inch flowers. The plants are dioecious ("two houses"), but both males and females have the same generous flowering response in sun to light shading where moisture is constant. A well-drained, humusy soil is best. Spring division is preferred, and in severe climates a winter mulch is required. Pests and diseases are no bother. The hybrids include *album,* a white form, and "Purple Cloud," a rosy purple.

Thalictrum dasycarpum (purpurascens) (Purple Meadow-
    rue) 48–72 in. Semi-shade
Flowering span: Mid-May to July
Color: Greenish yellow to white

Native habitat: Southeastern Canada to Ohio, west to Arizona

Here the loose clusters of flowers often appear on a purplish stem. Culture is the same as with *T. aquilegifolium.*

Thermopsis mollis (Soft Thermopsis) 24–36 in. Sun
Flowering span: Mid-May to mid-July
Color: Bright yellow
Native habitat: Virginia to North Carolina

Erect, hairy stems with 1- to 2-inch-long leaflets carry terminal, 6- to 10-inch spikes of showy, pealike blossoms. It does best in moist, well-drained, sandy loam in full sun, but will tolerate light shading. Seed is more reliable than division of the deep roots. Pests and diseases seem to shun it.

Thermopsis montana (Mountain Thermopsis) 18–30 in. Sun
Flowering span: Mid-May to mid-July
Color: Bright yellow
Native habitat: Northern California to British Columbia

Larger-flowered than its eastern cousin, *T. mollis,* the leaflets here are 4 inches long. Culture is identical for both.

Tiarella cordifolia (Allegany Foamflower) 6–12 in. Semi-shade
Flowering span: Early May to June
Color: White
Native habitat: Southeastern Canada to Alabama

A creeping, underground stem readily makes compact mats of long-stalked, 3-inch-broad, green leaves from this woodlot perennial groundcover. Erect, slender spikes of ¼-inch, star-shaped flowers rise well above the foliage in moist, cool, humusy soil from semi- to full shading. Best arranged in masses, it is easily grown from seed or division. Diseases and pests are unimportant. Occasionally these varieties are commercially offered: *purpurea,* purple; *purpurea major,* wine red; and *purpurea marmorata,* maroon with bronze foliage.

Tiarella wherryi 6–12 in. Semi-shade
Flowering span: Early May to June
Color: Creamy white
Native habitat: Virginia to Mississippi

A noncreeping relative of *T. cordifolia*, its clumps of decorative, heart-shaped foliage are bronze-green and turn reddish in the fall. The flower stalks are larger, too. Culture is the same for both.

Tradescantia virginiana (montana) (Virginia Spiderwort)
     18–30 in. Sun
Flowering span: Early May to July
Color: Violet blue
Native habitat: Maine to Georgia, west to Missouri and
     Minnesota

The straplike, 6- to 15-inch leaves of dull green are grass-like until flowering ends, when they sprawl erratically. Cut them back heavily for new foliage and possible reflowering in early autumn. The erect, hairy flower stems are gen-

A wide range of hybrid colorings makes *Tradescantia virginiana* showier than ever.

erously clustered terminally with 3-petaled, noticeable, 1-inch florets lasting but a day. Long-lived and long-blooming, these hardy perennials simply want a constantly moist, average-fertility soil in sun to light shade. Spring division of named varieties or seeding work equally satisfactorily. Pests or diseases are unknown. True varieties and hybrids are many: *alba*, white; *atrosanguinea*, dark red; "Blue Stone," strong deep blue; *caerulea*, bright blue; *coccinea*, bright red; *congesta*, purple; "Isis," deep blue, 3-inch flowers; "James C. Weguelin," porcelain blue, large-flowered; "Purple Dome," bright rosy purple; *rubra*, dark rosy pink; "Snowcap," pure white; and *violacea*, purple blue.

Trollius asiaticus (Siberian Globeflower) 18–24 in. Sun
Flowering span: Early May to June
Color: Orange yellow
Native habitat: Siberia

Finely divided, bronze-green leaves surround the slender flower stems with their solitary, 1- to 2-inch, globular blossoms. They thrive in damp locations enriched with peat, humus, or compost in sun or light shade. Division of the fibrous rootstock or seed work equally well. Mildew is an occasional nuisance but insects seem to avoid this plant. The variety *gigantea* is taller and more robust.

Trollius europeus (Common Globeflower) 12–15 in. Semi-shade
Flowering span: Early May to mid-June
Color: Lemon yellow
Native habitat: Northern Europe, British Isles

Here the globular flower is 2 inches wide with a darker-colored center. Culture is the same as with *T. asiaticus* except for a preference of sandy loam. The hybrids include: "Earliest of All," lemon yellow, 12 in; *loddigesii*, deep yellow; "Orange Princess," bright orange, 24 in.; and *superbus*, soft yellow, 24 in. Some of these hybrids are occasionally listed commercially under *T. chinensis* (Chinese Globeflower).

Trollius japonicus (Japanese Globeflower) 4–8 in. Semi-
   shade
Flowering span: Early May to June
Color: Orange yellow
Native habitat: Japan

Except for its low height, this species is similar to *T. asiaticus* and requires the same care. A double-flowered form,
flore-pleno, is known.

Tulipa (Tulip) 18–30 in. Sun
Flowering span: Early May to early June
Color: Every imaginable color and blending of color
Native habitat: Mostly horticultural hybrids are from Europe

As with the April-blooming tulips, these are also listed by
their *sequence of flowering.* This section of cultivated
tulips is entirely under the official Bulbgrowers' Society of
Holland classification of "Late" and covers the *Darwin,
Lily-flowered, Cottage, Breeder, Rembrandt, Parrot, Late
Double,* and *Fringed* types. Their culture is identical with
the comprehensive recommendations given under the April-
flowering tulips.

May-Flowering Sequence of Cultivated Tulips

LATE (Early May to June)
1. *Darwin* (Derived from selections of nineteenth century
   Cottage and further hybridized.)
   Description: Large, globular cups squared off at both
the base and the top, 24 to 32 inches, satiny texture, intense
colorings, sturdy stems.
   Examples (by colorings):
Mauve, lilac, purple, maroon: "Ace of Spades," 24 in., almost black, large; "Aberdeen," 28 in., silver mauve; "Aristocrat," 30 in., soft violet-rose with white edges; "Black
Forest," 28 in., deep reddish black; "Black Swan," 28 in.,
deep maroon with a violet-blue base; "Bleu Aimable," 26
in., bright lilac blue; "Blue Hill," 28 in., amethyst violet
with a white base; "Blue Perfection," 28 in., lavender-blue
with a white base; "Cum Laude," 28 in., deep violet-blue,

large; "Demeter," 28 in., plum purple, early; "Dorrie Overall," 26 in., dark purple violet with light mauve edges; "Gander," 26 in., pale magenta, early; "Insurpassable," 28 in., lilac; "La Fayette," 28 in., purple-violet; "La Tulipe Noire," 28 in., dark maroon-black with a dark violet center; "Madame Butterfly," 28 in., pale mauve with a violet flush; "Pandion," 26 in., purple with silvery edges; "Queen of Night," 28 in., deep velvety maroon, almost black, large; "Scotch Lassie," 28 in., deep lavender; "The Bishop," 28 in., clear lavender-purple with a blue base, large; and "William Copland," 26 in., lilac.

Pink, rose, orange: "Afterglow," 26 in., soft orange; "Azida," 30 in., rosy red with a white center, large; "Cantor," 26 in., coral pink with a white base; "Clara Butt," 24 in., bright rosy pink; "Elizabeth Arden," 22 in., deep salmon pink; "Etoile Du Midi," 26 in., orange with deep yellow edges; "Helen Madison," 28 in., rose pink with a white base, long-lasting; "Little Queen Bess," 28 in., white with a large flush of rose; "Mr. van Zyl," 28 in., pink with a pure white base; "Perry Como," 24 in., bright strawberry rose; "Picture," 26 in., soft rose; "Pink Supreme," 28 in., bright pink; "Pride of Zwanenburg," 28 in., salmon rose, large; "Princess Elizabeth," 26 in., light rose; "Queen of Bartigons," 24 in., pure salmon pink; "Smiling Queen," 28 in., pure rose, large, long-lasting; "Wilhelm Tell," 28 in., raspberry rose; and "William Copland Rose," 26 in., rose lilac.

Yellow: "Anjou," 26 in., canary yellow with buttercup yellow edges; "Golden Age," 28 in., deep yellow with an orange flush, large; "Golden Niphetos," 28 in., bright gold with light yellow center, long-lasting; "Gold Standard," 28 in., pure golden yellow, large; "Mamasa," 28 in., bright buttercup yellow; "Niphetos," 28 in., lemon yellow, long-lasting; "Silver Wedding," 28 in., yellow with silvery streaks; "Sunkist," 26 in., bright, deep yellow; "Sweet Harmony," 28 in., lemon yellow with ivory white edges; and "Tarakan," 24 in., bright buttercup yellow.

Scarlet and crimson: "Balalaika," 28 in., deep red with yellow base, large; "Charles Needham," 26 in., bright scarlet

with a black base; "City of Haarlem," 28 in., bright vermilion scarlet with a dark blue base; "Eclipse," 28 in., dark
blood-red with a violet base; "Florence Nightingale," 28 in.,
bright vermilion red; "Flying Dutchman," 27 in., bright
scarlet-red, long-lasting; "Koblenz," 26 in., deep wine red;
"Landseadel's Supreme," 28 in., rich cherry-red with a
creamy yellow base, late, long-lasting; "Margaux," 28 in.,
deep wine red with a blue base; "Nobel," 28 in., deep geranium red with a black center; "Pride of Haarlem," 28 in.,
cerise scarlet with a blue base; "Red Master," 28 in., deep
crimson with a blue base; and "Scarlett O'Hara," 28 in.,
bright scarlet with lighter edges.

White: "Anne Frank," 28 in., pure white; "Blizzard," 28 in.,
translucent white; "Duke of Wellington," 28 in., pure white
with a creamy white base; "Glacier," 26 in., white throughout; "Jeanne d'Arc," 26 in., ivory white, long-lasting;
"Snowpeak," 28 in., pure white, large; "White Elephant,"
28 in., pure white with a flush of icy green; and "White
Giant," white, large.

2. *Lily-flowered* (Derived from hybridizing between *T. re-
   troflexa* and *Cottage.*)
   Description: Slender, urn-shaped with long, curving
petals turning outward, 22 to 28 inches, long-lasting, blooming with the *Darwin.*
   Examples: "Aladdin," 22 in., scarlet with narrow yellow
edges; "Alaska," 26 in., clear yellow; "Ascona," 26 in., pale
yellow fading to white; "Beverley," 24 in., orange; "Captain
Fryatt," 24 in., reddish purple; "China Pink," 26 in., satin
pink with a white base; "Elegans Alba," 24 in., white with
narrow crimson edges; "Gisela," 28 in., pure rose; "Golden
Duchess," 28 in., golden yellow; "Inimitable," 26 in.,
golden yellow, large; "Kiruna," deep ruby red, long-lasting;
"Lilac Time," 26 in., deep lavender with white edges;
"Mariette," 25 in., deep rose, very long-lasting; "Maybole,"
24 in., bright pink; "Philemon," 22 in., creamy yellow;
"Queen of Sheba," 26 in., rusty red with yellow edges; "Red
Shine," 26 in., glowing, deep red; "West Point," 26 in., deep
primrose-yellow; "White Trimphator," 26 in., snowy white;
and "Yellow Triumphator," 26 in., soft yellow.

Dramatically colored, the flared petals of the lily-flowered tulip "Lilac Time" are a May delight.

3. *Cottage* (Named for types found in nineteenth-century English and French cottage gardens and later hybridized; also known as *Single Late.*)

Description: Long, egg-shaped, mostly pastel or light-colored, 18 to 30 inches, sturdy-stemmed. Included in this category are the *viridiflora* or "green" varieties, and the "bunch-flowering" or multiple-blossom types. They bloom with *Darwin* and *Lily-flowered.*

Examples:

Bunch-flowering: "Claudette," 24 in., white with red edges; "Georgette," 22 in., clear yellow with red edges; "Kuekenhof," 24 in., clear scarlet, large; "Madame Mottet," 24 in., bright rose with lighter edges; "Monsieur Mottet," 24 in., creamy white with a shell pink flush; "Orange Bouquet," 26 in., orange-red with pale yellow base outside, interior bright red with bright yellow base; "Rose Mist," 26 in., rich pink; and "Wallflower," 24 in., dark brown with a yellow base.

Viridiflora: "Angel," 20 in., white with greenish feathering; "Artist," 18 in., combined rose, yellow, purple, red, and green, long-lasting; "Court Lady," 20 in. pure white with dark green feathering; "Formosa," 14 in., greenish yellow with green feathering, late; "Golden Artist," 18 in., green and yellow mixed; "Greenland," 22 in., deep rose with wide green feathering, long-lasting; "Hummingbird," 20 in., yellow with green feathering, large; "Pimpernel," 18 in., carmine red with light green feathering; and "Viridiflora Praecox" or "Green Knight," 18 in., pale green with yellow edges.

Examples (by colorings):
White: "Albino," 25 in., pure white; "Carrara," 22 in., clear white, cup-shaped; "Ivory Glory," 26 in., ivory white, eggshaped; "Maureen," 28 in., translucent white, large; "Sigrid Undset," 30 in., creamy white, long-lasting; and "White City," 27 in., pure white.

Yellow: "Asta Nielsen," 26 in., creamy yellow outside, shining yellow inside; "Belle Jaune," 28 in., deep yellow outside, bright yellow inside; "Blushing Bride," 26 in., creamy white with a carmine red banding, long-lasting; "Bond Street," 26 in., buttercup yellow flushed with orange; "Elsie Eloff," 28 in., buttercup yellow; "Golden Harvest," 28 in., lemon yellow; "Golden Measure," 28 in., deep yellow, fragrant; "Mongolia," 28 in., soft yellow; "Mother's Day," 28 in., citron yellow, late; "Mrs. John T. Scheepers," 26 in., clear yellow, large; "Princess Margaret Rose," 23 in., canary yellow with orange-red edges; "Queen of Spain," 27 in., pale yellow flushed pink; and "Scaramouche," 27 in., brownish bronze with a yellow flush and clear yellow edges.

Red, Rose, and Pink: "Advance," 29 in., bright orange-scarlet with a silvery sheen; "Chappaqua," 28 in., violet-rose outside, interior carmine-rose with a yellow center; "City of Alkmaar," 28 in., bright cerise red; "Dido," 28 in., salmon-rose with orange-yellow edges; "General de la Rey," 27 in., salmon with a creamy white base, large; "G. W. Leak," 28 in., bright red with a light yellow base; "Halcro," 26 in., carmine red, large, long-lasting; "Majestic," 27 in., bright orange-scarlet with a black base; "Marjorie Bowen," 28 in., salmon rose; "Marshall Haig," 28 in., brilliant scarlet with a yellow base; "Mirella," 28 in., deep salmon; "Northern Queen," 25 in., white with wide pink edges; "Orange Diamond," 26 in., deep salmon orange with soft orange edges; "Oriental Queen," 24 in., bright red with greenish base; "Palestrina," 22 in., salmon pink flushed with rose; "Renown," 26 in., light carmine red; "Rosy Wings," 26 in., bright apricot-pink; "Sorbet," 28 in., exterior rosy white, interior white with red streaks; and "Unique," 28 in., white with broad streaks of carmine red, long-lasting.

4. *Breeder* (Derived from hybridizing older varieties for new colorings.)

Description: Similar to *Darwin* in shape and size, these are usually noticeably bicolored, 25–30 inches, blooming with *Darwin* and *Cottage.*

Examples: "Barcarolle," 28 in., bluish purple, large; "Cherbourg," 28 in., deep gold with light bronze overlay, large; "Dillenburg," 27 in., orange-terracotta with golden yellow edges; "His Highness," 26 in., clear orange flushed with bronze, very long-lasting; "Jessy," 30 in., deep coffee brown flushed with bronze-red; "J. J. Bouman," 28 in., tomato red, shaded orange with a yellow base; "Limnos," 28 in., salmon with orange flush and a yellow base; "Louis XIV," 28 in., steel-blue flushed with bronze and edged with golden brown, fragrant; "Maria Zamora," 28 in., burnt orange; "Orange Delight," 26 in., golden bronze with a flush of orange; "Papago," 28 in., poppy red exterior, interior orange-red; "Rayburn," 28 in., dark violet flushed with bronze; "Soir de Paris," 26 in., reddish purple with white edges and a green-blue base; "Tantalus," 28 in., light yellow with a violet flush and a dark yellow base; and "Winnetou," 27 in., red with bronze-orange edges outside, interior cardinal red with yellow base.

5. *Rembrandt* or *Broken* (Derived from virus-infected bulbs since the seventeenth century.)

Description: Striped or streaked with brown, bronze, black, red, pink, or purple on either, red, white, or yellow backgrounds, 24 to 30 inches, limited availability due to current lack of popular appeal, blooming with *Darwin* and *Cottage.*

Examples: "Absalon," 26 in., yellow feathered with coffee brown; "American Flag," 30 in., deep red with broad, white feathering and a blue base; "Cordell Hull," 24 in., carmine red with white feathering; "Insulinde," 24 in., yellow with violet feathering; "Madame de Pompadour," 24 in., white with lilac-purple feathering; "May Blossom," 24 in., creamy white with purple feathering; "Montgomery," 24 in., white with red feathering; "Union Jack," 25 in., ivory white feathered with raspberry-red and a white base; and "Victor Hugo," 24 in., white with cherry-red feathering.

6. *Parrot* (Known since the seventeenth century, many current varieties are chance mutations or "sports" of *Darwin*.)

Description: Fringed, scalloped, laciniated, or wavy petals, very large, 18 to 28 inches, often weak-stemmed, light green foliage, blooming with the *Darwin*.

Examples: "Black Parrot," 27 in., purple-black; "Blue Parrot," 28 in., lilac-blue; "Caprice," 24 in., violet-rose; "Discovery," 28 in., soft rose; "Doorman," 24 in., cherry red with deep yellow edges, large; "Fantasy," 26 in., salmon rose feathered with green; "Faraday," 26 in., white flushed with pale pink and green; "Firebird," 26 in., vermilion scarlet; "Ivory Parrot," 28 in., creamy white; "James V. Forrestal," 22 in., orange-red with yellow edges, large; "Muriel," 28 in., clear violet-blue; "Orange Favorite," 23 in., bright orange flushed green with yellow base, fragrant; "Orange Parrot," 20 in., deep bronze-orange, late, fragrant; "Parrot Wonder," 28 in., cherry red, large; "Red Champion," 24 in., carmine red; "Sunshine," 18 in., golden yellow; "Texas Flame," 20 in., buttercup yellow flushed with carmine red and a green base; "Texas Gold," 20 in., clear yellow with bright red edges; "Van Dyck," 28 in., bright rose pink, large; and "White Parrot," 23 in., pure white flushed green.

7. *Double Late* (Also called "Peony-flowered" because of their form.)

Description: Large cups filled with many rows of petals, 20 to 25 inches, stiff stems prone to flower loss in strong wind or storms, blooms as *Darwin* and *Cottage* fade.

Examples: "Brilliant Fire," 22 in., bright vermilion-red; "Clara Carder," 25 in., rose pink with pure white center, large; "Elite," 22 in., red with broad white edges; "Eros," 24 in., bold rose, large, fragrant; "Gerbrandt Kieft," 22 in., deep red edged with white, large; "Gold Medal," 20 in., deep golden yellow; "Grand National," 22 in., creamy yellow; "Lilac Perfection," 22 in., deep lilac-blue; "Mount Tacoma," 25 in., pure white, large; "Nizza," 22 in., soft yellow with red feathering; "Orange Triumph," 22 in., orange-red with deep yellow edges; "Symphonia," 25 in., cherry red; "Uncle Tom," 23 in., deep red, large; "Vincent Van Gogh," 22 in., wine red edged with yellow and creamy yellow; and "White Lady," 22 in., pure white.

8. *Fringed* (Also called "Orchid.")

Description: Resembling *Darwin* in general shape, except petal tips are finely cut and tend to fade greatly lighter than the main coloring for a "frosted" effect, 25 to 28 inches, blooming with the *Late Double.*

Examples: "Burgundy Lace," 28 in., rich wine-red; "Blue Heron," 25 in., lilac-blue; "Fringed Lilac," 26 in., lilac; "Humor," 26 in., purple-violet; "New Look," 28 in., creamy white flushed with pink; "Maja," 24 in., bright yellow; and "Swan Wings," 26 in., pure white.

Uvularia grandiflora (Big Merrybells) 12–24 in. Shade
Flowering span: Mid-May to mid-June
Color: Lemon yellow
Native habitat: Southeastern Canada to Georgia, west to
    Oklahoma and North Dakota

While hardly showy, this vigorous perennial offers a rich green, lanceolate foliage with soft hairs on the underside and 1- to 1½-inch, drooping, bell-shaped flowers. The arching stems appear to be growing from the center of the wraparound leaves. A rich, slightly acid, moist, humusy soil in deep to light shade is best. Propagate by cuttings of the thick, creeping rootstock or seed. There are no diseases or problematic pests.

Uvularia perfoliata (Wood Merrybells) 6–18 in. Shade
Flowering span: Mid-May to mid-June
Color: Pale yellow
Native habitat: Massachusetts to Florida, west to Louisiana

Similar in its groundcover habit and appearance to *U. grandiflora*, here the stems are thinner and the leaves are entirely smooth. Culture is identical for both.

Uvularia sessilifolia (Oakesia sessilifolia) (Little
   Merrybells) 6–10 in. Shade
Flowering span: Mid-May to mid-June
Color: Pale greenish yellow
Native habitat: Southeastern Canada to Alabama, west to
   South Dakota

Smaller and more delicately shaped than either of the other *Uvularias*, the flowers are only 1 inch long, surrounded by light green, somewhat oval leaves forming a long-lasting groundcover under the same cultural conditions as for *U. grandiflora*.

Veronica chamaedrys (Germander Speedwell) 12–18 in.
   Sun
Flowering span: Late May to late June
Color: Bright blue with a white eye
Native habitat: Northern and central Europe, Syria, Canary
   Islands

Slender, erect stalks with large, star-shaped, clustered florets appear above a creeping mat of mostly evergreen, thick, hairy, 1½-inch leaves. Enjoying any moist, average-fertility soil in sun to light shading, it can be easily propagated by division. Leaf spot is probably the only noticeable affliction, and insects fail to bother it.

Veronica gentianoides (glabra) (Gentian Speedwell) 6–24
   in. Sun
Flowering span: Early May to June
Color: Pale blue
Native habitat: Southeastern Europe

Tufts of smooth, somewhat thick, 1- to 3-inch glossy leaves form a heavy mat of durable summer foliage following the conspicuous bloom of erect flower stalks with noticeable, ¼-inch, cup-shaped florets. Culture is the same as with *V. chamaedrys*. Several varieties are known: *alba*, pure white; *pallida*, porcelain blue; and *variegata* with leaves streaked in creamy white.

Veronica officinalis (Common Speedwell) 6–12 in. Shade
Flowering span: Mid-May to mid-July
Color: Pale lavender-blue
Native habitat: Europe, Southeastern Canada to Tennessee

Prostrate, hairy, creeping stems root where they touch and form a durable, evergreen mat in densely shaded areas where little else will grow. Leaves are 1 inch, hairy, and elliptical. The ongoing flower display is from spikes of bell-shaped, ¼-inch florets. Any moist, average-fertility soil suits it from deep to semi-shade, and propagation is simplest by making cuttings of rooted stems. Pests and diseases are not problematic here.

Veronica pectinata (Comb Speedwell) 2–3 in. Sun
Flowering span: Early May to mid-June
Color: Deep blue
Native habitat: Asia Minor

Prostrate and creeping easily, this woolly-leaved rock garden plant has gray-green, evergreen foliage and carries short spikes of blue flowers with white centers. Tolerant of sun to semi-shade, it grows in almost any soil or exposure. Division is the simplest propagation method, and pests and diseases are not interested in it. The variety *rosea* has rose-pink flowers.

Veronica repens (Creeping Speedwell) ½–1 in. Sun
Flowering span: Early May to June
Color: Rose to pale blue
Native habitat: Corsica, Spain

Not heavily flowered, the mosslike, shining foliage works well as a prostrate groundcover mat, especially between stepping stones. It prefers a sandy soil and needs watering in dry spells. Division propagates it best, and diseases or pests are not evident. The variety *alba* has white flowers.

Veronica spuria (amethystina) (Bastard Speedwell) 12–18
   in. Sun
Flowering span: Mid-May to early June
Color: Pale blue
Native habitat: Southeastern Europe, southern Russia

Densely hairy, the plant has 1-inch, thick leaves and generous flowering stalks but tends to be weedy by late summer. Soil with average fertility in sun or light shade suits it well, and propagation is either by division or seed. Pests and diseases are unknown. The variety *elegans carnea* has rich pink flowers, more branching, and reaches only 12 inches.

Veronica teucrium (rupestris, latifolia) (Hungarian
   Speedwell) 12–18 in. Sun
Flowering span: Late May to July
Color: Bright lavender blue
Native habitat: Central and southern Europe, Central Asia

Slender spikes of long-blooming flowers are surrounded by narrow, dark green leaves in this species. It enjoys a well-drained, average soil in sun to light shade and has no particular pests or diseases. Several varieties are available: "Blue Fountain," 12 to 15 in., rich blue; "Crater Lake Blue," 12 to 18 in., purplish blue; and "Trehane," 9 in., light blue, yellow-green leaves.

Viola canadensis (Canada Violet) 3–12 in. Semi-shade
Flowering span: Early May to July
Color: White
Native habitat: Southeastern Canada to Maryland, west to
   Arizona

Thriving in cold areas best, the solitary, long-lasting flowers emerge from the leaf axils and are often flushed outside with magenta or lavender. The 2- to 4-inch leaves are heart-shaped and pointed. Preferring cool, moist, humusy woods, the husky, fibrous rootstock is difficult to divide when mature. Propagate by dormant spring or fall transplanting of seedlings. Nothing troublesome appears to bother it.

Viola hastata (Halberdleaf Yellow Violet) 4–10 in.
    Semi-shade
Flowering span: Early May to mid-June
Color: Lemon yellow
Native habitat: Pennsylvania to Florida

Showy when massed, the solitary, terminal flowers come from a top cluster of wedge-shaped leaves that are often splotched with silver. Best in moist, humusy woods, division is the preferred propagation method. Diseases and pests are no problem.

Viola lutea (European Yellow Violet)   2–6 in. Semi-shade
Flowering span: Early May to June
Color: Bright yellow
Native habitat: Central Europe, British Isles

Heavily flowered in moist, humusy rock gardens or wood-lot borders, this low-growing plant is compact and neat. The blossoms often have fine stripes of deep violet on the lower petals. Propagate by division in spring or fall. Pests and diseases are unknown.

Viola pedata (Birdsfoot Violet) 3–5 in. Sun
Flowering span: Mid-May to mid-June
Color: Lilac
Native habitat: Maine to Florida, west to Texas and Minnesota

The showy blossoms abundantly appear on sun-drenched, dry locations prior to the full emergence of the finely divided, green foliage resembling a bird's footprint. Typically, the 2 upper petals are velvety, dark violet with 3 pale lilac lower ones around a noticeable gold center. Requiring good drainage, it is best on rocky, acid, sandy soils of low fertility. Seed or dormant root cuttings work best, and there are no bothersome pests or diseases. The rare variety *alba* is nearly white.

Viola sagittata (Arrowleaf Violet) 2–3 in. Semi-shade
Flowering span: Mid-May to mid-June

Color: Violet purple
Native habitat: Massachusetts to Georgia, west to Texas and
  Minnesota

Elongated, narrow leaves surround the long-stalked, white-centered flowers here. Noninvasive, this wildflower likes moist, humusy sites in semi- to light shading. Propagate by seed, division, or offsets. Pests and diseases are unproblematic.

Waldensteinia fragaroides (Barren-strawberry) 3–4 in.
  Semi-shade
Flowering span: Early May to June
Color: Light yellow
Native habitat: Southeastern Canada to Georgia, west to
  Missouri

The deeply lobed, glossy, trifoliate leaves are very similar to the true strawberry and form evergreen tufts. Clusters of tiny, 5-petaled flowers appear above the foliage on slender stalks but produce no edible fruit. Suitable for dry to moist locations in semi-shade, it tolerates a wide variety of soils. Division of the underground rhizome propagates it best. It appears to be free of pests and diseases. The variety from eastern Europe and Japan, *ternata,* is similar but smaller and requires the same culture.

Xerophyllum asphodeloides (Turkeybeard Beargrass) 24–48
  in. Semi-shade
Flowering span: Mid-May to July
Color: Yellowish white
Native habitat: New Jersey to North Carolina, west to Tennessee

From a ground-hugging tuft of numerous, wiry green leaves comes a stout spike topped by a 6-inch, cylindrical head of star-shaped, ¼-inch florets of noticeable showiness, fragrance, and durability. Best in semi- to light shade in moist, sandy soils, it needs very careful division of the deep tap roots in spring for propagation. Small seedlings dug with intact roots provide greater success. Pests and diseases are not known. The Pacific variety, *tenax*, is similar with a pyramidal flower head.

JUNE

A *General Guide to the Color Values Available in June:*
(*Each division includes shades, tints, and tones of the dominant value.*)

WHITE: Achillea ageratifolia, Achillea argentea, Achillea nana, Achillea ptarmica, Anemone virginiana, Antennaria dioica, Anthericum liliago, Aquilegia flabellata nana alba, Aruncus sylvester, Asphodelus albus, Astilbe arendsi, Campanula carpatica *hybrids*, Campanula glomerata alba, Campanula latifolia alba, Campanula persicifolia *varieties*, Catananche caerulea alba, Centaurea montana alba, Centranthus ruber alba, Cerastium biebersteini, Cerastium boissieri, Cerastium tomentosum, Chimaphila maculata, Chimaphila umbellata, Chrysanthemum coccinea, Chrysanthemum maximum, Clematis integrifolia alba, Clematis recta, Coronilla varia, Cypripedium reginae, Delphinium cheilanthum *hybrids*, Delphinium elatum *hybrids*, Delphinium grandiflorum, Dianthus alpinus, Dianthus arenarius, Dianthus barbatus, Dianthus latifolius, Dictamnus albus, Digitalis lutea, Digitalis purpurea, Dipsacus fullonum, Eremurus himalaicus, Eremurus robustus albus, Erigeron speciosus *hybrids*, Filapendula hexapetala, Filipendula purpurea alba, Filipendula ulmaria, Gypsophila bodgeri, Gypsophila repens, Helianthemum nummularium *hybrids*, Hesperis matronalis *varieties*, Heuchera sanguinea *hybrids*, Heuchera villosa, Iris *"Dutch Hybrids,"* Iris sibirica *hybrids*, Iris spuria *hybrids*, Leontopodium alpinum, Leontopodium sibiricum, Lewisia cotyledon, Lewisia rediviva, Lilium *hybrids*, Lilium candidum, Lilium martagon album, Lupinus *"Russell Hybrids,"* Lychnis coronaria alba, Mitchella repens, Monarda didyma *hybrids*, Papaver orientale *hybrids*, Paradisea liliastrum, Penstemon gloxinoides, Phlox carolina, Platycodon grandiflorum, Polemonium richardsoni album, Salvia nemorosa alba, Saponaria ocymoides alba, Saxifraga aizoon, Saxifraga cotyledon, Scabiosa caucasica *hybrids*, Sedum pulchellum, Shortia galacifolia, Shortia uniflora, Sidalcea candida, Silene maritima, Tunica saxifraga, Valeriana officinalis, Verbascum hybrida

YELLOW: Achillea filipendulina, Achillea tomentosa, Alstroemeria aurantiaca lutea, Anthemis biebersteiniana, Anthemis tinctoria, Aquilegia longissima, Cephalaria alpina, Chrysogonum virginianum, Coreopsis auriculata, Coreopsis grandiflora, Coreopsis lanceolata, Coreopsis palmata, Delphinium zalil, Digitalis ambigua, Digitalis lanata, Gaillardia aristata, Helianthemum nummularium, Hemerocallis flava, Hemerocallis thunbergi, Hieracium bombycinum, Hieracium villosum, Iris *"Dutch Hybrids,"* Iris ochroleuca, Iris spuria *hybrids*, Kniphofia tucki, Lilium *hybrids*, Lilium canadense, Lilium hansoni, Lilium monadelphum, Linum flavum, Lotus corniculatus, Lupinus *"Russell Hybrids,"* Lysimachia nummularia, Lysimachia punctata, Lysimachia terrestis, Lysimachia vulgaris, Mecanopsis cambrica, Oenothera fruticosa, Oenothera missouriensis, Oenothera tetragona, Opuntia compressa, Potentilla argyrophylla, Potentilla grandiflora, Primula bullesiana, Primula bulleyana, Saxifraga aizoides, Saxifraga aizoon *varieties*, Sedum aizoon, Sedum middendorffianum, Sedum sexangulare, Sempervivum, Thermopsis caroliniana, Verbascum hybrida

ORANGE: Alstroemeria aurantiaca, Aquilegia skinneri, Helianthemum nummularium *hybrids*, Hemerocallis middendorffi, Hieracium auranticum, Iris *"Dutch Hybrids,"* Lilium *hybrids*, Papaver orientale, Primula bulleyana, Trollius ledebouri

RED: Alstroemeria aurantiaca *hybrids*, Aquilegia skinneri, Astilbe arendsi, Centaurea dealbata steenbergii, Centaurea montana rubra, Centranthus ruber, Dianthus alpinus *hybrids*, Dianthus barbatus, Dianthus latifolius, Dianthus sylvestris, Gaillardia aristata, Helianthemum nummularium *hybrids*, Heuchera sanguinea, Incarvillea grandiflora, Kniphofia tucki, Lilium *hybrids*, Lilium concolor, Lilium pomponium, Lupinus *"Russell Hybrids,"* Lychnis chalcedonica, Lychnis coronaria, Lychnis flos-cuculi, Monarda didyma, Papaver orientale, Penstemon barbatus, Penstemon gloxinoides, Penstemon hartwegi, Phlox ovata, Potentilla atrosanguinea *hybrids*, Primula bullesiana, Saponaria ocymoides splendidissima, Saxifraga aizoides atrorubens, Sidalcea hybrida, Silene virginica

PINK: Allium karataviense, Allium oreophilum ostrowskianum, Antennaria dioica rosea, Astilbe arendsi, Callopogon pallidus, Chimaphila umbellata, Coronilla varia, Delphinium elatum *hybrids*, Dianthus alpinus, Dianthus barbatus, Dianthus latifolius, Digitalis dubia, Digitalis lanata, Eremurus robustus, Erigeron speciosus *hybrids*, Filipendula purpurea, Filipendula rubra, Gypsophila bodgeri, Gypsophila repens, Helianthemum nummularium *hybrids*, Heuchera sanguinea *hybrids*, Heuchera villosa, Incarvillea delaveyi *hybrids*, Lewisia cotyledon, Lewisia rediviva, Lewisia tweedyi, Lilium *hybrids*, Lupinus *"Russell Hybrids,"* Lychnis chalcedonica salmonea, Lychnis coronaria *hybrids*, Lychnis flos-cuculi, Lychnis flos-jovis, Lythrum virgatum *hybrids*, Malva alcea, Mitchella repens, Monarda didyma *hybrids*, Papaver orientale *hybrids*, Penstemon barbatus *hybrids*, Penstemon gloxinoides, Phlox carolina, Phlox maculata *hybrids*, Phlox ovata, Platycodon grandiflorum, Primula bullesiana, Saponaria ocymoides, Saxifraga aizoon rosea, Scabiosa graminifolia *hybrids*, Sedum pulchellum, Sedum telephoides, Sempervivum, Shortia uniflora, Sidalcea hybrida, Silene schafta, Stachys macrantha robusta, Stachys olympica, Tunica saxifraga flore-pleno, Valeriana officinalis, Verbascum hybrida, Veronica incana rosea, Veronica spicata *hybrids*

PURPLE: Allium albopilosum, Callirhoe involuncrata, Campanula carpatica *hybrids*, Campanula glomerata, Campanula latifolia, Campanula persicifolia, Catananche caerulea, Centaurea dealbata, Centaurea gymnocarpa, Centaurea montana *hybrids*, Centaurea rutifolia, Delphinium brunonianum, Celphinium elatum, Dictamnus albus purpureus, Digitalis purpurea, Dodecatheon jeffreyi, Erigeron speciosus, Hesperis matronalis, Incarvillea delaveyi, Iris *"Dutch Hybrids,"* Iris sibirica, Iris spuria, Lupinus polyphyllus, Lychnis flos-jovis, Lythrum virgatum, Monarda didyma *hybrids*, Nepeta faassenii, Penstemon gloxinoides, Phlox maculata, Polemonium humile, Potentilla atrosanguinea, Primula beesiana, Primula bullesiana, Salvia nemorosa, Scabiosa caucasica *hybrids*, Scabiosa columbaria, Sedum pulchellum, Sedum rosea, Silene aucalis, Stachys macrantha, Thymus serphyllum, Tunica saxifraga, Valeriana officinalis, Verbascum hybrida

BLUE: Allium caeruleum, Allium cyaneum, Aquilegia flabellata, Campanula carpatica, Campanula glomerata superba, Campanula latifolia *hybrids*, Campanula persicifolia *hybrids*, Campanula portenschlagiana, Campanula rotundifolia, Centaurea montana, Clematis integrifolia, Delphinium cashmerianum, Delphinium cheilanthum, Delphinium elatum *hybrids*, Delphinium grandiflorum, Dracocephalum grandiflorum, Iris *"Dutch Hybrids,"* Iris sibirica *hybrids*, Iris spuria *hybrids*, Lupinus polyphyllus, Lupinus *"Russell Hybrids,"* Platycodon grandiflorum, Polemonium humile, Polemonium richardsoni, Scabiosa caucasica, Scabiosa graminifolia, Veronica incana, Veronica prostrata, Veronica spicata

BICOLOR: Cypripedium reginae, Dianthus barbatus, Erigeron speciosus, Gaillardia aristata, Iris *"Dutch Hybrids,"* Iris ochroleuca, Kniphofia tucki, Lilium *hybrids*, Lupinus *"Russell Hybrids,"* Papaver orientale *hybrids*, Penstemon gloxinoides *hybrids*, Primula bullesiana, Sempervivum, Verbascum hybrida

Achillea ageratifolia (Greek Yarrow) 6–12 in. Sun
Flowering span: Early June to July
Color: White
Native habitat: Greece

Flat clusters of 1-inch, daisylike blossoms stand above the woolly, silver-green, feathery foliage of this drought-resistant perennial best used in bright sun as a rock garden or plant wall accent. Any average, well-drained soil that is modestly moist is workable. Division in spring or fall propa-

gates it most easily. Pests and diseases avoid it. The variety
aizoon (*Anthemis aizoon*) has larger flowering and simple,
lancelike leaves.

Achillea argentea (Silver Yarrow) 5–6 in. Sun
Flowering span: Late June to August
Color: White
Native habitat: Yugoslavia

Preferring an alkaline soil, this moundlike perennial carries 3-parted leaves covered with white, silky hairs and
long-lasting clusterings of small flowers resembling daisies.
It thrives in full sun on sandy soils and is readily increased
by division. Occasionally, stem rot and rust bother it, but insects are no worry. The earlier-blooming and slightly larger
species, *clavennae*, is often mistaken for this plant.

Achillea filipendulina (*eupatorium*) (Fernleaf Yarrow)
    48–60 in. Sun
Flowering span: Mid-June to September
Color: Mustard yellow
Native habitat: Caucasus Mountains, Orient

Attractive, gray-green, feathery leaves up to 6 inches long
are capped by erect stems with 5-inch-wide, flat-topped
clusters of tightly packed florets. Stripped of leaves, the
flower stalks can be dried easily for winter bouquets. It
prefers full sun and an average-fertility soil with good drainage but may need staking in windy locations. Although it
takes drought comfortably, it prefers reasonable moisture at
all times. Seed, spring division, or summertime cuttings all
propagate it readily. Stem rot is a nuisance at times, but insects usually avoid the pungent foliage. The hybrids include: "Coronation Gold," 36 in., mustard-colored, 3-in.-
wide flower heads; "Gold Plate," 48 in., golden yellow, 6-
in.-wide flowering, blooming later; and "Parker's Variety,"
42 in., bright yellow with 4-in.-wide blossoms not quite so
dense as "Gold Plate."

Achillea nana (Dwarf Yarrow) 1–6 in. Sun
Flowering span: Early June to August

Color: White
Native habitat: Southern Europe

Useful for filling the spaces between stepping stones in full sun, this creeping mat of aromatic, downy, green foliage carries erect flower heads of daisylike, inconsequential flowers through most of the summer. Its leaves are importantly used as a flavoring, however, in the manufacture of the liqueur Chartreuse. Liking hot, dry locations with good drainage, it nevertheless tolerates a wide variety of soils. Division is the practical propagation method, and diseases or pests are not bothersome.

Achillea ptarmica (Sneezewort Yarrow) 12–24 in. Sun
Flowering span: Early June to September
Color: White
Native habitat: Europe, British Isles

Apt to become rangy and straggling in any of its forms, the species has an ongoing flower response worth inclusion in the cutting garden. The narrow, dark green leaves are long and smooth below much-branched flower heads with ball-shaped blossoming. Its dried roots were once used as homemade snuff, which accounts for the "sneeze" part of its naming. Any well-drained, average-fertility soil suits it in bright sunshine, and propagation can be handled by seed, division, or summer cuttings. It is known to escape cultivation and become wild. Stem rot is a pest at times, but insects are uncommon. Any of the double-flowered hybrids is superior to the parent: "Angel's Breath," 24 in., pure white; "Perry's Giant White," 24 in., having ¼-in. florets; "Snowball," 14 in. with ½-in. florets; and "The Pearl," 24 in., cultivated since 1900 for its ½-in., very double florets.

Achillea tomentosa (Woolly Yarrow) 2–10 in. Sun
Flowering span: Early June to September
Color: Canary yellow
Native habitat: Europe, Orient

Conspicuously woolly, gray-green leaves form ground-cover mats with 1- to 2-inch clusters of bright flower heads

The ongoing flowering of *Achillea tomentosa* is enhanced by woolly foliage.

all summer. Full sun, dryness, and a sandy soil provide its needs. Propagate by seed, division, or summer stem cuttings. Pests and diseases shun it. The variety "Moonlight" is pale yellow with light green leaves and slower growing.

Allium albopilosum (*christophi*) (Persian Onion) 20–30 in. Sun
Flowering span: Late June to late July
Color: Deep lilac
Native habitat: Turkestan, Afghanistan

One of the largest-flowering of the group, the bulb has football-shaped, 8- to 10-inch blossoms with ½-inch, silver-coated, starlike florets and worthwhile dried seed heads. The hairy, gray, strap leaves stretch to 18 inches. While not overly vigorous, it does best in full sun with good drainage and an average loam. Install new plantings in the autumn. Diseases and pests are unimportant, but in severe climates it requires a winter mulching.

Allium caeruleum (azureum) (Blueglobe Onion)   18–24 in.
   Sun
Flowering span: Late June to late July
Color: Sky blue
Native habitat: Siberia, Turkestan

Tight, 2-inch, globular flower heads rise above large, linear leaves with deep blue striping increasing the blossom vividness. Reasonably simple to grow, it requires the same culture as *A. albopilosum.*

Allium cyaneum   6–10 in.   Sun
Flowering span: Mid-June to mid-July
Color: Turquoise blue
Native habitat: China

The threadlike foliage here is unusual, along with the bright intensity of the flower coloring. The blossom heads are small and loosely clustered but make an attractive rock garden accent. Satisfactorily hardy, the bulb dislikes constantly damp sites and thrives best in sunny, average soil with good drainage. Plant these uniquely distorted bulbs in the fall. There are no difficulties with pests or diseases.

Allium karataviense (Turkestan Onion)   6–8 in.   Sun
Flowering span: Early June to mid-July
Color: Mauve pink
Native habitat: Turkestan

Grown as much for its long-lasting foliage as its sizable flower head, the bulb has only twin, gray-green, 4-inch-wide leaves mottled with purple at the ground level. The 4- to 8-inch, globular blossom stands erect on a stiff stem and does best in well-drained, sunny places of average fertility. Plant the bulbs in autumn. Pests and diseases are not bothersome, but in severely cold areas they may need winter protection.

Allium oreophilum ostrowskianum (Ostrowsky Onion)
   6–8 in.   Sun
Flowering span: Mid-June to mid-July
Color: Purple pink
Native habitat: Turkestan

Increasing readily in sunny, summer-dry locations, here the bulb has ½-inch florets in dense, rounded heads between 2 to 3 inches across. The narrow, green leaves are at ground level. Divide overcrowded plants after the foliage disappears, and install new colonies in the fall. It has no troublesome diseases or pests. The variety "Zwanenburg" is deep carmine-pink, more openly flowered, and 6 inches tall.

Alstroemeria aurantiaca (Peruvian Lily) 30–36 in. Sun
Flowering span: Mid-June to mid-July
Color: Orange
Native habitat: Chile

Not always hardy or reliable, this unusual, showy plant has fleshy roots that make no top growth during the first year after its spring or fall installation. The 4-inch, narrow, light gray-green leaves sparsely line the heavy stem that terminates in a loose cluster of 2-inch, lilylike florets streaked with red.

Tolerant of full sun where the climate is cool, it prefers half shade in hot areas. Best in a protected, south-facing border with a well-drained, sandy-humus soil that is annually enriched with compost or rotted manure, it should be mulched heavily in severe winter areas. The hybrid "Dover Orange" is 36 inches and orange-red, while *lutea* is bright yellow and 30 inches tall.

Anemone virginiana (Virginia Anemone) 24–30 in. Semi-
    shade
Flowering span: Mid-June to August
Color: White to greenish white
Native habitat: Southeastern Canada to Alabama, west to
    Kansas

Noticeable, 1- to 1½-inch, solitary flowers rise here above glossy, dark green, deeply incised leaves and display a wide ring of gold stamens. Best in moist, acid, humusy woodlots with dappled light, it produces an elongated, cylindrical seed head that gives it the name "thimbleweed" in some areas. Spring division is preferred, and there are no disease or pest nuisances.

Antennaria dioica (candida, tomentosa) (Common
    Pussytoes) 3–10 in. Sun
Flowering span: Early June to July
Color: Pinkish white
Native habitat: Europe, British Isles, Asia

While not distinguished for its erect flowering, the creeping, silvery green, woolly foliage mat has an easy adaptability for hot, dry, sunny rock garden sites. Seed or spring division suit it equally, and no pest or disease bothers it. The variety *rosea* has attractive rose pink blossoms. Removing the exhausted flowering keeps the plant decorative all season.

Anthemis biebersteiniana 5–10 in. Sun
Flowering span: Early June to July
Color: Bright yellow
Native habitat: Europe

Useful as a rock garden accent, its glistening, silvery-green foliage spreads neatly in dense mats and displays solitary, daisy-shaped flowers on thin stems. Accepting sun or light shade and any well-drained, average soil, it can be spring-divided or propagated by seed. Insects and diseases avoid it.

Anthemis tinctoria (Golden Camomile) 24–30 in. Sun
Flowering span: Mid-June to September
Color: Golden yellow
Native habitat: Europe

Here the feathery foliage is green and noticeably aromatic when bruised. The solitary, 2-inch, daisylike flowers come on stiff stems and seed prolifically if unchecked. Requiring no fertilizing to succeed, it thrives on dry, well-drained, average soil and can also be propagated readily by division or stem cuttings. Nothing seems to bother it. Quite a few hybrids are available but their seed proves erratic for exact color duplication: "Beauty of Grallagh," deep yellow, large-flowered; "E. C. Buxton," lemon yellow; "Grallagh Gold," deep orange-gold, 30 in.; *kelwayi*, deep yellow, 24 in.;

"Moonlight," pale yellow; "Perry's Variety," bright yellow; and "Wargrave Variety," lemon yellow with broad centers.

Anthericum liliago (St. Bernard's Lily) 18–24 in. Sun
Flowering span: Mid-June to August
Color: White
Native habitat: Central and southern Europe, northern Africa

Relatively simple to grow well, the tuberlike rhizomes require a year from planting to reestablish the large root system for blooming. Narrow, reedlike foliage appears in basal clumps and produces a slender flower stalk with 15 to 20 star-shaped, fragrant florets having golden stamens. Disliking hot, dry exposures, it needs rich, moist, sandy-humusy soils with generous watering when in blossom. Fall planting of new rootstock or careful division of crowded clumps propagates it readily, and there are no pests or diseases of consequence. The variety *major* is superior in size and noticeability.

Aquilegia flabellata (Fan Columbine) 12–18 in. Sun
Flowering span: Early June to July
Color: Lavender-blue
Native habitat: Japan

Pale green leaves with grayish pubescence surround stalks of waxy, 2-inch, wide-petaled flowers having short, gracefully incurved spurs. Enjoying a moist, sandy loam that is well-drained, this plant grows happily in sun or light shade and can best be propagated by seed or careful spring division of small plants. Crown rot and mildew are troublesome afflictions, along with root borer and leaf miner. The variety *nana alba* has icy-white flowers on 6- to 9-inch stems and blossoms slightly earlier.

Aquilegia longissima (Longspur Columbine) 18–30 in. Sun
Flowering span: Late June to August
Color: Pale yellow
Native habitat: Texas to Mexico

Parent to many of the long-spurred hybrids, this wildflower has greatly divided, green leaves with a somewhat silvery underside. Its typical columbine flower sports exceptionally long and slender spurs that stretch from 4 to 6 inches in a graceful curve. It likes very moist, sunny locations such as streamsides. Seed only from wild plants gives germination, but careful division is often workable in garden culture. No special pest or disease is bothersome.

Aquilegia skinneri (Skinner Columbine) 15–30 in. Sun
Flowering span: Mid-June to August
Color: Orange red
Native habitat: Mexico, Guatemala

A well-shaped plant with complex flowers having bright red spurs at the ends of green-orange petals, it likes full sun and a moist, sandy soil. Propagate by seeding. It appears to have no insect or disease difficulties. The scarce variety *flore-pleno* carries double flowers.

Aruncus sylvester (*Spiraea aruncus*) (Goats-beard)
      48–72 in. Semi-shade
Flowering span: Early June to July
Color: Creamy white
Native habitat: Europe, Asia, Pennsylvania to Georgia, west
    to Oklahoma

Useful as a background to a shaded border, this sizable wildflower has 12-inch, feathery plumes of tiny blossoms that appear terminally above large, light green, pinnately compound leaves. Thriving in consistently moist, humusy, well-drained soil, it is best propagated by division of the deep rootstock. Pests and diseases are no bother.

Asphodelus albus (Branching Asphodel) 18–30 in. Sun
Flowering span: Mid-June to mid-July
Color: Buff, fading to white
Native habitat: Southern Europe, northern Africa

Starry blossoms with brown-veined segments line the branched flower stalk of this relative to the true Asphodel,

Asphodeline, which has only a single spike. (The word daffodil is said to be a linguistic corruption of asphodel.) It tolerates light shading and prefers a sandy, well-drained location. In difficult climates it needs winter mulching. Division of the large, fleshy tubers in the autumn is recommended, and pests or diseases are uncommon.

Astilbe arendsi (Astilbe) 12–18 in. Semi-shade
Flowering span: Early June to mid-July
Color: White, pink, red
Native habitat: Horticultural hybrid

Although individual varieties have showy flower plumes of varying fullness, the semi-glossy, feathery foliage is common to all types. Shallow-rooted but quickly depleting soils, it likes a very humusy, moist, well-drained location (especially in winter) and requires fall division every 3 years to maintain its vigor. Easily grown in full sun if kept consistently moist all season, it offers a greater garden usefulness in semi-shaded areas needing noticeable color. Some red varieties hold their coloring when dried if picked at the

Showy plumes distinguish *Astilbe arendsi* in semi-shade or full sun.

moment a silvery sheen appears on most of the blossoms. None is prone to pest or disease problems.

The list of hybrids is extensive: "Bonn," rich, bright pink; "Deutschland," pure white, dwarfed; "Dusseldorf," deep salmon pink; "Emden," light rose; "Erica," rose, tall; "Etna," dark red; "Europa," clear pink; "Fanal," deep garnet; "Federsee," carmine red; "Feuer," deep red; "Gladstone," pure white; "Irrlicht," snowy white; "Koblenz," bright red; "Mainz," deep rose; "Peach Blossom," light pink; "Queen Alexandra," light rose; "Red Sentinel," scarlet red, late; and "White Gloria," white.

Callirhoe involuncrata (verticillata) (Low Poppy-mallow) 6–12 in. Sun
Flowering span: Early June to September
Color: Crimson purple
Native habitat: North Dakota to Texas

While not especially long-lived, these colorful perennials are easily propagated for quick replacement. The 2-inch, cup-shaped flower has a glistening sheen with hairy, finger-like, incised leaves on horizontally spreading stems. Growing rapidly in summer, it is useful for sunny rock gardens, borders, or to hang over walls where drainage is excellent and the soil is sandy and only slightly acid. Propagate by spring division of the deep taproots, seed, or summer stem cuttings. Diseases and pests are rare.

Callopogon pallidus (Pale Grass-pink) 12–18 in. Semi-shade
Flowering span: Early June to August
Color: Pale rose pink to white
Native habitat: Virginia to Florida, west to Louisiana

Happy in wet, boggy places with light to half-shading, this corm can adapt to porous rock gardens if kept very moist throughout the summer. The 1-inch, butterfly-shaped, orchid-looking flowers are plentiful on slender stems and have conspicuous orange beards. Foliage is limited to 2 or 3 reedlike leaves. Propagation can be made by using corm offsets, but nursery-grown stock is far superior. There are no diseases or pests of consequence. Several earlier species are native to the southern United States, blooming from March onward.

Campanula carpatica (Carpathian Harebell) 6–12 in. Sun
Flowering span: Early June to September
Color: Bright violet-blue
Native habitat: Eastern Europe, Carpathian Mountains

Readily growing into large mats of light green, lancelike foliage in full sun to light shade, this long-blooming perennial has 1½-inch, cup-shaped, up-facing blossoms on wiry stems in heavy masses. It thrives on moist, rich, well-drained soil and is easily propagated by spring division. Unfortunately, it also has a tendency to self-seed quickly throughout its growing area. Slugs and rust disease are often bothersome afflictions. Many hybrids exist: "Blue Carpet," clear blue; "Cobalt," deep blue; "Riverslea," dark blue, 15 in. tall with 2- to 3-in. flowers; *turbinata*, 4 in. tall; "Wedgwood," pale blue-violet; "White Carpet," white, profusely flowering; and "White Star," pure white.

Campanula glomerata (Danesblood Bellflower) 12–24 in. Sun
Flowering span: Early June to mid-July
Color: Deep violet
Native habitat: Europe, British Isles, Iran, Siberia

Heavy clusters of 1-inch, up-facing florets dominate the hairy, 2- to 3-inch leaves of this showy perennial. Culture is identical with *C. carpatica*. A few variations are known: *acaulis*, 4 in. tall with very large flowers; *alba*, white; *dahurica*, rich violet with 3-in. wide flower heads; "Joan Elliott," deep violet; "Purple Pixie," purple, dwarf, and *superba*, deep violet-blue in large heads.

Campanula latifolia (Great Bellflower) 36–48 in. Sun
Flowering span: Mid-June to August
Color: Bluish purple
Native habitat: Europe, British Isles, Iran

Easily grown in sun to half shade, the 8-inch flower spikes are lined with individual, 1-inch, bell-shaped blossoms and noticeably recurving petal edges. It likes a deep, moist, fertile soil and is best propagated by spring division of the thick roots or by stem cuttings. It appears to be unbothered by pests or diseases. Several varieties are available: *alba*, off-white, 48 in; "Brantwood," violet-purple, 48 in.; *eriocarpa*, pale lavender with very large leaves; "Gloaming," pale lilac-blue; and *macrantha*, with larger flowers, 60 in.

Campanula persicifolia (Peachleaf Bellflower) 24–36 in.
    Sun
Flowering span: Early June to mid-July
Color: Violet
Native habitat: Europe, British Isles

Here the 6- to 8-inch foliage is dark green, glossy, and narrow in a basal tuft. The erect flower stalks carry 1½-inch, cup-shaped florets, usually with several open at a time. Culture is the same as with *C. latifolia*. There are many hybrids: "Bernice," powder blue, double-flowered; "Blue Gardenia," rich blue, double; *grandiflora alba*, white, large-flowered; *marginata*, white with blue edges; *moerheimi*, white, double, 2- to 3-inch flowers; "Percy Piper," deep blue; "Snowdrift," white; "Telham Beauty," porcelain blue, 2- to 3-inch flowers, 48 inches tall; and "Wirral Blue," rich blue, double-flowered.

Campanula portenschlagiana (*muralis*) (Dalmatian
    Bellflower) 4–8 in. Sun
Flowering span: Early June to mid-July
Color: Light purple-blue
Native habitat: Yugoslavia

Abundantly flowering, this creeping perennial forms neat but large mats of shiny green, kidney-shaped leaves with ½- to ¾-inch star-shaped blossoms. It will take any average soil that is not dry in sun to light shade. Spring division is the simplest propagation method. Rust disease and slugs may prove troublesome. The variety *major* has 1½-inch flowers.

Campanula rotundifolia (Bluebells-of-Scotland, Harebell)
    6–12 in. Sun
Flowering span: Mid-June to September

Color: Bright violet-blue
Native habitat: Europe, Siberia, North America

Widely distributed throughout the north temperate areas of the world, these hardy, durable plants have very narrow foliage in grassy tufts (the round leaves are only occasional and located at the ground line) with branched, wiry flower stalks carrying 1-inch, drooping, bell-shaped blossoms for a lengthy period. Growing best in rich, well-drained loam, it readily adapts to sunlit crevasses in ledges or plant walls but can overseed quickly where it likes the conditions. Division, seed, or cuttings propagate it satisfactorily, and it appears unharrassed by pests or diseases of consequence.

Catananche caerulea (Cupid's-dart) 18–24 in. Sun
Flowering span: Mid-June to September
Color: Deep mauve
Native habitat: Mediterranean Europe

Although it offers a colorful garden accent, its favored use is as a durable dried flower. The narrow, hairy leaves appear in a clump at the base of the tall flower stems with their 2-inch, many-petaled, flattish blossoms that are much-incised at the edges. It prefers bright sun and a well-drained, light soil on the dry side. Fall root cuttings or seed readily propagate it. Nothing seems to bother it. The variety *alba* has white flowers, while *bicolor* displays a blue center with white edges.

Centaurea dealbata (Persian Centaurea) 8–24 in. Sun
Flowering span: Early June to August
Color: Rose purple
Native habitat: Asia Minor, Iran

Feathery, coarse-toothed leaves with a silvery underside produce erect flower stems and 2-inch solid blossoms with ragged edges much like its smaller, annual relative, the bachelor's-button. Any average garden soil on the dry side satisfies it well in full sun, and spring or fall division suit it. Rust and "yellows" can disfigure the leaves but are not customary problems. The hybrid "John Coutts" has bright pink-purple flowers with a noticeable yellow center, while *steen-*

bergii is long-flowering with grayish green foiliage and rose-crimson blossoms with white centers.

Centaurea gymnocarpa (argentea) (Velvet Centaurea)
    18–24 in. Sun
Flowering span: Late June to August
Color: Rose violet
Native habitat: Sardinia

Grown primarily for its intriguing silvery foliage, its small, insignificant flowers are mostly hidden by the fernlike, pubescent leaves. Useful as a trimmed border hedging, it likes the same culture as *C. dealbata.*

Centaurea montana (Mountain Bluet) 12–20 in. Sun
Flowering span: Mid-June to September
Color: Purple blue
Native habitat: Europe

The foliage here is rough-surfaced, green, and lance-shaped, but juvenile leaves are usually hairy and white. The 3-inch feathery flowers have florets more widely spaced than those of *C. dealbata.* Spreading quickly by underground stems, the plant is floppy and usually needs staking. Avoid rich soils and give it either sun or light shade in somewhat dry locations. Propagate by either spring or fall division. The variety *alba* is white-flowered; "Parham" is lavender purple; and *rubra* is rosy red.

Centaurea rutifolia (cineraria) (Dusty Miller) 24–36 in.
    Sun
Flowering span: Late June to August
Color: Purple
Native habitat: Mediterranean Europe

Similar to *C. gymnocarpa* in appearance, culture, and garden usefulness, this pinnate, velvet-leaved, many-branched perennial is entirely covered with downy, white hairs. Again, the blossoming is insignificant. It is best propagated by cuttings since seeds are very prone to damping-off.

Centranthus ruber (Kenthranthus ruber) (Red Valerian)
   12–36 in. Sun
Flowering span: Mid-June to September
Color: Deep crimson to pale red
Native habitat: Europe, British Isles

   Durable and long-flowering, the compact perennial has lancelike, gray green foliage with terminal, 3-inch clusters of tiny florets nicely perfumed. A sandy, humusy, moist soil close to neutral suits it best in full sun. Division or seed propagate it readily, and there are no troublesome pests or diseases. The variety *alba* is white-flowered but scarce.

Cephalaria alpina (Yellow Cephalaria) 60–72 in. Sun
Flowering span: Late June to August
Color: Sulphur yellow
Native habitat: Mediterranean Europe

   Although coarse in appearance, it is showy in flower with scabiosa-like blossoms on widely branched stems having slightly hairy, divided leaves. Undemanding, it likes an average-fertility soil in bright sun and has no known pests or diseases. It propagates easiest by self-seeding and may even become invasive.

Cerastium biebersteini (Taurus Cerastium) 4–6 in. Sun
Flowering span: Early June to July
Color: White
Native habitat: Asia Minor

   Useful in rock gardens or as a broad edging, the heavy mat of creeping foliage is neat and conspicuous with narrow, woolly-silver leaves. Tiny, bell-shaped flowers appear generously with full sun and any average soil that is well-drained. Division or summer cuttings are the usual methods of propagation. Pests and diseases are unknown.

Cerastium boissieri (gibraltaricum) (Spanish Cerastium)
   4–12 in. Sun
Flowering span: Early June to July

Color: White
Native habitat: Spain

Larger-flowered and taller in bloom than *C. biebersteini*, its foliage is more silvery and will tolerate light shading easily. Culture for both is identical.

Cerastium tomentosum (Snow-in-Summer) 3–6 in. Sun
Flowering span: Early June to July
Color: White
Native habitat: Europe

Easily rampant where it likes the conditions, this shallow-rooted, creeping perennial has narrow, gray-woolly leaves and loose sprays of bell-like flowers which should be severely cut back after bloom for greater plant compactness. Tolerant of any average soil in full sun or light shade, it is easily divided for propagation but generous self-seeding may provide an unwanted bonus of plants. Nothing bothers it.

Chimaphila maculata (Striped Pipsissewa) 3–6 in. Shade
Flowering span: Mid-June to August
Color: White
Native habitat: Southern Canada to Georgia, west to Illinois

An evergreen with 2-inch, spear-shaped, dark green, conspicuously toothed leaves centrally striped in cream, this slow-creeping plant has several fragrant, 1-inch, waxy flowers on erect stems when established in the dry woodlots it likes best. Very difficult to transplant from the wild, its long, underground runners require all the natural microorganisms of the gravelly, humusy soil to accompany them. Nursery stock assures more success. Diseases and pests are of no concern.

Chimaphila umbellata (Common Pipsissewa) 5–12 in.
     Shade
Flowering Span: Mid-June to August
Color: White to pale pink
Native habitat: Europe, Japan, southern Canada to Alaska,
     south to Utah, Illinois, and Georgia

Taller than *C. maculata*, its shiny, evergreen leaves are entirely without stripes and the ¾-inch flowers appear in clusters of 4 to 7 on erect stems. Culture is the same for both.

Chrysanthemum coccinea (Pyrethrum hybridum) (Painted Daisy, Pyrethrum) 9–36 in. Sun
Flowering span: Mid-June to mid-July
Color: Carmine, pink, white
Native habitat: Iran, Caucasus Mountains

Feathery, deep green foliage clumps produce thin-stemmed, unbranched flower stalks with showy, 3-inch blossoms having bright yellow centers. They thrive in well-drained, sandy loam with full sun but may need winter protection where climate is severe. Division in late summer or early spring, along with seeding, readily propagates this fibrous-rooted perennial. Aphids and red spider mites can be occasionally problematic, while mildew and rust are the disease nuisances. Many hybrids exist in both the single and double forms: "Brenda," bright cerise, single; "Carl Voight," white, double; "Eileen M. Robinson," salmon pink, single; "Helen," soft rose pink, double; "Madeleine," bright pink, double; "Marjorie Robinson," deep pink, single; "Vanessa," rosy carmine, double; and "Victoria," ruby red, single.

Chrysanthemum maximum (Pyrenees Chrysanthemum, Shasta Daisy) 12–36 in. Sun
Flowering span: Mid-June to August
Color: White
Native habitat: Pyrenees Mountains

Conspicuously showy, these large-flowered, yellow-centered perennials have long, glossy, narrow leaves and heavy stems. They want a rich, well-drained, constantly moist soil conditioned with lime and require regular division to survive. Single types enjoy full sun but the doubles do better in semi-shade. Spring division, cuttings, and seed all work well for propagation. Aphids and verticillium wilt are the main afflictions. Hybrid selections offer a broad range of blossom forms: "Aglaia," 3 in., frilled; "Cobham Gold,"

Chrysanthemum maximum offers snowy vividness to June gardening.

3 in., double, creamy white; "Esther Read," 3 in., double, very floriferous; "Majestic," 4 in., single; "Mayfield Giant," 3 in., single, 42 in. tall; "Thomas Killin," 5 in., semi-double; and "Wirral Supreme," 4 in., double.

Chrysogonum virginianum (Goldenstar) 4–12 in. Semi-shade
Flowering span: Early June to October
Color: Bright yellow
Native habitat: Pennsylvania to Florida, west to Louisiana

Five-petaled, 1-inch flowers on long stalks arise continually from the leaf axils of this wildflower throughout the summer and thrive in woodlot half shading to full sun (if kept well-watered). The hairy green leaves are scalloped at the edges. It adjusts to any average soil that is not overly limed. Division of the creeping rootstock is possible at any time and there are no bothersome pests or diseases.

Clematis integrifolia (Solitary Clematis) 18–24 in. Sun
Flowering span: Mid-June to August
Color: Indigo blue
Native habitat: Southern Europe, Siberia

Nonclimbing, this sun-loving perennial has solitary, 1½-inch, bell-shaped flowers with noticeably twisted petals above 4-inch leaves widely spaced on thin stems that may require staking. It grows well in ordinary garden soil that is moist and can be left undisturbed for many years. Propagation is by spring division, seed, or summer stem cuttings. Blister beetles and tarnished plant bugs are often bothersome, but diseases are not rampant. The variety *alba* has white blossoms, while *hendersoni* is lavender-blue.

Clematis recta (*erecta*) (Ground Clematis) 24–36 in. Sun
Flowering span: Mid-June to August
Color: White
Native habitat: Southern Europe

Large, terminal flower sprays with ¾-inch, fragrant florets rise above 6-inch, feathery leaves here, but the variety *mandshurica* is superior to the type by being taller, more vigorous, and having axillary flower clusters as well. Culture is identical with that for *C. integrifolia.*

Coreopsis auriculata (Eared Coreopsis) 12–36 in. Sun
Flowering span: Early June to mid-July
Color: Golden yellow
Native habitat: Virginia to Florida, west to Kentucky

The 2-inch, daisylike flower has the typical ragged petal edges of the group, but the simple leaves have a pair of noticeable protuberances or "ears" at right angles to the main blade. Easily adaptable to any well-drained, average soil in sun to light shading, this perennial can be spring-divided or seed-propagated with ease. Mildew is the main affliction. The dwarf variety *nana* has 1½-inch orange-yellow flowers on 8-inch stems, and dark green, often-persistent foliage forming thick mats readily for rock garden displays. "Golden

Star," a hybrid, is 18 to 24 inches tall with a brownish center.

Coreopsis grandiflora (Bigflower Coreopsis) 24–36 in. Sun
Flowering span: Early June to August
Color: Bright yellow
Native habitat: Florida to New Mexico, north to Kansas

Here the flowers are 2 to 3 inches wide and the lancelike leaves are entire. It does well naturally in dry woodlots and should not be planted in overly fertilized garden locations. The parent plant usually exhausts itself from blooming by one season, but self-seeded plants quickly fill any gaps. The worst problem is powdery mildew. Several hybrids with more permanent qualities are available: "Badengold," 36 in., golden yellow; "Goldfink," 8 in., bright yellow; "Perry's Variety," 30 in., deep yellow, semi-double; and "Sunburst," 30 in., semi-double.

Coreopsis lanceolata (Lance Coreopsis) 12–24 in. Sun
Flowering span: Early June to September
Color: Golden yellow
Native habitat: New England to Florida, west to New Mexico and Wisconsin

Similar to *C. grandiflora,* the flowers of this species are only 2 inches and may have a brownish center. The narrow-leaved foliage is mostly at ground level. Culture is the same for both, except that *C. lanceolata* is long-lived and available for spring division.

Coreopsis palmata (Finger Coreopsis) 24–36 in. Sun
Flowering span: Early June to August
Color: Bright yellow
Native habitat: Central Canada to Oklahoma

The narrow, 2½-inch leaves are deeply cleft into 3 finger-like sections on this midwestern wildflower, while the 2-inch flowers have rounded petal outlines at the tips. Culture is the same as with the other species.

Coronilla varia (Crown Vetch) 12–24 in. Sun
Flowering span: Mid-June to October
Color: Pinkish white
Native habitat: Europe

Rampantly invasive, this groundcover has its best use for steep banks in full sun where little else will grow. The fern-like, compound leaves appear generously on weak stems that trail, and the terminal heads of pealike blossoms are attractive throughout the summer but seed easily into nearby sites. Roots are deep and resist division. There are no diseases or pests, but the plant itself might become the real nuisance if not carefully located. The variety "Penngift," developed by the Pennsylvania State University for highway use, has solid pink flowering.

Cypripedium reginae (Showy Ladyslipper) 18–30 in.
    Semi-shade
Flowering span: Early June to July
Color: White, shaded with pink-purple
Native habitat: Newfoundland to New Jersey, west to Missouri

Unusually shallow-rooted for the group, the rootstock needs careful attention for needed leaf-mold mulching programs. The very broad leaves are entirely hairy and can cause a nuisance rash, but the sizable blossoms are worth the bother. Culture is the same guesswork as with the May-blooming *C. acaule.*

Delphinium brunonianum (Musk Larkspur) 10–15 in. Sun
Flowering span: Early June to July
Color: Violet purple
Native habitat: Afghanistan, Tibet

The broad, hairy leaves are musk-scented when bruised, while the ¾-inch, short-spurred florets appear on dwarfed spikes that should be removed after flowering for possible repeat bloom in early autumn. Culture is the same as for the May-blooming *D. nudicaule.*

Delphinium cashmerianum (Kashmir Larkspur) 12–24 in.
   Sun
Flowering span: Late June to August
Color: Azure blue
Native habitat: Himalaya Mountains

Here the bright green leaves are thick and multitudinous beneath the sturdy flower stalks with noticeably hairy, 2-inch florets. Again, culture is identical with *D. nudicaule.*

Delphinium cheilanthum (belladona) (Garland Larkspur)
    36–48 in. Sun
Flowering span: Mid-June to mid-July
Color: Dark blue
Native habitat: Siberia

Openly branched flower stalks provide many slender spikes of 1½- to 2-inch florets with long spurs in this species. The finely divided foliage adds another graceful detail, but its airy appearance still requires excellent air circulation to forestall mildew. As with most of these species, the plants dwindle quickly after several years and need replacement. Culture is given under *D. nudicaule.* Several hybrids are usually available: "Belladona," pale blue; "Bellamosum," dark blue; "Casa Blanca," white; "Cliveden Beauty," deep turquoise; "Lamartine," vivid gentian blue; and "Sapphire," delicate, pale blue. Removing the faded blossom stalks often produces repeat flowering in autumn.

Delphinium elatum (Bee Larkspur) 30–72 in. Sun
Flowering span: Mid-June to late July
Color: Blue purple
Native habitat: Siberia

The densely packed flower spikes of this well-appreciated perennial have recently been so cross-hybridized for increased vividness and larger floret size that clear identification of individual strains is no longer possible. The free-flowering "Connecticut Yankee" collection has an average height of 36 inches and white, blue, lavender, and purple colorings. The tall, mostly double, "Pacific Hybrid" mixture offers named shadings: "Astolat," pink; "Black Knight," deep violet-blue; "Blue Jay," rich blue with a white eye; "Cameliard," lavender blue; "King Arthur," purple; and "Galahad," all white. Each in this group usually has a contrasting set of deeper-colored sepals or "bee" in the middle of each floret. The English lists of Blackmore, Langdon, and Wrexham hybrids are also showy horticultural improvements requiring the same culture as described under the May-flowering *D. nudicaule*.

Delphinium grandiflorum (*chinense*) (Siberian Larkspur)
    12–18 in. Sun.
Flowering span: Late June to August
Color: Blue, white
Native habitat: Siberia

Although most plants are short-lived, seedlings can often flower the same year from spring-sown seeds. The long-spurred florets here are 1 inch and are loosely arranged on slender stems. The named hybrids include: "Azure Fairy," sky blue; "Blue Butterfly," deep blue; "Blue Mirror," gentian blue; "Cambridge Blue," rich blue; and "White Butterfly," pure white. Culture is the same as for the other species.

Delphinium zalil (Zalil Larkspur) 12–24 in. Sun
Flowering span: Mid-June to mid-July
Color: Lemon yellow
Native habitat: Iran

This species has dark green leaves and 1½-inch florets on weak stems. It often dies back completely by late summer but usually reappears in early autumn with new leafstalks and possible repeat flowering. It enjoys a sandy, enriched soil and seems to have no important pests or diseases.

Dianthus alpinus (Alpine Pink) 3 in. Semi-shade
Flowering span: Early June to mid-July
Color: Rose pink to white
Native habitat: Alps Mountains

Unusual by preferring some shading to full sun, the solitary, 1-inch, rounded flowers with a small, central ring of dark crimson rise out of a grass-green mat of slender leaves.

Mostly unscented, the blossoming can mask the entire foliage where drainage is excellent and the sandy soil highly alkaline. Topdress with humus yearly to prevent center dieout of the clump and divide after flowering or take summer stem cuttings. Crown rot and red spider mites are the most problematic afflictions. The variety "Little Joe" has silvery foliage, single, crimson flowers, and requires winter protection in most places.

Dianthus arenarius (Finland Pink) 4–12 in. Sun
Flowering span: Early June to mid-July
Color: White with purplish centers
Native habitat: Finland, Yugoslavia

Here the plant is very fragrant with multiflowered stems above blue-green foliage. Culture is the same as with *D. alpinus*, except for wanting a brightly sunny location.

Dianthus barbatus (Sweet William) 12–24 in. Sun
Flowering span: Early June to mid-July
Color: Crimson, scarlet, pink, white, often intermixed
Native habitat: Russia, China, central and southern Europe

Individual plants are actually biennial (requiring two years to blossom), but the generous self-seeding that results from an initial planting gives the effect of perennial bedding. The 4-inch, lance-shaped leaves appear along the stiff flower stems that terminate in 3- to 5-inch, rounded clusters of dense blossoming. Although separate colorings are available commercially, interblending of them quickly causes a reversion to a polyglot color mixture and weakened stems usually requiring total replacement. Culture is the same as for *D. alpinus*.

Dianthus latifolius (Button Pink) 6–12 in. Sun
Flowering span: Early June to August
Color: White, pink, red
Native habitat: Horticultural hybrid

Prolific for flowering, these plants often exhaust themselves so quickly that annual division in early spring assures more permanence for garden use. The 1-inch, double, scented flowers appear in clusters resembling the florists' carnation above gray green, linear foliage. Preferring a rich, sandy soil in full sun, they may need winter protection in severe climates. Leaf spot disfigures the foliage in muggy, summer weather, but insects appear to be no bother. Several hybrids are available: "Beatrix," salmon pink; "Furst Bismark," rose red; "Raven Rock Red," crimson; and "Silver Mine," white.

Dianthus sylvestris (Wood Pink) 6–12 in. Semi-shade
Flowering span: Mid-June to August
Color: Rose red
Native habitat: Mediterranean Europe, Austria

Adapting well to a reasonable amount of shading, this matlike perennial has gray green leaves in tufts and 1 to 3 odorless, single flowers per stem. Spring division is the best propagation method, and it has a liking for rich, light soil that occasionally becomes dry. Diseases and pests are not common. The Hungarian variety *frigidus* is dwarfed in all respects.

Dictamnus albus (*fraxinella*) (Gasplant Dittany) 24–36 in. Sun
Flowering span: Mid-June to mid-July
Color: White
Native habitat: Eastern Europe, Asia

Durably permanent once established, the deep roots adjust to drought well but resent transplanting except when young. The large, terminal flower spikes have 1- to 2-inch florets pleasantly scented with citron, while the attractive, compound, thick-leaved foliage also has a pronounced lemon odor when bruised. Supposedly, the blossom's volatile fragrance oils can be ignited on sultry evenings, but this curious bonus obviously has a limited appeal. Wanting rich, heavy soil in full sun to do its best, it is best propagated from easily germinated seeding. There are no pest or disease afflictions. The variety *giganteus* (*caucasicus*) is somewhat larger in every respect, while *purpureus* (*ruber*) has rosy purple blossoms with noticeably darker veining. The dried pods of any are useful for winter arrangements.

The lemon-scented blossoms of *Dictamnus albus* are surrounded by attractive foliage.

Digitalis ambigua (grandiflora) (Yellow Foxglove) 24–36 in. Semi-shade
Flowering span: Early June to mid-July
Color: Pale yellow
Native habitat: Europe, western Asia

Sometimes transitory as a biennial, the long flower stalks of this plant carry drooping, 2-inch, tubular flowers with brown markings. As with any of the species, early removal of the faded blossom spikes often stimulates fall reflowering. Here the 6-inch leaves are broad, toothed, and with downy hairs beneath. It likes a moist, acid-sandy loam with generous humus in light shade to full sun and can be reproduced by seed or spring division. There seem to be no insect pests, but mildew and leaf spot bother them in hot, humid weather. The variety "Canary Bird" has desirable, brighter color.

Digitalis dubia (Balearic Foxglove) 9–12 in. Semi-shade
Flowering span: Mid-June to mid-July

Color: Purple pink
Native habitat: Majorca

The species has slender florets and heavily tomentose leaves. Culture is the same as for *D. ambigua.*

Digitalis lanata (Grecian Foxglove) 24–36 in. Semi-shade
Flowering span: Late June to August
Color: Creamy yellow to pale pink
Native habitat: Southern Europe

Here the tall flower spikes are densely covered by 1- to 1½-inch, tubular blossoms with many fine hairs on each floret. Culture is identical with that for *D. ambigua.*

Digitalis lutea (Straw Foxglove) 12–24 in. Semi-shade
Flowering span: Mid-June to mid-July
Color: Yellowish white
Native habitat: Europe

All parts of the plant are nonhairy. Its culture is listed under *D. ambigua.*

Digitalis purpurea (Common Foxglove) 24–48 in. Semi-
shade
Flowering span: Mid-June to mid-July
Color: Purple, lavender, white
Native habitat: Europe, British Isles, Scandinavia

The commonest foxglove in cultivation, it often behaves more like a biennial than a perennial but self-seeds prodigiously to keep a patch ongoing satisfactorily. The 2-inch, dark-spotted blossoms appear above a basal clump of wrinkled, broad leaves that are mainly bothered by mildew where air circulation is sluggish. Give them a rich, light, moist soil. Propagate by seeding. The "Excelsior" strain of the Shirley hybrids from England is superior in a wide range of desirable color variations and has blossoming encircling the spike with a more upright thrust for each floret.

Dipsacus fullonum (Fullers Teasel) 48–72 in. Sun
Flowering span: Mid-June to early July

The dried seed heads of *Dipsacus fullonum* make novel displays inside and out.

Color: Purplish white
Native habitat: Europe

Coarse-growing and useful only in a wild background garden with full sun, the dense clusters of tiny flowers later produce 4-inch-tall, thimble-shaped seed heads with stiff, closely set scales once used extensively for teasing the nap of woolen cloth. They make interesting dried material for indoor arrangements. Grow in any ordinary soil and do not worry about pests or diseases.

Dodecatheon jeffreyi (Jeffrey Shooting-star) 18–24 in. Semi-shade
Flowering span: Early June to mid-July
Color: Rose purple
Native habitat: Northern California to Alaska, west to Nevada

In this species, the 1- to 1½-inch, linear leaves rise to the full height of the flower stalk with its clusters of ¾-inch blossoms. It wants a constantly moist, well-drained soil in semi- to full shade. Culture is the same as for the May-flowering *D. amethystinum.*

Dracocephalum grandiflorum (Bigflower Dragonhead)
    8–12 in. Semi-shade
Flowering span: Early June to July
Color: Rich blue
Native habitat: Siberia

Performing best in humid climates, the bright green foliage gives rise to heavily flowered spikes of 2-inch hooded flowers resembling those of its cousin, mint. It prefers a moist, sandy soil and can be propagated by division or seed. There are no pests or diseases.

Eremurus himalaicus (Himalayan Desertcandle) 60–84 in.
    Sun
Flowering span: Late June to August
Color: White
Native habitat: Himalaya Mountains

Strikingly impressive, the solitary, 3- to 4-inch-wide "candle," or flower stalk, of tiny, star-shaped florets blossoms for many weeks, but unfortunately the dormant flower bud is not always dependably hardy in northern climates. The 3-inch, persistent, thick, twisted leaves usually stretch to 18 inches. It needs full sun, a protected location, a rich, sandy soil with generous fertilizing, and perfect drainage at all times. Winter mulching should be porous and not hold water of itself or the flower bud may be lost. Although the brittle, fleshy roots of mature plants are easily damaged, seed is very difficult to germinate well, and division remains the better propagation method. Insects avoid it because of a natural repellent covering all flower parts, and diseases are unknown. This is a challenging plant with a rewarding flower display for a patient gardener.

Eremurus robustus (Giant Desertcandle) 72–120 in. Sun
Flowering span: Late June to August
Color; Salmon pink
Native habitat: Turkestan

Even more dramatic in bloom than *E. himalaicus,* the evergreen leaves here are up to 36 inches long and bright green with a 4- to 5-inch-wide flower stalk. It requires the same fussy cultural care, and there is a pure white variety, *albus.*

Erigeron speciosus (Oregon Fleabane) 28–30 in. Sun
Flowering span: Mid-June to August
Color: Violet with a yellow center
Native habitat: Coastal Oregon to British Columbia

Dependably vigorous, this Pacific coast perennial has smooth, lanceolate foliage surrounding branched flower stems with 2-inch, daisylike blossoms. It prefers a light, sandy, well-drained soil in full sun to light shade and can easily by increased by spring or fall division. When established, it tends to self-seed readily. Insects are no trouble, but "aster yellows" can stunt and disfigure the plant growth. Several European hybrids are available: "Azure Beauty," lavender blue, semi-double; "Foerster's Liebling," vivid pink; "Pink Jewel," bright pink; "Summertime," white; and "Wuppertal," deep amethyst-violet.

Filapendula hexapetala (*Spiraea filipendula*) (Dropwort)
    24–36 in. Sun
Flowering span: Early June to mid-July
Color: Creamy white
Native habitat: Europe, western Asia, Siberia

An attractive basal clump of narrow, fernlike, compound leaves, up to 18 inches long, surrounds slender flower stalks with many tiny florets clustered in 1-inch, flat groupings. Preferring sun or light shade and a moderately moist, rich soil, it propagates easily by division or seed. Pests and diseases apparently avoid it. The double-flowered variety, *flore-pleno,* is superior and grows only 15 to 18 inches tall.

Filipendula purpurea (*Spiraea palmata*) (Japanese
    Meadowsweet) 24–48 in. Semi-shade
Flowering span: Mid-June to August
Color: Carmine pink
Native habitat: Japan

Perhaps the handsomest of the group, the large, 5- to 7-lobed leaves are topped by sizable, flat-headed clusterings of tiny, fragrant flowers on crimson stems. It does best in a very moist, deep, rich soil and can tolerate full sun if kept very wet. Propagate by spring division only. It has no known insect or disease problems. There is a scarce form with white flowers, *alba*.

Filipendula rubra (Spiraea lobata) (Queen-of-the-Prairie)
    24–100 in. Semi-shade
Flowering span: Mid-June to mid-July
Color: Pink
Native habitat: Pennsylvania to Georgia, west to Kentucky
    and Minnesota

Bold, feathery plumes of fragrant flowers dominate the large, dark green, lobed leaves of this showy wildflower. It wants the same cultural conditions as *F. purpurea*. The variety *albicans* is pale pink; *magnifica* is carmine pink and 72 inches; *venusta* is deep pink and 48 inches.

Filipendula ulmaria (Spiraea ulmaria) (European
    Meadowsweet) 24–72 in. Semi-shade
Flowering span: Mid-June to August
Color: White
Native habitat: Europe, western Asia

Similar in appearance to *F. rubra*, the scented flowers appear in dense panicles. Culture is the same for both. The variety *aureo-variegata* has yellow-streaked leaves, while *plena* has double flowers.

Gaillardia aristata (grandiflora) (Common Perennial
    Gaillardia, Blanketflower) 18–36 in. Sun
Flowering span: Mid-June to October
Color: Red with yellow tips
Native habitat: Western United States

The 3- to 4-inch, daisylike flowers appear on slender, hairy stems with somewhat thick, lanceolate leaves in a basal clump. A raised, central disc is surrounded by a flattened or crinkly set of petals with noticeable, color-contrasted tips. Best in borders or wild areas with full sun in a well-drained, rich, light soil. It tolerates drought well but produces excessive foliage and is subject to crown rot in heavy, clay soils. Propagate by spring division, seed, or root cuttings. The only serious pest is the sow bug. Hybridization has produced interesting variations: "Burgundy," wine red, 24 in.; "Dazzler," golden yellow with a maroon center, 36 in.; "Goblin," crimson with cream tips, 8 in.; "Sun God," all yellow, 24 in.; and "Wirral Flame," entirely deep orange-red, 30 in. The annual species, G. pulchella, is practically indistinguishable except for its nondurability.

Gypsophila bodgeri (Bodger Baby's-breath) 12–18 in. Sun
Flowering span: Early June to July
Color: Pinkish white to white
Native habitat: Horticultural hybrid between G. *paniculata*
    and G. *repens rosea*

Filmy in appearance, this group of durable perennials all have topmost wiry stems and a profusion of small blossoms. Here the semi-double, ¼-inch flowers appear profusely in the initial bloom and then sporadically throughout the summer. It likes a well-drained, moist, neutral soil enriched with lime annually in full sun to light shading. Seed or spring division are the usual propagation methods, but be aware that many types are now grafted introductions and cannot be handled easily for further division. Pests and diseases are incidental.

Gypsophila repens (Creeping Baby's-breath) 2–6 in. Sun
Flowering span: Late June to September
Color: Pinkish white
Native habitat: Pyrenees and Alps Mountains

A hardy, vigorous creeper in the exposed, dry, rock garden locations it likes, the spreading, grasslike foliage here is topped by graceful clusterings of white, ¼-inch flowers that fade to pale pink. Any limed, well-drained soil in full sun suits it, and propagation can be handled by division, seed, or summer stem cuttings. Pests and diseases present no serious problems. The 6-inch variety, *rosea,* has rosy pink blossoms, but "Pink Star" and "Rosy Veil" swell to 18 inches in tangled mounds of flowering lasting for many weeks.

Helianthemum nummularium (chamaecistus) (Rock-rose)
9–12 in. Sun
Flowering span: Early June to July
Color: Bright yellow
Native habitat: Northern Europe, British Isles, northern Africa, Asia

Widely distributed, these shrublike, sprawling plants have narrow, 1-inch, gray-green leaves and terminal clusters of 1-inch, frosted-edged, crepe-paper-thin blossoms. They thrive on alkaline, well-drained, dry, sandy locations in bright sun and should be cut back heavily after bloom to induce reflowering in the autumn. Spring division, seed, or summer cuttings all work easily for propagation. Diseases and pests are not bothersome but protect where winters are severe. Hybrids abound: "Apricot Queen," apricot with glossy green leaves in a dense mound; "Ben Afflick," orange-yellow; "Ben Hope," pink-crimson; "Ben Ledi," crimson; "Ben Nevis," yellow-orange; "Buttercup," orange-red, gray foliage; "Gold Nugget," deep yellow, double; "Lemon Queen," bright yellow, double; "Mrs. Earle," red, double; "Mrs. Mould," salmon pink, silvery foliage; "Rose Peach," peach pink; "The Bride," white with gray foliage; and "Wisley Pink," clear pink. Seed of these hybrids may occasionally be offered as *H. mutabile*.

Hemerocallis flava (Lemon Daylily) 24–36 in. Semi-shade
Flowering span: Early June to July
Color: Lemon yellow
Native habitat: Europe, Asia

Individual blossoms of all daylilies last only 24 hours, but the tall, leafless flower scapes rising out of the center of the large mounds of fountainlike, narrow foliage carry many buds. The green leaves here are 18 to 24 inches long and the scapes have 6 to 9, slightly fragrant, 4-inch florets. Any species thrives for years in a well-drained, moist soil of average fertility in semi-shading to full sun. Division is the easiest propagation technique, better done in early autumn when foliage can be handled roughly, but seed is also dependable. There are no important pests or diseases for any of these remarkably adaptable and hardy plants.

Hemerocallis middendorffi (Middendorff Daylily) 12–18 in.
     Semi-shade
Flowering span: Early June to July
Color: Golden orange
Native habitat: Siberia

In this species the leaves are 15 to 18 inches long and the fragrant flowers 3 inches long. Culture is identical with that for *H. flava,* and it has a surprising adaptation for growing and blooming well under and near large deciduous plants.

Hemerocallis thunbergi (Thunberg Daylily) 24–36 in.
     Semi-shade
Flowering span: Mid-June to mid-July
Color: Lemon yellow
Native habitat: Japan

Similar in appearance but later-blooming than *H. flava,* the fragrant flowers appear on a scape that is also heavier and flattened about 6 inches from the top. Culture is the same for both.

Hesperis matronalis (Dame's Rocket) 24–36 in. Sun
Flowering span: Mid-June to August
Color: Purple, lilac
Native habitat: Europe, northern Asia

The   4-petaled   florets   in   pyramidal   heads   and 3-inch leaves somewhat resemble summer phlox but there is no botanical association. Nicely scented—and strongest in the evening—the showy flowering can be extended appreciably by removing the faded blossoms before they turn to seed. It likes a moist, well-drained, average-fertility soil in sun to light shade. Not especially long-lived as individual plants, their propagation is best handled by seeding, which grows readily. Cutworms are troublesome, as is a stunting mosaic disease spread by aphids. Several varieties are available: *alba-plena,* white, double, very fragrant; *nivea,* white;

nana candidissima, white, dwarfed; and *pumila,* purple, dwarfed.

Heuchera sanguinea (Coralbells) 12–18 in. Sun
Flowering span: Mid-June to September
Color: Bright crimson
Native habitat: New Mexico, Arizona, northern Mexico

Remarkably long-flowering, the profusion of wiry stems on an established plant carry hundreds of ¼-inch, bell-shaped florets above an attractive clump of bronze-green, heart-shaped, crinkled leaves with contrasting veining. Best in full sun, it wants a rich, well-drained, moist loam. Spring division, seed, and summer leaf cuttings with a stem piece attached work equally well for propagation. Mulch in severe climates to prevent winter heaving of the shallow root system. Mealy bugs are the worst pest. There is a natural white variety, *alba,* but popular appeal has brought out many hybrids: "Coral Mist," coral pink; "Fire Sprite," rose red; "Freedom," rose pink; "Garnet," deep rose; "Greenfinch," greenish white; "June Bride," white; "Pluie de Feu," bright red; "Red Spangles," deep red; "Rhapsody," clear rose pink; "Rosamundi," coral; "Scintillation," bright pink; "Splendour," salmon red; "Sunset," coral red; and "White Cloud," creamy white.

Heuchera villosa (Hairy Alumroot) 12–36 in. Sun
Flowering span: Mid-June to August
Color: White to pinkish white
Native habitat: Virginia to Georgia, west to Arkansas

The deeply incised, serrate-edged, green foliage is attractive throughout the season and is often covered with reddish hairs. Long, wiry, leafless stems carry heavy clusters of ⅛-inch florets for most of the summer. Culture is the same as for *H. sanguinea,* with perhaps slightly more tolerance for drier, rocky locations. It combines interestingly as a foliage look-alike with *Tiarella.*

Hieracium auranticum (Orange Hawkweed, Devil's
    Paintbrush) 6–24 in. Sun
Flowering span: Mid-June to September

Color: Red orange
Native habitat: Europe, southeastern Canada to Virginia,
    west to Iowa

A pesky weed from Europe with prolific self-seeding, this
showy plant should be restricted (if possible) to dry, sterile
sites where nothing else will grow. The entire plant is
coarse-haired, and the clusters of colorful, dandelion-like
flowers come on erect stems above a low-lying rosette of
green leaves. It unfortunately has no pests or diseases.

Hieracium bombycinum 2–6 in. Sun
Flowering span: Early June to August
Color: Golden yellow
Native habitat: Spain

Noninvasive, the decorative, 1½-inch flowering appears
above neat clumps of gray green, very hairy foliage throughout the summer. It needs a dry, gravelly soil in full sun and
can be propagated by spring division or seed. Pests and
diseases are unknown.

Hieracium villosum (Shaggy Hawkweed) 12–36 in. Sun
Flowering span: Mid-June to August
Color: Bright golden yellow
Native habitat: Europe

The most easily controlled of this group for spreading, its
basal, silvery foliage and white-haired flower stalks provide
a pleasant sheen for the 2-inch blossoms. It grows well in
any well-drained, sun-drenched soil and can be propagated
by spring division or seed. There are no problems with diseases or insects.

Incarvillea delaveyi (Delavey Incarvillea) 12–24 in. Sun
Flowering span: Mid-June to mid-July
Color: Rosy purple
Native habitat: China

Large, 3-inch-wide, trumpet-shaped blossoms somewhat
resembling a gloxinia often appear in clusters before the sizable, dark green, compound leaves that look like the lanceolate ones of an ash. Not always reliably hardy, this exotic

perennial needs a deep, sandy-humusy soil that is well-drained all year with ample moisture during flowering. Seed is more dependable for propagation than dividing the long tap roots, and winter mulching is recommended in almost all locations. Pests and diseases are not bothersome. A soft pink variety, "Bees' Pink," is available.

Incarvillea grandiflora (Bigflower Incarvillea) 9–12 in.
   Sun
Flowering span: Mid-June to mid-July
Color: Deep rosy red
Native habitat: China

Here the blossoming is up to 4 inches wide and the leaflets are rounded, but the culture is identical with that for *I. delaveyi.*

Iris "Dutch Hybrids" 12–18 in. Sun
Flowering span: Mid-June to mid-July
Color: White, yellow, blue, purple, mostly with contrasting
   colorings
Native habitat: Horticultural hybrid between *I. xiphium praecox* and *I. tingitana*

More reliably hardy than either the English or Spanish Iris, these small bulbs produce the familiar "florist's iris" of commerce. The narrow, tubular, grayish green foliage usually appears in early fall and persists, reasonably undamaged, through the winter. It likes any moist, well-drained soil in full sun but benefits from a loose winter mulch. Initial plantings should be made in the fall, and division of overcrowded clumps can be made after the foliage fades. Pests and diseases are not problematic. The hybrid list is extensive: "Blue Champion," bright blue with yellow falls; "Blue Giant," deep indigo blue; "Blue River," blue bi-tone; "Canarybird," bright yellow; "Delft Blue," blue bi-tone; "Heracles," a smoky blend; "Joan of Arc," white with yellow blotch; "King of the Blues," deep blue; "Lemon Queen," citron yellow; "Lilac Queen," lilac with white falls; "L'Innocence," pure white; "Melody," white with yellow falls; "Menelik," blue with white falls; "Orange King," deep orange; and "Wedgwood," light blue with yellow blotches.

Iris ochroleuca (*orientalis*) (Yellowband Iris) 18–36 in. Sun
Flowering span: Mid-June to mid-July
Color: Deep yellow with wide pale yellow or white margins
Native habitat: Asia Minor, Iraq

Dependable and vigorous, this species has gray-green, twisted foliage and several, large, "butterfly" blossoms per stem. It adapts to almost any moist, well-drained soil and can stand light shading. Division of the fibrous root system propagates it easily, and pests and diseases are not worrisome. White-flowered forms are occasionally found. The American Iris Society places this in the *Apogon* classification.

Iris sibirica (Siberian Iris) 24–36 in. Sun
Flowering span: Early June to July
Color: Deep violet with a whitened center
Native habitat: Central Europe

Cooperatively adaptive to almost any site, this very hardy member of the *Apogon* or "beardless" type has dense clumps of narrow, erect foliage with quantities of slender flower stalks bearing up to a half dozen 2- to 3-inch blossoms. At home most in a moist, acid soil well enriched with humus, it can also do reasonably well in heavier, drier soils and more shading. Spring or fall division of the fibrous rootstock suits it well, and seeding can be productive too. Pests and diseases are not common. Quite a few hybrid colorings exist: "Blue Brilliant," rich blue; "Blue Mere," violet-blue; "Blue Moon," medium blue; "Caesar's Brother," deep purple; "Congo Drums," deep blue-violet; "Cool Springs," pale violet-blue; "Ellesmere," vivid royal blue; "Eric the Red," reddish magenta; "Helen Astor," pink-purple; "Perry's Blue," sky blue; "Purple Mere," deep violet-purple; "Royal Ensign," red and blue bicolor; "Showy Egret," white; "Snow Crest," white; "Snow Queen," white; "Tealwood," blue-purple; "Tycoon," deep violet-blue; and "White Swirl," white.

Iris spuria (Seashore Iris) 15–40 in. Sun
Flowering span: Early June to July
Color: Blue purple
Native habitat: Turkestan, Iran

Growing the hybrids of this *Apogon* species is a gamble, but the results can be very rewarding. It likes a very moist growing condition when in flower but a hot, dry summer afterward. The glaucous, grasslike leaves produce sizable blossoms (moreso with the hybrids), and all resent transplanting, requiring an extra year to reflower well. Plant rootstock divisions for permanence in a well-drained, rich soil in full sun to light shade. Diseases and pests are not bothersome. Many showy hybrids are on the market: "Blue Pinafore," rich blue; "Bronze Butterfly," bronze; "Cambridge Blue," true blue; "Driftwood," bronze; "Golden Lady," deep yellow; "Lark Song," yellow and cream; "Lord Wolsely," rich purple-blue; "Monaurea," yellow; "Morningtide," white; "Wadi Zem Zem," creamy yellow, very adaptable for southern gardens; and "White Heron," white.

Kniphofia tucki (*Tritoma tucki*) 48–60 in. Sun
Flowering span: Mid-June to August
Color: Yellow, edged in red
Native habitat: South Africa

Showy in flower, this exotic plant has ¾-inch, sword-shaped foliage 12 to 18 inches long in a basal clump with leafless blossom spikes of drooping, tubular, 1½-inch florets heavily clustered in 5- to 6-inch terminal displays. Reasonably hardy in sun to light shade with some loose winter mulching, it wants a sandy, well-drained soil not overly rich and a location out of high winds. Although best left undisturbed when established, the deep, ropelike rootstock can be spring-divided, and it can also be propagated easily by seed. Insects are not pestiferous, but leaf spot can be a disease nuisance.

Leontopodium alpinum (*Gnaphalium leontopodium*)
    (Common Edelweiss) 4–10 in. Sun
Flowering span: Early June to mid-July

Leontopodium alpinum, famously associated with the Alps, can also be garden grown.

Color: White
Native habitat: Alps Mountains

Familiar, but not customarily planted here for unknown reasons, this rock garden asset has narrow, silvery-gray foliage close to the ground and woolly leaf bracts in a star shape surrounding the small, yellow, true flowers. The 1½-inch blossoms appear in clusters from each stem. Best in an alkaline soil, it prefers a well-drained, sandy loam that is moist in spring and dry during the winter. When established, it creeps slowly by underground stolons, but seed is recommended as more reliable for propagation. Nothing unusual bothers it.

Leontopodium sibiricum (Siberian Edelweiss) 4–10 in.
    Sun
Flowering span: Early June to mid-July
Color: White
Native habitat: Siberia

Here the flowers are almost twice the size of *L. alpinum*
and appear singly on a stem. Culture is the same for both.

Lewisia cotyledon 4–10 in. Semi-shade
Flowering span: Early June to mid-July
Color: Magenta, pink, white
Native habitat: Southwestern Oregon and northwestern
    California

Related to the summer annual *Portulaca,* these showy
wildflowers have thick, succulent rosettes of tongue-shaped
leaves 2 to 4 inches long. The branched flower stalks carry
many 1-inch blossoms with 8 to 10 petals striped in dark
red. Useful in rock gardens, they prefer a cool, semi-shaded
location with gritty, well-drained soil enriched with acid
leaf mould. Propagation is by seed or offsets. Pests and diseases are not worrisome.

Lewisia rediviva (Bitterroot Lewisia) 2–4 in. Sun
Flowering span: Mid-June to August
Color: Deep rose, white
Native habitat: Western Canada to California, east to Co-
    lorado and Montana

Here the 1-inch, chalice-shaped blossoms of this state
flower of Montana appear when the winter-persistent, needlelike foliage retreats into dormancy. It wants a rocky,
well-drained site in sun that is very dry in summer. Division
of the dormant, fleshy, red roots in late summer or seed
propagate it, and it appears to have no pests or diseases.

Lewisia tweedyi (Tweedy Lewisia) 4–8 in. Sun
Flowering span: Early June to mid-July
Color: Pale pink, apricot
Native habitat: Wenatchee Mountains of central Washing-
    ton

Fussy to grow well, it is a strikingly attractive plant with
2- to 3-inch, shimmering blossoms striped in yellow above a
set of glossy, lanceolate leaves at the base. Subject to crown
rot easily, it needs a gritty, well-drained soil and planting of

its long taproot vertically between rock garden stones with the lower feeding roots able to travel easily into rich, acid-humusy soil nearby. Propagate by removing offsets, and dust the wound with fungicide. In gardens the flowers need hand-pollination to set seed. Insects are no bother.

Lilium (Lily) 24–100 in.   Sun
Flowering span: Mid-June to mid-September
Color: White, yellow, red, orange, pink, plus many shadings
    and mixtures
Native habitat: The northern hemisphere around the globe,
    locally from southeastern Canada to Florida

Unique in blossom form, fragrance, height, and bulb type, the lily has maintained an historical association for 4,000 years with every culture of the north temperate climates. As symbols of royalty, religion, and purity, the clusters of sizable and pleasing flowers have been featured art forms for centuries. The proper classification of the newest types became unwieldy and confused, however, by the vast improvement in hybridization recently, and it took the joint effort of the Royal Horticultural Society in Britain and the North American Lily Society to evolve standards for the current horticultural system of 9 divisions based on the ancestral or geographical origin and the form of the blossom.

Lily Divisions

DIVISION 1:   *Asiatic hybrids* (June)

Having the earliest flowering, these are further subdivided into: (a) upright-blossoming, mostly stem-rooting, (b) outward-facing, mostly stem-rooting, (c) pendant, usually with elongated pedicels.

DIVISION 2:   *Martagon hybrids* (June)

Having the characteristics of *L. martagon* and *L. hansoni*, these have small, pendant flowers with recurved tips; stem-rooting.

DIVISION 3: *Candidum hybrids* (Late June, early July)

Having the characteristics of L. *candidum* and L. *chalcedonicum*, these have sharply recurving petals and wide, trumpet-shaped flowers; base-rooting.

DIVISION 4: *American hybrids* (Late June, early July)

Having turk's-cap flowers with elongated pedicels, these are tall-stemmed; stem-rooting.

DIVISION 5: *Longiflorum hybrids* (July)

Having the characteristics of L. *longiflorum* and L. *formosanum,* these have trumpet-shaped flowers.

DIVISION 6: *Aurelian* or *Trumpet hybrids* (Mid-July, early August)

Having the characteristics of the Asiatic hybrids, exclusive of the L. *auratum* and L. *speciosum* hybrids, these bloom later.

DIVISION 7: *Oriental hybrids* (August)

Having the characteristics of L. *auratum* and L. *speciosum,* these are further subdivided into: (a) bowl-shaped, (b) flat-faced, and (c) those with sharply recurved petals.

DIVISION 8: All hybrids not provided for in any previous division.

DIVISION 9: All true, wild species and their botanical forms.

Uncomplicated to grow for many years of endurance, the lily is a distinctive bulb having no outer skin or tunic covering its overlapping scales, which are actually modified, underground leaves. The round or egg-shaped bulb can be from 2 to 6 inches in diameter with white, pink, yellow, or brown scales either loosely or tightly attached. Fleshy, somewhat fragile roots come with each bulb and need careful handling to prevent breakage and drying out. Install lilies with only basal roots shallowly in the autumn, but plant those having additional stem roots in the spring and at a greater depth. Because lilies are dormant for only a brief period, get them into the ground immediately on receipt or after division. Always soak new plantings thoroughly to stimulate quick root response.

With the exception of at least the native, swamp-tolerant *L. superbum* and *L. canadense,* all lilies want excellent drainage throughout the year. Plant in raised beds if surface water movement is sluggish. The majority are best installed in a rich, sandy, acid soil deeply improved beforehand with generous amounts of humus, compost, spagnum peat moss, or leaf mold. Top-dress annually with several inches of humusy mulching to promote root coolness and to add ongoing nourishment, but avoid using fresh manure at any time since it spreads disfiguring diseases.

Fertilize lightly both before and after blossoming to improve the bulb's vigor. Most lilies are sun-lovers, but all dislike windswept and low elevation locations. Use sturdy staking early for the heavy-blossoming or very tall kinds to forestall stem breakage from downpour rains or wind gusts. Adequate watering at flowering is beneficial, but lilies dwindle into minor importance if too close to the moisture-seeking root competition or shading from nearby shrubs and trees. The single or whorled lancelike leaves are essential to future flowering and should not be collected indiscriminately when cutting blossoms for decoration. Unless wanted for propagation, the quick-forming seed capsules are best removed early to conserve the bulb's energies.

Propagating lilies is relatively simple and possible in several ways: seed, scales, division, offsets, and stem bulbils. Divide overcrowded, sparse-flowering colonies when the foliage yellows, but expect slow recuperation for generous reblooming until the roots have again become fully established.

Insects rarely create nuisances of themselves for lilies, but aphids are known to be the carrier of a virus mosaic disease which seriously mottles the foliage and distorts the blossoms. Infected plants require complete and prompt discard and no lily replanting in the same site for several years. Where the air is stagnant and consistently moist, another disease, *Botrytis elliptica*, can be troublesome and destructive. Mice and gophers relish the bulbs, requiring encasement of each bulb in loose-fitting, wire mesh barriers shaped with enough room for normal growth enlargement.

June-Blooming Hybrid Lilies

ASIATIC HYBRIDS: From 24 to 60 inches tall with 4- to 6-inch blossoms

Upright-flowering examples (Many are mid-century hybrids):
    "Cinnabar," crimson red; "Destiny," lemon yellow; "Enchantment," orange-red; "Golden Chalice," deep yellow; "Harmony," bright orange; "Joan Evans," golden yellow;

These upright-flowering lilies are mid-century hybrids for June displays.

"Tangelo," light orange; and "Vermilion Brilliant," bright red.

Outward-facing examples:

"Brandywine," orange; "Corsage," pale pink-lavender; "Fireflame," orange-red; "Fire King," vivid red; "Orange Triumph," orange-yellow; "Paprika," deep crimson; "Prosperity," bright yellow; "Tabasco," orange-red; and "Valencia," yellow-orange.

Pendant-flowering examples:

Burgundy strain, red shades; *Citronella* strain, yellow shades; *Fiesta* hybrids, pale yellow, orange, dark red; and *Harlequin* hybrids, ivory, buff, salmon, rose, lilac, purple.

MARTAGON HYBRIDS: From 36 to 72 inches tall with 3- to 4-inch, heavy-textured blossoms

Examples: "Achievement," yellowish white; *Paisley* strain, orange, yellow, white, brown, lavender, purple.

CANDIDUM HYBRIDS: From 36 to 48 inches tall with 4- to 5-inch blossoms

Example: L. testaceum (Nankeen Lily), apricot-yellow, the first recorded hybrid lily.

Lilium canadense (Canada Lily) 36–60 in. Semi-shade
Flowering span: Late June to August
Color: Bright orange-yellow
Native habitat: Southeastern Canada to Alabama, west to Minnesota and Missouri

Adaptable to wet, boggy soils of low meadows, the bulb is unusual by not requiring excellent drainage to survive. The nodding, 2- to 3-inch, bell-like flowers appear on sturdy stems in graceful clusters up to 10 and have a yellow exterior and an orange, dark-spotted interior coloring. The 2- to 4-inch leaves appear in whorls up the stem. Tolerant of full sun if kept wet and heavily mulched, it adapts perhaps best in open, acid woodlots with normal moisture and fertility. Propagate by seed or scales and plant the base-rooting bulbs initially in early autumn. No important pests or dis-

The pagoda-shaped flowers of *Lilium canadense* add special grace to borders.

eases bother it. The variety *coccineum* has orange-red blossoms, while *flavum* is lemon yellow.

Lilium candidum (Madonna Lily) 24–48 in. Sun
Flowering span: Mid-June to mid-July
Color: White
Native habitat: Greece, Asia Minor, northern Iran

The oldest European lily in cultivation, it has an attractive, heady fragrance and a surprising tolerance for heavily limed soils. The 4-inch, upturned blossom clusters are trumpet-shaped with noticeable golden stamens and reddish pedicels. The heavy stems are lined with small leaf bracts. Its durability in gardens remains curiously capricious with a preference for a rich, well-drained loam in full sun and a soil cover not exceeding 1 inch over the bulb. Seed is rarely fertile, and scales or offsets propagate it better. Fall planting is recommended for initial installations, and expect a rosette of winter-hardy foliage soon after. Pests and diseases are covered fully in the general information under *Lilium*. The variety *salonikae* blooms earlier, has green pedicels on the flowers, and is a prolific self-seeder. There are also scarce types with leaves edged in either yellow or white.

Lilium concolor (Morningstar Lily) 12–24 in. Sun
Flowering span: Late June to mid-July
Color: Bright scarlet
Native habitat: Central China

Tolerant of limed soils, this conspicuous but short-lived wildflower has generous clusters of star-shaped, 3- to 4-inch, upturned blossoms without the usual spotting. It prefers bright sun or light shading and a gravelly soil of moderate fertility. Seed or scales propagate it readily, and diseases and pests are not worrisome.

Lilium hansoni (Hanson Lily) 36–48 in. Semi-shade
Flowering span: Mid-June to mid-July
Color: Orange yellow
Native habitat: Korea, Japan

Pleasantly adaptable to both semi-shade or sun as well as to a wide range of soils, including limed ones, this spicy-fragrant lily has clusters of 2-inch, star-shaped, pendant blossoms with thick, waxy petals, spotted brown. Its 5-inch leaves appear in whorls, and the bulbs increase readily in a humusy, moist location. Propagate by offsets or scales. Diseases and pests are not commonplace.

Lilium martagon (Turk's-cap Lily) 24–48 in. Semi-shade
Flowering span: Early June to July
Color: Rosy purple
Native habitat: Most of Europe, Siberia, Mongolia

Here the bulb has up to 20 waxy, drooping, 2- to 3-inch blossoms on purplish stalks with dark green, 3- to 6-inch leaves. Unfortunately, the fragrance is disagreeably strong. It will grow well, and perhaps naturalize, in any light, moist, well-limed soil in light shade to full sun. Scales and offsets propagate it faster than seeding, and pests and diseases are not a serious concern. The variety *album* has pure white flowering; *cattaniae* is deep mahogany and unspotted; while *sanguineo-purpureum* is dark mahogany with yellow spots.

The flamboyant blossoms of *Papaver orientale* add an early summer glow to sunny borders with their many hybrid colorings.

Carpets of single (top) or double-flowered *Sanguinaria* give moist woodlots special appeal.

Majestic and showy, *Cypripedium reginae* naturally requires special attention to do its best.

Vibrant and versatile, the multihued hybrids of *Hemerocallis* belong in all summertime gardens.

Sparkling flowers and glossy foliage earmark both the domestic and Japanese *Shortia* types.

Sunshine favorites for autumn displays, the magnificent *Chrysanthemum* hybrids of today are without peer.

Spectacular masses of flowering can enliven any sunny rock garden with *Alyssum saxatile*.

Summer vividness can be yours annually with a wise selection of durable perennial plantings.

Hauntingly fragrant *Hyacinthus orientalis* combines handsomely with other springtime favorites such as these dwarfed
Iris.

Generous bedding of these hybrid *Narcissus* provides a naturalistic companion planting for this moist woodlot.

Impressively shaped lily-flowered tulips are here surrounded by mats of late spring white violets.

The flat-opening *Tulipa kaufmanniana* provides choice accenting
for all spring sun-pockets.

A well-grown clump of *Fritillaria* brings dramatic interest and flair with only moderate effort.

Serenely inviting even out of flower, these fragrant-leaved perennials show fascinating textural combinations.

Stately hybrid *Delphinium* towers contentedly above a massing of
Campanula glomerata as summer begins.

HAMPFLER

Naturalizing *Colchicum* is particularly effective for the surprise of autumn bulb color.

The doldrums of winter fade quickly when *Helleborus* can succeed as well as it does here.

Lilium monadelphum (Caucasian Lily) 36–60 in. Semi-
shade
Flowering span: Mid-June to mid-July
Color: Golden yellow
Native habitat: Caucasus Mountains, Turkey, Iran

The showy, 3- to 5-inch, bell-shaped flowers are purple-
spotted, thick-petaled and waxy, but its odor is strong and
not very pleasant. It likes any light, humusy soil in semi-
shade to sun but will adapt to heavier soils well. Reproduce
by offsets or scales. Diseases and pests are not worrisome.

Lilium pomponium (Pompon Lily) 18–24 in. Sun
Flowering span: Mid-June to mid-July
Color: Bright scarlet
Native habitat: Maritime Alps Mountains of France and
Italy

The glistening, thick-petaled, 2-inch blossoms are spotted
black and appear in clusters up to 10 on purplish stalks. Its
scent is disagreeably pungent, however. Tolerant of limed
soils, it grows well in any light, well-drained loam with
bright sun. Propagate by seed or scales, and do not worry
about pests or diseases.

Linum flavum (Golden Flax) 12–24 in. Sun
Flowering span: Mid-June to mid-July
Color: Golden yellow
Native habitat: Europe

Similar to the May-flowering species except for color, the
culture is the same for all. A dwarf variety, *compactum,* is
only 6 inches tall.

Lotus corniculatus (Birdsfoot Deervetch) 4–18 in. Sun
Flowering span: Mid-June to September
Color: Bright yellow
Native habitat: Europe, British Isles, Australia, North
America

Generally sprawling, this hardy creeper is useful for dry
embankments in full sun but can become weedy in ferti-

lized garden locations. The ongoing, pealike flowers appear in terminal clusters with tiny, 3-parted leaves. Propagate by seed or spring division. The double-flowered variety, *flore-pleno*, is showier and longer-lasting in bloom.

Lupinus polyphyllus (Washington Lupine) 24–60 in. Sun
Flowering span: Mid-June to September
Color: Deep blue, violet
Native habitat: Washington to California

Generous quantities of 8-inch flowering spikes appear on well-grown specimens of this wildflower above deeply cut, 2- to 6-inch palmate leaves. Preferring a cool site with full sun, but tolerant of light shading, the pealike florets continue blooming for an extended period where drainage is excellent and the soil deep, acid, and rich. Since they resent transplanting when established, they are best raised from seed. Mildew and rot are serious afflictions, along with aphid infestations. Many named varieties in various colorings are available but have been generally supplanted by the improved "Russell Hybrid" strain.

Lupinus "Russell Hybrids" 36–60 in. Sun
Flowering span: Mid-June to September
Color: Blue, white, yellow, red, pink, bicolorings
Native habitat: Horticultural hybrid of uncertain parentage

Here the long flower stalks are usually covered by 18 to 24 inches of crowded, 1-inch florets in a myriad of colorful shadings. Not long-lived beyond 4 years, they can be reproduced either by seeding or by early spring stem cuttings with a portion of root attached. Culture is the same as for *L. polyphyllus*, with the same aversion to limed soils.

Lychnis chalcedonica (Maltesecross Campion) 18–24 in.
   Sun
Flowering span: Mid-June to August
Color: Bright scarlet
Native habitat: Russia

Terminal heads of closely packed florets resembling small crosses appear on hairy stems above dull green, lanceolate leaves. Blossoming can be extended by removing the faded flowers. Best in full sun, it needs a well-drained, sandy loam and tolerates moderate drought satisfactorily. Spring or fall division, plus seeding, propagates it easily. Smut disease is the major affliction. The variety *salmonea* has pastel salmon blossoms.

Lychnis coronaria (*Agrostemma coronaria*) (Rose Campion)
      12–30 in. Sun
Flowering span: Mid-June to mid-July
Color: Vivid cerise
Native habitat: Europe, Asia

Distinguished by oblong, white-woolly foliage and silvery flower stalks, the solitary, 1½-inch, round blossoms appear on wide-branching stems. Not individually long-lived, it self-seeds generously. Culture is the same as with *L. chalcedonica*. The variety *alba* has white flowers, while the hybrid "Abbotswood Rose" is a vivid pink.

Lychnis flos-cuculi (Ragged Robin) 12–24 in. Sun
Flowering span: Mid-June to September
Color: Pink, red
Native habitat: Europe, northern Asia

Narrow, lanceolate, widely spaced leaves on slender stems produce quantities of terminal, serrated blossoming throughout most of the summer. It grows readily in any average-fertility soil and can be reproduced by seed, division or cuttings. Apparently it is unbothered by diseases or pests. The double-flowered form, *plenissima,* is superior to the type.

Lychnis flos-jovis (*Agrostemma flos-jovis*) (Flower-of-Jove)
      12–18 in. Sun
Flowering span: Mid-June to August
Color: Pink, carmine, purple
Native habitat: Alps Mountains

Here the broad, 3-inch foliage is gray-green and appears in a basal rosette. The ½-inch florets are tightly packed in terminal heads and endure for a long blooming time. It is readily adaptable to any ordinary, well-drained soil in full sun to light shading. Propagate by seed or division. It is not bothered by troublesome diseases or pests.

Lysimachia nummularia (Moneywort, Creeping Jenny) 1–2 in. Semi-shade
Flowering span: Early June to August
Color: Deep yellow
Native habitat: Northern Europe, British Isles

Remarkably adaptive to any soil and almost any light condition, this invasive, rapidly creeping groundcover has quantities of cup-shaped, ½-inch flowers on short, erect stems above deep green, ¾-inch rounded leaves. Propagate by division or cuttings. Pests and diseases are usually no bother. The scarce variety *aurea* has bright yellow foliage.

Lysimachia punctata (Spotted Loosestrife) 18–30 in. Semi-shade
Flowering span: Mid-June to mid-July
Color: Bright yellow
Native habitat: Asia Minor, Europe

This plant is unusual in that both its 3-inch, lanceolate leaves and the 1-inch blossoming appear in clustered whorls above each other all along the slender, erect stems. Rapid growth from the below-ground stems can become quickly invasive, especially in moist, rich soils. Preferring some shading, it adapts to full sun if kept well-watered. Division or seed propagate it readily. White fly and rot are an occasional nuisance.

Lysimachia terrestis (Swampcandle Loosestrife) 8–30 in. Sun
Flowering span: Mid-June to August
Color: Bright yellow
Native habitat: Southeastern Canada to Georgia, west to Iowa

Usually found wild in consistently moist to wet locations, the showy ½-inch florets with dark markings appear generously on the terminal spikes above paired, narrow, lanceolate leaves with gray undersides. Propagate by seed or division and provide it with a moist garden location in sun to light shading. It appears unbothered by disease or insect problems.

Lysimachia vulgaris (Golden Loosestrife) 24–36 in. Sun
Flowering span: Mid-June to mid-July
Color: Golden yellow
Native habitat: Europe, southeastern Canada to Maryland, west to Illinois

Here the stems are somewhat sticky-hairy with dull green, pointed leaves in pairs or circles. The showy, terminal clusters of cup-shaped, 1-inch flowers are erect, and occasionally the blossoms are edged in red. Found wild in wet, streamside locations, it can adjust to a moist, average soil in bright sun to light shading. Division or seed reproduces it well, and it seems to be untroubled by pests or diseases.

Lythrum virgatum (Wand Lythrum) 24–36 in. Sun
Flowering span: Late June to August
Color: Purple
Native habitat: Europe, northern Asia

Slender, graceful spikes covered with ½-inch florets in threes appear from dark green, lancelike foliage during most of the summer. It prefers a moist, average-fertility location in full sun. Division or stem cuttings readily propagate it, but it also self-seeds generously and may become invasive in borders. It is unlikely to be nuisanced by either diseases or insects. The hybrids are few: "Dropmore Purple," 30 in., rosy-purple in cool areas but muddy rose in hot ones; and "Rose Queen," 18 to 24 in., bright rose in any growing condition.

Malva alcea (Hollyhock Mallow) 36–48 in. Sun
Flowering span: Late June to September
Color: Deep rose
Native habitat: Europe

Downy, deeply incised, light green foliage gives rise to numerous spikes with several long-blooming, 1½-inch flowers usually open at one time. Adjustable to any soil and tolerant of drought, this perennial can be left undisturbed indefinitely. Seed, division, or stem cuttings propagate it readily, and it has no pests or diseases worth mentioning. The variety *fastigiata* is deeper-colored, erect, and carries 2-inch blossoms.

Mecanopsis cambrica (Welsh Poppy) 12–18 in. Semi-shade
Flowering span: Mid-June to mid-July
Color: Yellow, occasionally orange
Native habitat: Western Europe, British Isles

The attractive foliage clump has light green, deeply cut, lanceolate leaves and 1½-inch, round, papery flowers on slender stems. It prefers a humusy, well-drained soil and can be propagated by spring division or seed. Nothing appears to bother it. The variety *flore-pleno* has very double yellow blossoms with conspicuous scarlet veining.

Mitchella repens (Partridge-berry) 2–3 in. Semi-shade
Flowering span: Mid-June to early July
Color: White, pale pink
Native habitat: Southeastern Canada to Florida, west to Mexico and Minnesota

Creeping, wiry stems have pairs of small, dark green, shiny leaves with conspicuous white veining and tiny, trumpet-shaped flowers that produce bright red fall fruiting. Adaptable for indoor use in a terrarium, it is a slow-growing outdoor groundcover even where the soil is consistently moist, humusy, and in light to heavy shading. Division or early summer stem cuttings work better than seeding. It has no pests or diseases of note.

Monarda didyma (Oswego Bee-balm, Bergamot) 18–30 in. Sun
Flowering span: Mid-June to September
Color: Bright scarlet
Native habitat: Newfoundland to Florida, west to Tennessee and Michigan

Ragged-looking, 3-inch heads of many tubular flowers terminally appear on the squared, hollow stems of this vigorous wildflower in sun to semi-shade. Its rough-haired, bronze-green leaves are aromatic when bruised. Enjoying a moist, well-drained, average soil, they are best spring-divided. Rust damage to the foliage is the chief annoyance. The hybrids are many and superior to the parent: "Adam," bright red; "Cambridge Scarlet," crimson; "Croftway Pink," clear, rose pink; "Granite Pink," pink; "Prairie Glow," salmon red; "Prairie Night," violet-purple; "Snow Maiden," white; "Snow Queen," white; "Snow White," white; and "Violet Queen," lavender-violet. All are attractive to hummingbirds.

Nepeta faassenii (mussini) (Persian Catmint) 12–18 in. Sun
Flowering span: Early June to August
Color: Lavender
Native habitat: Iran, Caucasus Mountains

Useful as a rampant groundcover in full, hot sun, this spreading perennial has silvery gray, tiny leaves with the aroma of mint and billowy mounds of trumpet-shaped florets on slender spikes. It does best in a sandy, well-drained soil and can easily be propagated by spring division. Rust on the foliage is the only nuisance. The hybrid "Six Hills Giant" is 24 inches tall with gray leaves and violet-blue, sterile flowering.

Oenothera fruticosa (Common Sundrops) 12–24 in. Sun
Flowering span: Early June to mid-July
Color: Bright yellow
Native habitat: New England to Florida, west to Oklahoma

Highly variable in appearance, the erect, woody stems and lanceolate leaves are usually covered with noticeable hairs. The 1- to 2-inch flowers appear terminally in clusters. Shallow-rooted, it thrives in any moist, well-drained soil in full sun to light shade. The stem foliage often turns reddish in the fall and a basal rosette of evergreen leaves (generally bronze-toned in winter) readily marks their location. Spring division is recommended, and it appears to have no bothersome diseases or pests, except occasional white fly infestations in dry weather. The variety *youngi* is shorter and more floriferous.

Oenothera missouriensis (macrocarpa) (Ozark Sundrops)
    6–9 in. Sun
Flowering span: Mid-June to August
Color: Lemon yellow
Native habitat: Illinois to Colorado, south to Texas

Often confused with the night-blooming Evening Primrose, this daytime plant has 5-inch, funnel-shaped blossoms and long-tapered, red-spotted buds. The lance-shaped, glossy leaves appear on trailing stems. Best in full sun, it likes an excellently drained soil that is deep, rich, limed, and only moderately moist. Division is the simplest propagation method. White fly and rot are the chief pests.

Oenothera tetragona 18–24 in. Sun
Flowering span: Mid-June to August
Color: Lemon yellow
Native habitat: Eastern North America

Here the cup-shaped, 1½-inch blossoms appear with linear foliage that may grow to 8 inches. Culture is the same as with *O. missouriensis*. There are several hybrids: "Fireworks," 12 in., large, golden yellow flowers on red-brown stalks with leathery, bronze leaves; *riparia*, 18 in., large, bright yellow flowers, exceptionally long-blooming; and "Yellow River," 24 in., lemon yellow, 2-in. flowers.

Opuntia compressa (vulgaris) (Common Prickly-pear)
    10–12 in. Sun
Flowering span: Mid-June to mid-July
Color: Chrome yellow
Native habitat: Massachusetts to Georgia, west to Oklahoma
    and Minnesota

In sandy or rocky, well-drained locations in bright sun, this hardy cactus variant can thrive. It has thick, oval, 6-inch sections joined end to end and carries no spines. Frilly, 2- to 3-inch blossoms can appear in dense clusterings, followed by 1-inch, dark red fruit that is not palatable for eating. The small, red-brown hairs on the smooth stem parts can be troublesome since they detach easily and work themselves under the skin to produce an annoying inflammation. Propagate by making cuttings to be rooted in barely moist sand. Pests and diseases are uncommon.

Papaver orientale (Oriental Poppy) 24–48 in. Sun
Flowering span: Early June to July
Color: Scarlet with blackish base
Native habitat: Armenia

Noticeably conspicuous when in flower, the 6- to 12-inch, crinkly, tissue-paper blossoms appear on hairy, erect stems that are easily distorted by heavy rain and their own weight. The center of each flower is also noticeable for the high, broad ring of black stamens. When collecting for arranging, sear the milky sap with flame and place in warm water for "hardening-off." The 12-inch, greatly divided, silvery green leaves are rough-textured and fade soon after flowering. Its deep taproots need a well-drained, average soil in full sun, and root cuttings made in late summer dormancy are the easiest propagation method. Aphids and stem blight are the worst nuisances. A number of colorful hybrids exist: "Glowing Embers," 30 in., orange-red; "Indian Chief," 30 in., deep red; "Marcus Perry," 30 in., orange-red; "Mrs. Perry," 36 in., salmon pink; "Perry's White," 30 in., white; "Pinnacle," 30 in., white with an orange-red rim; "Salome," 30 in., rose pink; "Show Girl," 36 in., bright pink; and "Sultana," 30 in., peach pink.

Paradisea liliastrum (*Anthericum liliago*) (St. Bernard's
    Lily) 18–24 in. Sun
Flowering span: Mid-June to mid-July
Color: White
Native habitat: Central and southern Europe

This nonbulbous member of the lily family has fleshy tubers producing sedgelike foliage and long, thin stems of trumpet-shaped, 1½-inch flowers with golden stamens. It grows well in borders and at the edges of woods that are humusy, moist, and very fertile. Both seeds or divisions of the brittle tubers in autumn are satisfactory, but divisions require more than one season to flower again after separation. Pests and diseases are uncommon.

Penstemon barbatus (Chelone barbata) (Beardlip
      Penstemon) 36–48 in. Sun
Flowering span: Mid-June to August
Color: Bright red
Native habitat: Southern Colorado to southern Utah

Pendant, 1-inch, tubular blossoms appear widely spaced on slender, erect stems with smooth, dark green, narrow leaves. It likes a well-drained, average-fertility soil in full sun and can be reproduced by seed or spring division. Crown rot is the chief nuisance. A hybrid, "Rose Elf," is 30 inches tall with deep rose flowering.

Penstemon gloxinoides (Gloxinia Penstemon) 24–30 in.
      Sun
Flowering span: Mid-June to September
Color: Red, pink, lavender, white
Native habitat: Horticultural hybrid between *P. cobaea* and
      P. hartwegi

Here the blossoms are 2 inches long and in heavy clusters. Culture is identical with that for *P. barbatus* but not all types are reliably hardy. Removing the faded flower stalks prolongs bloom. Several hybrids are available: "Firebird," 18 to 24 inches, crimson, somewhat tender; "Indian Jewels," 18 to 24 inches, mixed colorings; and "Prairie Fire," 36 inches, orange red.

Penstemon hartwegi (gentianoides) (Hartweg Penstemon)
      36–48 in. Sun
Flowering span: Mid-June to September
Color: Deep red
Native habitat: Mexico

This species has erect, purple flower stalks and drooping, tubular blossoms. Best propagated by stem cuttings wintered over in cold frames, its general culture is the same as that for *P. barbatus*.

Phlox carolina (*suffruticosa*) (Carolina Phlox) 12–30 in.
    Sun
Flowering span: Early July to mid-July
Color: White, pink, rose
Native habitat: Maryland to Florida, west to Illinois

The 4- to 5-inch, high-headed clusterings of ¾-inch florets make a long-lasting display that can be extended by removing the faded blossoming before it sets seed. Slender-pointed, glossy foliage is an asset that is also less susceptible to the disfiguring mildew of other upright phlox types. Grow in well-drained, airy, sunny locations that are consistently moist and enriched liberally with compost, humus, or peat moss. Division or top stem cuttings in summer propagate it easily. When too dry, the leaves develop red spider mite infestations. The choice hybrid "Miss Lingard" is pure white and does not produce seed. This entire species is sometimes listed as *P. glaberrima* or *P. ovata*.

Phlox maculata (Meadow Phlox) 12–30 in. Sun
Flowering span: Early June to August
Color: Reddish purple
Native habitat: Southeastern Canada to Mississippi, west to
    Arkansas and Minnesota

Here the fragrant flower heads appear on purple-spotted stems with 2- to 4-inch, very smooth and slender leaves. It needs the same cultural conditions as *P. carolina*. The hybrid "Alpha" is deep pink, while *purpurea* is a rich purple.

Phlox ovata (Mountain Phlox) 12–18 in. Sun
Flowering span: Early June to mid-July
Color: Pink, light red
Native habitat: Pennsylvania to Georgia, west to Indiana

These stems are unfortunately weak and prone to lie on the ground. Its 3-inch leaves are widest at the tip ends, and the 1-inch florets come in small, dense, terminal clusters. It creeps by underground stems to form large mats. Culture is identical with that for *P. carolina*.

The puffed-up budding of *Platycodon grandiflorum* eventually unfurls some showy blue blossoms.

Platycodon grandiflorum (Balloonflower) 24–36 in. Sun
Flowering span: Mid-June to August
Color: Blue, white, pale pink
Native habitat: Japan, western China

Slow to indicate any growth in early spring, these showy perennials may want marking to identify their locations. The slender stems usually need staking and carry gray green foliage with terminal spikes of unusual puffed buds that open into 2- to 2½-inch-wide, saucer-shaped stars. Sear the milky stems after cutting for use in arrangements. They do best in a consistently moist, well-drained, sandy loam in full sun to light shading. Propagation by seed is best since the deep, brittle roots on established plants do not take kindly to transplanting. Pests and diseases are unknown. The variety *mariesi* is 18 inches tall with blue or white flowering only; "Mother of Pearl" is a pale pink hybrid, while "Snowflake" has white, semi-double blossoms.

Polemonium humile (pulcherrimum) (Skunkleaf Jacob's-ladder) 6–9 in. Semi-shade

Flowering span: Early June to July
Color: Pale blue to purple
Native habitat: Arctic regions

Good for rock gardens and naturalized areas, the bell-shaped florets have golden stamens and appear on airy stems with the usual, pinnate leaves of the group. Its culture is the same as with the May-flowering *P. caeruleum.* The variety *pulchellum* has smaller, violet-colored florets.

Polemonium richardsoni (Richardson's Jacob's-ladder)
    18–24 in. Semi-shade
Flowering span: Early June to July
Color: Bright blue
Native habitat: Arctic regions

Erect stems of this compact and hardy plant carry profuse flowering above the fernlike, basal leaves. Its culture is the same as that for *P. caeruleum.* The variety *album* has white blossoms.

Potentilla argyrophylla (Undersnow Cinque-foil) 12–18 in.
    Sun
Flowering span: Early June to mid-July
Color: Yellow
Native habitat: Himalaya Mountains

The distinctive, strawberrylike foliage is probably more interesting than the 1-inch flowers that are loosely arranged on wide-branched, silky stems. The underside of the leaves has a coating of silver. Thriving in full sun with only moderate moisture, it can be grown in any soil from poor and dry to average and damp. Spring division and fall basal cuttings propagate it equally well, and leaf spot is the only nuisance.

Potentilla atrosanguinea (Ruby Cinque-foil) 12–18 in. Sun
Flowering span: Mid-June to August
Color: Reddish purple
Native habitat: Himalaya Mountains

Similar to *P. argyrophylla,* the 5-fingered foliage here is slightly larger with less silvery coating. Culture is identical. The hybrid collection includes: "Etna," deep crimson, 18 in.; "Firedance," red-centered with wide yellow borders, 15 in.; "Gibson's Scarlet," blood-red, 15 in.; "Monsieur Rouillard," copper red, double, 18 in.; and "William Rollisson," flame orange, 18 in.

Potentilla grandiflora (Sunny Cinque-foil) 6–15 in. Sun
Flowering span: Late June to mid-August
Color: Golden yellow
Native habitat: Alps Mountains

Conspicuous 1½-inch flowers on erect stems rise above a basal clump of mostly 3-parted, green leaves. Culture is the same as with *P. argyrophylla.*

Primula beesiana (Bee's Primrose) 18–24 in. Semi-shade
Flowering span: Mid-June to mid-July
Color: Rose purple
Native habitat: China

Similar to *P. japonica* by having candelabrum-type blossoming in tiers, the florets are distinguished by a noticeable golden eye and leaves that can stretch to 8 inches. Performing best in a cool, very moist, almost boggy soil—well-enriched with humus or compost—these showy perennials are best propagated by division and partitioning of the long taproots after flowering. Red spider mite is the main affliction where the soil and air are too dry. This plant benefits from a winter mulching in almost every area.

Primula bullesiana (Bulle's Primrose) 18–24 in. Semi-shade
Flowering span: Mid-June to mid-July
Color: Cream, rose, purple, mauve, deep red
Native habitat: Horticultural hybrid between *P. beesiana* and *P. bulleyana*

A rainbow-colorful addition to the primrose garden that requires the same culture as *P. beesiana.*

Primula bulleyana (Bulley's Primrose) 24–30 in. Semi-shade
Flowering span: Mid-June to August

Color: Deep yellow, reddish orange
Native habitat: China

Paper-thin leaves in a basal clump give rise to a stout stalk with from 5 to 7 tiers of heavily flowered rosettes. It, too, prefers a very moist soil at all times and should be cultivated like *P. beesiana.*

Salvia nemorosa (Violet Sage) 24–36 in. Sun
Flowering span: Late June to September
Color: Bright violet
Native habitat: Europe, western Asia

Ornamental for a long time, the 12- to 15-inch flower stalks carry rosettes of tiny blossoms on reddish stems above 2- to 3-inch, gray-green foliage. Any average soil well-drained and on the dry side suits it, but fertilizing should be low in nitrogen to produce a better flower display. Division in spring or fall, plus seeding, reproduces it easily, but white fly infestations occasionally bother the leaves. A white variety, *alba,* is only 18 inches tall.

Saponaria ocymoides (Rock Soapwort) 4–8 in. Sun
Flowering span: Early June to mid-July
Color: Deep pink
Native habitat: Alps Mountains

The wide, creeping mats of tiny, semi-evergreen foliage produce a total covering of star-shaped flowers where it has full sun and a well-drained site. Adaptable to very sandy soils, this perennial is easily propagated by seed or rootstock divisions, and there are no problems with pests or diseases. Several varieties exist: *alba,* pure white; *rubra compacta,* rich pink, dwarfed; and *splendidissima,* deep crimson. Shearing back heavily after flowering helps keep them compact-growing.

Saxifraga aizoides (Yellow Mountain Saxifrage) 2–6 in.
     Semi-shade
Flowering span: Mid-June to August
Color: Yellow

Native habitat: Canada, south to Vermont, New York, and
  Michigan

The narrow, 1-inch, untoothed leaves at ground level are
green or reddish green on this slow-creeping wildflower.
The high-branched, often solitary blossoms have wide-
spaced petals and prominent stamens. Easy to grow in
moist, average soil with good drainage, it dislikes hot, dry
summer weather. Division at almost any time is satisfactory,
but seeding is workable too. Occasionally, aphids and rust
bother it. The variety *atrorubens* has orange-red blossoms.

Saxifraga aizoon (Aizoon Saxifrage) 3–12 in. Semi-shade
Flowering span: Mid-June to August
Color: Creamy white
Native habitat: Europe, Asia, Canada

Here the rosette of toothed, basal leaves is thick and
leathery with silvery encrustations of lime, and good-sized,
open sprays of clustered flowers endure for lengthy periods.
It likes a well-drained, sandy, humusy, moist location in
light shading. Division or seed propagate it readily, and
aphids and rust are sometimes problematic. These are some
of the many varieties: *atropurpurea*, rose purple; *baldensis*,
white, 2 to 3 inches tall; *flavescens*, lemon yellow; *lutea*,
creamy yellow; *paradoxa*, white, blue leaves; *rosea*, bright
pink; and *rosularis*, white, generous-flowering.

Saxifraga cotyledon (Jungfrau Saxifrage) 6–24 in. Semi-
  shade
Flowering span: Early June to mid-July
Color: Pinkish white
Native habitat: Europe

A robust plant with long, spoon-shaped, grayish leaves, 4
inches wide, and large, airy panicles of flowers. Culture is
the same as with S. *aizoon*. Numerous side shoots easily
propagate it.

Scabiosa caucasica (Caucasian Scabious, Pincushion-flower)
  18–24 in. Sun
Flowering span: Mid-June to September

Color: Light lavender blue
Native habitat: Caucasus Mountains

The 3-inch, round flowers come on slender stems with grayish, lancelike foliage having irregular outlines. An outer circle of flat petals surrounds a raised center of prominent, protruding stamens with a pincushion effect. It thrives in full sun on a very well-drained, limed site that is consistently moist. Divide only in the spring or start from seeds. Slugs appear to be its only nuisance. Several varieties are available: "Bressingham White," white; "Clive Greaves," mauve; "Loddon Anna," light blue; and "Moerheim Blue," deep blue. Removing faded flowers extends the bloom.

Scabiosa columbaria (Dove Scabious) 18–24 in. Sun
Flowering span: Mid-June to September
Color: Bluish purple
Native habitat: Europe, Asia, Africa

Here the 1½-inch, globular flowers rest on very hairy stems and are arranged above gray-green, much-cut foliage. Average soil, not too rich, suits it best in full sun. Spring division is recommended. It appears to have no bothersome pests or diseases, and a protective winter mulch is helpful in most areas.

Scabiosa graminifolia (Grassleaf Scabious) 8–12 in. Sun
Flowering span: Mid-June to September
Color: Pale blue
Native habitat: Europe

Its silvery gray foliage is grasslike in a low mound and gives rise to stiff flower stems with dense-headed blossoming. Culture is the same as with *S. caucasica.* The variety "Pinkcushion" has lilac-pink flowering.

Sedum aizoon (Aizoon Stonecrop) 12–18 in. Sun
Flowering span: Mid-June to August
Color: Dull yellow
Native habitat: Siberia, Japan

A multitude of erect stems carry broad, 3-inch, coarsely toothed, shiny leaves and terminate in 2- to 3-inch, flat-topped clusters of starry blossoms. Most stonecrops prefer full sun but will tolerate light shading. These do best in a sandy-humus soil, well-drained, and have no problematic pests or diseases. Late summer division is preferred.

Sedum middendorffianum (Middendorf Stonecrop) 4–16 in.
    Sun
Flowering span: Late June to August
Color: Bright yellow
Native habitat: Manchuria

Here the dark green, 2-inch, needlelike leaves are arranged compactly on trailing stems that only reluctantly bloom with flat heads of ½-inch florets. Deep-rooted when established, the plant grows into a heavy clump with the same cultural needs as those for S. *aizoon.* The foliage usually changes to bronze in late fall.

Sedum pulchellum (Texas Stonecrop) 3–6 in. Semi-shade
Flowering span: Early June to mid-July
Color: Rose purple, pink, white
Native habitat: West Virginia to Georgia, west to Texas

Unusual in its liking for more shading and a moist soil, this stonecrop has sparse flowering appearing (when it does) as 3- to 4-inch, branched heads of long, graceful sprays underlaid with a leafy bract. The unpaired, 1-inch leaves are on trailing stems that easily root to form a wide mat and become red, brown, and purple in the autumn. Division is the easiest propagation method, and there are no especially troublesome pests or diseases.

Sedum rosea (Roseroot Stonecrop) 4–8 in. Sun
Flowering span: Mid-June to August
Color: Reddish purple
Native habitat: Arctic regions

Terminal, dense clusters of upright blossoms appear above a crowded collection of 2-inch, gray green, linear leaves arranged circularly on a thick stem. The stems and rootstock have the surprising fragrance of rosewater when cut or bruised. Its culture is identical with that for S. *aizoon.*

Sedum sexangulare (Hexagon Stonecrop) 2–4 in. Sun
Flowering span: Early June to July
Color: Bright yellow
Native habitat: Europe

Resembling S. *acre* when flowering, the dense foliage of this species is crisply spiral with minute, 6-ranked, bronze-green leaves. Useful as a compact groundcover, its simple needs are the same as S. *aizoon.*

Sedum telephoides (Allegany Stonecrop) 6–10 in. Sun
Flowering span: Early June to July
Color: Flesh pink
Native habitat: Southern Pennsylvania to North Carolina

Here the 2-inch leaves are paired, thick, and smooth-edged. The pyramidal flower heads are 2 inches across and occasionally blossom yellowish. Care is the same as for S. *aizoon.*

Sempervivum (Houseleek, Hen-and-chickens) 1–24 in.
    Sun
Flowering span: Mid-June to August
Color: Purplish rose, pink, greenish yellow, yellow, various
    hybrid blends
Native habitat: Mountains of Europe and northern Africa

The name translates to "live forever," and this close relative of *Sedum* seems to do just that. Practically indestructible when provided with full sun and excellent drainage, the typically compact rosettes of fleshy leaves multiply easily in any light soil from offsets that appear (like baby chicks) from beneath the bottom leaves of the larger parent. Star-shaped flowers appear in disproportionately large clusters atop heavy stalks rising from the center of the leaf whorl. The blossoming rosette then slowly dies and is soon replaced by a younger neighbor.

Houseleeks readily form solid mats of evergreen foliage, and while they require no fertilizing to perform well, they appreciate a light mulching of moist peat moss or compost annually in the heat of summer. Highly tolerant of a thin soil layer and the driest conditions, they suffer only from oc-

Thriving on scanty soil, *Sempervivum* enjoys the crevices of rocky plant walls.

casional crown rot or foliage rust. Separation of the shallow-rooted offsets can be made at any time, and seeding works well for propagation, too. Self-seeding is practically assured.

The hundreds of available species and hybrids are completely muddled botanically at this time and pin-pointing specific recommendations seems futile. Offered widely by nurseries and specialist growers (where mail ordering brings no greater assurance of correct identities), these plants are perhaps best selected by eye appeal for their colorful foliage, which ranges from red, pink, purple, blue, brown, gray, and green into every blending imaginable. The rosette spread can be from ¼ inch to 12 inches, and all types hardy for an area intermingle satisfactorily. If any one type can be touted, *S. arachnoideum* (Spiderweb Houseleek) is the winner with bright pink flowering and silver strands of webbing covering the entire rosette of leaves. It is commonly available and unmistakable in appearance.

Shortia galacifolia (Oconee-bells) 4–8 in.   Shade
Flowering span: Early June to July

Color: White
Native habitat: Mountains of North and South Carolina

Attractive in all seasons for its glossy, evergreen foliage, this choice wildflower produces solitary, 1-inch, heavily fringed blossoms on 6- to 8-inch stems above round, scallop-edged, 3-inch leaves that turn bronze red in fall if sun reaches the clump. Adaptable to shaded woodlots favoring azaleas and rhododendrons, it can develop into large mats where the soil is acid, moist, well-drained, humusy, and cool. Spring division of the creeping rootstock is recommended since seed requires years of patience to produce flowering plants. Pests and diseases are uncommon.

Shortia uniflora (Nippon-bells) 4–8 in. Shade
Flowering span: Early June to July
Color: Shell pink, white
Native habitat: Japan

Similar in appearance to S. *galacifolia,* this oriental cousin is not so easily cultivated and seems to prefer more moisture and coolness to succeed. The fringed blossoms are usually 1½ inches wide above heart-shaped, evergreen leaves turning red in the fall. The variety *grandiflora* has showy flowers almost 2 inches wide.

Sidalcea candida (White Checkermallow) 24–36 in. Sun
Flowering span: Early June to mid-July
Color: White
Native habitat: Southern Wyoming to Colorado, Utah, and
    Nevada

The 3-inch, heart-shaped leaves are deeply divided and appear widely spaced with palm-shaped leaves on the same plant. Blossoms are 1 inch and heavily clustered up lengthy spikes. Removing the faded flowering extends the bloom appreciably. They do well in any moist, well-drained average-fertility soil in full sun, and can be easily propagated by division in spring or fall or by seed. Pests and diseases are not commonly troublesome.

Sidalcea hybrida (Hybrid Prairie Mallow, Miniature
    Hollyhock) 18–48 in. Sun
Flowering span: Mid-June to August
Color: Crimson to pale pink
Native habitat: Horticultural hybrid

The improved colorings and increased branching from hybridization contribute a long-lasting, showy perennial addition for the garden border. The sturdy, hollyhock-like spikes
are crowded with 1- to 2-inch bowl-shaped blossoms above
large, finger-cut leaves. Removing the old flowering extends
the flowering and promotes new basal growth for over-win-
tering successfully. Not fussy about soil, it thrives in full sun
with reasonable moisture on a well-drained site, and is unbothered by diseases or pests of consequence. The named
hybrid list is extensive: "Croftway Red," deep pink, 36 in.;
"Elsie Heugh," light pink, 48 in.; "Loveliness," shell pink,
30 in.; "Reverend Page Roberts," light pink, 48 in.; "Rose
Queen," rose, 48 in.; "Wensleydale," rosy red, 48 in.; and

Resembling a miniature hollyhock, *Sidalcea* "Elsie Heugh"
blooms continuously until fall.

"William Smith," salmon pink, 36 in. Reproduce them by division or seeding.

Silene aucalis (Moss Campion) 1–2 in. Sun
Flowering span: Mid-June to August
Color: Reddish purple
Native habitat: Europe

Reluctant to bloom profusely in cultivation, this mosslike creeper has miniature, pointed, green leaves tightly. packed along the short stems and solitary, ½-inch flowers. Providing a gravelly, well-drained, lean soil in full sun helps it thrive and may encourage solid flowering. Propagate only by division or stem cuttings carried over in pots for at least a year. Nothing troubles it except sparse blooming.

Silene maritima (Sea Silene) 8–16 in. Sun
Flowering span: Mid-June to August
Color: White
Native habitat: Europe, northern Africa

A rambling, weak-stemmed perennial useful in sunny rock gardens and woodlot borders, this long-blooming plant has small, fleshy, gray green leaves and 1½-inch blossoms with cleft petals that end in noticeably bulbous inflations. Tolerant of dryness and a low-fertility soil, it remains more compact if given these growing conditions. Propagate by cuttings. Pests and diseases are uncommon. The double-flowered form, *flore-pleno,* is noticeably superior with 3-inch-wide blossoms.

Silene schafta (Schafta Silene) 3–6 in. Sun
Flowering span: Mid-June to October
Color: Bright rose pink
Native habitat: Caucasus Mountains

Dependable and simple to grow well, this compact species has light green, narrow, hairy leaves arranged in rosettes along with a profusion of pinwheel-like flowers with notched ends. It thrives in any sandy loam in either full sun or light shading and is readily propagated by seed, division or cuttings. There are no pests or diseases worth mentioning.

Silene virginica (Firepink Silene) 12–24 in. Semi-shade
Flowering span: Early June to August
Color: Bright crimson
Native habitat: Western New York to Minnesota, south to Oklahoma and Georgia

Vividly showy in light shading to full sun, the 1-inch, 5-parted flowers are arranged in loose clusters on sticky, branched stems above a persistent, basal collection of smooth, dark green leaves often up to 12 inches long. It does best in a moist, sandy, humusy soil and can be propagated by root cuttings, spring division, or seed. Pests and diseases are not usual.

Stachys macrantha (grandiflora) (Big Betony) 12–24 in. Sun
Flowering span: Mid-June to August
Color: Deep violet
Native habitat: Caucasus Mountains

Durable and sturdy, this perennial has whorls of closely set flowers on erect spikes much like its cousin mint, and thick, wrinkled, hairy, oval leaves. It likes full sun in any average-fertility soil with good drainage and can be divided or propagated by seed readily. It has no pests or diseases. The variety *robusta* has rosy pink flowers and a height of 18 to 24 inches, while *superba* is somewhere between mauve and purple-violet.

Stachys olympica (lanata) (Woolly Betony, Lamb's-ear) 12–18 in. Sun
Flowering span: Mid-June to August
Color: Purplish pink
Native habitat: Caucasus Mountains, Iran

Welcomed for its thick, silvery foliage, this perennial has noneffective blossoming perhaps best cut off as it appears. The elliptical, gray-white leaves are heavily tomentose like felt and make a display of themselves. It enjoys full sun in any well-drained, average soil but will tolerate light shading satisfactorily. Spring division or seed propagate it well, and there are no likely nuisances from insects or diseases. The hybrid "Silver Carpet" is nonflowering and quickly makes a dense groundcover.

Thermopsis caroliniana (Carolina Thermopsis) 36–48 in.
    Sun
Flowering span: Mid-June to mid-July
Color: Bright yellow
Native habitat: Mountains of North Carolina

Slender spikes with closely packed, conspicuous, pea-shaped florets rise well above the 3-parted, cloverlike foliage of this wildflower. It works well in open woodlots having fertile, well-drained loam in sun to light shading and is best reproduced from new seed. Nothing bothers it.

Thymus serphyllum (Mother-of-thyme) 3–4 in. Sun
Flowering span: Mid-June to August

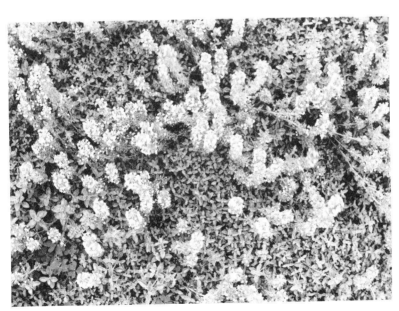

Aromatic *Thymus serphyllum* easily forms a groundcover mat in full sun.

Color: Reddish purple, lilac
Native habitat: Europe, British Isles, Asia, northern Africa

Familiar to most for the dense, aromatic foliage, these matlike creepers are truly at home in full sun with dry, niggardly soil. Division is the best propagation method, and little affects them from insects or diseases. There are several varieties: *argenteus,* with silver-streaked leaves; *aurens,* with golden leaves; *citrodorous,* with green, lemon-scented leaves; and *languinosus,* with downy, gray leaves.

Trollius ledebouri (Ledebour Globeflower) 18–24 in.
    Semi-shade
Flowering span: Mid-June to mid-July
Color: Deep orange
Native habitat: China, Siberia

Similar in appearance to other cultivated types, this species has larger, 2- to 2½-inch blossoms, which extend the blooming season. Its cultural needs are the same as those for the May species, *T. asiaticus.* The hybrid "Golden Queen" has bright orange coloring.

Tunica saxifraga (Saxifrage Tunicflower) 6–10 in. Sun
Flowering span: Late June to September
Color: Rosy white, pale purple, lilac
Native habitat: Southern Europe, Asia

The minute, dark green, grassy foliage produces a full carpet of wispy flowering on wiry stems through most of the summer. Useful for rock garden layouts, this perennial has ½-inch, *dianthus*-like blossoms. Preferring a well-drained, average soil in full sun, it is a prolific self-seeder in the single form. The preferred, double-flowered types are best reproduced by cuttings made close to the deep taproot. Pests and diseases are unknown. The variety *alba* has white blossoms but is readily superseded by *albo-plena* with double, carnationlike flowers. There is also a double pink type called *flore-pleno.*

Valeriana officinalis (Common Valerian, Garden
    Heliotrope) 24–48 in. Sun

Stately and profuse, *Valeriana officinalis* has perfumed generations of garden plots.

Flowering span: Late June to August
Color: Pink, lavender, white
Native habitat: Europe, Asia

These roots have been used in the manufacture of perfumes for ages, and the delightfully scented blossoms in the garden border or on the edges of a sunny woodlot have their own appeal. Its dense heads of tiny blossoms smell like heliotrope and appear terminally and axially on hollow-stemmed stalks with ferny foliage. Best in a very moist, well-drained, average soil, it can readily be divided or started from seed. Black aphid is the worst pest, but diseases are uncommon.

Verbascum hybrida (Hybrid Mullein) 36–48 in. Sun
Flowering span: Late June to September
Color: White, yellow, pink, lavender
Native habitat: Horticultural hybrid

The bold flower stalks carry 1-inch, saucer-shaped florets, often with color-contrasted centers, above a flat-laying rosette of very hairy, gray-green leaves. It needs a very well-drained soil of moderate fertility in full sun to do its best. Taking root cuttings in early spring is the only workable propagation method for specific colorings; seed is highly variable for true reproduction. Pests and diseases are of little concern. A partial list of hybrid colorings includes: "C. L. Adams," deep yellow; "Cotswold Gem," pale yellow with a purple center; "Cotswold Queen," apricot; "Gainsborough," canary yellow; "Mont Blanc," white; and "Pink Domino," rosy pink with a purple center.

Veronica incana (Woolly Speedwell) 12–24 in. Sun
Flowering span: Mid-June to August
Color: Lavender blue
Native habitat: Southern Europe, northern Asia

The 2- to 3-inch silvery, lance-shaped foliage is highly attractive even out of flower, while the 6-inch spikes of small florets contribute showy color worth displaying in garden borders. Requiring a well-drained, fertile soil in full sun to light shading, it is easily reproduced by division in spring or fall. Insects and diseases are rarely prevalent. The varietal listing includes: *candidissima*, pale blue; *glauca*, deep blue; *rosea*, pink; and "Saraband," deep violet.

Veronica prostrata (rupestris) (Harebell Speedwell) 6–8 in.
    Sun
Flowering span: Early June to July
Color: Bright blue
Native habitat: Europe, northern Asia

Sometimes invasive, the creeping foliage mat offers a brilliant but brief color display of erect flower stalks above ½-inch, dark green foliage. It needs the same culture as *V. incana*. A pale blue hybrid, "Spode Blue," is sometimes available. This plant is occasionally listed as *V. latifolia prostrata*.

Veronica spicata (Spike Speedwell) 12–24 in. Sun
Flowering span: Mid-June to August
Color: Bright blue
Native habitat: Europe, British Isles

Vividly sparkling, the slender spikes of *Veronica spicata* create choice accents.

Here the vivid flowers appear on many densely crowded spikes above 1½-inch narrow, toothed, green foliage. Culture is the same as for *V. incana*. Several pink hybrids exist: "Barcarolle," deep pink; "Minuet," soft pink; and "Pavane," rose pink.

JULY

*A General Guide to the Color Values
Available in July*

(Each division includes shades, tints, and tones of the dominant value.)

WHITE: Achillea millefolium, Althaea rosea, Anthericum ramosum, Boltonia latisquama *hybrids*, Calluna vulgaris *hybrids*, Campanula garganica, Campanula lactiflora, Cardiocrinum giganteum, Cephalaria tatarica, Chelone glabra, Cimicifuga racemosa, Coreopsis rosea, Delphinium carolinianum, Echinacea purpurea *hybrids*, Eryngium aquaticum, Eupatorium perfoliatum, Eupatorium rugosum, Euphorbia corollata, Filipendula camtschatica, Galtonia candicans, Gaultheria procumbens, Gentiana asclepiadea alba, Gypsophila acutifolia, Gypsophila paniculata, Iris kaempferi, Lilium *hybrids*, Lilium auratum, Lilium regale, Lobelia cardinalis alba, Lysimachia clethroides, Macleaya cordata, Malva moschata alba, Mentha, Phlox paniculata *hybrids*, Physalis franchetii, Physostegia virginiana *hybrids*, Salvia farinacea alba, Sedum album, Sedum hispanicum, Veronica longifolia alba, Yucca filamentosa, Yucca flaccida

YELLOW: Aconitum lycoctonum, Allium flavum, Althaea rosea, Arnica montana, Cassia marilandica, Centaurea macrocephala, Centaurea ruthenica, Coreopsis pubescens, Coreopsis verticillata, Erigeron aureus, Gentiana lutea, Helianthus decapetalus, Heliopsis helianthoides, Heliopsis scabra, Hemerocallis citrina, Hemerocallis hybrida, Hibiscus moscheutos, Inula ensifolia, Inula hookeri, Inula orientalis, Lilium *hybrids*, Lilium auratum wittei, Lilium pardilinum giganteum, Rudbeckia fulgida, Rudbeckia laciniata, Ruta graveolens, Sedum kamtschaticum, Sedum reflexum, Senecio cineraria, Senecio clivorum, Senecio przewalski, Solidago hybrida, Solidaster luteus, Thalictrum speciosissimum

ORANGE: Asclepias tuberosa, Belamcanda chinensis, Delphinium cardinale, Erigeron aurantiacus, Heliopsis scabra *hybrids*, Hemerocallis fulva, Hemerocallis hybrida, Lilium *hybrids*, Lilium pardilinum

RED: Achillea millefolium *hybrids*, Althaea rosea, Calluna vulgaris *hybrids*, Delphinium cardinale, Echinacea purpurea, Hemerocallis hybrida, Hibiscus palustris *hybrids*, Iris kaempferi *hybrids*, Lilium *hybrids*, Lilium bulbiferum, Lilium chalcedonicum, Lilium philadelphicum, Lilium superbum, Lilium tigrinum, Lobelia cardinalis, Lythrum salicaria *hybrids*, Phlox paniculata *hybrids*, Potentilla nepalensis *hybrids*, Sedum spurium coccineum, Stachys coccinea

PINK: Allium cernuum, Althaea rosea, Aster linarifolius, Bletilla striata, Calluna vulgaris, Coreopsis rosea, Dianthus superbus, Echinacea angustifolia, Erigeron hybrida, Hemerocallis hybrida, Hibiscus palustris, Iris kaempferi, Lathyrus latifolius, Lilium *hybrids*, Lythrum salicaria *hybrids*, Macleaya cordata, Malva moschata, Mentha, Phlox paniculata *hybrids*, Physostegia virginiana, Potentilla nepalensis, Sedum hispanicum, Sedum spurium

PURPLE: Aconitum commarum, Allium aflatunense, Allium giganteum, Allium pulchellum, Allium rosenbachianum, Allium sphaerocephalum, Althaea rosea, Anemonopsis macrophylla, Astilbe chinensis, Boltonia latisquama, Calluna vulgaris *varieties*, Campanula rapunculoides, Coreopsis rosea, Dianthus superbus, Echinacea purpurea *hybrids*, Erigeron hybrida, Hemerocallis hybrida, Hosta crispula, Hosta fortunei, Hosta sieboldiana, Hosta undulata, Iris kaempferi, Lathrus latifolius, Lavandula officinalis *hybrids*, Liatris spicata, Limonium latifolium *hybrids*, Liriope spicata, Lycoris squamigera, Lythrum salicaria, Lythrum vigatum, Mentha, Phlox paniculata *hybrids*, Salvia haematodes, Teucrium chamaedrys, Thalictrum rocquebrunianum

BLUE: Aconitum autumnale, Aconitum commarum, Aconitum napellus, Amorpha canescens, Aster frikarti, Campanula lactiflora, Campanula sarmatica, Delphinium carolinianum, Echinops ritro, Echinops spaerocephalum, Eryngium alpinum, Eryngium amethystinum, Ga-

lega officinalis, Gentiana asclepiadea, Gentiana lagodechiana, Gentiana septemfida, Hosta caerulea, Iris
kaempferi, Lavandula officinalis, Limonium latifolium,
Veronica longifolia

BICOLOR: Aconitum napellus *hybrids*, Echinacea purpurea
hybrids, Hemerocallis hybrida, Hibiscus moscheutos,
Iris kaempferi *hybrids*, Lilium *hybrids*, Lilium auratum,
Lilium superbum, Phlox paniculata *hybrids*

Achillea millefolium (Common Yarrow) 12–36 in. Sun
Flowering span: Early July to September
Color: Off white, occasionally reddish
Native habitat: Europe, British Isles, Asia, North America

Generally considered an invasive weed without garden
appeal, the delicately cut, ferny lancelike leaves of the
parent plant are topped by densely packed, flat clusters of
flowers. Any ordinary, well-drained soil that is very sunny
and moderately dry suits it best. Division is the simplest
propagation method, but summer stem cuttings work well
too. Mildew and stem rot are occasionally problematic in
humid, overcast weather. The horticultural hybrids are far
superior: "Cerise Queen," bright cerise, 18 in.; "Crimson
Beauty," bright red, 18 in.; "Fire King," deep red, silvery
foliage, 18 in.; and the variety *roseum*, soft rosy pink, 18 to
24 in.

Aconitum autumnale (*henryi*) (Autumn Monkshood) 48–60
    in. Semi-shade
Flowering span: Late July to September
Color: Deep blue
Native habitat: Northern China

Attractive for a long time by flower or foliage, the dark
green, glossy leaves are deeply cut into 5 fingerings with
neatly serrated edges. Its closed, helmetlike, 1-inch florets
appear terminally in clusters on open-branched stems and
are useful for border backgrounds or the edges of woods
with light shading. Except for the flowers, all parts of any

monkshood—roots, leaves, and seeds—are highly poisonous if eaten or if their juices enter an open wound. Thriving best in a rich, moist, humusy soil, they resent moving but can be propagated in late fall or early spring by careful division of the tuberous, turniplike roots or by fully matured seeds. Crown rot, verticillium wilt, and mildew are often serious afflictions, but insects are chary with the plant, perhaps with cause.

Aconitum commarum (exaltatum) (Hungarian Monkshood)
    36–48 in. Semi-shade
Flowering span: Mid-July to mid-August
Color: Purple, blue
Native habitat: Hungary

The leaves of this species have short, blunt lobes, while the closed, hemispherical florets are arranged loosely on the branched stems. Its culture is identical with that for *A. autumnale.* The variety *sparkianum* grows 60 to 72 inches and carries deep violet-blue flowering.

Aconitum lycoctonum (Wolfbane Monkshood) 36–48 in.
    Semi-shade
Flowering span: Early July to September
Color: Creamy yellow
Native habitat: Europe, northern Asia

Here the plant has slender stems and deeply cut leaves with 5 to 9 lobes. Its flowers are conelike and have a pinched appearance on elongated petioles. Care for it is the same as for *A. autumnale.*

Aconitum napellus (Aconite Monkshood) 36–48 in. Semi-
    shade
Flowering span: Early July to September
Color: Deep purple-blue
Native habitat: Europe, Asia

Ornamentally popular, but also the most poisonous of the group, this species offers deeply cut leaves with lobes further divided into fine, lacy segments. The helmet flowers have a beaklike visor and come on sturdy, erect stems. Cultivate it the same as for *A. autumnale*. Aside from the almost white variety, *album*, several hybrids are available: "Bicolor," white with blue edges, 42 in.; "Blue Sceptre," blue and white, 24 in.; "Bressingham Spire," violet-blue, 36 in.; and "Newry Blue," deep blue, 48 in.

Allium aflatunense 36–48 in. Sun
Flowering span: Early July to August
Color: Lilac purple
Native habitat: Central China

The star-shaped florets appear in large, globular heads above wide, gray green, straplike leaves. The bulb is about 2½ inches wide and should be cultivated similar to the June-blooming *A. albopilosum*.

Allium cernuum (Nodding Onion) 12–18 in. Sun
Flowering span: Early July to August
Color: Deep rose, occasionally white
Native habitat: Southeastern Canada to Georgia, west to Arizona

The open-headed, semi-rounded flower clusters have ¼-inch florets on long peduncles and narrow, linear clumps of foliage. The flower becomes pendulous from a bend in the stalk just below the blossom. This is an easily adaptable, hardy bulb and requires the simple care given *A. albopilosum*. The closely related species *stellatum* from the midwestern United States has completely erect stems and pinkish flowers.

Allium flavum (Yellow Onion) 12–15 in. Sun
Flowering span: Mid-July to mid-August
Color: Bright yellow
Native habitat: Southern Europe, Turkey

Loose, 2-inch-wide heads of showy, bell-shaped, drooping florets appear on upright but variable stems above grasslike foliage here, and culture of the bulb is the same as with *A. albopilosum*.

Allium giganteum (Giant Onion) 36–48 in. Sun
Flowering span: Early July to August
Color: Violet
Native habitat: Central Asia

Probably the tallest-flowering of the group, the 3- to 4-inch-wide, ground-hugging leaves produce tubular stalks with solitary, 4-inch heads of star-shaped florets. Again, it is cared for like the June-flowering *A. albopilosum.*

Allium pulchellum 12–24 in. Sun
Flowering span: Mid-July to mid-August
Color: Reddish violet
Native habitat: Southern Europe

A narrow set of leaves produces erect stems with loose flower heads having pendulous, tiny florets. Culture is identical with that for *A. albopilosum.* Occasionally this bulb is sold as *A. flavum pumilum roseum.*

Allium rosenbachianum (Rosenbach Onion) 24–36 in. Sun
Flowering span: Mid-July to mid-August

All the *Allium*s attract showy visitors.

Color: Purplish violet
Native habitat: Central Asia

Similar in leaf appearance to *A. aflatunense,* the stout flower stalk carries decorative, 4- to 5-inch, round blossom heads. Its needs are the same as for *A. albopilosum.*

Allium sphaerocephalum (Ballhead Onion)   12–24 in.   Sun
Flowering span: Early July to August
Color: Reddish purple
Native habitat: Europe, Asia

Here the flowers appear generously in dense, egg-shaped heads with slender, tubular and sparse foliage. Cultivate it the same as *A. albopilosum.*

Althaea rosea (Hollyhock) 60–100 in.   Sun
Flowering span: Early July to September
Color: White, pink, red, lavender, yellow
Native habitat: China

Cultivated in Europe with appreciation since the sixteenth century, the 3- to 5-inch, showy blossoms appear on 4 to 6 erect, stout stems of each plant. Flowering begins at the bottom with an ascending 18 to 24 inches of the stalk covered in bloom for a long period. The basal, 6- to 8-inch leaves are coarse, hairy, and prone to serious disfigurement from rust and leaf spot diseases; Japanese beetles relish the large, crepe-paper blossoms. They do best in full sunlight in a moist, well-drained, average-fertility soil on a site with good air circulation. Seed is the best propagation method, followed by fall planting of the seedlings in permanent locations. Although not long-lived individually, self-seeding usually reproduces them well. Several hybrid improvements are available: "Begonia-flowered" with pastel, fringed, single blossoms; "Charter's Double," mostly double-flowered; and "Powder Puffs," a fully double and impressive strain in novel colorings.

Amorpha canescens (Leadplant Amorpha) 12–36 in.   Sun
Flowering span: Early July to August

Color: Deep blue
Native habitat: Michigan to New Mexico

Adaptable to dry conditions in full sun, the plant is more a compact shrub than a true herbaceous perennial. It has pinnately compound leaves made up of nearly 30, ½-inch leaflets. All parts of the plant are covered with fine, white hairs, and the flower spike has 1-petaled blossoms. Provide a well-drained, average soil and propagate by seed or by summer stem cuttings. Pests and diseases are unknown.

Anemonopsis macrophylla 24–36 in. Semi-shade
Flowering span: Late July to September
Color: Light purple
Native habitat: Japan

The large, multiple-compounded leaves resemble those of the April-blooming *Actaea*, but here the nodding, half-open, 1½-inch flowers come on loose branching resembling the Japanese anemone. Hardy in most locations, it likes a deep, rich, well-drained soil in semi-shading. Spring division or seed propagate it well, and nothing appears to bother it seriously.

Anthericum ramosum (Branching Anthericum) 18–24 in.
    Sun
Flowering span: Early July to August
Color: White
Native habitat: Europe

Very similar to the *A. liliago* of May, these flowers are smaller and appear on branched stems. Culture for both is identical.

Arnica montana (Mountain Arnica, Mountain Tobacco)
    8–12 in. Sun
Flowering span: Mid-July to mid-August
Color: Orange yellow
Native habitat: Europe

Daisylike, 2-inch flowers appear singly or paired on erect stems from a basal clump of broad, oval leaves. Easily grown in any moist, well-drained, average soil in sun to semi-shade, the deep rootstock of established plants resists division or transplanting and it is best propagated by separating young plants or from seed. It has no diseases or pests of concern.

Asclepias tuberosa (Butterfly Milkweed) 24–36 in.   Sun
Flowering span: Early July to mid-August
Color: Bright orange
Native habitat: New Hampshire to Florida, west to Colorado

Strikingly colorful, the 2-inch clusters of tiny, waxy flowers stand erect on branched stems and offer fragrant nectar to a host of flying insects, especially butterflies. The long, pointed, rough-hairy leaves are a bright green, and the slender seed pods turn a rich mahogany in the autumn. It grows best in a well-drained, acid, sandy soil with full sun and can take drought well because of its deep tap roots. Spring growth is slow to appear and planting locations should be well marked to avoid ripping out the dormant

Fascinating to butterflies, the rich coloring of *Asclepias tuberosa* perks up sunny borders.

roots inadvertently. Propagate by division only since seeds are reluctant to germinate well. There are no pests or diseases.

Aster frikarti   24–30 in.   Sun
Flowering span: Early July to October
Color: Lavender blue
Native habitat: Horticultural hybrid between *A. amellus* and *A. thomsoni*

Long in bloom, the 2½-inch, daisylike flowers have a bright yellow center above oblong, dark green, roughened leaves. It does well in full sun with any well-drained, average-fertility soil and can be readily spring-divided for reproduction. Insects are uncommon but mildew may be a nuisance in humid weather.

Aster linarifolius (Savoryleaf Aster, Bristle Aster)   6–20 in. Sun
Flowering span: Mid-July to September
Color: Lavender pink
Native habitat: Maine to Florida, west to Texas and Wisconsin

The needlelike, dark green leaves are not only stiff but roughened and surround erect, many-branched flowering stems with long-enduring ¾-inch florets of daisylike blossoms with deep yellow centers. Growing compactly neat in any light, well-drained, dry soil, it is readily reproduced by spring division. Pests and diseases are minor.

Astilbe chinensis (Chinese Astilbe)   18–24 in.   Semi-shade
Flowering span: Late July to September
Color: Deep pinkish purple
Native habitat: China

The narrow, compound leaves of this species have hairy leaflets 2 to 3 inches long and tiny flowers in small, erect plumes. Best in semi-shaded locations that are constantly moist and cool, it thrives in any ordinary, well-drained soil. Division in spring or late fall propagates it most easily, and there are no troublesome diseases or pests. The dwarf vari-

Annual geraniums surround the spiked flowering from *Astilbe chinensis pumila.*

ety *pumila* is 10 inches tall and noticeably different by carrying stiff spikes of raspberry-colored flowering above a flat foliage mat of much-divided leaves. It blooms in mid-August.

Belamcanda chinensis (Pardanthus chinensis) (Blackberry
    Lily) 30–36 in. Sun
Flowering span: Late July to September
Color: Orange, spotted red
Native habitat: China, Japan

Although the 2-inch, star-shaped flowers last individually only a day, they appear from large, slender, branched clusters of buds. Its irislike, lanceolate foliage is 12 to 18 inches long in basal clumps, and the ripening pods open to reveal glossy black seeds resembling blackberry fruit that are attractive if dried for indoor use. They like a rich, moist, sandy soil in full sun to light shade, and the fleshy rootstock can be divided in spring or fall. Seed is slower but works satisfactorily. Pests and diseases are rare, but mulch where winters are severe to prevent heaving.

Bletilla striata (hyacinthina) (Terrestial Orchid) 10–15 in. Semi-shade
Flowering span: Early July to mid-August
Color: Carmine pink
Native habitat: China, Japan

While only moderately hardy in cold areas even with winter mulching, these unusual summer flowers can be worth a growing attempt. The broad, glossy, gladioluslike leaves stretch 10 to 12 inches and are noticeably ribbed. A slender flower stalk carries between 6 to 10 tiny, Cattleya-type orchid blossoms when grown in semi- to light shading. Provide a well-drained, constantly moist, peat-sandy soil for the pseudobulbs and make the initial installation in either autumn or early spring. Divide crowded colonies after flowering. They are less bothered by pests and diseases than full winter hardiness.

Boltonia latisquama (Violet Boltonia) 42–48 in. Sun
Flowering span: Late July to October
Color: Blue violet
Native habitat: Missouri, Arkansas, Kansas

Profuse, long-lasting flowering accents this perennial's usefulness in borders or at the edges of sunny woodlots. The daisylike, 1-inch blossoms have a yellow center and appear on erect but willowy, much-branched stalks with 2- to 3-inch, gray green, narrow foliage. Adaptable to almost any soil in full sunlight or light shading, they are easily propagated by spring division and have no bothersome diseases or insect pests. The dwarf variety *nana*, has pinkish lavender flowers and is 30 to 36 inches tall; a hybrid, "Snowbank," has white blossoms and a 48-inch height.

Calluna vulgaris (Scotch Heather) 6–36 in. Sun
Flowering span: Mid-July to October
Color: Rosy pink
Native habitat: Europe, Asia Minor

Outstandingly adaptive to drought and seashore conditions, these shrubby, evergreen, groundcover plants provide an ongoing flower display and wintertime foliage colorings

Remarkably adaptable to infertile, sunny sites, *Calluna vulgaris* carries months of blossoming.

few other plantings can match. The tiny, ⅛-inch, scalelike leaves clasp tightly the slender stems for an almost squarish appearance, and the long, thin, terminal spikes of blueberry-like florets remain colorful and natural-looking when dried. Best in a sandy, peaty, well-drained, acid soil low in fertility, they can be spring-pruned to keep them neat and compact since flowering comes from new wood. Covering with evergreen boughs in winter prevents foliage discoloration on exposed sites, yet the plants themselves are hardy without protection. Spring division, late summer cuttings, and stem layerings all work conveniently for reproduction. Supply generous watering to all new plantings until established. A fungus in hot, humid weather occasionally browns the tips, but insects are no bother.

The list of natural varieties and hybrids is impressive: *alba*, white, 24 in.; *alba erecta*, white, 18 in.; *alba minor*, white, 12 in.; *alba plena*, white, double, 12 in.; *alporti*, deep crimson, 24 in.; *aurea*, gold foliage, 12 in.; "Camala," soft rose, double, 18 in.; "County Wicklow," soft pink, double, 12 in.; *crispa*, white, 18 in.; *cuprea*, gold foliage, lavender;

hammondi, white, 30 in.; *hammondi aurea,* gold foliage, white, 24 in.; "H. E. Beale," silvery pink, double, 24 in.; "J. H. Hamilton," clear pink, double, 10 in.; *kupholdi,* deep lavender, 6 in.; *minima,* bright purple, 6 in.; "Peter Sparkes," pale purple-pink, double, 24 in.; *plena,* purple, double, 18 in.; *plena multiplex,* pink, double, 18 in.; *pygmaea,* purple, 3 in.; *rigida,* white, 10 in., the only foliage not turning bronze with fall frost; *rosea,* rosy lavender, 18 in.; *rubra,* dark red-purple, 30 in.; "Sister Anne," lavender, 6 in.; "Tib," deep red-purple, double 30 in.; and *tomentosa,* bright purple, 30 in.

Campanula lactiflora (Milky Bellflower) 30–60 in. Sun
Flowering span: Mid-July to mid-August
Color: Off white, pale blue
Native habitat: Caucasus Mountains

The 1½-inch florets come massed in large, terminal clusters above narrow, sharp-toothed, robust foliage. Doing best with full sun in a deep, fertile, constantly moist soil, it will also grow well in light shading. Spring division of the thick, fleshy rootstock or spring stem cuttings reproduce it easily, and it appears unbothered by serious pests or diseases. The variety *alba* has pure white blossoms; *coerulea,* light blue; and the hybrid "Loddon Anna," pinkish white bloom.

Campanula rapunculoides (Creeping Bellflower) 24–48 in.
    Semi-shade
Flowering span: Early July to September
Color: Bright blue violet
Native habitat: Europe, Siberia, Newfoundland to Maryland, west to Missouri

Apt to become weedy unless controlled, the creeping rootstock and self-seeding of this sturdy perennial can crowd out choicer material quickly. The 1-inch, funnel-shaped, pendulous florets appear generally on only one side of the unbranched, slender stems with broad-based, lanceolate leaves. Thriving in any rich, moist, well-drained soil, it willingly adapts to almost any other growing conditions from full sun to shade. Division, seed, or stem cuttings propagate it perhaps all too readily. Pests and diseases are uncommon.

Campanula sarmatica (Sarmatian Bellflower) 12–24 in. Sun

Flowering span: Early July to September
Color: Light blue
Native habitat: Caucasus Mountains

Unusual for both its velvety, nodding flowers and the leathery, wrinkled, gray foliage, this species grows readily in any well-drained, rich soil and is best reproduced by seed. It has no troublesome diseases or pests.

Cardiocrinum giganteum (*Lilium giganteum*) (Giant Himalaya Lily) 48–100 in. Semi-shade

Flowering span: Early July to August
Color: Glistening white
Native habitat: Himalaya Mountains of Nepal and northeast Burma

Imposing in leaf or in flower, this close relative of the lily has 18-inch, heart-shaped leaves on very sturdy, erect stems and generous clusters of fragrant, 6-inch, trumpet-shaped flowers with a reddish base in a pendulous arrangement. Lime-tolerant, it prefers a damp, well-drained, light soil in dappled to semi-shading coupled with generous feeding and a thick, humusy mulch at all times. In severe climates, protect with a heavy winter covering. The initial bulb can be from 3 to 6 inches wide and up to 8 inches tall, but since it dies after flowering, only offsets or scales (which are very few) keep it propagated. Seed is tediously slow, taking perhaps 8 years to flower. New plantings require a full year to adjust before making much growth, but there appears to be no problem with diseases or pests. The scarce variety *yunnanense* has slightly greenish, smaller flowering and blooms from the top down.

Cassia marilandica (Wild Senna) 36–60 in. Sun
Flowering span: Late July to September
Color: Bright yellow

Native habitat: Massachusetts to North Carolina, west to Tennessee and Wisconsin

This tall wildflower has 6- to 10-inch pinnately compound leaves with individual segments up to 3 inches long and clusters of leaf axil blossoms showing rich, brown anthers. Suitable for wild areas and the rear of large flower borders, it is hardy and adaptable for almost any soil in sun to light shading. Seed or division propagate it easily, and there are no difficulties with pests or diseases.

Centaurea macrocephala (Globe Centaurea)   36–48 in.   Sun
Flowering span: Mid-July to September
Color: Bright yellow
Native habitat: Armenia

The bold, 3-inch, round, thistlelike blossoms are long-lasting and appear above broad and coarse, 4-inch-wide, rough-hairy leaves. Best placed in the background, it likes full sun and any well-drained, average-fertility soil. Seed is the surest propagation method, and it is untroubled from diseases or pests.

Centaurea ruthenica (Ruthenian Centaurea)   24–36 in.   Sun
Flowering span: Early July to mid-August
Color: Pale yellow
Native habitat: Central Europe

Here the species has finely dissected foliage and 1½-inch solitary flowers. Its culture is the same as that for *C. macrocephala.*

Cephalaria tatarica (Tatarian Cephalaria)   60–72 in.   Sun
Flowering span: Early July to September
Color: Creamy white
Native habitat: Europe, Asia Minor, Siberia

Although the pinnately compound foliage is coarse in appearance, the plant produces an ongoing abundance of flat flower heads on long stems resembling the annual scabiosa. Any moist soil in sun to semi-shade satisfies it, and division or seeding made propagation simple. Nothing appears to bother it.

Chelone glabra (White Turtlehead) 24–36 in. Semi-shade
Flowering span: Mid-July to September
Color: Off white
Native habitat: Newfoundland to Georgia, west to Missouri
    and Minnesota

The ¾-inch, egg-shaped flowers appearing in leafy terminal stalks resemble the animal of its name. Its paired foliage is lanceolate, dark green, and widely spaced on the stems. Thriving in rich, consistently moist, humusy soil, especially along streams and swamps, it adapts to garden use if kept well-watered and mulched. Division is the practical propagation method. It appears to be pest- and disease-free.

Cimicifuga racemosa (Cohosh Bugbane) 60–84 in. Semi-
    shade
Flowering span: Early July to August
Color: Creamy white
Native habitat: Massachusetts to Georgia, west to Missouri

Bee-attracting *Cimicifuga racemosa* gently illuminates any moist, woodlot setting.

Dramatically bold in foliage, the 18-inch, dark green, compound leaves are thrice-divided and then subdivided 3 times more. Erect spikes with strongly scented, bee-attracting, fuzzy flowers dominate shadowy woodlots and shaded borders where the soil is well-drained, acid-humusy, constantly moist, and deep. Spring division is the best reproduction method to follow. True to its naming, it has no difficult pests or diseases. The species *americana* from West Virginia is very similar, blooms later, and is shorter in growth. The wandlike spikes of any species dry well for indoor arrangements when in the seed stage.

Coreopsis pubescens 12–48 in. Sun
Flowering span: Early July to September
Color: Deep yellow
Native habitat: Virginia to Florida, west to Louisiana and
    Missouri

The thick, oval-to-lanceolate leaves are generally hairy and appear sparsely on slender, erect stems with 1½- to 2½-inch, daisylike flowers having yellow or brownish centers. Easily grown in any average-fertility soil, it is best propagated by seeding and is prone mainly to powdery mildew attacks.

Coreopsis rosea (Rose Coreopsis) 12–24 in. Sun
Flowering span: Early July to September
Color: Rose-purple, pink, white
Native habitat: Nova Scotia to Georgia

Not overly showy, the unusual coloring in this species offers some interest. The ¾-inch flowers appear on much branched stems with very narrow, lancelike foliage. It prefers constantly moist to wet locations in average soil, and division is the recommended propagation method. Nothing critical bothers it.

Coreopsis verticillata (Threadleaf Coreopsis) 12–24 in. Sun
Flowering span: Early July to mid-August
Color: Golden yellow
Native habitat: Maryland to Florida, west to Arkansas

The hairlike, compound leaves create a filmy foliage mass (resembling dwarfed *cosmos*) that is topped by 2-inch, jagged-tipped blossoms on wiry stalks. The plants easily creep by underground stems to form large, but not invasive, clumps and are readily tolerant to semi-shade. It also has a surprising liking for dry soil that is well-drained at all times. Division in spring or fall is the simplest method for increasing the plants. No pest or disease seriously disfigures it.

Delphinium cardinale (Cardinal Larkspur) 24–48 in. Sun
Flowering span: Early July to August
Color: Orange-scarlet
Native habitat: Southern California

Similar in appearance and culture to the May-blooming *D. nudicaule*, here the flowers are slightly larger on taller stems (it can reach 7 feet in its native habitat). It needs a winter mulching in severe climates.

Delphinium carolinianum (Carolina Larkspur) 18–30 in.
   Sun
Flowering span: Early July to August
Color: Azure blue, white
Native habitat: Ohio to Florida, west to Texas and Missouri

Downy stems carry deeply divided leaves and erect flower stalks with 1-inch, pendulous florets on this wildflower. It grows best in a deep, rich, sandy soil and can be propagated by seed, division, or stem cuttings in spring or fall. Possible reflowering comes if the first blooms are cut off when faded. Mildew is undoubtedly the worst affliction.

Dianthus superbus (Lilac Pink) 12–24 in. Sun
Flowering span: Early July to August
Color: Lilac, pale rose, pink
Native habitat: Europe, Japan

The lacy, deeply fringed, very fragrant blossoms appear on slender, branched stems with small, light green, glossy foliage but can overbloom themselves into extinction in a short time. Enjoying a rich, moist soil in full sun, they are probably best grown from seed started annually. Pests or diseases affect them less than self-exhaustion.

Echinacea angustifolia (Blacksampson Echinacea) 4–20 in. Sun
Flowering span: Early July to mid-August
Color: Purplish pink
Native habitat: Montana to Oklahoma

The 8-inch, blue-green, silvery foliage is narrow and surrounds long flower stems with individual, 2- to 3-inch asterlike flowers having prominent, raised, brownish centers. Tolerant naturally of gravelly, well-drained soil, it can be utilized in the garden in any sandy, rich loam. Seed and division suit it equally for propagation, and it has no bothersome pests or diseases.

Echinacea purpurea (*Rudbeckia purpurea*) (Purple Coneflower) 12–48 in. Sun
Flowering span: Early July to mid-September
Color: Purplish crimson
Native habitat: Pennsylvania to Georgia, west to Louisiana and Iowa

Easily tolerant to drought, this species carries many 4-inch, daisylike flowers with drooping, widely spaced petals and raised, mahogany-colored centers. The 8-inch, coarse, lanceolate, green leaves look unkempt and shabby if placed prominently in view. Any well-drained, sandy loam satisfies it, and clump division or root cuttings propagate it readily. Pests and diseases seem to avoid it. The hybrids are all superior: "Bright Star," rose red with maroon centers; "Robert Bloom," carmine purple with orange centers; "The King," coral red with maroon centers; and "White Lustre" ("White King"), white with bronze centers.

Echinops ritro (Small Globe-thistle) 24–36 in. Sun
Flowering span: Mid-July to mid-August
Color: Steel blue
Native habitat: Southeastern Europe

The blue globes of *Echinops ritro* vie with its thistlelike foliage.

The striking foliage of this plant is matched by the unusual, ball-shaped flower heads. Its deeply lobed, 12-inch, dark green leaves have a heavily downy underside and are tipped with fragile spines. Branched flower stems carry terminal, 2-inch globes of tightly packed, star-shaped florets. Any average, well-drained, somewhat dry soil is satisfactory, and propagation can be achieved by division, root cuttings, or seeds. Nothing important affects its growth. The hybrid, "Taplow Blue," has 3-inch flower heads and stretches to 48 inches, while "Veitch's Blue" is a bright, deep blue in color.

Echinops spaerocephalum (Common Globe-thistle) 60–84
    in. Sun
Flowering span: Mid-July to mid-August
Color: Pale blue
Native habitat: Southern Europe

Here the stems are ribbed and greenish white while the foliage is a lighter green, rough-surfaced, and only silver-hairy beneath. The flower heads are between 1½ to 2 inches

and may occasionally be almost white. Culture is identical
with that for *E. ritro.*

Erigeron aurantiacus (Orange Fleabane) 8–10 in. Sun
Flowering span: Mid-July to mid-August
Color: Bright orange
Native habitat: Turkestan

Somewhat twisted, oblong, velvety leaves clasp the thin
stems below the 2-inch, solitary, semi-double, daisylike flowering of this plant. Performing better if given some noon-
day shading, it thrives in any sandy, low-fertility soil that is
well-drained and yet reasonably moist. Seeds or division
propagates it readily, and only the "aster yellows" disease
appears to be troublesome.

Erigeron aureus (Gold Fleabane) 2–6 in. Semi-shade
Flowering span: Mid-July to mid-August
Color: Bright golden yellow
Native habitat: Cascade Mountains of Washington

This rock garden accent has a basal grouping of downy,
warped leaves and 1-inch, double flowers. Except for a decided preference to have an acid, humusy soil in light shading, its culture is the same as for *E. aurantiacus.*

Erigeron hybrida (Hybrid Fleabane) 18–30 in. Sun
Flowering span: Late July to early October
Color: Pink, purple
Native habitat: Horticultural hybrid

These showy and long-blooming hybrid introductions are
on sturdy stems carrying 2-inch, yellow-eyed flowers with
rows of usually whisker-thin outer petals. Culture is the
same as that for *E. aurantiacus,* except that only spring division will successfully propagate the named varieties such
as: "Amity," lilac rose; "Charity," light pink; "Darkest of
All," violet blue; "Dignity," violet; "Felicity," deep pink;
"Festivity," lilac pink; "Gaiety," deep pink; "Lilofee,"
mauve blue; "Sincerity," lavender-blue; and "Wuppertal,"
deep violet.

Eryngium alpinum (Bluetop Eryngo) 18–30 in. Sun
Flowering span: Mid-July to September
Color: Metallic blue
Native habitat: Europe

Unusual in form throughout, the 3-inch, terminal blossoms sport noticeably raised, pineapplelike cones surrounded by jagged, flat ray petals on steel blue stems that also carry stiff, prickly, much-divided green foliage. The plant can easily be dried for indoor, decorative use and prefers a somewhat dry, light, rich, sandy soil in full sun. Division of the fanglike root system shocks the plant badly, and although root cuttings are feasible, seed is the recommended propagation method. Leaf miner and beetles can disfigure the plant, along with rot and leaf spot diseases. The variety "Donard" has bluish-silver flower heads.

Eryngium amethystinum (Amethyst Sea-holly) 12–18 in.
    Sun
Flowering span: Early July to September
Color: Deep blue
Native habitat: Yugoslavia

Much-branched and bushy in appearance, the blossoms, bracts, and upper stems are here shaded from steel blue to amethyst. Its ½-inch, oval flower heads are surrounded by ragged collars of spiny bracts above deeply cut, green foliage. Culture is the same as for *E. alpinum.*

Eryngium aquaticum (Button Snakeroot) 24–72 in. Sun
Flowering span: Mid-July to mid-August
Color: White
Native habitat: New Jersey to Florida

Native to bogs and marshes, this wildflower has 2-inch, conelike flower heads on steel blue stems and distinctive, narrow, bristly leaves with noticeable veining carried to the edges. Effective as a sunny border accent, it strangely likes either a dry or very moist soil when used in gardens, where it may need winter protection. Seed is still the most assured method for reproduction, and the plant appears unbothered by serious pests or diseases.

Eupatorium perfoliatum (Boneset) 36–60 in. Sun
Flowering span: Early July to September
Color: Dull white
Native habitat: Southeastern Canada to Florida, west to
    Texas

Although the dense, flat-topped flower clusters, which resemble its relative, ageratum, are somewhat ill-smelling up close, the sturdy, vigorous plants have a wildflower value in woodlots by their long blooming period. Its lanceolate, wrinkled, light green leaves are joined together around the stem, giving the impression the foliage is being perforated by the stalk. The entire plant is hairy and does well in any rich, very moist soil in full sun to light shade. Division of the coarse, fibrous rootstock is difficult on mature plants; nursery stock or young seedlings propagate it better. Seed fails to germinate well, and there is rarely any self-seeding. Crown rot and botrytis blight are occasionally serious diseases, but insects present no problems.

Eupatorium rugosum (White Snakeroot) 24–48 in. Sun
Flowering span: Mid-July to September
Color: White
Native habitat: Southeastern Canada to Virginia

Showier than *E. perfoliatum*, this heavily branched plant has loose clusters of tiny, buttonlike blossoms and wide-ended leaves on distinct petioles. Poisonous if chewed in any of its parts, it probably needs restriction to wild areas infrequently visited. Best in a constantly moist location well-endowed with humus, it can flower satisfactorily even in semi-shading. Remaining dormant long into spring, it is best propagated by nursery-grown stock or collected seedlings, although division is workable if only the vigorous portions of the plant are used.

Euphorbia corollata (Flowering Spurge) 18–36 in. Sun
Flowering span: Early July to mid-August
Color: White
Native habitat: Massachusetts to Florida, west to Texas and
    Minnesota

A tough and dependable plant, its true, minuscule flowers are surrounded by showy white bracts above narrow, blunt-tipped, 1½- to 2-inch, smooth leaves that turn wine red in autumn, adding to its usefulness. Attractive in borders and woodlots as an erect baby's breath, it prefers a light, sandy, well-drained soil held on the dry side. Seed, division, or summer cuttings readily propagate it, and it appears to be unaffected by pests or diseases.

Filipendula camtschatica (*Spiraea camtschatica*)
　　(Kamchatka Meadowsweet) 48–100 in. Semi-shade
Flowering span: Early July to August
Color: Creamy white
Native habitat: Manchuria, Siberia

These airy, graceful plants have very large plumes of tiny flowers that are especially noticeable at dusk. Culture is identical as that for the June-blooming *F. purpurea.*

Galega officinalis (Common Goat's-rue) 24–36 in. Sun
Flowering span: Early July to September
Color: Purplish blue
Native habitat: Western Asia, southern Europe

Uncommonly grown, this easily adaptable and long-flowering plant has graceful, pinnately compound foliage and showy, pea-shaped florets on 4- to 6-inch, terminal spikes, making it a useful summer border addition. Preferring full sun, it also grows well in light shade on any moist, average-fertility soil. Division in spring or fall or seed reproduce it satisfactorily. Unfortunately, aphids and cutworms bother the stems and leaves, and mildew can be a problem in hot, humid weather. The similar species, *orientalis,* flowers entirely in July and has slightly larger foliage.

Galtonia candicans (*Hyacinthus candicans*) (Giant Summer
　　Hyacinth) 36–48 in. Sun
Flowering span: Mid-July to mid-August
Color: Milky white
Native habitat: South Africa

Showy in the background of borders, the stiff, erect flower spikes of these bulbs carry 20 to 30, slightly fragrant, 1½-inch, drooping florets above a basal clump of straplike, gray-green leaves that stretch, perhaps, to 30 inches. Easily grown in any constantly well-drained, sandy-humusy, moist soil in full sun, they need winter mulching in severe winter climates, where lifting and replanting in spring may be the wiser culture. Late spring planting of new bulbs or offsets from established colonies propagate them, and there appear to be no serious afflictions.

Gaultheria procumbens (Checkerberry Wintergreen) 4–6 in. Semi-shade
Flowering span: Early July to August
Color: White, pinkish white
Native habitat: Manitoba to Newfoundland, south to Georgia and Alabama

Widely distributed in acid woods and tolerant of a variety of soils and exposures, this evergreen wild plant has dark, glossy green, 1- to 2-inch, oval leaves shielding waxy, drooping, ½-inch flowers that produce ¼-inch, edible red fruit with a somewhat minty flavor. Best treated as a shady woodlot groundcover, it prefers a sandy-peaty, moist, well-drained soil, free of excessive root competition from vigorous shrubs or other perennials. Propagate by division or nursery-grown stock since seed and cuttings are difficult to manage. Nothing seems to bother it.

Gentiana asclepiadea (Willow Gentian) 18–30 in. Semi-shade
Flowering span: Mid-July to September
Color: Deep blue
Native habitat: Southern Europe, Caucasus Mountains

The slender arching stems carry light green, lancelike, 2- to 3-inch leaves and are terminally ended by 6 to 8 inches of conspicuous, tubular, 1½-inch flowers. Best in an acid-humusy, constantly moist and cool soil, they prefer locations which avoid transplanting. Spring division of young plants is workable but risky, and seeding, although slow for results, is preferred. Rust disease is the main disfigurement of the foliage. There is a white form, *alba*, but it is rare.

Gentiana lagodechiana 6–12 in. Sun
Flowering span: Mid-July to mid-August
Color: Deep blue
Native habitat: Russia

Large, 1½-inch, solitary flowers with green-speckled throats appear terminally on short, upright stems, along with 1-inch, ovate-shaped leaves. Easily grown in full sun to light shading, it prefers a moist, gravelly, well-drained soil, either acid or slightly alkaline. Propagated best by seeds, the young plants should be carried in pots until ready for permanent locations in the rock garden or border. Avoid damaging the roots at any time. Pests and diseases are no serious threat.

Gentiana lutea (Yellow Gentian) 24–36 in. Semi-shade
Flowering span: Mid-July to mid-August
Color: Rich yellow
Native habitat: Europe, Asia Minor

Here the terminal flowering is in flat-topped, dense clusters. Treat as for *G. asclepiadea,* but only seeding will propagate it.

Gentiana septemfida 8–12 in. Semi-shade
Flowering span: Mid-July to mid-August
Color: Deep blue
Native habitat: Asia Minor

In this species the trumpet blossoms have white throats and appear in headlike clusters on squarish, trailing stems that turn upward when flowering. Its culture is identical with that for *G. lagodechiana,* except in its preference for some shading.

Gypsophila acutifolia (Big Gypsophila) 36–48 in. Sun
Flowering span: Mid-July to September

Color: Pinkish white
Native habitat: Caucasus Mountains

All of the species are chalk- or lime-loving plants (convert acid soils easily by annual applications of garden lime). The airy sprays of tiny flowers provide a mistlike effect in borders and are good for drying as indoor decorations. This plant has narrow green foliage sketchily provided on the brittle stems and is remarkably similar in overall appearance to the larger-flowered *G. paniculata* most commonly sold by nurseries. It wants a sunny location in an average-fertility, fairly dry soil and can be reproduced by seed, division or stem cuttings. Pests and diseases are unknown.

Gypsophila paniculata (Baby's-breath) 24–36 in. Sun
Flowering span: Mid-July to mid-August
Color: White
Native habitat: Europe, Siberia

Usually as broad as it is tall, it carries 3-inch, gray-green leaves and tiny, single flowers on a multitude of much-

Myriads of tiny, double flowers float effusively on wiry stems with *Gypsophila paniculata flore-pleno.*

branched, wiry stems. Its culture is identical with that of *G. acutifolia*, which it closely resembles. Only seed, however, will reproduce it satisfactorily. The natural double form *flore-pleno* has generally been superseded today by the hybrid "Bristol Fairy," which has larger and more-doubled flowering, although the newest variety, "Perfecta," claims still larger florets.

Helianthus decapetalus (Thinleaf Sunflower) 24–60 in. Sun
Flowering span: Late July to October
Color: Bright yellow
Native habitat: Southeastern Canada to Georgia, west to Kentucky and Michigan

The loose, 10-petaled flowers have a darker yellow center and appear with 3- to 8-inch, wide, coarse-textured, lanceolate leaves that are rough above and slightly hairy beneath. Adaptable to any light, moist soil in full sun, they prefer a slightly alkaline condition easily created by adding garden lime annually. Regular division not only propagates them readily but maintains vigor since they spread—and crowd—enthusiastically. Aphids, beetles, and leaf miners are a nuisance, but diseases are not prevalent. The double form *flore pleno* has 4-inch, showy blossoms and is visually superior. It is sometimes listed as *multiflorus*. Overcrowding of the double-flowered type will cause some quick reversion to single flowers.

Heliopsis helianthoides (*laevis*) (Sunflower Heliopsis, Oxeye) 36–60 in. Sun
Flowering span: Mid-July to October
Color: Golden yellow
Native habitat: Southern Canada to New Mexico, east to Georgia

Widely distributed throughout much of the United States, this wildflower carries 3- to 5-inch, mostly smooth, stalked, thin leaves on erect stems and 1½- to 2½-inch, long-stemmed, daisylike flowers in generous branching abundance. Drought-resistant, it does nicely in any sunny, well-drained, average-fertility soil on the dry side. Division, seed, or cuttings propagate it well, but it also has the same general nuisances as its relative *Helianthus*. The deeper-colored variety, *pitcheriana*, is dwarfed with a 24- to 36-inch height and a 36- to 48-inch spread.

Heliopsis scabra (Rough Heliopsis) 36–48 in. Sun
Flowering span: Early July to September
Color: Golden yellow
Native habitat: Maine to New Jersey, west to Missouri

Very similar to *H. helianthoides* in color and appearance, the chief difference is the roughness of the stems and leaves throughout the plant. The 3-inch flowers also often appear singly on long stems. Any sunlit, moist, average-fertility soil enriched with humus is satisfactory, and division reproduces it well, although self-seeding may become a slight problem. There are several hybrid introductions: "Gold Greenheart," double, golden yellow with an emerald green center as it opens; "Golden Plume," double, orange-yellow; "Light of Loddon," single, bright yellow; "Orange King," single, bright orange; and "Summer Sun," single, orange-yellow.

Hemerocallis citrina (Citron Daylily) 24–48 in. Sun
Flowering span: Early July to August
Color: Pale yellow
Native habitat: China, Japan

The individual flower of any daylily normally has only the daylight-hours' life span, but the many leafless scapes supporting the prolific buds and blossoms offer an ongoing display worth including in any garden development. In this species, the flowering is surprisingly nocturnal, beginning in late afternoon and continuing until dawn. Its dark green, 1½-inch, strap leaves are between 30 to 45 inches long, arranged in a graceful, fountainlike but compact mound. The trumpet-shaped, 3- to 4-inch flowers are slightly fragrant. The parent of many hybrids, it enjoys any moist, humusy, well-drained, average-fertility soil in sun to light shade. Division in spring or fall is simply handled, although seeds reproduce well, too. The entire genus is remarkably free of diseases and pests of consequence as well as tolerant to both drought and heat. The variety *baroni* has larger blossoms, freely produced, and is also a night-bloomer.

Hemerocallis fulva (Tawny Daylily) 48–6o in. Sun
Flowering span: Early July to August
Color: Rusty orange
Native habitat: Europe, Asia

Often mistakenly labelled "tiger lily," these durable plants have 18- to 24-inch grasslike leaves and clusters of 6 to 12 blossoms on erect, tall scapes. Culture is identical with that for *H. citrina.* The double-flowered form "Kwanso" (from the Chinese word *Hsuan-ts'ao*) has 2-inch-wide leaves, longer-lasting blossoms, and sets no fruit.

Hemerocallis hybrida (Hybrid Daylily) 15–5o in. Sun
Flowering span: Late June to mid-August
Color: Solid and blended colorings of yellow, orange, red, pink, and mahogany from pale to vivid, along with many bicolors

Confidently sturdy, hybrid *Hemerocallis* adapts handsomely to gardens of every size.

Native habitat: Horticultural hybrids from European and
   North American sources

The continued development interest in daylily hybridization over the past few decades has given us a wealth of
colorings and flower shapes that is both astounding and confusing. Annually, dozens of new introductions appear from
amateur and commercial sources with either a larger blossom, heavier petal texture, greater color intensity, improved
durability, differing blooming span, or several of these attri-
butes combined. Separation of the meritorious is frequently
a matter of very subtle differences and involves the personal
opinion of the viewer. It is fascinating to discover—but awe-
somely difficult to untangle—these overlapping choices, and
no listing of recommended types can be entirely helpful or
up-to-date for long. Local nursery offerings can sensibly provide a starting place for reliable named varieties.

   Although hybrid daylilies are readily tolerant of a wide
range of growing conditions from southern Canada to the
Mexican border (and perhaps beyond both), not every kind
will be fully dependable for every area. The types with persistent, evergreen foliage are generally better suited to the
southerly parts of the United States, although the plants
themselves are reasonably hardy elsewhere even without
foliage in winter. Whether used as border specimens or lush
groundcover bedding, daylilies are tough, adaptable plants
with a long life span. If carefully handled, they can even be
transplanted while in full flower. Daylilies deserve inclusion in every sunny garden, and their relevant culture is
listed under *H. citrina*.

   The following arbitrarily brief listing of named hybrids
with sustained popularity will provide some clue to at least
the colorings available today: "Autumn Gold," yellow;
"Bess Ross," red; "Big Mamou," brown blend; "Black
Magic," black purple; "Buried Treasure," yellow; "Capitol
Dome," gold; "Cartwheels," gold; "Colonial Dame," apricot; "Cream Glory," buff; "Crestwood Ann," melon pink;
"Daafu," red; "Dorcas," melon pink; "Dream Mist," cream
and salmon bicolor; "Easter Anthem," cream and purple
bicolor; "Evelyn Claar," coral; "Exotic Gold," gold;
"Francis Fay," melon pink; "Golden Chimes," gold;

"Grand Canyon," peach blend; "Green Envy," buff; "Gusto," red; "Heaven Sent," purple; "Hyperion," yellow; "Jack Frost," yellow; "Kindly Light," yellow; "Lady Inara," peach; "Lexington," yellow; "Lime Painted Lady," yellow; "Lucky Strike," pink; "Luxury Lace," lavender pink; "May Hall," rose blend; "Nob Hill," pink bitone; "Petite Violette," lavender bitone; "Pink Damask," pink; "Pink Lightning," pink; "Porcelain Doll," orange; "Prairie Sunset," pastel blend; "Primrose Mascotte," yellow; "Rare China," rose; "Red Siren," red; "Ringlets," gold; "Royal Fashion," purple bitone; "Satin Glass," pastel melon; "Sea Gold," peach blend; "Shining Plumage," red; "Smiling Through," apricot; "Spring Fantasy," lilac and yellow bicolor; "Tinker Bell," orange; "'Tis Midnight," black purple; and "Tom Boy," red. There are hundreds more in cultivation.

Hibiscus moscheutos (Swamp Rose-mallow) 60–100 in. Sun
Flowering span: Late July to September
Color: Cream with a red center
Native habitat: Maryland to Florida, west to Alabama and Indiana

The giant, 6- to 8-inch, saucer-shaped flowers appear terminally clustered on erect stems with narrow green leaves sometimes having 3 points. Native to marsh areas, it is hardy and does well in gardens with rich, moist, well-drained loam in sun or light shade. Division or seed readily propagate it, but it is pestered by aphids, white fly, stem rot, and leaf spot disease.

Hibiscus palustris (Common Rose-mallow) 60–100 in. Sun
Flowering span: Late July to September
Color: Pink, occasionally white or purple
Native habitat: Massachusetts to North Carolina, west to Illinois and Michigan

Here the flowers are only 4 to 6 inches across and the sharply tapered leaves are covered with light downy hairs on the under surface. Its culture is the same as for *H. moscheutos*, which some believe is merely a form of this species. Named varieties are available: "Cotton Candy," soft

Late summer emphasis comes pleasantly from *Hibiscus palustris*.

pink; "Crimson Wonder," deep red; "Ruby Dot," white with a red center; "Satan," deep crimson; and "Strawberry Blonde," deep pink.

Hosta caerulea (Funkia caerulea) (Blue Plantainlily) 18–24 in. Semi-shade
Flowering span: Early to late July
Color: Deep to pale blue
Native habitat: Japan, Siberia, northern China

All plantainlilies not only possess the remarkable duality of having attractive foliage and noticeable flowering, but their reliable hardiness, tolerance of drought, and willing adaptability to deep shading (for a show of leaves and little flowering) extend their usefulness far beyond most other perennials. They all dislike constant sun, strong winds, and poor drainage, but will yet attempt to cope with almost any growing condition. Their popularity is richly deserved, but the correct identification of the separate species and varieties is still puzzling botanists and growers.

This species has 5- to 10-inch, heart-shaped, dark green leaves half again as wide and slender flower stalks strung loosely with 1½- to 2-inch tubes that flare into bell shapes at the ends. All *Hostas* (formerly called *Funkia*) thrive and spread widely in a consistently moist, humusy, well-drained soil of average fertility in light to semi-shading. Early spring or fall division of the thick, ropelike rootstock readily propagates them, but seed is also reliable. Few diseases are a serious bother, and only slugs and snails seem to relish the foliage. The variety *marginata* has wide, white leaf edges, while *aurea* has yellowish streaking.

Hosta crispula (fortunei albo-marginata) (Whiterim
    Plantainlily) 18–24 in. Semi-shade
Flowering span: Mid-July to early August
Color: Pale lilac
Native habitat: Japan, China

Here the somewhat wavy, white-margined, medium green leaves extend to 12 inches and are about 6 inches wide on 12-inch or longer petioles. A vigorous, wide-spreading plant, its showy leaves are far superior to the flowering. Culture is identical with that for *H. caerulea.*

Hosta crispula foliage adds contrast and color to shaded locations.

Hosta fortunei (Fortunes Plantainlily) 18–36 in. Semi-
    shade
Flowering span: Early July to August
Color: Pale lilac
Native habitat: Japan

Here the 5- to 8-inch, narrow leaves are entirely green
with a moderately grayish cast, while the 1- to 1½-inch
florets appear on tall scapes well above the foliage. Culture
is identical with that for *H. caerulea*.

Hosta sieboldiana (glauca) (Siebold Plantainlily) 18–24
    in. Semi-shade
Flowering span: Early July to August
Color: Creamy lavender
Native habitat: China, Japan

Strikingly colorful in foliage, the rounded, 15-inch by 10-
inch leaves are metallic blue-green with noticeable, wrinkled ribbing. The low-set flower stalk has 2-inch florets compactly arranged. Cultivate as for *H. caerulea*. The variety
elegans displays larger and more intensely colored leaves.

Hosta undulata (Wavyleaf Plantainlily) 12–15 in. Semi-
    shade
Flowering span: Mid-July to mid-August
Color: Light purple
Native habitat: Japan, China

This common species has 5- to 8-inch, oval, broadly undu-
lating leaves centrally splashed with white, plus long petioles longitudinally striped in green and white. Its culture is
the same as for *H. caerulea*.

Inula ensifolia (Swordleaf Inula) 18–24 in. Sun
Flowering span: Mid-July to September
Color: Bright yellow
Native habitat: Caucasus Mountains

Long-lasting, 2-inch, asterlike flowers appear above slender, pointed, dull green leaves on this vigorous perennial. It
does well in any average-fertility, moist, well-drained soil in
full sun and can be reproduced by division or seed. Mildew

is the chief problem. The variety *compacta* has 1-inch flowers and is 9 inches tall. A hybrid, "Golden Beauty," carries golden yellow flowering and stands 24 inches tall.

Inula hookeri (Hooker Inula) 18–24 in. Sun
Flowering span: Late July to mid-September
Color: Lemon yellow
Native habitat: Himalaya Mountains

These 3-inch, daisylike flowers have yellow centers and long, slender ray petals above downy, soft green, 3- to 5-inch linear leaves. The plant has a tendency to flop over and usually needs staking. Its culture is identical with that for *I. ensifolia.*

Inula orientalis 18–24 in. Sun
Flowering span: Early July to August
Color: Golden yellow
Native habitat: Himalayan Mountains

Here the flowers are 4 to 5 inches across and have a noticeably raised central disc surrounded by rows of narrow petals broader than those on *I. hookeri.* The lanceolate foliage is also broad and from 4 to 7 inches long. Cultivate it the same as *I. ensifolia.*

Iris kaempferi (laevigata) (Japanese Iris) 24–36 in. Sun
Flowering span: Early July to August
Color: Rose, purple, blue, white
Native habitat: Japan, eastern Siberia

The flat-opening, beardless flowers can reach 8 inches across and usually appear 3 to a stem. Its swordlike green foliage is 12 to 18 inches tall, and while the assumption often is that this species demands a waterside, marshy location, it merely prefers generous moisture while blooming. Grow them in a consistently damp, humusy, well-drained (especially in winter), acid soil in full sun or light shading. Avoid using lime, bone meal, or wood ashes near them since the roots react fatally to all of these ingredients. Easily divided because of the fibrous root system, spring separation alone is recommended. Few pests or diseases are bothersome. The hybrid list is extensive: "Attraction," purple over a gray background; "Geihan," white; "Jeweled Kimona," blue lavender, double; "Juno," rosy purple; "Mahogany," mahogany red; "Pillar of Fire," reddish purple; "Pink Frost," rosy lavender, double; "Pink Pearl," flesh pink; "Purple Splendor," rich purple, double; "Pyramid," bluish violet with a white center, double; "Rose Anna," wine red; and "Snowy Hills," white, double.

Lathyrus latifolius (Perennial Pea) 48–100 in. Sun
Flowering span: Mid-July to September
Color: Rose magenta
Native habitat: Europe

A scrambling vine undaunted by soil, exposure, or most climates, this vigorous perennial has nonfragrant clusters of 1½-inch, pealike blossoms at the ends of 8- to 12-inch stalks which come from the axils of the gray green, parallel-veined, lanceolate leaves. As a disguiser of fences, rock piles, and trellises, it is readily adaptable to almost any growing condition, but it flowers best in full sun. Seed is the recommended propagation method, and nothing seems to bother it. Pink, purple, red, and white varieties are available, but many of these do not always come true to color from seeding.

Lavandula officinalis (*vera, spica*) (True Lavender) 24–36
     in. Sun
Flowering span: Late July to September
Color: Lavender blue
Native habitat: Mediterranean Europe and Africa

The familiar sweet scent of the leaves or flowers of this woody herb is known to almost everyone since it has been cultivated for countless generations and used in aromatic sachets. The 1-inch, blunt, needlelike leaves are silvery green in tight placement along the stems. Tall, gray-colored spikes produce terminal heads of ½-inch, fragrant florets which can be successfully dried for indoor use. A light, sandy, somewhat dry soil in full sun encourages good growth with occasional fertilizing. Mulch heavily in winter and prune back to old wood each spring. Propagate by spring cuttings only. There are no troublesome pests or diseases. A few hybrids exist: "Gray Lady," deep lavender, 24 in.; "Hidcote" (*nana atropurpurea*), deep purple, compact, 12 in.; and "Twickel Purple," deep lavender, 36 in.

Liatris spicata (Spike Gayfeather) 24–60 in. Sun
Flowering span: Mid-July to September
Color: Deep purple
Native habitat: Southeastern Canada to Florida, west to Louisiana and Wisconsin

Spirals of very narrow, dark green leaves thread their way up the slender, unbranched stems of this wildflower that is ended with a long spike of ½-inch, ragged-edged florets densely crowded along the stem. Peculiarly, they open from the top down. Often found wild near streams and marshes, they can be garden-cultivated in any constantly moist, light, well-drained loam in full sun to light shade. Division or seed readily propagate it, and nothing unusual bothers its growth. The variety "Kobold" is 18 inches, compact, and dark purple; while "Silver Tips" is 36 inches tall and lavender.

Lilium (Lily) 24–100 in. Sun
Flowering span: Early July to mid-September
Color: White, yellow, red, orange, pink, along with many shadings
Native habitat: The northern hemisphere, worldwide

The midsummer-blooming hybrid lilies have some tendency for larger blossoms, heavier clusterings of buds, and greater size throughout. Their care and culture, however, are identical with that provided in depth under the same lily entry for June.

July-Blooming Hybrid Lilies

AMERICAN HYBRIDS: From 48 to 100 inches tall with 4- to 6-inch turks-cap blossoms and derived from native American species

Examples: "Bellingham Hybrids," speckled orange and red shadings, vigorous, easy-to-grow; "Buttercup," deep yellow, heavily spotted with brown, only partly recurved petals; and "Shuksan," gold, spotted in crimson maroon, strongly recurved petals.

LONGIFLORUM HYBRIDS:　From 36 to 72 inches with 6- to 8-inch, trumpet-shaped, scented blossoms

Examples: "Holland's Glory," pure white, 36 to 48 in., the hardiest variety; "Mount Everest," waxy white with a gold flush inside, 60–72 in.; and "White Queen," white with a greenish throat, 36–48 in.

AURELIAN OR TRUMPET HYBRIDS:　From 48 to 60 inches tall with 6- to 10-inch fragrant blossoms of varying shapes

Chinese trumpet or funnel-shaped flowering examples:
"Black Dragon," white with extensive dark maroon flush outside and golden inside; "Golden Splendor," deep gold, prefers light shade; "Limelight," chartreuse yellow; "Olympic Hybrids," ranges from soft pink to cool green with darker shadings on the outside; "Pink Perfection," green buds open to purplish pink, then fade to deep pink, likes semi-shade; and "Royal Gold," bright golden yellow.

Bowl-shaped flowering examples:
"First Love," pink outside and gold inside with a pale green throat; and "Heart's Desire," white, cream, and yellowish orange blends.

Pendant-flowering examples:
"Golden Showers," butter yellow with a brown outside, vigorous grower; and "Reliance," golden yellow.

Sunburst or star-shaped flowering examples:
"Bright Star," ivory white with an apricot center; "Golden Sunburst," deep gold; "Pink Sunburst," fuchsia-pink; "Silver Sunburst," white to cream with a gold throat; and "Thunderbolt," buff-apricot.

Lilium auratum (Goldband Lily) 60–84 in. Sun
Flowering span: Mid-July to mid-August
Color: White
Native habitat: Japan

These spectacularly large, 10- to 12-inch, bowl-shaped flowers are sweetly scented and appear in generous quantities above lustrous, 6- to 8-inch, lanceolate leaves about 2 inches wide. Each petal is centrally banded in rich yellow with brown freckle-spotting, and the plant is striking against an evergreen background that still allows the fullest possible sunlight to reach the bulb. Disliking lime, overfertilizing, and poor drainage, it is also highly troubled by mosaic disease. Generally, the bulb can be expected to be short-lived, but where it is likely to grow for several seasons, provide a peat-rich, humusy, well-drained soil with reasonable moisture, especially when in bloom. Offsets or scales propagate it best since seed, which is generally mosaic-free, germinates poorly and sluggishly. The varieties include: *pictum*, gold banding terminating in crimson tips with crimson spotting; *platyphyllum*, larger in all respects; *rubro-vittatum*, deep crimson banding and spotting; and *wittei* (*virginale*), pale yellow banding and almost white spots without any crimson overtones.

Lilium bulbiferum (Bulbil Lily) 24–48 in. Sun
Flowering span: Early July to August
Color: Bright orange-red
Native habitat: Southern Europe

Easy to grow in almost any soil, this bulb carries erect, chalice-shaped, 3- to 4-inch sterile flowers with brown to orange spotting. It has the unusual habit of providing tiny bulbs (*bulbils*) in the axils of its 3- to 4-inch, slender leaves near the top of the stem. Any light, rich, well-drained soil in sun to light shade is satisfactory, and quick reproduction is probably best accomplished from offsets or scales. Nothing important bothers it. The variety *croceum* has light orange, 5-inch blossoms, while *latifolium* is slightly larger in all respects.

Lilium chalcedonicum (Scarlet Turks-cap Lily) 24–48 in.
    Sun
Flowering span: Early July to August
Color: Bright scarlet
Native habitat: Greece, Ionian Islands

Strikingly colorful but unhappily provided with a disagreeable odor, these vivid 2- to 3-inch flowers appear tightly clustered above slender stems crowded with 2- to 6-inch, grasslike foliage. Of simple culture, the bulbs have become recently susceptible to many virus infections and may now be of short garden duration. A light, well-drained, average-fertility soil in sun to light shade is suitable, and propagation is achieved best from scales and offsets. The rare variety *maculatum* often has solitary flowers with noticeable purple spotting.

Lilium pardilinum (Leopard Lily) 48–84 in. Semi-shade
Flowering span: Early July to August
Color: Light red-orange
Native habitat: California, Oregon

Easily grown and vigorous to spread, this lily has 3- to 4-inch, turks-cap, pendulous flowers with a heavy sprinkling of red or maroon spots, mainly around the orange center. The leaves are linear and arranged in whorls. It likes a constantly damp but well-drained location and a light, humusy soil. Propagate it by offsets or scales, and do not be concerned about pests or disease. The variety *giganteum*, also known as the "Sunset Lily," has larger, bright orange-yellow blossoms; it is sometimes listed as a true species, *harrisianum*.

Lilium philadelphicum (Wood Lily) 12–36 in. Sun
Flowering span: Early July to August
Color: Orange red
Native habitat: Southern Canada to Missouri, east to North
    Carolina

This up-facing, wild lily has 3- to 4-inch blossoms in clusters to 5 above narrow, linear leaves arranged in whorls. The wide petals are arranged on very tapered ends and have deep purple spotting. Easily grown in any light, rich soil with full sun or light shading, it is not always adaptable to garden culture. Propagate by scales or offsets since seed is very slow. Pests and diseases are not troublesome.

Lilium regale (Regal Lily) 36–72 in. Sun
Flowering span: Early July to early August
Color: White
Native habitat: China

One of the most popular garden additions, it has an enticing fragrance from the heavy clustering of 3- to 6-inch, trumpet-shaped flowers that perch atop the sturdy, wiry stems with their deep green, 3- to 6-inch, narrow leaves. The coloring inside the throat is canary yellow, while the outside is flushed with rosy-purple between dark purple veining. Lime-tolerant, it is readily grown in full sun or light shade in any well-drained, light, rich soil. It also prefers having shading around the roots. Reproduce it by scales or offsets and forget being bothered by any serious pests or diseases.

Lilium superbum (Turks-cap Lily) 36–100 in. Sun
Flowering span: Late July to September
Color: Bright orange-scarlet
Native habitat: Eastern North America

Native in meadows and marshes, it becomes a sizable plant with 15 to 20 turban-shaped, brown-spotted flowers arranged pyramidally atop generally tall stems with whorls of 2- to 5-inch linear leaves. Since it dislikes lime, any damp, peaty soil is acceptable with sun or light shading, and propagation is still easiest from offsets or scales because seed is sluggish to germinate. Pests and diseases are not usual, but it can become susceptible to mosaic infection if grown with Asiatic lilies. It is very similar in appearance to *L. pardalinum* but differs by having a green "star" in the center of each flower.

Lilium tigrinum (Tiger Lily) 24–48 in. Sun
Flowering span: Mid-July to late August

Color: Salmon red
Native habitat: Korea, Japan, western China

Sharing honors with *L. candidum* for thousands of years of cultivation, it carries up to 15, unscented, black-spotted, 3- to 5-inch flowers on dark-colored stems. Disliking excess lime, it performs satisfactorily in any well-drained, average-fertility soil with sun to light shade. The sterile blossoms produce no seed but tiny bulbils are evident in the axils of the glossy, linear leaves, which contribute to dense colonization. Offsets and scales also propagate it easily. It is not susceptible to diseases or pests of itself but can readily be the carrier of mosaic infection to any nearby Asiatic types. The double-flowered variety, *flore-pleno,* is striking, while *splendens* is darker-colored and blooms several weeks later.

Limonium latifolium (Wideleaf Sea-lavender) 12–24 in.
     Sun
Flowering span: Mid-July to September
Color: Lilac blue
Native habitat: Mediterranean Europe

Highly resistant to salt spray and even to salt-water coverage, this border or rock garden, semi-evergreen perennial has a flat, basal rosette of leathery, broad leaves and airy panicles of staticelike, horizontal flowering on wiry, branched stems. If cut and dried, these flower stalks can be used for long-lasting indoor decorations. Any well-drained, sandy loam is suitable, and reproduction is most satisfactorily handled by seed. Nothing apparently bothers it. The hybrid "Violetta" has violet-colored florets.

Lobelia cardinalis (Cardinal-flower) 24–60 in. Sun
Flowering span: Late July to September
Color: Bright scarlet
Native habitat: Southeastern Canada to Florida, west to
     Texas and Minnesota

Erect, slender, unbranched stems produce showy, terminal blossoming with many 1- to 2-inch tubular florets ending in 3-fingered sets of down-turned lobes. The narrow leaves are tapered at both ends. It thrives in a constantly moist, peaty, rich soil in sun to semi-shade and can be pro-pagated, where it does not self-seed readily, by division or spring softwood cuttings. Rust disease on the leaves and rhizoctonia crown rot are problematic, but insects are not bothersome. The hybrid "Bees Flame" has intensely scarlet coloring, while "The Bishop" displays a velvety scarlet ap-pearance and carries bronze-green foliage. A rare white vari-ety, *alba*, exists but does not come true to color from seed-ing.

Lycoris squamigera (Amaryllis hallii) (Autumn Lycoris)
    12–30 in. Sun
Flowering span: Mid-July to early August
Color: Rose lilac
Native habitat: Japan

This hardy bulb behaves like the Meadow Saffron by pro-ducing a spring set of leaves which fade well before the ac-tual blossoming. Here the straplike foliage disappears and a slender, leafless stalk soon emerges with a terminal cluster of 2- to 3-inch, lilylike flowers that are fragrant and banded in yellow. Any moist, well-drained, average-fertility soil in sun to light shade is satisfactory, and propagation is easiest from bulb offsets. It seems to be free of disfiguring pests and diseases.

Lysimachia clethroides (Clethra Loosestrife, Gooseneck)
    24–36 in. Sun
Flowering span: Mid-July to September
Color: White
Native habitat: Japan, China

The vigorously extensive underground rootstock quickly spreads this durable perennial over wide areas. Its erect stems carry 3- to 6-inch lanceolate leaves plus nodding and recurved spikes composed of densely packed star-shaped florets. Any well-drained, average fertility soil in full sun to light shading is suitable, and division is the easiest repro-duction method to follow. Pests and diseases are unimpor-tant.

The goose-necked flowering of *Lysimachia clethroides* captivates any audience.

Lythrum salicaria (Purple Lythrum) 24–48 in. Sun
Flowering span: Mid-July to late August
Color: Reddish purple
Native habitat: North temperate zones of the globe

Widely dispersed throughout the world, these marsh-loving plants generously enhance any moist soil area with their graceful, leafy, branched spikes of slender flowering. The 1-inch, star-shaped blossoms have wavy petals and the deep green foliage is smooth and willowlike. Simple division or seeding propagates it readily, and no important diseases or pests hamper its development. There are a surprising number of hybrids: "Morden Gleam," carmine pink, 48 in.; "Morden Pink," rose pink, 36 in.; "Morden Rose," rose, 36 in.; "Robert," fuchsia pink, 24 in.; and "The Beacon," dark carmine red, 24 in.

Lythrum vigatum (Wand Lythrum) 24–36 in. Sun
Flowering span: Early July to August
Color: Rose purple
Native habitat: Europe, northern Asia

The colorful wands of *Lythrum salicaria* "Morden Pink" provide generous summer bouquets.

Similar to *L. salicaria*, this species is generally more compact and smaller in all its parts. Culture for both is identical.

Macleaya cordata (Bocconia cordata) (Pink Plume-Poppy)
    72–120 in. Sun
Flowering span: Mid-July to mid-August
Color: Pinkish white
Native habitat: China, Japan

Boldly tropical in appearance, its 8- to 18-inch, thin, round-lobed leaves are very widely spaced along the un-branched, gray stems that terminate with sizable, feathery masses of petal-less florets and can be cut and dried for later indoor use. The conspicuous, gray-green foliage is roughly heart-shaped in outline with numerous scalloped margins and a silvery underside. Vigorously invasive, it requires isolation to restrain encroachment throughout a border planting. Adaptable to either sun or light shade, it prefers a constantly moist, rich loam and can be propagated by division, root cuttings, or seed. Pests and diseases are unknown.

Malva moschata (Musk Mallow) 12–24 in. Sun
Flowering span: Early July to September
Color: Rose pink
Native habitat: Europe

Similar to the June-flowering *M. alcea*, here the leaves are more cleft in their fingered appearance, and the silhouette is more compact. Culture is the same for both, and there is also a white form, *alba*.

Mentha (Mint) 3–30 in. Sun
Flowering span: Early July to September
Color: Purple, pink, white
Native habitat: North temperate zones of the world

The aromatic leaves of these well-known perennial herbs have been utilized for centuries horticulturally and commercially as flavoring and in perfume-making. Naturalized throughout most of the northern parts of the globe, its squared stems with opposite leaves terminate with insignificant spikes of tiny florets. Generously invasive in any moist, well-drained, average-fertility soil in sun or semi-shade, all can readily be propagated by division or stem cuttings. Rust disease is the main foliage affliction. The most commonly used species are *citrata* (Bergamot Mint), *piperita* (Peppermint), *piperita citrata* (Orange Mint), *rotundifolia* (Apple Mint), *rotundifolia variegata* (Pineapple Mint), and *spicata* (Spearmint).

Phlox paniculata (decussata) (Perennial or Summer Phlox)
    24–48 in. Sun
Flowering span: Mid-July to late September
Color: Purplish pink
Native habitat: New York to Iowa, south to Arkansas and
    Georgia

The poorly colored parent plant is scarcely seen except as a wildflower because of the vast array of hybrid improvements now in cultivation. These have sweetly scented, 1-inch, disc-shaped florets generously massed in wide heads atop erect, woody stems with thin, dull green, lanceolate leaves that are highly susceptible to mildew where air

Sweet-scented *Phlox paniculata* handsomely dominates summertime borders.

drainage is sluggish and the weather is hot and humid. Thriving in full sun or light shade in any moist, average soil improved with generous compost or humus allotments, all will rebloom with smaller, axillary heads if the terminal blossoming is removed before it sets seed. This is a desirable chore, because hybrids quickly revert to vigorous seedlings with muddier colorings if left untended. Thinning out the new multitude of spring stem growth contributes to larger flowering and more resistance to mildew and red spider mite infestations. Spring or fall division is the recommended propagation method.

The hybrid list is extensive and includes an extended blooming range, color-contrasted centers or "eyes," massive flower heads, and a palette of white, pink, salmon, red, pale blue, lavender, and plum in shades and tints. The English strain *Symons-Jeune* contains a remarkably brilliant and fragrant set of choices, although pure white is not yet included. The following examples illustrate the wide range of options from all manner of hybridizers: "American Legion," 48 in., vivid rose red; "Ann," 36 in., mauve; "B. Compte," 30 in., deep plum red; "Blue Ice," 40 in., pink, fading white; "Bonny Maid," 30 in., pale blue-violet; "Bright Eyes," 24 in., pale pink with crimson eye; "Cecil Hanbury," 30 in., salmon-orange with carmine eye; "Charmaine," 36 in., cherry red; "Chintz," 36 in., pink with red eye; "Colorado," 36 in., salmon orange; "Dodo Hanbury Forbes," 36 in., clear pink, massive head; "Dresden China," 36 in., shell pink; "Eva Forester," 18 in., salmon rose with white eye; "Excelsior," 48 in., rich magenta; "Fairest One," 36 in., pale pink with cerise eye; "Fairy's Petticoat," 42 in., pale pink with darker pink eye, immense heads; "Gaiety," 42 in., cherry red; "Juliet," 24 in., pale pink; "Lilac Time," 48 in., clear lilac blue; "Mary Louise," 30 in., white; "Mother of Pearl," 36 in., white; "Olive Wells Durrant," 42 in., light rose with carmine eye; "Prince Charming," 48 in., glowing scarlet; "Prince George," 36 in., scarlet; "Prince of Orange," 36 in., orange-scarlet; "Rembrandt," 36 in., white; "Royalty," 42 in., rich purple; "Sir John Falstaff," 30 in., salmon pink, enormous florets and heads; "Snowdrift," 30 in., bluish white; "Spitfire," 30 in., salmon orange; "Starfire," 30 in., brilliant red; "Vintage Wine," 36 in., claret red; "White Admiral," 36 in., white with giant-sized heads; and "World Peace," 36 in., white.

Physalis franchetii (Chinese Lantern) 12–24 in. Sun
Flowering span: Early July to August
Color: White
Native habitat: Japan

Not grown for its inconspicuous flowering, this vigorously creeping perennial has late summer, inflated, papery capsules of orange-red about 2 inches long containing an edible but bland-tasting red fruit. When cut as the "lantern" coloring strengthens, its zig-zag stems can be hung and dried for indoor use. Any moist, rich soil in full sun is suitable, and division of the fleshy roots or seed works equally well. Flea beetles are a serious foliage pest, but diseases are uncommon. A smaller species, *alkekengi*, is not reliably hardy in northern areas, but the 8-inch variety, *pygmea*, is satisfactorily adaptable over a wide range.

Physostegia virginiana (Dracocephalum denticulatum)
(Virginia Lions-heart, False Dragonshead) 24–48 in.
Semi-shade
Flowering span: Early July to September
Color: Purplish rose
Native habitat: Vermont to Alabama, west to Texas and Oklahoma

The erect, squarish stems carry dark green, deeply toothed, willowlike, 3- to 5-inch leaves and 8- to 10-inch, terminal spikes of tubular florets arranged in 4 matched rows. Another common name is "obedient plant" from the oddity that individual florets, when bent, retain that position. Although tolerant of full sun if kept constantly moist, it behaves better in light to semi-shading on any average-fertility, humusy soil. Spring division is preferred, and only occasional rust disease bothers it. The several hybrids offer more interesting colors: "Bouquet Rose," 36 in., rose, late-blooming; "Rosy Spire," 42 in., deep rose, late-blooming; "Summer Glow," 42 in., pale pink; "Summer Snow," 24 in., white; and "Vivid," 24 in., bright rose, late-blooming. There is also a type with striking green-and-white foliage but pallid flower color.

Potentilla nepalensis (Nepal Cinque-foil) 18–24 in. Sun
Flowering span: Mid-July to September
Color: Deep rose
Native habitat: Himalaya Mountains

Here the compound leaves are green on both sides and have segments up to 3 inches long, while the branched flower heads have 1-inch, somewhat furry, cup-shaped blossoms. It likes a rich, well-drained soil in full sun and should not be overwatered. Seed or division reproduce it well, and only occasionally is it troubled by anything more than leaf spot. The variety "Miss Wilmott" is crimson with a darker center.

Rudbeckia fulgida (Orange Coneflower) 30–36 in. Sun
Flowering span: Late July to October
Color: Deep orange-yellow

Native habitat: New Jersey to Florida, west to Missouri and
Michigan

The narrow, coarsely toothed leaves are generally hidden
by the masses of daisylike flowers on a well-grown plant.
Creeping stems easily enlarge into a sizable, bushy display
of 3-inch blossoms with slightly down-turned petals, surrounding a black center. Best in full sun, it tolerates light
shading and dryness well and prefers a well-drained, heavy
soil. Division is the preferred propagation method, and
there are no important diseases or pests. The hybrid variety
"Goldsturm" is 24 inches with golden yellow, 3- to 4-inch
flowers. This species is sometimes listed lately as *R. deamii.*

Rudbeckia laciniata (Cutleaf Coneflower) 30–80 in. Sun
Flowering span: Mid-July to September
Color: Golden yellow
Native habitat: Southeastern Canada to Florida, west to
New Mexico and Montana

In this species the deeply incised, broad foliage is dark
green and the flowers have a raised, greenish yellow center.
It enjoys a moist, average soil in sun or light shade and can
easily be propagated by division. Again, there are no problematic pests or diseases. The double variety "Golden
Glow" has 3-inch flowers on 48- to 60-inch stems, spreads
rapidly, and blooms later. The hybrid "Goldquelle" carries
chrome yellow, double blossoms on 30-inch plants and also
blooms later in the summer.

Ruta graveolens (Common Rue) 18–24 in. Sun
Flowering span: Mid-July to mid-August
Color: Dull yellow
Native habitat: Asia, southern Europe

Primarily raised for its unique blue-green foliage instead
of its nondescript flowering, this evergreen sub-shrub
requires a sheltered location and heavy winter mulching in
severe-climate areas. The much-divided, round-lobed leaves
are pungently aromatic when bruised, and in mild sections
it can successfully be trained into a low hedge. Any moist,
average-fertility soil is satisfactory, and it is best increased

by spring division or seed. The hybrids "Blue Beauty" and "Jackman's Blue" are similar and have intensely blue-green, glaucous leaves.

Salvia farinacea (Mealycup Sage) 24–36 in. Sun
Flowering span: Mid-July to mid-August
Color: Deep violet-blue
Native habitat: Texas, eastern New Mexico

These showy blossoms appear in dense whorls terminally on branched stems with 3-inch lancelike leaves attached by 1½-inch petioles. Felted, white hairs cover the outside of the lobelia-like blossoms, giving a "mealy" appearance. Rich, well-drained soil is best and only seed seems to work well for reproduction since the plant usually dies after flowering. Occasionally, white fly can be a pest. There is a scarce white variety, *alba*. Perhaps both are better treated as annuals.

Salvia haematodes (Bloodvein Sage) 12–36 in. Sun
Flowering span: Early July to September
Color: Blue violet
Native habitat: Greece

In this durable species the 9-inch, heart-shaped, blue-green leaves have noticeable red veining and remain in a basal rosette below the tall, much-branched flowering stalks with their loosely arranged, ½-inch florets. It needs the same cultural conditions as S. *farinacea*.

Sedum album (White Stonecrop) 4–8 in. Sun
Flowering span: Early July to August
Color: White
Native habitat: Europe, northern Asia

Another in the fine list of groundcover plants of the same genus, this species has sausage-shaped, ½-inch leaves with a red tint and airy clusters of starry flowers. Full sun is best but it does satisfactorily in light shade, although with reduced blossoming. A light, sandy loam of average fertility encourages rapid growth, and division is the simplest way to make more plants. There are no bothersome diseases or pests. A pink-flowered variety, *murale,* has deep purple foliage.

Sedum hispanicum (Spanish Stonecrop) 3–4 in. Sun
Flowering span: Early July to August
Color: Pinkish white
Native habitat: Central and southern Europe

Here the ¼-inch, tightly compressed, gray-green foliage of this creeping plant turns reddish as it ages. The tips of the leaves are pimpled, and the branched flowering is flat-topped. Culture is the same as for *S. album.* This species is sometimes marketed under the name *S. glaucum.*

Sedum kamtschaticum (Orange Stonecrop) 4–9 in. Sun
Flowering span: Early July to August
Color: Golden yellow
Native habitat: Japan, Korea, Kamschatka Peninsula

A clump-forming species with trailing stems, this one has bright green, pulpy, 1½-inch leaves and large flower clusters with ¾-inch, star-shaped florets. The seed pods later turn dark red and remain effective all season. It has a surprising tolerance for light shade and should be cared for in other respects like *S. album.*

Sedum reflexum (Jenny Stonecrop) 8–10 in. Sun
Flowering span: Early July to August
Color: Bright greenish yellow
Native habitat: Europe

The ¾-inch flowers here have pale chocolate markings and the ½-inch pulpy leaves are crowded toward the growing tip. It has a marked preference for a dry soil but should otherwise be cultivated like *S. album.* Some botanists prefer to include this plant as a part of *S. rupestre*'s forms.

Sedum spurium (Two-row Stonecrop) 6 in. Sun
Flowering span: Mid-July to early August
Color: Purplish pink, occasionally white
Native habitat: Asia Minor, northern Iran

A rampant creeper even in semi-shade, its 1-inch, oval, wavy-edged leaves are paired on trailing stems that root as they touch. The star-shaped, ragged flowering comes in tight, 2-inch clusters on reddish stalks and produces best in full sun. This durable plant even grows satisfactorily under branches of maples and should have the same care as S. *album*. The variety *coccineum* carries erect, rosy crimson flowering and foliage, while the hybrid "Dragon's Blood" is ruby red in blossom with bronze leaves.

Senecio cineraria (*Cineraria maritima*) (Silver Groundsel)
 18–24 in. Sun
Flowering span: Mid-July to September
Color: Yellow
Native habitat: Mediterranean Europe

Primarily grown for its white-woolly foliage, the insignificant, terminal flower clusters of ¼-inch, rounded, daisylike blossoms can be removed to make a compact edging plant. The lancelike, deeply cut leaves are 2 to 6 inches long and

Silver tracery of foliage is the hallmark of *Senecio cineraria* throughout the summer.

have rounded lobes. Full sun to light shade, plus a consistently moist, well-drained, rich soil, is best. In severe climates it needs winter protection. Division, stem cuttings, or seed readily reproduces it, and aphids appear to be the chief nuisance. The variety *candicans* or *candididissimus* has very silvery white foliage.

Senecio clivorum "Desdemona" (*Ligularia clivorum*) 24–36 in. Semi-shade
Flowering span: Late July to mid-September
Color: Deep yellow
Native habitat: Horticultural hybrid

The origin of this unusual plant is clouded, but its showiness is conspicuous. The rounded, 6- to 12-inch leaves appear first as deep purple and turn green with age, while branched, sturdy stems produce loose clusters of 2-inch, fragrant, daisylike flowers with brown centers. Except for a preference for some shading, its culture is identical with that for S. *cineraria.*

Senecio przewalski (*Ligularia przewalski*) 48–60 in. Sun
Flowering span: Late July to mid-September
Color: Bright yellow
Native habitat: Northern China

The deeply cut and serrated, 8- to 12-inch, arrow-point leaves form generous mounds prior to the striking appearance of the narrow 10- to 12-inch spikes of ragged-looking florets on almost-black stems. It thrives in any rich, moist, sunny location and can readily be propagated by spring or fall division. Nothing serious seems to bother it. A hybrid, "The Rocket," blooms later and has leaves slightly more rounded.

Solidago hybrida (Hybrid Goldenrod) 12–60 in. Sun
Flowering span: Late July to November
Color: Yellow
Native habitat: Horticultural hybrids, probably derived mainly from S. *canadensis* of eastern North America

Blamed incorrectly for domestic hay-fever allergies more properly assigned to ragweed (*Ambrosia* species), the fluffy plumes of these colorful, long-flowering perennials are more appreciated in Europe, where hybridization has evolved a wealth of sizes, colorings, and blooming times worth investigating. Rampant if overfertilized, they like a well-drained, average-fertility, somewhat dry soil in full sun or light shading, and can readily be moved even in full flower. Division is the easiest propagation method, and only rust disease on the narrow, willowlike foliage is a serious problem. Some of the popular hybrids are: "Crown of Rays," mustard yellow, 24 in.; "Goldenmosa," golden yellow, 36 in.; "Golden Shower," yellow, 42 in.; "Golden Thumb," yellow, 12 in.; "Golden Wings," bright gold, 60 in.; "Lemore," lemon yellow, 30 in.; "Leraft," bright gold, 36 in., late; "Peter Pan," canary yellow, 36 in., late; and "Queenie," deep yellow, 12 in.

Solidaster luteus 18–30 in. Sun
Flowering span: Mid-July to September
Color: Bright yellow
Native habitat: Horticultural hybrid between *Solidago* and Aster

The heavy clusters of ½-inch flowers appear on widely branched stems that can billow to 48 inches in width. The leaves are willowlike as on the goldenrod; the flowering is similar to an aster. Any average soil, well-drained and moderately moist, suits it in sun or light shade. Fall and spring division are equally satisfactory, and there appear to be no bothersome pests or diseases of consequence.

Stachys coccinea (Texas Betony) 4–24 in. Semi-shade
Flowering span: Mid-July to mid-August
Color: Scarlet red
Native habitat: Western Texas to Arizona

Brightly conspicuous, the ¾-inch, tubular flowers appear interruptedly in whorls along the slender flower stalks above a basal rosette of broad, lanceolate foliage. Any average-fertility soil in light to half-shade is workable, and seed or division reproduces it easily. Pests and diseases are uncommon. It requires winter protection in severe climates, where it may behave like an annual.

Teucrium chamaedrys (Chamaedrys Germander) 12–24 in. Sun
Flowering span: Mid-July to mid-August
Color: Rose purple
Native habitat: Europe

Useful either as an airy groundcover or as a clipped edging in sunny borders, the erect, woody stems have dark green, oval, hairy, ¼-inch leaves tightly arranged and ¾-inch, tubular flowers often spotted with white or rose. Generally evergreen in mild areas, it may need winter protection in severe climates. Any light, well-drained, average-fertility soil is suitable, and propagation is simplest by division. Diseases and pests are not bothersome.

Thalictrum rocquebrunianum (Lavender Mist Meadow-rue) 36–60 in. Sun
Flowering span: Late July to September
Color: Rose lavender
Native habitat: Uncertain, but probably northern Asia

The dainty, fernlike, green foliage is robust and appears on blue-green, hollow stems below airy panicles of ½-inch, globular florets with densely conspicuous, yellow, protruding stamens. Its culture is identical to that for the May-blooming species, *T. aquilegifolium.* This one may prove to be the hardiest of the group.

Thalictrum speciosissimum (glaucum) (Dusty Meadow-rue) 24–60 in. Sun
Flowering span: Mid-July to September
Color: Light yellow
Native habitat: Southern Europe

The blue-green, compound leaves and fragrant flowering give this species extra distinction. It should be cultivated the same as *T. aquilegifolium* of May.

Veronica longifolia (maritima) (Clump Speedwell) 24–36 in. Sun
Flowering span: Mid-July to September
Color: Lilac blue
Native habitat: Central Europe, northern Asia

Here the gray-green, lanceolate leaves appear either in pairs or in whorls of 3, and the narrow, densely flowered spikes are numerous. Any moist, well-drained, average-fertility soil in sun to light shade is satisfactory, and division is the practical reproduction method, although seed is workable, too. Pests and diseases are not common. The varieties include: *alba*, ivory white; "Blue Giant," lavender blue; *rosea*, pink; and *subsessilis*, royal blue, erect, densely flowered.

Yucca filamentosa (Adams-needle Yucca) 60–120 in. Sun
Flowering span: Early July to mid-August
Color: White, creamy white
Native habitat: Southern New Jersey to Georgia

The tropical-looking foliage of this evergreen plant is conspicuous throughout the year. Its swordlike leaves are 1-inch wide and from 12 to 36 inches long with curly threads along the margins. The stem is stout and short, and its stiff, sharply pointed leaves are tightly arranged in radiating whorls around it. In this species the foliage ends in a recurved, spoonlike shape. A solitary, stiff, asparaguslike flower stalk develops many side branches and 1- to 2-inch, down-hanging, bell-like florets. It prefers a sun-drenched, sandy soil that is consistently well-drained and moderately dry. Propagate by division of young plants only since the deep rootstock resents moving; older plants can be completely dug up and the roots sliced into 4- to 6-inch pieces for reproduction. Leaf blotch sometimes affects the foliage, while caterpillars and beetles may disfigure the blossoms.

Yucca flaccida (Weakleaf Yucca) 60–120 in. Sun
Flowering span: Early July to mid-August
Color: Off white
Native habitat: North Carolina to Alabama

Often confused with its look-alike relative *Y. filamentosa,* the thick foliage here hangs downward and the leaf margin fibers are straight. Its flower head is generally more openly constructed, but the florets are the same size for both. Culture is identical. The hybrid "Ivory Tower" has showier blossoming.

AUGUST

A General Guide to the Color Values Available in August:
(*Each division includes shades, tints, and tones of the dominant value.*)

WHITE: Anaphalis margaritacea, Anaphalis yedoensis, Artemesia albula, Artemesia lactiflora, Artemesia schmidtiana nana, Aster novae-angilae *hybrids,* Boltonia asteroides, Chrysanthemum parthenium, Chrysanthemum uliginosum, Hosta *"Honeybells,"* Hosta lancifolia minor alba, Hosta plantaginea, Liatris pycnostachya *hybrids,* Lilium *hybrids,* Lilium philippinense, Lilium speciosum, Liriope spicata, Lobelia syphilitica alba, Phalaris arundinacea, Salvia azurea alba, Sedum spectabile *hybrids,* Stokesia laevis alba

YELLOW: Artemesia absinthium, Artemesia stelleriana, Chrysopsis falcata, Chrysopsis mariana, Helenium autumnale, Kniphofia uvaria *hybrids,* Lilium henryi citrinum, Rudbeckia hirta, Rudbeckia speciosa, Santolina chamaecyparissus, Santolina virens

ORANGE: Helenium autumnale *hybrids,* Kniphofia uvaria hybrids, Lilium henryi, Rudbeckia hirta gloriosa

RED: Aster novae-angilae *hybrids,* Helenium autumnale *hybrids,* Kniphofia uvaria, Lilium *hybrids,* Lilium speciosum *hybrids,* Polygonum reynoutria, Sedum spectabile *hybrids,* Sedum telephium *hybrids*

PINK: Aster amellus *hybrids,* Aster novae-angilae, Boltonia asteroides, Boltonia latisquama nana, Chelone obliqua, Dianthus cinnabarinus, Kniphofia uvaria *hybrids,* Lilium *hybrids,* Lilium speciosum *hybrids,* Sedum sieboldi, Sedum telephium

PURPLE: Aster amellus, Aster novae-angilae, Aster spectabilis, Boltonia asteroides, Boltonia latisquama, Chelone lyoni, Crocus kotschyanus, Hosta decorata, Hosta lancifolia, Liatris pycnostachya, Liatris scariosa, Liatris squarrosa, Liriope spicata, Sedum spectabile, Thalictrum dipterocarpum

BLUE: Aster amellus *hybrids*, Ceratostigma plumbaginoides, Clematis heracleaefolia, Eupatorium coelestinum, Gentiana andrewsi, Hosta ventricosa, Lobelia syphilitica, Salvia azurea, Stokesia laevis

BICOLOR: Helenium autumnale *hybrids*, Kniphofia uvaria *hybrids*, Lilium *hybrids*, Lilium speciosum *hybrids*, Rudbeckia hirta gloriosa

Anaphalis margaritacea (Antennaria margaritacea)
(Common Pearly Everlasting) 12–24 in. Semi-shade
Flowering span: Early August to October
Color: Pearl white
Native habitat: Northeast Asia, North America, Europe

Adaptable to a wide range of soils and exposures, this wildflower produces unbranched, erect stems with 2- to 4-inch, lanceolate, woolly, silvery gray foliage and 2-inch, terminal clusters of tiny blossoms composed mainly of whitened leaf bracts. Tolerant of both full sun or shade and dry, poor soils, it performs best in any well-drained, average-fertility location. The flower stems can be cut and dried easily for indoor use. Propagate by division, spring stem cuttings, or seed. Nothing bothers it.

Anaphalis yedoensis (Japanese Pearly Everlasting) 24–30 in. Semi-shade
Flowering span: Early August to October
Color: Off white
Native habitat: Himalaya Mountains

Here the leaves are ½ inch wide and are not produced on the bottom part of the stems. The flowers appear in tighter bunchings and dry easily. Growth is neat but not invasive from underground stems, and its culture is the same as for *A. margaritacea.*

Anemone vitifolia (Grapeleaf Anemone) 24–36 in. Semi-shade
Flowering span: Late August to October

Color: Silvery pink
Native habitat: Nepal

The earliest of the windflower anemones to bloom, this plant produces a heavy basal clump of grapelike, much-cut foliage and erect, thin stems with 2-inch, saucer-shaped flowers having raised, yellowish centers. A rich, moist, humusy soil with morning light and afternoon shading is preferred, and propagation is best handled by division or seeding. Pests or diseases are not common, but the plant is somewhat tender and needs winter protection. The variety *robustissima* is sturdier and reliably hardy.

Artemesia absinthium (Common Wormwood) 30–40 in. Sun
Flowering span: Early August to October
Color: Greenish yellow
Native habitat: Europe

Its fernlike, silver-coated foliage is useful, when dried, as the flavoring for the liqueur absinth, and for a home-brewed tea with medicinal powers. The somewhat woody stems carry insignificant but numerous terminal flower clusters. Any dry, well-drained location in sun or light shade is suitable, and reproduction is accomplished by division or seed. Rust is the main cultural problem. The hybrid "Lambrook Silver" is 36 inches tall, rapid-growing, and more silvery.

Artemesia albula (Silver King Wormwood) 30–36 in. Sun
Flowering span: Mid-August to October
Color: White
Native habitat: Colorado to Texas

With its flowers inconsequential, the plant is grown mainly for its silver-gray, aromatic, feathery foliage, which can easily be dried for decorative, indoor uses. Any light, well-drained, somewhat dry soil in full sun or light shade is best, and either spring division, summer stem cuttings, or seed reproduces it quickly. Rust disease on the valued leaves is a nuisance, but insects have no especial fondness for it. In severe winter climates it needs to be mulched

Silvery *Artemesia albula* refreshingly lowers the visual temperature of August borders.

heavily. A hybrid, "Silver Queen," is said to have more glistening foliage.

Artemesia lactiflora (vulgaris lactiflora) (Ghostplant
     Wormwood, White Mugwort) 48–60 in. Semi-shade
Flowering span: Mid-August to October
Color: Creamy white
Native habitat: China, India

Here the 6- to 9-inch, deeply cut, fragrant leaves are deep green above and silvery beneath. Clusters of scented flowers appear in decorative plumes on purplish stems, and this species prefers a moist, well-drained soil in some shading. Spring division is recommended, although seeds and summer stem cuttings also work well. Foliage rust is still the chief affliction.

Artemesia schmidtiana nana 6–12 in. Sun
Flowering span: Mid-August to October
Color: Creamy white
Native habitat: Japan

The parent plant seems to have faded from view, while the variety listed here has already been supplanted by the hybrid selection "Silver Mound" (sometimes listed as "Silver Dome"). Its silvery, feathery, moundlike habit is retained best in full sun and in a sandy or gravelly soil low in fertility. Overfeeding and shade cause the slender stems to flop over, exposing the center. Remove the unimportant, disclike flowering when it appears to retain symmetry, and propagate by spring division or summer stem cuttings. This type is not bothered by pests or diseases of consequence.

Artemesia stelleriana (Beach Wormwood) 18–24 in. Sun
Flowering span: Early August to October
Color: Yellow
Native habitat: Northeast Asia, Massachusetts to Delaware

Prized for its strikingly white, woolly foliage, the species carries small, globe-shaped flowers in heavy clusters and thrives in seacoast conditions. For garden use it wants a well-drained, sandy soil in full sun. Propagate by spring division or summer cuttings. It has no important diseases or pests.

Aster amellus (Italian Aster) 24–30 in. Sun
Flowering span: Early August to mid-September
Color: Purple
Native habitat: Italy, Asia

Showy for a long time, the 2-inch, fragrant flowers have yellow centers and appear in clusters with oblong, lanceolate, gray-green leaves having rough surfaces. Although satisfactorily resistant to drought, the plant still prefers a moist, average-fertility soil in sun to light shading. Spring division, seeds or summer stem cuttings all work well for reproduction, and only mildew is occasionally bothersome. There are several attractive hybrids: "King George," deep violet; "Perry's Variety," almost red; "Rudolph Goethe," deep lavender; "Sonia," clear pink; "Triumph," violet blue, early; and "Violet Queen," rich violet.

Aster novae-angilae (New England Aster) 36–72 in. Sun
Flowering span: Late August to October

Color: Deep violet-purple, lavender, pink
Native habitat: Eastern North America

Widely distributed in fields and meadows, the erect, woody stalks carry distinguishing stem-clasping leaves that are 3 to 5 inches long, gray green, and hairy. The clusters of 40 to 50 florets have yellow-centered, 2-inch blossoms. A moist, average-fertility soil in full sun to light shade is suitable. If kept heavily mulched and cool, the stems retain their lower leaves. Division, seeding, or stem cuttings reproduce it well. Mildew may become a problem in very dry weather, but insects are not troublesome. There are many hybrid improvements: "Barr's Pink," rose pink; "Harrington's Pink," clear pink, semi-double; "Incomparabilis," fuchsia purple; "Mount Rainier," creamy white; "September Glow," ruby red; and "September Glory," deep rose red.

Aster spectabilis (Seaside Aster) 18–24 in. Sun
Flowering span: Mid-August to October
Color: Bright violet
Native habitat: Massachusetts to North Carolina coastlines

Spreading quickly by slender, underground runners, this wildflower carries 3- to 5-inch, dark green, oval leaves and 1½- to 2-inch blossoms with yellowish centers arranged in terminal clusters. Tolerant of a sandy, acid location in full sun or light shade, it also grows well in gardens with heavy, lean soils. No pests or diseases of consequence annoy its growth.

Boltonia asteroides (White Boltonia) 24–96 in. Sun
Flowering span: Late August to October
Color: White, violet, pink, purple
Native habitat: New York to Florida, west to Texas and
    North Dakota

In general appearance they resemble perennial asters, but here the 1-inch flower's yellow, central disc is raised and rounded in shape. Its narrow, somewhat thick, 3- to 5-inch, pale green leaves appear on willowy stems but rarely need staking as a border background grouping. Any average-fertility soil is suitable in sun or light shade, and division is the best method for propagation, although seed can give fair results. Nothing bothers it. The hybrid "Snowbank" is 48 inches tall and pure white.

Boltonia latisquama (Violet Boltonia) 36–48 in. Sun
Flowering span: Early August to October
Color: Blue violet
Native habitat: Kansas, Missouri, Arkansas

In this species the flowers are 1½ to 2 inches broad and appear more generously than on *B. asteroides*. Culture is the same for both. The variety *nana* is 36 inches tall and pale pink in coloring.

Ceratostigma plumbaginoides (*Plumbago larpentae*) (Blue Leadwort) 6–12 in. Sun
Flowering span: Mid-August to October
Color: Cobalt blue
Native habitat: China, India

Vividly colorful when grown in the full sun it likes best, this long-blooming groundcover has trailing, wiry stems and bright green, 2- to 3-inch, bristle-tipped leaves wider at the far end. The ¾-inch phlox-shaped blossoms appear in tight clusters along the reddish stems, and at the end of the flowering season the foliage takes on a bronze cast. A consistently well-drained, humusy soil suits it best, with propagation coming either from spring division or summer cuttings. There are no pests or diseases as nuisances. Mulch heavily for winter in severe climates.

Chelone lyoni (Pink Turtlehead) 24–36 in. Semi-shade
Flowering span: Early August to mid-September
Color: Rose purple
Native habitat: Mountains of North Carolina, South Carolina, and Tennessee

Native to swampy places, it demands a consistently moist, humusy soil in the shade garden and is intolerant of full sun at any time. The deep green, 4- to 6-inch, glossy foliage is terminated by short spikes of tubular, hooded florets. Spring division, seed, and summertime cuttings all propagate it readily, and there are no nuisances from diseases or pests.

Chelone obliqua (Rose Turtlehead) 18–24 in. Semi-shade
Flowering span: Early August to mid-September
Color: Deep rose
Native habitat: Maryland to Georgia, west to Arkansas and
　　Minnesota

Less vigorous but more attractively colored than its relative, *C. lyoni,* this species has 6- to 8-inch, glossy leaves back-tapering to a broad stalk instead of a slender petiole. Culture for both is identical, and each benefits from having a thick compost mulch at all times.

Chrysanthemum parthenium (Pyrethrum parthenium)
　　(Feverfew) 12–36 in. Sun
Flowering span: Early August to mid-September
Color: White
Native habitat: Europe, Caucasus Mountains

Because it is not reliably hardy but self-seeds eagerly, this perennial should perhaps be treated as an overproductive annual. The 1-inch, daisylike flowers have a prominent yellow center and appear on much-branched stalks above pungent, oval, bisected foliage. A well-drained, sandy soil extends its potential lifespan, and winter mulching is recommended. Seed is obviously the better reproduction method, although summer cuttings root with ease. Pests and diseases can come in multiples but most do not have any serious affect on its seasonal growth. There are several single and double forms available, but the doubles cannot be reproduced except from cuttings.

Chrysanthemum uliginosum (Pyrethrum uliginosum) (Giant
　　Daisy) 48–84 in. Sun
Flowering Span: Mid-August to October
Color: White
Native habitat: Hungary

Impressive in the background of a border, this densely upright plant carries 2½- to 3-inch, yellow-centered blossoms in terminal clusters above narrow, coarsely toothed, light green leaves. It has a decided liking for very moist locations and enjoys a heavy, rich soil. Seed, division, and root suckers all reproduce it well, and there are no bothersome pests or diseases.

Chrysopsis falcata (Sickleleaf Goldaster)　4–16 in.　Sun
Flowering span: Early August to mid-September
Color: Golden yellow
Native habitat: Coastal Massachusetts to coastal New Jersey

A hardy, trailing plant suitable for acid, sandy soils with a seacoast exposure, it can be grown in gardens satisfactorily. The slender, dark green, curved leaves appear on hairy stems with erect, solitary, 1-inch, daisylike flowering. Spring division or seed propagates it, and there appear to be no nuisances from diseases or pests. Pinching back new growth in springtime encourages heavier flowering.

Chrysopsis mariana (Maryland Goldaster)　8–28 in.　Sun
Flowering span: Mid-August to mid-September
Color: Bright yellow
Native habitat: New York to Ohio, south to Texas and
    Florida

Smooth, 2- to 3-inch, broad leaves on silky stems usually have a noticeable, lighter colored mid-vein in this species, and the blossoming of 1½- to 2-inch, daisylike flowers is on showy, terminal clusterings. Its culture is the same as for *C. falcata.*

Clematis heracleaefolia (Tube Clematis)　36–48 in.　Sun
Flowering span: Mid-August to mid-September
Color: Pale blue
Native habitat: China, Japan

The 3-parted, 4- to 6-inch, bright green leaves of this vigorous plant may appear coarse, but the hyacinth-like, 1-inch, tubular flowers in terminal clusters have a welcome fragrance and a useful coloring for late summer borders. Any well-drained, humusy soil is suitable, and reproduction can be handled by seed, division, or stem cuttings. Unfortunately, the large foliage is prone to disfigurement from either the tarnished plant bug, blister beetle, red spider mite, or from leaf spot disease. The fragrant variety *davidiana* grows between 36 to 48 inches with deep blue florets, while the hybrid "Crepescule" has slightly scented blossoms of sky blue. "Wyevale" is flax blue, fragrant, and 48 inches tall.

Crocus kotschyanus (*zonatus*) 3–4 in. Sun
Flowering span: Late August to mid-September
Color: Rose lilac
Native habitat: Asia Minor

Probably the earliest of the fall-blooming crocus, it carries fine, short leaves and blossoming distinguished by 2 yellow-orange spots on the inside of each petal base. The flower throat is yellow. Any well-drained, sunny location with soil of average fertility is suitable, and there are no insect or disease nuisances. It spreads freely. The variety *leucopharynx* (*karduchorum*) flowers later and has a white throat with no orange spotting.

Dianthus cinnabarinus (Cinnabar Pink) 10–12 in. Sun
Flowering span: Mid-August to mid-September
Color: Magenta pink
Native habitat: Greece

Rigid, grasslike leaves produce 4-angled stems with narrow, linear stem foliage and tight flower clusters. A rich, moist soil is best, and division is the recommended propagation method. It appears to be unaffected by pests or diseases.

Eupatorium coelestinum (*Conoclinium coelestinum*)
　　(Mistflower Eupatorium) 18–36 in. Sun
Flowering span: Mid-August to mid-September
Color: Bright violet-blue
Native habitat: New Jersey to Florida, west to Texas and
　　Kansas

Slender stems with widely spaced, elongated, triangular, wrinkled leaves produce 3- to 4-inch clusters of ageratumlike, fuzzy florets in full sun or light shade. Rapid-growing, this wildflower prefers a light, well-drained, humusy soil. Spring division, summer cuttings, or seed propagate it equally well, but it is susceptible to serious affliction from either crown rot, rhizoctonia rot, or botrytis blight. Insects, however, are not troublesome.

Gentiana andrewsi (Andrews Gentian, Closed Gentian)
    18–24 in. Semi-shade
Flowering span: Early August to mid-September
Color: Purple blue
Native habitat: Southeastern Canada to Georgia, west to Arkansas

Novel because the football-shaped blossoms never open (it self-fertilizes in complete privacy), its long, oval leaves tightly surround the stemless, clustered flowers on slender, upright stems. Growing any of the gentians well is hardly a simple process since they are individually finicky. This species wants a deep, cool, humusy, shaded location that is constantly moist, acid, and well-drained. Seed, although slow, is by far the easiest propagation method, and only rust disease on the foliage is a nuisance. Often confused with its lookalike, *G. clausa,* perhaps only a botanist would be able to distinguish them correctly.

Helenium autumnale (Common Sneezeweed) 24–60 in.
    Sun
Flowering span: Early August to October
Color: Bright yellow
Native habitat: Southern Canada, most of the United States

Free-flowering through many months, this prolific wildflower carries 1½- to 2-inch, daisylike flowers with a raised central cone above 4- to 6-inch, lancelike, smooth leaves. It enjoys a consistently moist, rich soil in full sun and can be easily propagated by division, summertime cuttings, or seed. Root aphids are the only affliction. There is a generous listing of hybrids: "Brilliant," 36 in., blendings of orange, brown, and yellow; "Bruno," 42 in., deep red-brown; "Butterpat," 42 in., clear, golden yellow; "Chippersfield Orange," 48 in., gold; "Coppelia," 36 in., deep coppery orange; "Copper Spray," 42 in., orange; "Crimson Beauty," 24 in., brown-red; "Golden Youth," 36 in., deep yellow; "Gold Fox," 36 in., orange-brown; "Mahogany," 36 in., bronze red; "Moerheim Beauty," 36 in., reddish brown; "Pumilum Magnificum," 24 in., butter yellow; "Riverton Beauty," 48 in., orange-yellow; and "Wyndley," 24 in., copper-orange.

Hosta decorata (*Funkia decorata*) (Blunt Plantainlily)
    10–12 in. Semi-shade
Flowering span: Early August to September
Color: Violet
Native habitat: China, Japan

Slow to spread, the dark green, 6-inch, blunted leaves are enlivened with a ½-inch white margin in this later-blooming type that requires the same cultural care as the July-flowering *H. caerulea.* It is sometimes listed as "Thomas Hogg."

Hosta "Honeybells" 18–24 in. Semi-shade
Flowering span: Mid-August to mid-September
Color: Violet white
Native habitat: Horticultural hybrid

This hybrid has light green, 12-inch leaves that are 6 inches wide and erect flower stalks with pleasantly fragrant blossoming. Its culture is identical to that for the July-flowering *H. caerulea.*

Hosta lancifolia (Narrow Plantainlily) 15–18 in. Semi-
    shade
Flowering span: Mid-August to mid-September
Color: Pale lilac
Native habitat: Japan

The 6-inch leaves here are 2 to 3 inches wide and make a dense mound even under very dry conditions. Its 1½-inch florets appear 6 to 10 on slender stems. Care for it the same as for the earlier blooming *H. caerulea.* There are several varieties: *albo-marginata,* 15 inches, with mostly green leaves brushed with white and showing violet flowering; *minor alba,* 10 inches, glossy green leaves with sparse white flowering; and *tardifolia*, 15 inches, mauve-purple blossoms appearing weeks later than the type.

Hosta plantaginea (subcordata) (Fragrant Plantainlily)
　　12–20 in.　Semi-shade
Flowering span: Mid-August to mid-September
Color: Waxy white
Native habitat: China, Japan

Delightfully scented, late-blooming, and showy, this plantainlily has noticeably veined, light green, 12- to 18-inch, heart-shaped leaves ending in a sharp point. The 3- to 5-inch, tubular blossoms generally open by late afternoon and persist fragrantly until dawn. Its cultural needs are the same as for the July-flowering *H. caerulea*. The variety *grandiflora* has longer, wider blossoms, while the hybrid "Royal Standard" grows 18 to 24 inches tall with smaller, fragrant florets and tolerance to more sun without foliage damage.

Hosta ventricosa　12–18 in.　Semi-shade
Flowering span: Mid-August to mid-September
Color: Violet blue
Native habitat: Japan, China

On this species the leaves are a rich green and up to 8 inches long. Flowering comes on erect stems usually accompanied by widely spaced tiny leaflet forms. It requires the same cultural care as *H. caerulea*.

Kniphofia uvaria (Tritoma uvaria) (Common Torchlily, Red-
　　hot Poker)　24–30 in.　Sun
Flowering span: Early August to mid-September
Color: Red, turning yellow with age
Native habitat: South Africa

Similar to the June-blooming *K. tucki*, the gray-green, slender foliage here often stretches to 36 inches and usually falls into mild disarray by the time its leafless flower stalks emerge. The 4- to 8-inch heads have 1½- to 2-inch, down-hanging, tubular florets tightly packed into a noticeable 2- to 3-inch wide blossom attractive to hummingbirds. It prefers a rich, deep, constantly moist soil that is very well drained and generally requires protective mulching in winter. Where climates are severe, it is best to treat the ropelike roots as tender and to dig them for winter storage. Propagate by seed (which is very likely to produce mixed colorings) or by spring division of the thick rootstock (which then requires 2 to 3 years to flower). Leaf spot is the only nuisance. A striking list of hybrids is available: "Ada," 42 in., deep orange; "Bees Lemon," 36 in., lemon yellow; "Bees Sunset," 30 in., gold with light red shading; "H. C. Mills," 42 in., gold and red; "Maid of Orleans," 42 in., creamy white, tinged pink; "Modesta," 24 in., ivory with a pink cast; "Royal Standard," 42 in., bright red and yellow; and "Samuel's Sensation," 60 in., fiery red.

Liatris pycnostachya (Kansas Gayfeather) 36–60 in. Sun
Flowering span: Mid-August to mid-September
Color: Rosy lavender
Native habitat: North Dakota to Oklahoma

The wandlike spikes of this species carry closely set, fuzzy blossoms and more densely arranged linear foliage; otherwise, it is quite similar to the July-blossoming *L. spicata*. It prefers a moderately fertile soil that is consistently moist, and while it will also do nicely in semi-shade, the stems will grow crookedly instead of stiffly erect. Seed is sluggish to germinate, so that division of the large corms is the recommended propagation method. Mulch in severe climates for successful wintering. The later hybrid "September Glory" carries deep purple flowering up to 60 inches tall, while "White Spire," also late, has white blossoming at 60 inches.

Liatris scariosa (Tall Gayfeather) 12–60 in. Sun
Flowering span: Mid-August to mid-September
Color: Deep lavender
Native habitat: Pennsylvania to Georgia

The stems here are usually covered with downy white hairs and the basal leaves often become 2 inches wide. The flowering is distinctly stalked and appears very openly arranged. A rich, moist soil is best, and additional plants can come from seed or from division. Leaf spot is an occasional nuisance.

Liatris squarrosa (Lacinaria squarrosa) 12–36 in. Sun
Flowering span: Early August to September
Color: Bright purple
Native habitat: Delaware to Florida, west to Texas and
 South Dakota

Although producing only a few flowering stalks, the ones that do appear often carry up to 60 florets in a showy but irregularly shaped head. Its basal leaves are grasslike, but the upper ones are narrow and stiff on stems that are generally hairy. A light, rich, moist soil is preferred, and it grows well in semi-shade, too. Fall seeding or offsets readily reproduce it, and there is little to be concerned about with pests or diseases.

Lilium (Lily) 24–100 in. Sun
Flowering span: Early August to October
Color: White, pink, crimson
Native habitat: Global northern hemisphere locations

These late-flowering hybrid lilies continue in a display of greater size and sturdiness along with improved colorings. Culture is explained at length under the lily entry for June.

August-Blooming Hybrid Lilies

ORIENTAL HYBRIDS: From 24 to 100 inches tall with 6- to 12-inch, highly fragrant blossoms and derived from *L. auratum, L. speciosum, L. japonicum, L. rubellum,* plus any crosses made with *L. henryi*

Bowl-shaped flowering examples:
"Empress of India," dark crimson inside, deep pink outside; "Empress of Japan," white, heavily spotted with deep crimson; and "Pink Glory" strain, clear deep pink with pale crimson spotting

Flat-faced flowering examples:
"Imperial Crimson," mostly crimson with white margins with heavy spotting; "Imperial Gold," white with gold

center banding and heavy dark red spotting; and "Imperial Silver," white with moderate dark brown-red spotting

Recurved flowering examples:

"Allegra," pure white with slightly recurved petals; "Everest" strain, pure white with a slightly greenish throat; and "Sprite," deep crimson with silvery edges

Trumpet flowering example:

"Parkman" strain, various tints and shadings of white or crimson

Lilium henryi (Henry Lily) 60–90 in. Semi-shade
Flowering span: Early August to September
Color: Salmon orange
Native habitat: China

Not only lime-loving but detesting acidity (do not use peat), the large bulb develops thick, glossy, dark green foliage that is lanceolate (5 inches) at the bottom and almost oval (1 inch) near the blossoms on purplish stems that flop over easily and require early staking or placement to hang over a wall. The 4-inch, turks-cap, black-spotted flowers

A pervading spicy fragrance accompanies the flowering exuberance of *Lilium* "Imperial Crimson."

have no fragrance. It needs fall division every 3 to 4 years and planting in a heavily composted soil with excellent drainage (*a must* for all lilies, except swamp types) that is not exposed to more than a half day of filtered sunshine. It fortunately appears unaffected by the troublesome mosaic disease. The rare variety *citrinum* has pale yellow flowering.

Lilium philippinense (Philippine Lily) 24–36 in. Sun
Flowering span: Early August to September
Color: White
Native habitat: Philippine Islands

Although not reliably hardy and often treated as a biennial, the unusual 10-inch, narrow, trumpet-shaped blossoms are nicely fragrant. Only 1 to 2 flowers appear on the slender stems along with widely spaced, bright green leaves. The outside of the flower is greenish white with some red streaking near the base, but the interior is pure white. Plant new bulbs in the spring in a well-drained, humusy soil with ample moisture and a cool location. Seed germinates easily for bloom the following year if planted as soon as it is ripe. There appear to be no problems except its outdoor tenderness.

Lilium speciosum (Speciosum Lily) 48–72 in. Sun
Flowering span: Mid-August to mid-September
Color: White or pink with crimson spotting
Native habitat: Japan, China

Very hardy and reliable, this fragrant lily has many outward-facing, 4- to 6-inch flowers on long pedicels above deep green, lanceolate leaves. Its thick, waxy petals are strongly recurved and wavy-margined around noticeable, elongated stamens. Disliking any lime, it does best in a rich, deep, humusy location. Scales or offsets propagate it readily, and new plantings can be made in the spring. There are many varieties and hybrids: *album,* pure white; *album-novum,* white with yellow spotting and yellow anthers; "Grand Commander," crimson with deep red spotting and white edges; *kraetzeri,* white with orange-brown stamens; "Lucy Wilson," rose pink edged in white; *magnificum,* rose with deep crimson spots; "Melpomene," white margins around heavy carmine spotting, 8-in. blossoms, *roseum,* pink; *rubrum,* carmine pink with a broad, white margin, 8-in. blossoms; and "Uchida," deep crimson with a white edge.

Liriope spicata (*graminifolia*) (Creeping Lilyturf) 8–12 in.
    Semi-shade
Flowering span: Early August to mid-September
Color: Pale lilac, white
Native habitat: China, Japan

Useful as a neat border planting, the linear foliage tufts of this evergreen perennial produce short, 6- to 8-inch spikes of ¼-inch florets tightly crowded along the stalks. While not reliably hardy in severe climates, it has a late summer appeal if given good drainage and a semi-shaded location in a moderately rich, constantly moist soil. Reducing the winter-damaged foliage each spring soon produces new, bright green leaves which darken with age. It grows rapidly by underground runners and can be easily spring-divided. It appears to be pest-free and disease-resistant, and if grown well, clusters of blue-black berries will appear in late fall. The showier southern species, *muscari,* is a plant of dubious hardiness in most northern locations.

Lobelia syphilitica (Bigblue Lobelia) 24–36 in. Sun
Flowering span: Mid-August to late September
Color: Bright blue
Native habitat: Maine to Alabama, west to Texas and Minnesota

Toothed, lanceolate, thin leaves crowd the stems and terminate with a 6- to 8-inch spike of 1-inch, ribbed, tubular florets generously noticeable for their vivid color and down-turned, pointed lobes. Thriving best in a boggy, neutral soil, it can be garden-planted if kept consistently wet. Division (spring for cold climates and fall for mild ones), seed, and offsets readily propagate it. Rust and rhizoctonia rot are serious diseases, but insects are no problem. The white-flowered rarity, *alba,* is especially needful of wintertime mulching.

Phalaris arundinacea (Reed Canary-grass) 24–60 in. Sun
Flowering span: August
Color: White
Native habitat: Northern North America

Ornamentally useful along wet embankments of streams or ponds, the grasslike, ½-inch leaves are topped by open plumes of tiny florets. It grows eagerly by underground stems and can become invasive in gardens. Division is the usual propagation method, and there appear to be no problems with pests or diseases. The colorful variety *picta* (*variegata*) has leaves attractively striped in white and is less ambitious to spread.

Polygonum reynoutria (Reynoutria Fleeceflower) 12–18 in. Sun
Flowering span: Late August to October
Color: Pinkish red
Native habitat: Horticultural hybrid

A bright note of variegated foliage from *Phalaris arundinacea picta* punctuates sunny wet spots.

Vigorously able to withstand a variety of soils and exposures, this groundcover is best suited to sun-drenched, semi-dry embankments since its rapid-growing underground stems quickly make a thick mat of the 1-inch, heart-shaped foliage marked with reddish veining and reddish stems. Noticeable, heavy clusterings of tiny florets generously cover the plant in late summer from red buds. Any average-fertility soil suits it, and spring division is the most reliable propagation method. Nothing appears to pester it, but it can become invasive if not restrained.

Rudbeckia hirta (Black-eyed Susan) 24–30 in. Sun
Flowering span: Early August to October
Color: Golden yellow
Native habitat: Massachusetts to Georgia, west to Alabama
    and Illinois

Usually treated as a prolifically seeding annual or biennial, this plant carries 5-inch, lanceolate, coarsely toothed, roughened leaves and hairy stems with 3-to 4-inch, daisylike flowering having dark brown centers. Best suited to dry, open sites in full sun or light shading, its vigor is often overwhelming in gardens. Occasionally a leaf miner bothers the foliage, but it is usually pest- and disease-resistant. The earlier-blooming variety, *gloriosa*, has single, 5-to 7-inch, yellow flowers variously shaded with orange and red-brown, while the double form has golden yellow blossoms.

Rudbeckia speciosa (*newmani*) (Showy Coneflower) 12–42
    in. Sun
Flowering span: Early August to October
Color: Golden yellow
Native habitat: Pennsylvania to Alabama, west to Arkansas
    and Michigan

A true perennial, this species has 6- to 8-inch blunt-tipped, broad leaves on 8- to 12-inch petioles arranged in a heavy basal clump. Both the green purplish stems and the dark green foliage are rough with bristle hairs. The wide-apart outer petals surround a dark purple-brown central disc that is only slightly domed. Tolerant to light shading, it

Flamboyantly colorful *Rudbeckia speciosa* glows until frost.

prefers full sun and a moist, average-fertility soil. Spring division and seed propagate it easily, and it can become invasive. The large leaves are sometimes noticeably disfigured by a leaf miner, but no disease is bothersome. In silhouette it forms a denser mass of flowering than R. *hirta*, which it closely resembles.

Salvia azurea (Azure Sage) 12–60 in. Sun
Flowering span: Mid-August to mid-September
Color: Sky blue
Native habitat: North Carolina to Florida, west to Texas and
    Nebraska

A species with 4-inch, narrow, dark green leaves prominently veined with lighter green, it has terminal spikes of loosely arranged, 1-inch, wide-lipped flowers on slender stems. The plant usually goes into dormancy after flowering and does best in any well-drained, average-fertility soil on the dry side. Division is the easiest propagation method, although seed works satisfactorily, too. Summer stem cuttings are reluctant to make roots. White fly is the worst difficulty, and the plants need winter protection since they have only marginal hardiness in very cold areas. There is a white form, *alba,* and a western type with deeper blue flowering, *grandiflora,* which recently has been separated by some botanists into its own species, *S. pitcheri.*

Santolina chamaecyparissus (incana) (Lavender-cotton)
    18–24 in. Sun
Flowering span: Early August to mid-September
Color: Yellow
Native habitat: Southern Europe

Since it is generally used only as a tightly clipped, low hedging, its ¾-inch, buttonlike flowering is rarely given a chance to develop. The silver-gray, minutely divided, aromatic foliage appears in tightly packed closeness along the stems, and if left unpruned, the plant has a great tendency to fall open and become bedraggled-looking. Any well-drained, average soil in full sun is suitable to its needs, and summer stem cuttings root very easily in sand. Severe climates cannot grow this plant except as an annual, and winter mulching is recommended in all but the mildest

Santolina chamaecyparissus makes a fine-leaved accent or a border edging of gray foliage.

areas. The variety *nana* is a natural dwarf. Cut all plants back severely each spring to encourage attractive new growth.

Santolina virens (viridis) (Green Lavender-cotton) 18–24 in. Sun
Flowering span: Early August to mid-September
Color: Creamy yellow
Native habitat: Southern Europe

Here the foliage is deep green, and its culture is identical with that for *S. chamaecyparissus.*

Sedum sieboldi (Siebold Stonecrop) 6–9 in. Sun
Flowering span: Late August to October
Color: Bright pink
Native habitat: Japan

An outdoor trailing plant also adaptable for indoor pot culture, this perennial has thick, leathery, ¾-inch, round, bluish green leaves in whorls of 3 with faint red margins. The numerous, ½-inch florets appear in 2- to 3-inch, terminal clusterings. Any well-drained soil in full sun or light shade suits it, and it is easily propagated by division or stem cuttings. These are pest- and disease-free plants. The colorful variety *medio-variegatum* has a prominent yellow center on each leaf.

Sedum spectabile (Showy Stonecrop) 18–24 in. Sun
Flowering span: Late August to October
Color: Rose purple
Native habitat: Japan

Drought-resistant and sturdy, the species has thick, succulent stems and heavy, oval, 3-inch leaves appearing in whorls of 3 or in pairs. Its 3- to 4-inch, flat-topped clusters of star-shaped florets are attractive to butterflies and bees. While tolerant of almost any well-drained soil in full sun or light shading, it seems to do best in a clay soil. Reproduce by division or summer stem cuttings. Nuisances are nonexistent. The list of varieties and hybrids is fairly wide: *album,*

Durable, late summer flowering from *Sedum spectabile*'s many hybrids adds luster to the garden.

creamy white; *atropurpureum*, rose crimson, 18 in.; "Brilliant," raspberry red, 18 in.; "Carmen", rose red, 12 in., silvery green leaves; "Meteor," deep red, 18 in.; "Ruby Glow," deep ruby red, 12-in., purplish green leaves; and "Star Dust," ivory, 18-in., blue-green leaves.

Sedum telephium (Liveforever Stonecrop) 12–18 in. Sun
Flowering span: Mid-August to October
Color: Rose pink
Native habitat: Europe, northern Asia, southeastern Canada
    to New Jersey, west to Indiana

An upright-growing plant with few flower heads of 3- to 4-inch clusterings, it has 2- to 3-inch, ovate, toothed leaves scattered along the succulent stems. Easily grown in any sandy loam in sun or light shading, this wildflower is best propagated by seed or offsets. There are no insect or disease nuisances. Its hybrids include: "Autumn Joy," 24 in., rosy salmon with bright green foliage; and "Indian Chief," 18 in., coppery red with dark gray-green leaves.

Stokesia laevis (cyanea) (Stokes' Aster) 12–24 in. Sun
Flowering span: Early August to mid-September
Color: Lavender blue
Native habitat: South Carolina to Florida

While not reliably hardy in northern areas without winter mulching, it has a good resistance to drought everywhere. The 3- to 4-inch, ragged-looking, asterlike flowers appear on hairy, purplish stems above shiny, lanceolate leaves sparsely arranged. Disliking standing water around the roots in any season, this perennial wants a moist, well-drained, sandy loam to perform vigorously in sunshine or light shade. Seed, division, or spring stem cuttings readily duplicate it, and there appear to be no nuisances from diseases or pests. Improved types include: *alba,* white, 12 in.; "Blue Star," blue, 12 in.; *praecox,* lavender, 12 in.; "Silver Moon," ice blue, 12 in.; and *superba,* lavender blue, 9 in.

Thalictrum dipterocarpum (Yunnan Meadow-rue) 36–60 in.
    Semi-shade
Flowering span: Mid-August to October
Color: Deep lavender
Native hatitat: Western China

Here, fernlike, graceful foilage surrounds airy panicles of tiny flowers with prominent yellow stamens. It does best in a moist, humusy soil and will tolerate full sun if kept constantly watered. Seed is the recommended propagation method, and nothing bothersome afflicts it. The fully double hybrid, "Hewitt's Double," needs the same care but cannot successfully be propagated except from side shoots.

SEPTEMBER

**A General Guide to the Color Values
Available in September:**

(Each division includes shades, tints, and tones of the dominant value.)

WHITE: Anemone hupehensis *hybrids*, Aster novi-belgi *hybrids*, Aster *"Oregon Hybrids,"* Chrysanthemum morifolium, Chrysanthemum nipponicum, Cimicifuga simplex, Colchicum autumnale *varieties*, Colchicum speciosum album, Crocus cancellatus, Crocus sativus cartwrightianus albus, Crocus speciosus albus, Polygonum amplexicaule

YELLOW: Chrysanthemum morifolium

ORANGE: Chrysanthemum morifolium

RED: Aster novi-belgi *hybrids*, Chrysanthemum morifolium, Colchicum speciosum atrorubens, Polygonum amplexicaule

PINK: Anemone hupehensis *hybrids*, Aster novi-belgi, Aster *"Oregon Hybrids,"* Chrysanthemum morifolium, Colchicum autumnale, Colchicum speciosum *hybrids*, Crocus sativus, Polygonum amplexicaule album

PURPLE: Anemone hupehensis, Aster laevis, Aster novi-belgi, Aster *"Oregon Hybrids,"* Chrysanthemum morifolium, Colchicum autumnale minor, Colchicum speciosum, Crocus cancellatus, Crocus longiflorus, Crocus sativus *varieties*, Crocus speciosus

BLUE: Aster novi-belgi *hybrids*, Aster *"Oregon Hybrids,"* Crocus pulchellus, Crocus speciosus *hybrids*

BICOLOR: Chrysanthemum morifolium, Colchicum speciosum *hybrids*, Crocus speciosus *hybrids*

Anemone hupehensis (japonica) (Japanese Anemone) 24–36 in. Semi-shade

Flowering span: Early September to mid-October
Color: Rosy purple
Native habitat: Japan, China

Dark green, unequally 3-lobed, toothed leaves form a husky basal mound of attractive foliage. It sends up generous, erect flower stems branched well to produce many 2-inch, saucer-shaped blossoms with noticeable yellow centers. Thriving best in a sheltered location with full morning sun and dappled afternoon light, they want a rich, deep, moist, humusy soil. Division in spring or seed reproduces them well, and root cuttings are also workable. Root decay, smut, rust, and beetles can be occasional problems. Generally, they require some light mulching for winter, especially in very cold areas. The list of hybrids is impressive: *alba* ("Honorine Jobert"), single, white; "Kriemhilde," semi-double, blush pink; "Lady Gilmour," semi-double, pink; "Louise Uhink," single, white; "Margarette," double, rose pink; "Marie Manchard," semi-double, white; "Profusion," single, deep rose; "Queen Charlotte," semi-double, pink; "September Charm," single, clear pink; "September Sprite," single, rose pink; and "White Giant," single, white. Some cataloguers assign *A. japonica* to the taller types and *A. hupehensis* to the dwarf ones.

Aster laevis (Smooth Aster) 24–36 in. Sun
Flowering span: Early September to mid-October
Color: Violet
Native habitat: Maine to Georgia, west to New Mexico and
     Oregon

Showy in bloom, the erect stems carry 1½-inch-wide, lanceolate leaves which occasionally have a whitened cast. The foliage is stem-clasping beneath the flower cluster of 1-inch blossoms with gold centers. Any well-drained, average-fertility soil is suitable, and they endure drought well. Division or seed reproduces them easily, and there are no bothersome diseases or pests.

Aster novi-belgi (New York Aster) 24–48 in. Sun
Flowering span: Early September to mid-October

Fall asters provide heavy blossoming in a wide range of colors.

Color: Purple, lavender, pink, occasionally white
Native habitat: Coastal Newfoundland to coastal Georgia

This noticeable species is similar in effectiveness to *A. nova-angliae* of August but differs by its lower height and its smooth, 2- to 5-inch, lanceolate leaves with evident teeth. The bracts beneath the 2-inch flowers extend either outward or downward, also. Its culture is identical, and early summer pinching-back of the stems encourages more plant compactness. The list of hybrid developments is extensive: (Tall, 30 to 48 in.): "Ada Ballard," mauve blue; "Autumn Glory," claret red; "Clarity," white; "Crimson Brocade," bright red; "Ernest Ballard," rose crimson; "Eventide," purple; "Glorious," carmine-pink; "Marie Ballard," pale blue; "Patricia Ballard," pink; "Winston Churchill," ruby red; (Dwarf, 9 to 18 in.): "Audrey," pale blue; "Jean," lilac blue; "Jenny," cerise red; "Little Red Boy," rose red; "Niobe," white; "Peter Harrison," rose pink; and "Snowsprite," white.

Aster "Oregon Hybrids"   10–15 in.   Sun
Flowering span: Early September to mid-October

Color: White, pink, violet, blue
Native habitat: Horicultural hybrid between *A. douglasi* and *A. novi-belgi*

A compact group of plants covered with solid flowering, these hybrids have 2-inch blossoms with mostly yellow "eyes." Any well-drained, moist, rich soil in full sun or light shading is suitable, and they can be reproduced by spring division, seed, or summer stem cuttings. Mildew is the worst problem if air circulation is sluggish, while rust and wilt (which turns the entire plant bright yellow) are also troublesome. Fortunately, they are insect-resistant. The colorful list of variations is sizable: "Bonny Blue," wisteria blue; "Canterbury Carpet," gentian blue; "Pacific Amaranth," red-purple; "Persian Rose," rose pink; "Pink Bouquet," rose pink; "Romany," plum purple; "Snowball," white; "Snow Flurry," pure white; "Twilight," deep violet-blue; and "White Fairy," clear white.

Chrysanthemum morifolium (hortorum) (Hardy
   Chrysanthemum) 9–42 in. Sun
Flowering span: Early September to November
Color: All but blue in every shade, tint, and hue
Native habitat: China, Japan

It would be difficult to find a more adaptable perennial since it easily transplants in full flower, is readily propagated by several methods, grows well in a variety of soils, and offers a wide array of colorings, flower shapes, heights, and blooming spans. They also keep amazingly well when cut for decoration.

All are distinguished by incised, aromatically pungent foliage and semi-woody stems with multiple florets. Shallow-rooted, they require a rich, well-drained, constantly moist soil with frequent fertilizer applications throughout the growing season. While described as hardy, many types are not truly reliable left in the garden—even lightly mulched—and winter safely only in cold frames. Spring division of the old clump means discarding the woody parts in favor of fleshy, new growth. Pinching back the growing stems until mid-July (unnecessary for the "cushion" type) provides additional plant material that will readily root, when treated with a hormone, in a moist mix of half sand and peat moss for bloom the same season. Disbudding for larger, terminal flowering is rarely used with garden-grown plants since it negates much of their natural appeal.

All types appreciate a loose mulch in summer, and tall varieties benefit as much from early, loosely arranged staking. Shorter plants can be successfully, and inconspicuously, supported by defoliated, twiggy branches cut from trees and shrubs needing pruning maintenance. This economical staking usually requires no tying up. Unfortunately, there are many potential afflictions to good growth from aphids, root nematodes, red spider mites, blister beetles, leaf miners, and thrips, along with mildew, leaf spot, black spot, rust, and botrytis blight. None of these problems is consistently damaging to all types, however, and with reasonable care chrysanthemums are productively rewarding.

The "cushion" type generally grows from 9 to 15 inches high and self-branches readily and early to produce up to 30 inches of spread with intermittent, midsummer flowering before the main fall display obscures all the foliage. The various kinds of upright varieties have led to some confusion about their correct placement, and recently the National Chrysanthemum Society has catalogued the differing flower types as follows:

Pompon: 1½- to 2-inch blossoms in clusters formed of stiff, short petals creating a ball shape or a yellow-centered, daisy-type blossom with one row of loosely arranged petals; both are generally 24 inches tall.

Button: Blossoms are less than an inch across, clustered, and formed mainly of tightly packed petals; height is 24 inches.

Decorative: 2- to 4-inch double blossoms without any noticeable yellow center or "eye"; between 18 to 36 inches tall.

Single: Daisylike, 2- to 3-inch blossoms with a conspicuous yellow center that is either flat or slightly raised; 12 to 18 inches tall.

The 6 other hardy types are difficult to grow well since they flower very late and are easily bothered by frost damage unless carefully sheltered. These are: *spoon, quill, ane-*

mone, spider, exhibition, and *cascade.* Each is better suited to greenhouse culture except, perhaps, in very mild areas.

Because there are hundreds of varieties available in commercial cultivation throughout the country, any listing of recommended types here would quickly become outdated and have little guidance value. Their low cost and adaptability to being moved when in bloom make chrysanthemum experimentation a simple, eye-appealing pleasure for anyone, whether browsing illustrated garden catalogues or garden center displays. All types make long-blooming additions for the perennial border or in terrace tubs and planters.

Chrysanthemum nipponicum (Leucanthemum nipponicum)
    (Nippon Oxeye Daisy) 12–24 in. Sun
Flowering span: Mid-September to November
Color: White
Native habitat: Japan

Similar in flower to the daisylike forms of the summertime Shasta Daisy, here the light green leaves are thick and blunt, 3 to 4 inches long, with toothed margins only on the

Showy, solitary blossoms appear at each branch tip with *Chrysanthemum nipponicum.*

farther end. Unusual by having woody stems that often per-sist through the winter, the plant generally dies to the ground where climates are severe. The 2- to 3-inch flower has a greenish yellow center, and the blossoms appear sin-gly only at the tip of each stem. Thriving in seashore condi-tions, it adapts well to any average, well-drained, humusy soil in full sun. Spring division or summer stem cuttings readily reproduce it, and there are no important pests or diseases.

Cimicifuga simplex (foetida intermedia) (Kamchatka
    Bugbane) 24–36 in. Semi-shade
Flowering span: Mid-September to mid-October
Color: White
Native habitat: Siberia

Except for its height, this species is very similar to the July-blooming *C. racemosa*, and its culture is the same. The white hybrids "Armleuchter" and "White Pearl" offer slight flower variations.

Colchicum autumnale (Meadow Saffron, Autumn Crocus)
    4–8 in. Sun
Flowering span: Early September to October
Color: Lilac pink
Native habitat: British Isles, Europe

An initial planting of these large corms should be made as soon as they appear in the marketplace in August or the blooming will possibly take place out of the earth. Capable of producing elongated flowering from sitting openly on a windowsill because the bud has been long preformed, these novel plants naturally do better if planted logically in the garden. The 6-petaled blossom can open between 2 to 3 inches in diameter and appears in ongoing clusters, all with-out foliage at the time of bloom. The straplike, broad, 6- to 8-inch, upright leaves appear the following spring—to many gardeners' great amazement—and persist until late June. Do not remove before fading or the bulb will diminish and probably fail to flower. Any well-drained, average soil is sat-isfactory in full sun or light shading, and division of over-crowded colonies is the recommended propagation method, but only after the foliage properly withers. Pests and diseases are uncommon. The few varieties offer color contrasts: *album*, 6 in., off-white; *album plenum*, 6 in., double, off-white; *major (byzantium)*, 6 in., purple-pink, the hardiest and most prolific for bloom; and *minor*, 5 in., lilac, later-blooming.

Colchicum speciosum (Showy Meadow Saffron) 8–12 in. Sun
Flowering span: Mid-September to mid-October
Color: Pale lilac to rosy lavender
Native habitat: Asia Minor

The largest and showiest of all, these clustered, 6- to 8-inch, tulip-shaped blossoms open widely and offer a striking fall accent in shrub beds or mixed borders where the long-lasting spring foliage can properly develop without being overly conspicuous. The leaves require a longer time to ripen than those of *C. autumnale*, but the culture for both is the same. Its hybrid list is extensive: *album*, pure white; *atrorubens*, purple crimson; "Autumn Queen," rose-violet; "Conquest," deep violet, late; "Disraeli," deep mauve; "Huxley," deep rose lilac, scarce; "Lilac Wonder," mauve pink with a white base, very late; "Premier," pale rose-lilac; "Princess Astrid," light violet; "The Giant," dark lilac with a white base, late; "Violet Queen," deep purple; and "Waterlily," double, lilac-mauve, late, top-heavy. Any of these can be naturalized in grassy, wild areas that are infrequently mowed.

Crocus cancellatus 3–4 in. Sun
Flowering span: Early September to October
Color: Lilac, white
Native habitat: Greece, Asia Minor

Unusual in that the foliage appears right after flowering, this fall accent has slender, grasslike leaves and large flowers with noticeable purple veining. The stigma and anthers are pale yellow. Any well-drained, average soil in full sun is suitable, but rich soil encourages larger bulb colonies faster. Division of the overcrowded plantings after the foliage fades will increase them, but they are better left undisturbed. The variety *cilicicus* is pale lilac with white anthers. Neither is bothered by any debilitating diseases or pests.

Crocus longiflorus (Longflower Crocus) 4–5 in. Sun
Flowering span: Late September to late October
Color: Lilac purple
Native habitat: Southern Italy, Sicily, Malta

Fragrant and hardy, this species has long, sharp-pointed petals and is distinguished by an orange throat and a deep orange stigma. Its culture is identical with that for *C. cancellatus.*

Crocus pulchellus 3–4 in. Sun
Flowering span: Mid-September to mid-October
Color: Pale lavender blue
Native habitat: Turkey, Greece

Easy to grow but slow to colonize, this species has a deep yellow throat, an orange-yellow stigma, and white anthers. Cultivate it the same as *C. cancellatus.*

Crocus sativus (Saffron Crocus) 4–5 in. Sun
Flowering span: Late September to late October
Color: Pale pink to purple mauve
Native habitat: Southern Europe, Asia Minor

Its feathery stigma, when dried, has become the saffron of commerce. While not easy to grow well, this species can be rewarding if provided with a very warm, sunny location and culture similar to that for *C. cancellatus.* Abundant leaves appear with the large, globular blossoms, which open into wide-spreading stars. The bloom is unusual by staying open constantly, even at night and in poor weather. The flower is sterile and only division of the bulb colonies can propagate it. There are several varieties: *cashmirianus,* deep lilac; *cartwrightianus,* deep mauve; and *cartwrightianus albus,* white.

Crocus speciosus 3–4 in. Sun
Flowering span: Early September to October

Color: Bright lilac
Native habitat: Eastern Europe, Asia Minor

One of the easiest crocus to grow satisfactorily, it is noticeably attractive with its funnel-shaped, fragrant blossoms striped in dark lilac veining. The stigma is a deep orange-red, and it flowers either before or with the start of the leaves. Any rich, well-drained soil in full sun helps it thrive, and there are no problematic pests or diseases. It benefits from, and is not harmed by, a light forking of the bed when the corms are dormant since this redistributes the many tiny cormlets more widely. Self-seeding also promotes large colonies easily. Several varieties and hybrid types are available: *aitchisoni*, pale lavender, very large-flowered; *albus*, white; "Artabir," pale lavender blue; "Cassiope," blue-lavender with a cream base; "Oxonian," closest to blue and not as vigorous as the parent; and "Pollox," pale violet blue.

Polygonum amplexicaule (Mountain Fleeceflower) 24–36
   in. Sun
Flowering span: Early September to mid-October
Color: Rose red, white
Native habitat: Himalaya Mountains

Making a wide-spreading mat of attractive foliage where it becomes well-established, this perennial has 5- to 7-inch, wavy-margined, heart-shaped leaves and slender flower stalks with 4- to 6-inch, narrow spikes of ¼-inch florets tightly arranged. Any well-drained, average soil is suitable, and it will tolerate light shading. Spring division is recommended, and only leaf spot is an occasional nuisance. The variety *album* has pinkish white blossoming, *atrosanguineum*, ruby red, "Firetail," scarlet, and *speciosum*, deep red.

Hardy Ferns

Whether evergreen or deciduous in foliage, hardy ferns are reliable perennials of many heights used for the texture and luxuriance of their leaves in a variety of light exposures and soil conditions. They belong to a major division of the plant kingdom called *Pteridophyta*, a Latinized Greek word translating to "feathery plant." Botanically they are an evolutionary step below the seed-producing plants, since they have no true flowering or fruiting. Their chief method of natural reproduction is by means of fertile *spores* (a Greek word meaning "seed") often arranged in clustered, tiny heaps on the backside of the leaf forms or *fronds*. The dominant frond type is compound, and the primary leafy divisions from the main stem are called *pinnae*.

There are two major kinds of fern growth related to how the often varicolored stems grow: creeping and clustered. Those rootstocks with below-ground, creeping rhizomes form sizable masses, continually develop new foliage throughout the growing season, and can readily become invasive in mixed borders. Those with raised crowns of clustered stems produce central foliage concentrations, maintain the original number of spring stems, and are more restrained in their expansion. Creeping types can generally be transplanted at any time, while clustered forms usually prefer dormant digging. Some kinds are so sturdy they can be mowed without harm or dug up in thick sods like grass for transplanting. The emerging fronds are colloquially called "fiddleheads" because of their tightly rolled, crozier-like shape, and several kinds can be collected and eaten as a gourmet delicacy.

Generally, ferns do best where moisture is evenly available at all times and the soil is rich in humus to allow easy penetration of the fine roots. A loose, sandy loam balanced in content between clay and humus provides a basic soil mix for permanent growth of most ferns.

Because they resent having mud splashed on their foliage, ferns also benefit from a loose mulching at all times. In natural distributions they are often found growing satisfactorily with moss, leaf litter, and twiggy debris. New plantings can be helped by an initial top-dressing of moist peat moss, pine bark, compost, shredded plant parts, or any other vegetative mulching material not likely to generate great heat as it decays. Ferns are no more difficult to establish than other perennials once their basic growing needs are understood.

Adiantum pedatum (American Maidenhair) 8–20 in. Semishade
Foliage color: Light to medium green
Native habitat: Southeastern Canada to Georgia, west to Louisiana and Minnesota

The emerging wiry stems are somewhat reddish but mature to a shiny, black-brown with flat-spreading, delicate fronds horizontal to the ground. The leaf outline is almost circular, and the foliage is durable when cut for indoor use. Spores form on the underside outer edge of the pinnae. Best in a loose, rich, slightly acid, well-drained but constantly moist soil, it slowly spreads by a creeping rhizome. Spores or rootstock cuttings propagate it readily, and only snails and slugs are serious afflictions.

Asplenium platyneuron (*ebeneum*) (Ebony Spleenwort) 6–20 in. Sun
Foliage color: Deep green
Native habitat: Southeastern Canada to Florida, west to Texas and Kansas

Here the plant displays two kinds of foliage: tightly compressed pinnae, 2 to 6 inches long, of prostrate, evergreen, sterile fronds, and stiffly erect, fertile fronds stretching to 20 inches and tapering at both ends. These 1- to 2-inch wide fertile fronds have noticeable spacing between alternate pinnae and appear on purple-brown, glossy petioles. A gravelly soil enriched with humus or compost is to its liking, but it must also be moist and reasonably cool, although this fern tolerates dryness and light shading well. Propagate by spores located on the midrib. There are no problematic diseases or pests.

Asplenium trichomanes (Maidenhair Spleenwort) 2–8 in.
    Semi-shade
Foliage color: Dark green
Native habitat: Europe, Asia, Nova Scotia to Georgia, west
    to Arizona and Alaska

Here, too, the evergreen, sterile fronds are prostrate and
the fertile ones upright as with *A. platyneuron,* but these
shorter fronds have lustrous, dark brown stems and roundish
pinnae which are notched at the upper edges. Their spores
are arranged along the midribs. Protect from too much wind
and provide a cool, moist, well-drained location high in
humus between limestone rocks. Rootstock division or
spores reproduce it easily. Tolerant of occasional dryness, it
is bothered mostly by the destructive eating habits of slugs
and snails.

Athyrium felixfemina (*Asplenium felixfemina*) (Lady Fern)
    18–36 in. Sun
Foliage color: Yellow green to medium green
Native habitat: Europe, southeastern Canada to Pennsyl-
    vania and Ohio

The constantly produced, lance-shaped fronds are often
15 inches wide with pinnae that are twice divided and have
fine teeth on the edges. Mature fronds often have a reddish
or brownish cast on the upper surface, while the tightly
clustered pinnae near the top carry the curved spore cases.
Slow to spread, this fern needs constant wetness since it is
found naturally in swamps and streamsides. A neutral,
average, reliably moist soil out of high winds gives good
results in garden developments. Spores or division of the
thick, horizontal rootstock readily reproduces it. There are
no pests or diseases of consequence.

Anthyrium pycnocarpon (*Asplenium angustifolium*)
    (Narrowleaf Spleenwort) 20–40 in. Shade
Foliage color: Bright green changing to dark green, finally to
    russet
Native habitat: Southeastern Canada to Georgia, west to
    Louisiana and Missouri

The pronounced triangular shape of the 6-inch-wide frond carries simple, elongated pinnae that are widely spaced along the petiole and appear above brown stems. Often found growing in association with *Drypopteris goldiana,* this fern is slow to spread but produces ongoing fronds into summer, and does best in a limestone soil that is moist, cool, rich, and deep. Spores or dividing the surface rootstock propagates it satisfactorily. The spore cases make a herringbone pattern along the midvein of each fertile pinnae. Diseases and pests are uncommon.

Anthyrium thelypteroides (Asplenium acrostichoides)
  (Silvery Spleenwort) 20–36 in. Sun
Foliage color: Yellow green changing to deep green, then to russet green
Native habitat: Asia, Nova Scotia to Georgia, west to Missouri and Minnesota

The yellow stems produce 7-inch-wide, lanceolate fronds with noticeable deep notches between the simple, often toothed pinnae. Silvery spore cases are attached to the veining of the fertile fronds and change to blue gray at maturity. A rich, moist, acid soil in sun or light shade is suitable, and division seems to be best for reproduction. Nothing bothers it.

Botrychium virginianum (Rattlesnake Fern) 6–30 in.
  Shade
Foliage color: Yellow green changing to rich green
Native habitat: Europe, Asia, most of southern Canada and the entire United States

One of the earliest ferns to provide foliage in spring, the succulent stems are very brittle and carry triangular fronds with lacy-looking pinnae. The sterile frond also terminally carries, when it appears at all, a fertile stalk that has rows of circular capsules. A moist, rich, loose, humusy, neutral soil in medium to deep shade helps it thrive, but slugs, cutworms, rabbits, and rodents enjoy feeding on the juicy stems. Spore reproduction is superior to division.

Camptosorus rhizophyllus (Walking Fern) 4–12 in. Semi-shade
Foliage color: Medium green
Native habitat: Southeastern Canada to Georgia, west to Oklahoma and Minnesota

Unusual and novel, this fern has simple, evergreen, wedge-shaped leaves with very elongated, tapering points that can vegetatively produce new plants where the tips touch the ground and root. Its spore cases are haphazardly arranged on the underside of the leaves, and while it tolerates moderate dry spells satisfactorily, its preference is for a moist, humusy location, preferably in the damp crevice of a limestone rock. Propagate it by spores or by careful separation of a leaf-tip colony from the parent. Slugs are devastating in humid, steamy weather.

Chelianthes lanosa (Hairy Lip Fern) 6–10 in. Semi-shade
Foliage color: Medium yellow green
Native habitat: Connecticut to Georgia, west to Kansas and Wyoming

Here the narrow, twice-divided fronds have purple-brown to blackish petioles covered with fine hairs above very short, brown stems. The spores outline the outside edge of each fertile pinnae, which are also hairy. Dry weather can cause the plant to collapse, but rainfall soon brings its quick recovery. Its preference is for an acid, average soil somewhat on the dry side, and it appears to have no problem except drought. Reproduce it from spores.

Cystopteris bulbifera (Filix bulbifera) (Berry Bladder Fern) 24–42 in. Shade
Foliage color: Yellow green
Native habitat: Southeastern Canada to Georgia, west to Arizona and Wisconsin

A graceful, tapering, twice-divided frond, 3 to 4 inches wide, appears from a pink-green stem, carrying two neat rows of spore cases along each pinnae. At the junction of the pinnae and the petiole, however, there develops a pea-shaped bulblet which easily reproduces this fern. A cool, humusy, moist soil is generally suitable, but superior performance comes from having the slender rhizome packed tightly into a limestone rock crevice. There are no disease or insect nuisances, and either rootstock division or frond bulblets are recommended for reproduction.

Cystopteris fragilis (*Filix fragilis*) (Brittle Bladder Fern)
   4–18 in. Shade
Foliage color: Medium green
Native habitat: Southeastern Canada to Pennsylvania, west
   to Texas and Alaska

The twice-pinnate foliage is widely spaced on the slender, somewhat brittle stems which are brown at the base and green above. Its round-lobed pinnae carry only a few scattered spore cases attached prominently to the veins. Foliage appears very early in springtime, and the plant has a preference for a limestone soil that is humusy and moist at all times. Drought withers the foliage but rain quickly renews it again. Division is the better propagation method, and snails and slugs have a fondness for its semi-drooping foliage.

Dennstaedtia punctilobula (*Dicksonia punctilobula*)
   (Hayscented Fern) 18–36 in. Sun
Foliage color: Yellow green
Native habitat: Southeastern Canada to Georgia, west to
   Missouri and Minnesota

Rapid-growing to the point of becoming invasive, this feathery, thin-textured fern is useful for slope coverage since it tolerates a wide variety of exposures from full sun to heavy shade and almost any soil condition. The 10- to 12-inch-wide, lanceolate frond has a brown stem, and its pinnae have glands which secrete an odor of hay. Cup-shaped spore cases regularly dot the backsides of the pinnae. Its preference is for an acid location with a humusy, average soil, either wet or dry or both in turn. Division of the surface rootstock is the simplest propagation method. Snails and thrips are often bothersome.

Dryopteris cristata (*Aspidium cristatum*) (Crested Wood
Fern) 12–36 in. Shade
Foliage color: Dark green
Native habitat: Europe, southeastern Canada to Virginia,
west to Arkansas

The sterile fronds here are short, somewhat evergreen and
leathery, while the 5-inch-wide fertile leaf forms are taller,
erect, and carry the pinnae turned horizontally in a steplike
fashion which is characteristic of this fern group. The spores
are round dots supplied generously. Very wet, mucky locations are best with a cool, somewhat acid soil, although it
also tolerates more average garden conditions satisfactorily
if kept constantly moist. Division or spores work equally
well for propagation, and it appears to be unbothered by
problems.

Dryopteris dilatata (Mountain Wood Fern) 20–40 in.
Semi-shade
Foliage color: Dark green
Native habitat: Europe, southern Canada to Alaska, south to
Washington, Michigan, and North Carolina

Impressively attractive, the 12-inch-broad fronds appear
from stems generously covered with dark scales. The overlapping pinnae give a solid foliage appearance. It grows best
in a cool, very acid, rich soil from moist to wet, and can occasionally be found in rocky sites as well. Division of the
nearly horizontal rootstock or spores reproduces it satisfactorily. Apparently nothing is troublesome about growing it.

Dryopteris disjuncta (*Phegopteris dryopteris*) (Oak Fern)
4–15 in. Semi-shade
Foliage color: Yellow green
Native habitat: Southern Canada to Alaska, south to Arizona, Iowa, and Virginia

These doubly pinnate fronds have broad-based triangular
shapes with a graceful appearance. Creeping widely from
black-colored rootstalks, it produces only a sparse amount of
foliage in the acid, moist, cool woodlots it prefers. Rootstock

cuttings, spores, or dividing established plants reproduces it, and it is unencumbered by nuisances.

Dryopteris goldiana (Aspidium goldiana) (Goldie Wood Fern) 48–60 in. Shade
Foliage color: Yellow green to deep green
Native habitat: Southeastern Canada to Virginia, west to Iowa and Minnesota

Having both the tallest and widest fronds—up to 14 inches across—of this group, it makes a dramatic inclusion for the woodlot garden. The foliage is oval in outline and appears from stems that have pale brown scales very shaggily arranged at the base. The spore cases are precisely and generously set along the veins of the pinnae. Thriving in a cool, moist, deep, humusy soil, it tends to like a neutral to slightly acid condition. Division or spores propagate it well, and there appear to be no difficult problems with diseases or pests.

Dryopteris hexagonoptera (Phegopteris hexagonoptera) (Broad Beech Fern) 12–24 in. Shade
Foliage color: Medium green
Native habitat: Southeastern Canada to Louisiana, north to Minnesota

Highly variable in its form, here the fronds are broadly triangular with leafy ridges along the petiole connecting the lacy divisions of pinnae. Fragrant when bruised, it usually forms dense mats in the rich, moist, humusy, acid soils it enjoys best. Spore cases are tiny and round. New plantings can be made from division, rootstock cuttings, and spores. Nothing bothers it.

Dryopteris intermedia (Common Wood Fern) 16–30 in. Semi-shade
Foliage color: Deep green
Native habitat: Southeastern Canada to Alabama, west to Missouri and Wisconsin

This is a crown-forming species which spreads only by dropping its spores nearby. The 10-inch-wide, evergreen fronds are on stems with light brown scales, while the spore case coverings are kidney-shaped. Popular when dried for decorative use, this is called "fancy fern" in the florists' trade. Succeeding in a constantly moist, deep, rocky, humusy soil, it tolerates growing conditions ranging from acid to slightly alkaline. Spores or division of the crown readily propagates it, and it is untroubled by pests or diseases of consequence.

Dryopteris marginalis (*Aspidium marginale*) (Leather Wood
   Fern) 15–30 in. Shade
Foliage color: Dark bluish green
Native habitat: Southeastern Canada to Alabama, west to
   Oklahoma and Minnesota

Slow-creeping, it forms a raised crown of inward-bending, dormant fronds for the next season's growth, which then become a uniform circle of foliage. The 5- to 8-inch-wide, erect, broadly oval, leathery leaves carry large, round, blue-black spore cases arranged along the edges of the pinnae, and the stems have large and coarse brown scales. A moist, deep, stony, leaf-composted soil from acid to slightly alkaline is suitable, and it will tolerate anything from full shade to intermittent sunlight if kept moist. Spores or division creates additional plants readily, and it appears to be unbothered by insect or disease problems.

Dryopteris noveboracensis (*Thelypteris noveboracensis*)
   (New York Fern) 8–24 in. Semi-shade
Foliage color: Yellow green to medium green
Native habitat: Southeastern Canada to Georgia, west to
   Arkansas and Minnesota

Rapid-growing to a point of overcrowding itself quickly, these narrow, tapered-at-both-ends fronds have pale green stems and spore cases located at the edges of the pinnae. Consistently sending up new foliage into the summer, this fern can be readily divided or grown from spores. An acid, humusy soil, either moist or dry, is satisfactory, and it seems to be insect- and disease-free.

Dryopteris phegopteris (*Thelypteris phegopteris*) (Narrow
   Beech Fern) 6–18 in. Semi-shade

Foliage color: Light green to yellow green
Native habitat: Southern Canada to Alaska, south to Washington and Pennsylvania

Another candidate for spreading invasively in a short time, this fern is also one of the easiest to grow. The 5-inch-wide, triangular fronds appear on yellow-brown stems with brown scales and are generally hairy throughout. Unique in outline, the lowest set of pinnae are longer and point downward away from the others. A constantly moist, acid, rich, leaf-compost soil encourages good growth, and propagation can be accomplished either from division, rootstock cuttings, or spores. There are no nuisances.

Dryopteris spinulosa (Thelypteris spinulosa) (Toothed
    Wood Fern) 15–30 in. Semi-shade
Foliage color: Deep green
Native habitat: Europe, southeastern Canada to Virginia,
    west to Idaho

Mostly evergreen, this lacy, narrowly lanceolate, 7-inch-wide fern is collected in late summer and used commercially as "florist's fern." Its stems have pale brown scales, while the pinnae display many shiny black, kidney-shaped spore cases as the fertile fronds mature. A deep, stony, humusy soil kept in the neutral range is suitable, and the plant will tolerate more sun if kept constantly moist. Spores or division reproduce it, and pests and diseases generally avoid it.

Dryopteris thelypteris (palustris) (Marsh Fern) 10–30 in.
    Semi-shade
Foliage color: Bright green changing to gray green
Native habitat: Europe, Asia, southeastern Canada to
    Florida, west to Oklahoma

Native to bogs, marshes, and other wet locations, it creeps extensively from a cordlike rootstalk. The narrow, fertile fronds have spore cases along the edges of the pinnae, which fold over to cover them. Tolerant of full sun to dense shade if kept wet at all times, it needs a rich, acid soil.

Division and spores reproduce it readily. It has little to bother it.

Lygodium palmatum (Hartford Fern) 24–60 in. Semi-
  shade
Foliage color: Light green
Native habitat: New Hampshire to Florida, west to Tennessee and Michigan

While not easy to grow well, its novel, vinelike appearance is worth a trial. The 1- to 3-inch-wide, palmate-shaped
leaves appear in pairs widely spaced along the stringy, dark
brown, trailing or climbing stem. Its sterile foliage is evergreen, and the spores come independently clustered in
branched stalks. Almost swampy, very acid soil helps it
thrive, while reproduction is probably best accomplished
from spores. Snails and strong winds seriously affect its
growth.

Onoclea sensibilis (Sensitive Fern) 12–30 in. Sun
Foliage color: Yellow green to brownish green
Native habitat: Eastern Europe, western Asia, southern
  Canada to Texas and Florida

Its sensitivity is to late spring and early autumn frosts,
which quickly brown the foliage. Otherwise, it is a generally
easy plant to grow and can become too wide-spreading
from the pencil-thick, creeping, surface rootstocks. The tri-
angular-outlined, deeply lobed, simple leaves can be up
to 10 inches wide and are separately produced from the fertile portions, which are erect and slender and carry only
heavy clusters of green balls that turn dark brown with maturity. These are collectible for indoor decorative use and
are sometimes colloquially called "bead sticks." A wet,
marshy, acid-to-alkaline soil in good sunlight is best, but the
plant will do well in semi-shading, too. Propagate by division or spores. Frost-damage is the only hindrance to vigorous growth.

Osmunda cinnamonia (Cinnamon Fern) 24–60 in. Semi-
  shade
Foliage color: Yellow green to deep green

Favoring constant moisture, *Onoclea sensibilis* adapts uncon-
cernedly to a variety of growing conditions.

Native habitat: Eastern Europe, western Asia, South
    America, West Indies, southeastern Canada to Florida,
    west to New Mexico and Minnesota

Widely distributed throughout the world, this almost fool-
proof fern is not only attractive but provides a nutritious,
gourmet foodstuff when the undeveloped fronds or "fiddleheads" are boiled or eaten raw in salads. Slow to spread, its
erect, fertile leaves are entirely separated from the outward-
facing, fountainlike sterile ones. The thick-stemmed, stiff,
spore-carrying fronds produce a terminally thick collection
of rounded cases which are first bright green, then change to
a gold-brown color like cinnamon before finally withering to
a dark brown remnant. It needs a wet or consistently moist
location with acid soil. Duplicate it from spores or division
and do not worry about pests or diseases.

Osmunda claytoniana (Interrupted Fern) 36–60 in. Semi-
    shade
Foliage color: Yellow green to dark green

Native habitat: Asia, South America, West Indies, eastern North America

As easy to grow as its relative, *O. cinnamonea*, it prefers somewhat less soil acidity and will tolerate dry conditions satisfactorily, although the plants will be shorter. Both the sterile and the fertile leaves are similar in size and appearance here, except that the fruiting fronds are interrupted by a noticeable, branched clustering of spore cases about halfway up the stem. It is unbothered by nuisances, and it can readily be propagated by division or spores.

Osmunda regalis (Royal Fern) 36–60 in. Semi-shade
Foliage color: Light reddish green changing to deep green
Native habitat: Europe, Asia, Africa, South America, North America

A cluster of golden, spherical, spore capsules crown the top of an otherwise sterile frond and give this fern the odd appearance of displaying true flowering. The foliage resembles that of a honeylocust with its bi-pinnate, openly spaced pinnae. Very sluggish to spread, it maintains its ferny individuality for a long time in one place. Only a very wet, highly acid soil will make it thrive happily, and it will actually grow successfully even if flooded with water around its base. Spores are the practical propagation method, short of digging up an entire plant, which is easily handled. There are no nuisances from pests or diseases.

Pellaea atropurpurea (Purple Cliffbrake) 6–15 in. Semi-shade
Foliage color: Pale green changing to gray green, then to blue green
Native habitat: New Hampshire to Florida, west to Arizona and South Dakota

Semi-evergreen, it has purple brown, hairy stems and oddly divided, stalked pinnae with more subdivisions appearing on the lowest segments. The spores line the under edges of the pinnae, which curve in to protect them. Tolerant of a good amount of sun, it prefers some shading and grows perhaps best on dry, limestone rocks. Spores are probably the better propagation method, and there appear to be no difficult diseases or pests.

Polypodium vulgare (Common Polypody) 4–12 in. Semi-
   shade
Foliage color: Yellow green to medium green
Native habitat: Europe, southern Canada to Alaska, south to
   Arkansas and Georgia

Often called the "rock's cap" fern because it can completely swath a small boulder in a mat of foliage when well grown, this plant has 2-inch-wide, evergreen, leathery, persistent leaves and many spore cases on the upper part of the frond. Doing best in moist, northerly exposures of open shade and semi-sunny sites elsewhere, it is so easily propagated by division or rootstock cuttings that collecting spores should be ignored for reproduction. Nothing bothers it.

Polystichum acrostichoides (*Dryopteris acrostichoides*)
   (Christmas Fern) 12–30 in. Shade

Persistent foliage with *Polystichum acrostichoides* makes it a year-round favorite for shade.

Foliage color: Light green changing to very dark green
Native habitat: Southeastern Canada to Florida, west to Texas and Wisconsin

Useful for cutting, this durable, evergreen fern has 5-inch-wide, narrowly tapered fronds with dense clusters of brown spore cases at the tip ends of the fertile leaf forms. White stem scales on emerging foliage turn brown and persist until the following spring. A slow-creeping plant, it has many variations in form, and some have been selected and given specific varietal names for the marketplace. Tolerant to sun if kept consistently moist, it grows nicely in any rich, humusy, damp, well-drained soil. Division is the preferred reproduction method, and there appear to be no serious nuisances.

Polystichium brauni (Aspidium brauni) (Braun Holly Fern)
18–30 in. Shade
Foliage color: Deep green
Native habitat: Southeastern Canada to Pennsylvania, west to Wisconsin

The 8-inch-wide, gracefully arching, glossy fronds of this fern are, unfortunately, not evergreen, but its summertime attractiveness is worth having just the same. Long, brown scales appear on the short stems, and the lancelike leaves taper sharply at both ends. A cool, consistently moist, rich, woodlot humus is preferred, slightly toward an alkaline condition. Spores and dividing the heavy rootstock are the propagation methods. It has no pests or diseases of note.

Pteridium latisculum (Eastern Bracken) 36–60 in. Semi-shade
Foliage color: Deep green
Native habitat: Almost worldwide in temperate zones

Apt to become weedy in a short time, these leathery, thrice-divided, triangular leaves appear irregularly spaced from wide-creeping, deep rootstalks. The emerging fronds can be collected and cooked like asparagus. It grows equally well on moist or dry sites that are very acid and prefers a sandy, humusy soil. Division is the easiest propagation method, and insects and diseases appear to avoid it.

Pteretis nodulosa (*Matteuccia struthiopteris*) (Ostrich Fern)
   24–60 in. Semi-shade
Foliage color: Deep green
Native habitat: Europe, southern Canada to Alaska, south to
   Iowa and Virginia

The leathery, erect, plumelike sterile fronds are graceful and durable except in periods of drought. They appear from raised domes that poke several inches above the ground, and the shorter, fertile fronds come from the center in late summer. These spore-bearing parts are almost 2 inches wide, feathery-looking but stiff, and turn dark brown at maturity. They make good indoor decorations. If kept constantly moist, this fern tolerates full sunlight, but it generally is more satisfied in a damp, humusy, average-fertility soil in semishading. Division is simpler than spores for reproduction, and nothing seems to be overly troublesome except summer dryness.

Pteretis nodulosa spreads graceful plumes in evenly moist, semishaded locations.

Woodsia ilvensis (Rusty Woodsia) 3–6 in. Sun
Foliage color: Light gray green changing to yellow brown
  on the underside
Native habitat: Cold, northern areas of Europe, Asia, North
  America

The 1-inch-wide, thick fronds are tapered at both ends,
and although they brown completely in drought, they re-
cover quickly after adequate rain. A neutral to slightly acid,
loose soil, slightly moist, is preferred, and this fern is
usually associated growing among rocks, making it highly
suitable for garden rockeries. Division is by far the simplest
propagation technique, and there are no difficulties with
diseases or other nuisances.

Woodsia obtusa (Common Woodsia) 6–16 in. Shade
Foliage color: Gray green
Native habitat: Southeastern Canada to Florida, west to
  Texas and Arizona

The yellow green stems produce 3-inch-wide fronds that
remain somewhat evergreen where the climate is mild. Tiny
white hairs cover both leaf surfaces, and the ends of the pinnae are unusual by being blunt. A well-drained, rocky, neutral, moist soil is to its liking, and it can be readily reproduced by spores or division. It appears unbothered by
much.

Woodwardia areolata (angustifolia) (Netvein Chain Fern)
  15–24 in. Sun
Foliage color: Dark green
Native habitat: Coastal southeastern Canada to Florida,
  west to Texas

These glossy fronds are 3 to 4 inches wide and the sterile
one has a slight resemblance to the outline of *Onoclea sensibilis,* but here there is less leaf width and more space between the divisions. Quick to spread over wide areas, it
does best in an acid, swampy soil but will accept a well-
drained, drier garden location without flinching. Division or
spores propagate it equally well, and it seems to be disease-
and insect-free.

Woodwardia virginica (*Anchistea virginica*) (Virginia Chain
 Fern) 36–60 in. Semi-shade
Foliage color: Dark green to yellow green, depending on
 light conditions
Native habitat: Coastal New Jersey to Florida, west to
 Texas

Growing so rapidly it may overtake a garden space, this
fern has 5-inch-wide fronds on green-brown stems that become black as they meet the earth. The spores are interestingly arranged on the back of the pinnae both parallel to the
midrib and also in an ascending herringbone pattern up the
segments. Natively it enjoys an acid, swampy site, but it can
grow satisfactorily—if perhaps too vigorously—on a moist,
average-fertility location in a garden. Division is by far the
easiest way to make more plants. Nothing bothers it.

Useful Lists

Perennials with a Blooming Period of Eight Weeks or More

(Carried under the monthly listing indicated for the light intensity given.)

MARCH:

Erica carnea (*Sun*)
Helleborus niger (*Semi-shade*)
Helleborus orientalis (*Semi-shade*)

APRIL:

Brunnera macrophylla (*Semi-shade*)
Dicentra eximia (*Semi-shade*)
Polemonium reptans (*Semi-shade*)
Vinca minor "Bowles" (*Sun*)
Viola cornuta (*Sun*)

MAY:

Anemone canadensis (*Semi-shade*)
Anemonella thalictroides (*Semi-shade*)
Aquilegia chrysantha (*Sun*)
Arenaria verna caespitosa (*Semi-shade*)
Campanula garganica (*Sun*)
Campanula portenschlagiana (*Semi-shade*)
Cerastium arvense (*Sun*)
Corydalis lutea (*Semi-shade*)
Delphinium nudicaule (*Sun*)
Dianthus alwoodi (*Sun*)
Dicentra formosa (*Semi-shade*)
Doronicum caucasicum (*Sun*)
Doronicum pardalianches (*Sun*)
Erigeron glaucus (*Sun*)
Geranium endressii (*Sun*)
Geranium sanguineum (*Sun*)
Geum borisi (*Sun*)
Geum chiloense (*Sun*)
Geum peckii (*Semi-shade*)
Geum triflorum (*Semi-shade*)
Hypoxis hirsuta (*Sun*)
Lamium maculatum (*Semi-shade*)

Myosotis alpestris (*Semi-shade*)
Myosotis scorpiodes (*Sun*)
Myosotis sylvatica (*Semi-shade*)
Polemonium caeruleum (*Semi-shade*)
Potentilla argentea (*Sun*)
Potentilla anserina (*Sun*)
Potentilla tridentata (*Sun*)
Silene alpestris (*Sun*)
Silene caroliniana (*Sun*)
Symphytum officinale (*Sun*)
Thermopsis mollis (*Sun*)
Thermopsis montana (*Sun*)
Tradescantia virginiana (*Sun*)
Veronica officinalis (*Shade*)
Viola canadensis (*Semi-shade*)

JUNE:

Achillea filipendulina (*Sun*)
Achillea nana (*Sun*)
Achillea ptarmica (*Sun*)
Achillea tomentosa (*Sun*)
Anthemis tinctoria (*Sun*)
Callirhoe involuncrata (*Sun*)
Callopogon pallidus (*Semi-shade*)
Campanula carpatica (*Sun*)
Campanula rotundifolia (*Sun*)
Catananche caerulea (*Sun*)
Centaurea dealbata (*Sun*)
Centaurea montana (*Sun*)
Centranthus ruber (*Sun*)
Chrysanthemum maximum (*Sun*)
Chrysogonum virginianum (*Semi-shade*)
Clematis integrifolia (*Sun*)
Clematis recta (*Sun*)
Coreopsis grandiflora (*Sun*)
Coreopsis lanceolata (*Sun*)
Coreopsis palmata (*Sun*)
Coronilla varia (*Sun*)
Delphinium elatum (*Sun*)
Dianthus latifolius (*Sun*)

Eremurus himalaicus (*Sun*)
Eremurus robustus (*Sun*)
Gaillardia aristata (*Sun*)
Gypsophila repens (*Sun*)
Heuchera sanguinea (*Sun*)
Hieracium auranticum (*Sun*)
Hieracium bombycinium (*Sun*)
Lotus corniculatus (*Sun*)
Lupinus polyphyllus (*Sun*)
Lupinus "Russell Hybrids" (*Sun*)
Lychnis flos-cuculi (*Sun*)
Malva alcea (*Sun*)
Monarda didyma (*Sun*)
Nepeta faassenii (*Sun*)
Penstemon gloxinoides (*Sun*)
Penstemon hartwegi (*Sun*)
Phlox maculata (*Sun*)
Salvia nemerosa (*Sun*)
Scabiosa caucasica (*Sun*)
Scabiosa columbaris (*Sun*)
Scabiosa graminifolia (*Sun*)
Silene schafta (*Sun*)
Silene virginica (*Semi-shade*)
Tunica saxifraga (*Sun*)
Verbascum hybrida (*Sun*)

JULY:

Achillea millefolium (*Sun*)
Aconitum lycoctonum (*Semi-shade*)
Aconitum napellus (*Semi-shade*)
Althaea rosea (*Sun*)
Anemonopsis macrophylla (*Semi-shade*)
Aster frikarti (*Sun*)
Boltonia latisquama (*Sun*)
Calluna vulgaris (*Sun*)
Campanula rapunculoides (*Semi-shade*)
Campanula sarmatica (*Sun*)
Cephalaria tatarica (*Sun*)
Coreopsis pubescens (*Sun*)
Coreopsis rosea (*Sun*)

Echinacea purpurea (*Sun*)
Erigeron hybrida (*Sun*)
Eryngium amethystinum (*Sun*)
Eupatorium perfoliatum (*Sun*)
Galega officinalis (*Sun*)
Helianthus decapetalus (*Sun*)
Heliopsis helianthoides (*Sun*)
Heliopsis scabra (*Sun*)
Malva moschata (*Sun*)
Mentha *species* (*Sun*)
Phlox paniculata (*Sun*)
Physostegia virginiana (*Semi-shade*)
Rudbeckia fulgida (*Sun*)
Salvia haematodes (*Sun*)
Solidago hybrida (*Sun*)

AUGUST:

Artemesia absinthium (*Sun*)
Artemesia stelleriana (*Sun*)
Aster spectabilis (*Sun*)
Boltonia latisquama (*Sun*)
Helenium autumnale (*Sun*)
Rudbeckia hirta (*Sun*)
Rudbeckia speciosa (*Sun*)
Sedum telephium (*Sun*)

SEPTEMBER:

Anemona hupehensis (*Semi-shade*)
Chrysanthemum morifolium (*Sun*)
Polygonum amplexicaule (*Sun*)

Perennials Having the Bonus of Foliage Effects with or after Blooming

(Carried under the monthly listing indicated for the light intensity given.)

APRIL:

Alchemilla alpina (*Sun*)
Bergenia cordifolia (*Semi-shade*)
Bergenia crassifolia (*Semi-shade*)
Caulophyllum thalictroides (*Shade*)
Euphorbia epithymoides (*Sun*)
Euphorbia myrsinites (*Sun*)
Pachysandra terminalis (*Semi-shade*)
Tulipa greigi (*Sun*)
Vinca minor (*Sun*)

MAY:

Amsonia angustifolia (*Semi-shade*)
Amsonia tabernaemontana (*Semi-shade*)
Asarum europaeum (*Semi-shade*)
Asperula odorata (*Semi-shade*)
Baptisia australis (*Sun*)
Baptisia leucantha (*Semi-shade*)
Cornus canadensis (*Shade*)
Corydalis lutea (*Semi-shade*)
Dryas octopetala (*Sun*)
Epimedium *species* (*Semi-shade*)
Galax aphylla (*Semi-shade*)
Geranium sanguineum (*Sun*)
Iberis sempervirens (*Sun*)
Lamium maculatum (*Semi-shade*)
Paeonia lactiflora (*Sun*)
Polygonatum biflorum (*Semi-shade*)
Polygonatum canaliculatum (*Semi-shade*)
Polygonatum multiflorum (*Semi-shade*)
Potentilla tridentata (*Sun*)
Saxifraga virginiensis (*Sun*)
Sedum *species* (Sun)

Tiarella cordifolia (*Semi-shade*)
Tiarella wherryi (*Semi-shade*)

JUNE:

Antennaria dioica (*Sun*)
Centaurea gymnocarpa (*Sun*)
Centaurea rutifolia (*Sun*)
Cerastium biebersteini (*Sun*)
Cerastium boissieri (*Sun*)
Chimaphila maculata (*Shade*)
Dianthus *species* (*Sun*)
Dictamnus alba (*Sun*)
Filipendula ulmaria aureo-variegata (*Semi-shade*)
Heuchera sanguinea (*Sun*)
Heuchera villosa (*Sun*)
Iris sibirica (*Sun*)
Leontopodium alpinum (*Sun*)
Mecanopsis cambrica (*Semi-shade*)
Mitchella repens (*Semi-shade*)
Opuntia compressa (*Sun*)
Potentilla argyrophylla (*Sun*)
Saxifraga aizoides (*Semi-shade*)
Saxifraga aizoon (*Semi-shade*)
Saxifraga cotyledon (*Semi-shade*)
Sedum *species* (*Sun*)
Sempervivum (*Sun*)
Shortia galacifolia (*Shade*)
Shortia uniflora (*Shade*)
Stachys olympica (*Sun*)
Thymus *species* (*Sun*)

JULY:

Aconitum *species* (*Semi-shade*)
Calluna vulgaris *species* (*Sun*)
Cardiocrinum giganteum (*Semi-shade*)
Cassia marilandica (*Sun*)
Coreopsis verticillata (*Sun*)
Echinops ritro (*Sun*)
Echinops spaerocephalum (*Sun*)
Eryngium aquaticum (*Sun*)

Euphorbia corollata (*Sun*)
Hosta *species* (*Semi-shade*)
Iris kaempferi (*Sun*)
Limonium latifolium (*Sun*)
Macleaya cordata (*Sun*)
Ruta graveolens (*Sun*)
Salvia haematodes (*Sun*)
Sedum *species* (*Sun*)
Senecio cineraria (*Sun*)
Senecio przewalski (*Sun*)
Thalictrum speciosissimum (*Sun*)
Yucca filamentosa (*Sun*)
Yucca flaccida (*Sun*)

AUGUST:

Anaphalis margaritacea (*Semi-shade*)
Artemesia absinthium (*Sun*)
Artemesia albula (*Sun*)
Artemesia schmidtiana nana (*Sun*)
Artemesia stelleriana (*Sun*)
Hosta *species* (*Semi-shade*)
Liriope spicata (*Semi-shade*)
Phalaris arundinacea picta (*Sun*)
Santolina chamaecyparissus (*Sun*)
Sedum *species* (*Sun*)
Polygonum amplexicaule (*Sun*)

FERNS:

Most species (*Sun, semi-shade, shade*)

Perennials Enjoying Constantly Moist or Wet Conditions

(Carried under the monthly listing indicated for the light intensity given.)

APRIL:

Anemone nemerosa (*Semi-shade*)
Anemone quinquefolia (*Semi-shade*)
Anemone ranunculoides (*Semi-shade*)
Caltha palustris (*Semi-shade*)
Leucojum aestivum (*Sun*)
Leucojum vernum (*Sun*)
Polemonium reptans (*Semi-shade*)
Primula *species* (*Semi-shade*)
Trillium grandiflorum (*Semi-shade*)
Trillium nivale (*Semi-shade*)
Trillium sessile (*Semi-shade*)
Trillium undulatum (*Semi-shade*)
Vinca minor (*Sun*)
Viola blanda (*Semi-shade*)

MAY:

Anemone canadensis (*Semi-shade*)
Baptisia leucantha (*Semi-shade*)
Camassia quamash (*Sun*)
Cornus canadensis (*Shade*)
Cyprepedium candidum (*Semi-shade*)
Dodecatheon amethystinum (*Semi-shade*)
Geum montanum (*Sun*)
Geum rivale (*Semi-shade*)
Geum triflorum (*Semi-shade*)
Hutchinsia alpina (*Semi-shade*)
Iris prismatica (*Sun*)
Iris pseudacorus (*Sun*)
Mazus reptans (*Semi-shade*)
Myosotis alpestris (*Semi-shade*)
Myosotis scorpiodes (*Sun*)
Patrinia triloba (*Sun*)
Phlox divaricata (*Semi-shade*)
Polemonium caeruleum (*Semi-shade*)

Polygala paucifolia (*Shade*)
Polygonatum canaliculatum (*Semi-shade*)
Primula *species* (*Semi-shade*)
Tradescantia virginiana (*Sun*)
Trollius asiaticus (*Sun*)
Trollius europeus (*Semi-shade*)
Trollius japonicus (*Semi-shade*)

JUNE:

Aquilegia longissima (*Sun*)
Aruncus sylvester (*Semi-shade*)
Callopogon pallidus (*Semi-shade*)
Chrysanthemum maximum (*Sun*)
Dodecatheon jeffreyi (*Semi-shade*)
Filipendula purpurea (*Semi-shade*)
Filipendula rubra (*Semi-shade*)
Filipendula ulmaria (*Semi-shade*)
Lilium canadense (*Semi-shade*)
Lysimachia terrestis (*Sun*)
Lysimachia vulgaris (*Sun*)
Mitchella repens (*Semi-shade*)
Platycodon grandiflorum (*Sun*)
Polemonium humile (*Semi-shade*)
Polemonium richardsoni (*Semi-shade*)
Primula *species* (*Semi-shade*)
Trollius ledebouri (*Semi-shade*)
Valeriana officinalis (*Sun*)

JULY:

Astilbe chinensis (*Semi-shade*)
Bletilla striata (*Semi-shade*)
Campanula lactiflora (*Sun*)
Chelone glabra (*Semi-shade*)
Cimicifuga racemosa (*Semi-shade*)
Coreopsis rosea (*Sun*)
Eupatorium perfoliatum (*Sun*)
Filipendula camtschatica (*Semi-shade*)
Gentiana asclepiadea (*Semi-shade*)
Gentiana lutea (*Semi-shade*)
Hibiscus moscheutos (*Sun*)

Hibiscus palustris (*Sun*)
Hosta *species* (*Semi-shade*)
Iris kaempferi (*Sun*)
Liatris spicata (*Sun*)
Lilium pardilinum (*Semi-shade*)
Lilium superbum (*Sun*)
Lobelia cardinalis (*Sun*)
Lythrum salicaria (*Sun*)
Lythrum vigatum (*Sun*)
Macleaya cordata (*Sun*)
Senecio cineraria (*Sun*)
Senecio clivorum (*Semi-shade*)

AUGUST:

Chelone lyoni (*Semi-shade*)
Chelone obliqua (*Semi-shade*)
Chrysanthemum uliginosum (*Sun*)
Gentiana andrewsi (*Semi-shade*)
Hosta *species* (*Semi-shade*)
Kniphofia uvaria (*Sun*)
Liatris pycnostachya (*Sun*)
Lilium philippinense (*Sun*)
Liriope spicata (*Semi-shade*)
Lobelia syphilitica (*Sun*)
Phalaris arundinacea (*Sun*)

SEPTEMBER:

Cimicifuga simplex

FERNS:

Adiantum pedatum (*Semi-shade*)
Anthyrium felixfemina (*Sun*)
Dennstaedtia punctilobula (*Sun*)
Dryopteris cristata (*Shade*)
Dryopteris dilatata (*Semi-shade*)
Dryopteris phegopteris (*Semi-shade*)
Dryopteris thelypteris (*Semi-shade*)
Lygodium palmatum (*Semi-shade*)
Onoclea sensibilis (*Sun*)

Osmunda cinnamonia (*Semi-shade*)
Osmunda regalis (*Semi-shade*)
Polystichum brauni (*Shade*)
Pteretis nodulosa (*Semi-shade*)
Woodwardia areolata (*Sun*)
Woodwardia virginica (*Semi-shade*)

Perennials for Deep Shading

(Carried under the monthly listing indicated for the soil moisture given.)

APRIL

Actaea alba (*Moist*)
Actaea rubra (*Moist*)
Caulophyllum thalictroides (*Moist*)
Hepatica acutiloba (*Moist*)
Hepatica americana (*Moist*)
Trillium nivale (*Moist*)
Trillium sessile (*Moist*)

MAY:

Clintonia borealis (*Moist*)
Clintonia umbellata (*Moist*)
Cornus canadensis (*Moist*)
Polygala paucifolia (*Moist*)
Uvularia grandiflora (*Moist*)
Uvularia perfoliata (*Moist*)
Uvularia sessilifolia (*Moist*)
Veronica officinalis (*Moist*)

JUNE:

Chimaphila maculata (*Dry*)
Chimaphila umbellata (*Dry*)
Shortia galacifolia (*Moist*)
Shortia uniflora (*Moist*)

JULY:

Hosta *species* (*Moist or dry*)

AUGUST:

Hosta *species* (*Moist or dry*)

FERNS:

Anthyrium pycnocarpon (*Moist*)
Botrychium virginianum (*Moist*)

Cystopteris bulbifera (*Moist*)
Cystopteris fragilis (*Moist*)
Dryopteris cristata (*Wet*)
Dryopteris goldiana (*Moist*)
Dryopteris hexagonoptera (*Moist*)
Dryopteris marginalis (*Moist*)
Polystichum acrostichoides (*Moist*)
Polystichum brauni (*Moist*)
Woodsia obtusa (*Moist*)

Perennials Tolerant to Periods of Partially or Fully Dry Conditions

(Carried under the monthly listing indicated for the light intensity given.)

MARCH:

Crocus tomasinianus (*Sun*)
Eranthis cilicica (*Sun*)
Erica carnea (*Sun*)

APRIL:

Alyssum saxatile (*Sun*)
Anemone patens (*Sun*)
Anemone pulsatilla (*Sun*)
Arabis alpina (*Sun*)
Arabis caucasicus (*Sun*)
Aubretia deltoides (*Sun*)
Euphorbia epithymoides (*Sun*)
Iris bucharica (*Sun*)
Iris magnifica (*Sun*)
Ornithogalum nutans (*Sun*)
Phlox procumbens (*Sun*)
Phlox subulata (*Sun*)
Tulipa aucheriana (*Sun*)
Tulipa eichleri (*Sun*)
Tulipa greigi (*Sun*)
Tulipa kaufmanniana (*Sun*)
Tulipa kolpakowskiana (*Sun*)
Tulipa linifolia (*Sun*)
Tulipa stellata chrysantha (*Sun*)
Tulipa tarda (*Sun*)
Tulipa turkestanica (*Sun*)
Tulipa whittali (*Sun*)
Viola palmata (*Semi-shade*)
Viola pubescens (*Semi-shade*)

MAY:

Aethionema cordifolium (*Sun*)
Aethionema grandiflora (*Sun*)

Aethionema warleyense (*Sun*)
Ajuga brockbanki (*Sun*)
Anemone alpina (*Sun*)
Camassia cusicki (*Sun*)
Campanula garganica (*Semi-shade*)
Cerastium arvense (*Sun*)
Corydalis lutea (*Semi-shade*)
Cyprepedium acaule (*Semi-shade*)
Delphinium nudicaule (*Sun*)
Douglasia laevigata (*Sun*)
Douglasia vitaliana (*Sun*)
Erigeron bellidifolius (*Sun*)
Erigeron glaucus (*Sun*)
Iberis saxatilis (*Sun*)
Lamium maculatum (*Semi-shade*)
Lithospermum canescens (*Sun*)
Lithospermum caroliniensis (*Sun*)
Lychnis viscaris (*Sun*)
Ornithogalum umbellatum (*Sun*)
Oxalis adenophylla (*Sun*)
Phlox pilosa (*Sun*)
Polygala senega (*Sun*)
Polygonatum biflorum (*Sun*)
Potentilla argentea (*Sun*)
Potentilla tridentata (*Sun*)
Saxifraga virginiensis (*Sun*)
Sedum acre (*Sun*)
Silene carolinana (*Sun*)
Veronica pectinata (*Sun*)
Viola pedata (*Sun*)
Waldensteinia fragaroides (*Semi-shade*)

JUNE:

Achillea ageratifolia (*Sun*)
Achillea argentea (*Sun*)
Achillea nana (*Sun*)
Achillea tomentosa (*Sun*)
Allium oreophilum ostrowskianum (*Sun*)
Antennaria dioica (*Sun*)
Anthemis tinctoria (*Sun*)

Catananche caerulea (*Sun*)
Centaurea dealbata (*Sun*)
Centaurea gymnocarpa (*Sun*)
Centaurea montana (*Sun*)
Centaurea rutifolia (*Sun*)
Chimaphila maculata (*Shade*)
Chimaphila umbellata (*Shade*)
Coronilla varia (*Sun*)
Delphinium brunonianum (*Sun*)
Delphinium cashmerianum (*Sun*)
Delphinium cheilanthum (*Sun*)
Delphinium elatum (*Sun*)
Delphinium grandiflorum (*Sun*)
Dianthus latifolius (*Sun*)
Dianthus sylvestris (*Semi-shade*)
Dictamnus albus (*Sun*)
Erigeron speciosus (*Sun*)
Gaillardia aristata (*Sun*)
Helianthemum nummularium (*Sun*)
Hemerocallis middendorffi (*Semi-shade*)
Hieracium auranticum (*Sun*)
Hieracium bombycinium (*Sun*)
Hieracium villosum (*Sun*)
Iris spuria (*Sun*)
Kniphofia tucki (*Sun*)
Lewisia cotyledon (*Sun*)
Lewisia rediviva (*Sun*)
Lewisia tweedyi (*Sun*)
Lotus corniculatus (*Sun*)
Lychnis chalcedonica (*Sun*)
Lychnis coronaria (*Sun*)
Lysimachia nummularia (*Semi-shade*)
Malva alcea (*Sun*)
Oenothera missouriensis (*Sun*)
Oenothera tetragona (*Sun*)
Opuntia compressa (*Sun*)
Potentilla argyrophylla (*Sun*)
Potentilla atrosanguinea (*Sun*)
Potentilla grandiflora (*Sun*)
Salvia nemorosa (*Sun*)
Saponaria ocymoides (*Sun*)

Sedum aizoon (*Sun*)
Sedum middendorffianum (*Sun*)
Sedum rosea (*Sun*)
Sedum sexangulare (*Sun*)
Sedum telephoides (*Sun*)
Sempervivum (*Sun*)
Silene auculis (*Sun*)
Thymus serphyllum (*Sun*)

JULY:

Achillea millefolium (*Sun*)
Amorpha canescens (*Sun*)
Asclepias tuberosa (*Sun*)
Aster linarifolius (*Sun*)
Boltonia latisquama (*Sun*)
Calluna vulgaris (*Sun*)
Cassia marilandica (*Sun*)
Coreopsis verticillata (*Sun*)
Delphinium cardinale (*Sun*)
Echinacea angustifolia (*Sun*)
Echinacea purpurea (*Sun*)
Echinops ritro (*Sun*)
Eryngium alpinum (*Sun*)
Eryngium amethystinum (*Sun*)
Euphorbia corollata (*Sun*)
Gypsophila acutifilia (*Sun*)
Gypsophila paniculata (*Sun*)
Hemerocallis citrina (*Sun*)
Hemerocallis fulva (*Sun*)
Hemerocallis hybrida (*Sun*)
Hosta *species* (*Semi-shade*)
Lathyrus latifolius (*Sun*)
Lavandula officinalis (*Sun*)
Limonium latifolium (*Sun*)
Malva moschata (*Sun*)
Potentilla nepalensis (*Sun*)
Rudbeckia fulgida (*Sun*)
Sedum album (*Sun*)
Sedum hispanicum (*Sun*)
Sedum kamtschaticum (*Sun*)

Sedum reflexum (*Sun*)
Sedum spurium (*Sun*)
Solidago hybrida (*Sun*)
Yucca filamentosa (*Sun*)
Yucca flaccida (*Sun*)

AUGUST:

Anaphalis margaritacea (*Semi-shade*)
Anaphalis yedoensis (*Semi-shade*)
Artemesia absinthum (*Sun*)
Artemesia albula (*Sun*)
Artemesia schmidtiana nana (*Sun*)
Artemesia stelleriana (*Sun*)
Aster spectabilis (*Sun*)
Chrysanthemum parthenium (*Sun*)
Chrysopsis falcata (*Sun*)
Chrysopsis mariana (*Sun*)
Hosta *species* (*Semi-shade*)
Polygonum reynoutria (*Sun*)
Rudbeckia hirta (*Sun*)
Salvia azurea (*Sun*)
Santolina chamaecyparissus (*Sun*)
Santolina virens (*Sun*)
Sedum sieboldi (*Sun*)
Sedum spectabile (*Sun*)
Sedum telephium (*Sun*)
Stokesia laevis (*Sun*)

SEPTEMBER:

Aster laevis (*Sun*)
Aster novi-belgi (*Sun*)

FERNS:

Dennstaedtia punctilobula (*Sun*)
Dryopteris noveboracensis (*Semi-shade*)
Osmunda claytoniana (*Semi-shade*)
Pellaea atropurpurea (*Semi-shade*)
Pteridium latisculum (*Semi-shade*)

Perennials Having Persistent Winter Foliage

(Carried under the monthly listing indicated for the light intensity given.)

MARCH:

Erica carnea (*Sun*)
Helleborus niger (*Semi-shade*)
Helleborus orientalis (*Semi-shade*)

APRIL:

Alyssum saxatile (*Sun*)
Arabis mollis (*Sun*)
Bergenia cordifolia (*Semi-shade*)
Bergenia crassifolia (*Semi-shade*)
Epigaea repens (*Semi-shade*)
Muscari *species* (*Sun*)
Pachysandra procumbens (*Semi-shade*)
Pachysandra terminalis (*Semi-shade*)
Vinca minor (*Sun*)

MAY:

Aethionema cordifolium (*Sun*)
Aethionema grandiflora (*Sun*)
Aethionema warleyense (*Sun*)
Armeria maritima (*Sun*)
Asarum europaeum (*Semi-shade*)
Cornus canadensis (*Shade*)
Dianthus gratianopolitanus (*Sun*)
Dryas octopetala (*Sun*)
Epimedium *species* (*Semi-shade*)
Galax aphylla (*Semi-shade*)
Iberis saxatilis (*Sun*)
Iberis sempervirens (*Sun*)
Phlox stolonifera (*Semi-shade*)
Potentilla tridentata (*Sun*)
Sedum acre (*Sun*)
Veronica chamaedrys (*Sun*)
Veronica officinalis (*Shade*)
Veronica pectinata (*Sun*)

JUNE:

Cerastium tomentosum (*Sun*)
Chimaphila maculata (*Shade*)
Chimaphila umbellata (*Shade*)
Coreopsis auriculata (*Sun*)
Eremurus himalaicus (*Sun*)
Eremurus robustus (*Sun*)
Helianthemum nummularium (*Sun*)
Heuchera sanguinea (*Sun*)
Lewisia rediviva (*Sun*)
Mitchella repens (*Semi-shade*)
Oenothera fruticosa (*Sun*)
Opuntia compressa (*Sun*)
Saponaria ocymoides (*Sun*)
Saxifraga *species* (*Semi-shade*)
Sedum sexangulare (*Sun*)
Sempervivum (*Sun*)
Shortia galacifolia (*Shade*)
Shortia uniflora (*Shade*)
Thymus *species* (*Sun*)

JULY:

Calluna vulgaris (*Sun*)
Gaultheria procumbens (*Semi-shade*)
Lavandula officinalis (*Sun*)
Ruta graveolens (*Sun*)
Sedum album (*Sun*)
Sedum spurium (*Sun*)
Yucca filamentosa (*Sun*)
Yucca flaccida (*Sun*)

AUGUST:

Liriope spicata (*Semi-shade*)
Santolina chamaecyparissus (*Sun*)
Santolina virens (*Sun*)

FERNS:

Asplenium platyneuron (*Sun*)
Asplenium trichomanes (*Semi-shade*)

Camptosorus rhizophyllus (*Semi-shade*)
Dryopteris cristata (*Shade*)
Dryopteris intermedia (*Semi-shade*)
Dryopteris spinulosa (*Semi-shade*)
Lygodium palmatum (*Semi-shade*)
Pellaea atropurpurea (*Semi-shade*)
Polypodium vulgare (*Semi-shade*)
Polystichum acrostichoides (*Shade*)
Woodsia obtusa (*Shade*)

Perennials with Showy Fruit or Dried Flower Part Potential

(Carried under the monthly listing indicated for the light intensity given.)

APRIL:

Actaea alba (*Shade*)
Actaea rubra (*Shade*)
Anemone pulsatilla (*Sun*)
Caulophyllum thalictroides (*Semi-shade*)
Trillium undulatum (*Semi-shade*)
Tulipa tarda (*Sun*)

MAY:

Anemone alpina (*Sun*)
Arisaema triphyllum (*Semi-shade*)
Cornus canadensis (*Shade*)
Dryas octopetala (*Sun*)
Jeffersonia diphylla (*Semi-shade*)
Podophyllum emodi (*Semi-shade*)
Podophyllum peltatum (*Semi-shade*)
Smilacina racemosa (*Semi-shade*)

JUNE:

Achillea filipendulina (*Sun*)
Allium albopilosum (*Sun*)
Anemone virginiana (*Semi-shade*)
Catananche caerulea (*Sun*)
Dictamnus albus (*Sun*)
Dipsacus fullonum (*Sun*)
Mitchella repens (*Semi-shade*)
Opuntia compressa (*Sun*)

JULY:

Belamcanda chinensis (*Sun*)
Cimicifuga racemosa (*Semi-shade*)
Eryngium alpinum (*Sun*)
Eryngium amesthystinum (*Sun*)
Gaultheria procumbens (*Semi-shade*)

Lavandula officinalis (*Sun*)
Limonium latifolium (*Sun*)
Macleaya cordata (*Sun*)
Physalis franchetii (*Sun*)

AUGUST:

Anaphalis margaritacea (*Semi-shade*)
Anaphalis yedoensis (*Semi-shade*)

BIBLIOGRAPHY

Bailey, Liberty Hyde. *The Standard Cyclopedia of Horti-culture*, vols. 1–3. New York: The Macmillan Company, 1944 edition.

Baumgardt, John Philip. *Bulbs for Summer Bloom*. New York: Hawthorn Books, Inc., 1970.

Birdseye, Clarence and Eleanor G. *Growing Woodland Plants*. New York: Dover Publications, 1951.

Bloom, Alan. *Perennials for Your Garden*. Nottingham, England: Floraprint, Ltd., 1971.

Crockett, James Underwood. *Bulbs*. New York: Time-Life Books, 1971.

————— *Lawns and Groundcovers*. New York: Time-Life Books, 1971.

————— *Perennials*. New York: Time-Life Books, 1972.

Cumming, Roderick W., and Lee, Robert E. *Contemporary Perennials*. New York: The Macmillan Company, 1960.

De Graaf, Jan, and Hyams, Edward. *Lilies*. New York: Funk & Wagnalls, 1968.

Doerflinger, Frederick. *Complete Book of Bulb Gardening*. Harrisburg, Pennsylvania: Stackpole Books, 1973.

Foster, F. Gordon. *Ferns to Know and Grow*. New York: Hawthorn Books, Inc., 1971.

Foster, H. Lincoln. *Rock Gardening*. Boston: Houghton Mifflin Company, 1968.

Harrison, Richmond E. *Know Your Lilies*. Wellington, Australia: A. H. & A. W. Reed, 1971.

Hylander, Clarence J. *The Macmillan Wild Flower Book*. New York: The Macmillan Company, 1954.

Klaber, Doretta. *Rock Garden Plants*. New York: Bramhall House, 1959.

Kolaga, Walter A. *All About Rock Gardens and Plants.* New York: Doubleday & Company, 1966.

May, Roy, and Synge, Patrick M. *The Color Dictionary of Flowers and Plants for Home and Garden.* New York: Crown Publishers, 1969.

Mathew, Brian. *Dwarf Bulbs.* New York: Arco Publishing Company, 1973.

Morse, H. K. *Gardening in the Shade.* New York: Charles Scribner's Sons, 1953.

Nehrling, Arno and Irene. *Peonies, Outdoors and In.* New York: Hearthside Press, 1960.

Pettingill, Amos. *The White Flower Farm Garden Book.* New York: Alfred A. Knopf, 1971.

Potter, Charles H. *Have You Tried Perennials?* Chicago: Florists' Publishing Company, 1959.

Price, Molly. *The Iris Book.* Princeton, New Jersey: D. Van Nostrand Company, 1966.

Rickett, Harold W. *Wild Flowers of the United States,* vols. 1–6. New York: McGraw-Hill, 1966.

Sedgwick, Mabel Cabot. *The Garden Month by Month.* New York: Frederick A. Stokes Company, 1907.

Schauenberg, Paul. *The Bulb Book.* London: Frederick Warne & Company, Ltd., 1965.

Sperka, Marie. *Growing Wildflowers.* New York: Harper & Row, 1973.

Synge, Patrick M. *Collins Guide to Bulbs,* 2nd ed. London: Collins, 1971.

Wister, John C. *The Peonies.* Washington, D.C.: American Horticultural Society, 1962.

INDEX OF
COMMON AND SCIENTIFIC NAMES